ORGANIC ORCHARDING
A Grove of Trees to Live In

By Gene Logsdon

Rodale Press ® Emmaus, Pennsylvania

Printed in the United States of America on recycled paper,
containing a high percentage of de-inked fiber.

Design by Linda Jacopetti
Illustrations by Mark Grounard

Library of Congress Cataloging in Publication Data

Logsdon, Gene.
  Organic orcharding.

  Includes index.
  1. Fruit trees.   2. Nuts.   3. Organic gardening.
I. Title.
SB357.24.L63   634′.0484   81-8639
ISBN 0-87857-356-9   hardcover   AACR2

2   4   6   8   10   9   7   5   3   1   hardcover

Dedicated to the men and women of the North American Fruit Explorers and the Northern Nut Growers Association who have helped me so much in the writing of this book, with both their knowledge and inspiration.

TABLE OF CONTENTS

iv

ACKNOWLEDGMENTS

Every book is a cooperative venture, and this one is no exception. I wish to thank first of all my Rodale editors, Bill Hylton and, particularly, Dan Wallace—the first for his guidance in the early days of this book, the second for his long hours spent editing the manuscript.

Various members of the North American Fruit Explorers and the Northern Nut Growers Association have been extremely helpful to me, giving unstintingly of their time and their experience in fruit and nut production. In particular, my thanks to: Robert Kurle, Elwood Fisher, R. Douglas Campbell, Harold Schroeder, Art Weaver, Ray Walker, John English, William Davie, Lois Davie, Les Wilmoth, Norm Hansen, Gene Wild, T. O. Warren, Michael McConkey, Edward Myrzynski, William McKentley, J. C. McDaniel, Eugene Carpovitch, Jerry Frecon, Fred Ashworth (deceased), E. M. Meader, John Bonn, Greg Williams, Ed Fackler, Corwin Davis, Henry Hartman, Fred Janson, and Gus Rutledge.

Others who have helped with information or inspiration are: Wendell Berry, Bee Williams, Craig Dremann, Paul Lanphere, Bill Johnson, Norman Letsinger, Steve Page, Deke Dietrick, Ric Lassiter, George Geiger, and Newt Schertzer.

Timothy White was kind enough to lend his expertise as a professional orchard pest manager, making much-needed corrections, especially in my chapters on pest control.

My daughter Jennifer helped type the manuscript, and she and my son Jerry drew many of the reference drawings for Mark Grounard's finished illustrations.

INTRODUCTION

...We should accept as a fundamental concept, the proposition that crops should be grown primarily for the purpose of satisfying man's food requirements and not as a means of making particular human activities commercially profitable regardless of the overall effect on human welfare.
  A. D. Pickett, *"A Critique on Insect Chemical Control Methods," in* The Canadian Entomologist, *vol. 81, no. 3, March, 1949.*

For nearly a decade I tried not to write this book. One of my editors at Rodale Press, Bill Hylton, would suggest it, and I would change the subject. I did not know how to go about telling people how to grow fruit trees in a totally "organic" (or biological, as I prefer to say) system. There were, in my experience, diseases of fruit and nut trees that in unfavorable weather could not be controlled even with the most potent chemicals, let alone without them. In addition, there was a growing number of virus problems in some tree fruits that defied all control methods, natural or man-inspired, making fruit production in some instances a fit venture only for poker players with a desire to lose money.

I fretted a long time over what seemed to me to be flaws in the organic argument: the seeming inability to cope adequately with fungal disease in tree fruits, and the rather vague insect-control program that applied to a medium- or large-size orchard. (It was at that time only beginning to be realized that the same criticism applied to chemical controls, too.) After some years of study and experimentation, I think I have the answers to my frettings, but ten years ago I certainly did not. I was raised on and worked on farms where financial worries dominated every decision. In the face of heavy debt, or in striving to avoid heavy debt, we felt unable to farm in as ecological a manner as we would have liked. As an agricultural writer, I came to know many fruit growers in the same situation. They grappled with staggering debt loads; with rigid and often senseless market standards; with a shrinking number of market buyers who often seemed to act in collusion with each other when they bid on farmers' produce; with enormous competition from other growers; and with crop risks that would give a racetrack gambler ulcers. I found unsavory the idea of writing a book that would espouse methods these growers would only consider naive and pompously insulting. No matter how carefully I worded my argument for a more natural and less financial approach to tree crop agriculture, I would insinuate that these farmers, who scratched out their livings raising fruit, were the bad guys ecologically, while I, who raised fruit without toxic chemicals but only for my own table, was one of God's little ecological angels. I did not want to assume such a sanctimonious posture.

In realizing, though, that finance, not biology, was the root of the farmers' predicament, I was closer to a solution to my fretting than I understood at the time. I recall some turning points in my thinking that finally led to a decision to try this book. I remember sitting on a steep hillside pasture at Wendell Berry's farm, telling him about my dilemma—that I championed organic farming but at the same time feared that tree fruit could not be grown organically. His reply turned my head around on the subject. "Why don't you write a book about why you *can't* grow tree fruit organically?" We passed on to other matters, but that suggestion stuck in my mind, not as the subject of a book exactly but as the proper question to ask. When I asked it often enough, I was finally convinced, by the answers, that the core of the dilemma facing me was economical, not biological.

"If I don't use toxic sprays, the apples aren't cosmetically acceptable for top price."

"If I don't spray, there will be worms in some of the apples, and people won't buy them at any price."

"There may be some fruits or varieties of fruits we could grow without much spraying, but the fruits for which we have a good market have to be sprayed every week."

"We have to spray every 10 to 14 days regardless as insurance, just in case a disease or insect infestation pops up. When you've borrowed money up to your neck, you can't afford to take chances."

Only rarely did anyone answer my question by saying, "If I don't spray, the trees will all die." When I did get that answer, it propelled me toward a second turning point in my changing attitude toward writing this book. Logically, if all fruit trees really would die without spraying, or if the whole crop would be ruined, a fruit industry could not have arisen in the first place, during a time when toxic sprays hadn't yet been invented.

I began to study the history of chemical pest control in fruit trees. I can make no claim for completeness in this research for the simple reason that no such critical history has been written as far as I know. But what I did glean—from observations of entomologists, naturalists, and the recollections of orchardists— is that trees die from fungal or insect attack only if something has upset the ecological balance that formerly protected that particular tree species, or if a particular species is introduced into a region where it did not evolve and, therefore, is not biologically acclimated to that region. In either case, the trees are grown in spite of their vulnerability because of the possibility of making money from them, over and above the high cost of maintaining them artifically by using chemicals toxic to the environment. The history of chemical pest control is a history of conflict between profiteering humans and natural biology. My conclusions about the orchard were the same as those of R. W. Stark about the forest in a paper he gave at the 1970 Third Annual Northeast Forestry Institute Workshop Conference (United States Department of Agriculture [USDA] Forest Service research paper NE–194, 111–29):

It seems to me that the tremendous economic growth of forestry in the past has blinded us to the fact that prior to our exploitation of the forests, forest pest problems were much less. In many of those areas that are still relatively undisturbed, problems are usually minimal. . . . The majority of our pests are man-made.

But it is Robert Van Den Bosch, a professor of entomology at the University of California until his recent and untimely death, who summed up best the history of chemical intrusion by man into the natural world. In his book, *The Pesticide Conspiracy* (New York, Doubleday, 1978), he pointed out that about 30 years ago, when the synthetic insecticide era really got rolling, the United States used roughly 50 million pounds of insecticides a year and insects destroyed about 7% of our crops. Thirty years later, he said, we dump 600 million pounds of insecticide on our land and lose 13% of our crop to insects! Van Den Bosch went on to say, "This reflects incredibly bad technology and extremely poor economics—unless, of course, one is selling insecticides."

The renewed emphasis on biological pest controls that came during the 1970s further motivated me to write this book. Even the most dyed-in-the-wool chemical-user realizes today that total reliance on poisons doesn't work in the long run. You can't poison just part of an ecosystem. Persistence in trying to do so leads to a collapse of the whole system. The Southeast peach industry and the Northwest pear industry both verged on collapse in 1980 for precisely this reason. To stave off the collapse, scientists and orchardists are trying to work out a compromise—a combination of biological controls with some continued but decreased use of chemicals. This method is called integrated pest management (IPM) and, for success, demands an extremely disciplined and knowledgeable attention to the orchard environment. If fruit growers are prepared to accept IPM, then it is my hope that they will at least entertain (I do not expect them to agree yet) the idea that a *total* biological-control system would be better yet and a goal possible to attain.

If I needed a last straw to move me toward this book, it occurred a couple of summers ago. I happened to be in a peach-growing area and passed a roadside stand in front of a large peach orchard. People were milling around the stand. The owner, as it turned out, had just sold out all the ripe peaches he and his family had been able to pick, working frantically since 4:00 that morning. Scores of customers, who had driven from some distance, were turned away, angry, without peaches. Those who had gotten there early enough had paid $8 a *half*-bushel— "and bitched about the price all the way home," the peach grower remarked sourly.

There was something out of whack in that scenario, at least to my way of thinking. Most of the customers, I'm sure, were homeowners with yard enough for at least two peach trees. Since the locale had a good peach-growing climate, they could have raised a few bushels of peaches with very little time or trouble. In that area, some folks I know *do* grow a few peaches, and without any spraying at all. These disgruntled customers chose rather to depend on an orchardist who had to grow many peach trees in a concentrated area and spend many long hours at his job in order to earn enough money to make a living. Naturally, he had to spray, and spray, and spray ten more times. What was achieved? Disease continued to mount in his orchard despite the spraying. The grower's bank account, by his own admission, dwindled rather than increased. His customers paid exorbitant prices for the fruit. Or got none at all. Nature was wasted and no one was satisfied, save perhaps the chemical companies who supplied the spray materials and the government regulators who parasitized a living from the fruit industry under the pretense of protecting consumers.

And so to this book. It is intended neither for the commercial grower trapped in a financial situation over which he has no control, nor for consumers who prefer to support that financial situation because they are too lazy to grow their own fruit. Biological orcharding won't work in that kind of "progressive" society. Biological orcharding is economical in the original meaning of "economy"—the management of a household with a careful and thrifty use of resources. The truly biological orchard is a grove of trees to live in—*literally* to live in and from. The establishment of such a grove and its maintenance are quite different from that of a commercial orchard. For those who yearn for such a tree grove, for those who like the independence of raising their own food and wish now to advance beyond vegetable and berry gardens, for those I hope this book will be helpful.

In establishing my own grove, I've committed my share of blunders, and some of them will inevitably creep into this book. For this, I apologize. Let us all seek and learn together, for there is much more to be learned about biological food production than is known now. A nation of nearly self-subsistent grove dwellers is not an impossible dream. If you have a home or plan to have one, you are more than halfway there now.

PART I

ESTABLISHING AND MAINTAINING A HOMESTEAD ORCHARD

CHAPTER 1

LIFE IN A GROVE OF TREES: AN OVERVIEW

Even those who know little about the complex and intrinsically beautiful world of the orchard like the sound of the word. It echoes the essence of the good old days and the timeless solidity of supposed rural virtue in American tradition even as the reality disappears sentimentally into the names of roads and subdivisions: Old Orchard Lane; Peach Orchard Hills; Crab Orchard Park. Like windmills and smokehouses, sitting porches, and well pumps, the old home orchard exists as an anachronism only. The trees have all marched off to join the armies commanded by commercial fruit growers.

Or so it seems. Actually, the home orchard is not really disappearing but has only changed its appearance. Nurserymen are selling more fruit and nut trees to homeowners than ever before. But the backyard gardener does not always have the space for the formal orchard of yesterday's family farm. Instead of a prim, white-fenced block of apple and peach trees along the road, handy to barn and house, today's home-food producer scatters food trees of many varieties around his property wherever he can find room, to serve double duty both as food and for landscaping beauty, not to mention as shade, fuel, or protection

1

from the wind. His orchard becomes something more than the orchard that we are accustomed to thinking of—it becomes an orchard in the oldest and truest sense, a grove of trees not only to eat from but to live in.

In this sense, the orchard or tree grove becomes a habitat for man. Look closely at our origins. Those primates from whom we

presumably evolved were certainly orchard creatures. The monkey swinging through the trees with a banana in his mouth or a coconut in his arm holds, woven into his genetic code, a partnership with trees and tree food that is revealed again in the human strolling through his grove, munching an apple or gathering a pocketful of hickory nuts. Give any person the choice, and he will pay homage to these primal instincts. He will surround an abode with trees whenever able to do so. What nutritionist does not insist that the diet of our primate forerunners, which consisted mainly of fresh fruit and nuts, is not still a good basic diet for us? What psychologist will not agree that the serene environment of a grove of trees can promote mental health? What poet will not recognize the certain sacredness of a tree grove?

It is this broad view of the "orchard" that I take in this book—a grove of food trees that provides a natural and healthful habitat for man. This view—perhaps I should call it a vision—is quite different from the conventional notion of an orchard. Today's commercial tree groves are specialized, streamlined, and stripped of everything not directly related to making a profitable crop. So specialized is the culture of some fruits and nuts, in fact, that during many parts of the growing season the orchard habitat is distinctly *in*hospitable to man, rendered so by the

Photos 1-1 and 1-2—A Commercial Orchard and a Backyard Grove— The commercial orchardist lines his trees up in geometric rows, all of the same species. The backyard, organic grove-owner attempts to foster a more natural habitat of which he is an integral part. Rodale Press photographs.

toxicity of chemicals used in an effort to exclude forms of life that threaten the profits from the fruit crop. Man, bird, animal, bees, and countless other beneficial forms of life come to the orchard in the summer spraying-time at their own risk. Few plants are tolerated there, either, other than the trees themselves. Even the trees are no longer desirable in their natural forms. They must be dwarfed with rootstocks or interstems of other species, then pruned for the benefit of machines. Or roots of a tree may be of one species for hardiness, with a dwarfing interstem length of trunk and a second interstem to make the varietal graft compatible with the dwarfing interstem. Some trees may have yet a fifth addition, a branch of another variety grafted on to improve pollination. All of this technological progress is looked upon as good, and in many ways it may be good. But the result is not a grove of trees to live *in*. And the result is achieved at such great cost that, after listening to orchardists complain, I'm not too sure it provides a grove of trees that one can make a good living *from,* either.

The home orchardist, on the other hand, does not have to look at his tree grove with bankers' eyes. He plants his trees to establish a healthy living environment. He sees the totality of that environment, not money, as his profit. The fleshy fruits provide fiber, vitamins, and carbohydrates in his diet; the nut fruits provide protein and energy. His "orchard" includes both kinds of food. Variety is his objective. A mulberry tree is as legitimate as a plum; a wild papaw as appropriate as an apple; a hickory nut as practical as a walnut, or maybe more so.

Home processing uses of the fruits and nuts are as important as fresh uses. Less than perfect apples make for applesauce, butter, pie, and cider just as good as perfect ones. Secondary uses of the trees are also important to the grove-owner's scheme. Hickory nuts are delicious; hickory wood is an excellent firewood.

The home grove-owner sees his "orchard" as a community of interrelated living things. He has an idea and a vision of how varied and complex that community should be if it is to interact correctly in the maintenance of an environment healthy for him. That is his goal, not just the production of fruit and nuts. He knows that if he can promote ecological completeness in his grove, then the foods and fibers he needs will come as a fringe benefit.

His apple blossoms herald another fruit crop but also another honey crop—the honey indeed a much surer proposition than the fruit. The sod floor of his grove may be graze for sheep, hens, or hogs, who by keeping the fallen fruit cleaned up help control harmful insects, too. He expects to find aphids in his trees, but, to help control them, he'll also find ladybugs. If damaging mites are present, he knows that predator mites will also come to prevent serious crop losses.

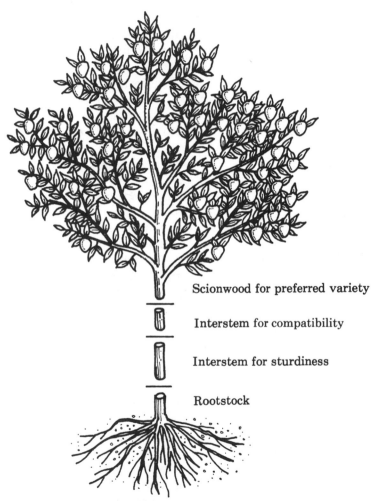

Scionwood for preferred variety

Interstem for compatibility

Interstem for sturdiness

Rootstock

Illus. 1-1—The Makeup of a Grafted Tree—Rootstocks are planted for their strength to support the grafted varieties, with various interstems grafted in to assure the compatibility of the variety to be grafted for its fruit.

The home grove-owner does everything in his power to bring not only a variety of insects to his orchard but every bird as well. Some birds will do "good," some "bad," some both. All will contribute to the tenuous, dynamic balance of pest and predator he desires. Hairy and downy woodpeckers feed on codling moth. Flickers tongue down ants that carry aphids into the trees. Woodpeckers staccato holes into dead branches of old fruit trees in their search for bugs, and then bluebirds use the holes for nests. The bluebird is a great friend of the orchard, eating bugs but no fruit. Cuckoos are one of the few bird species that can eat tent caterpillars. The hairy hides of the worms, repulsive to many other birds, matter not to the cuckoo. When the lining of its throat becomes rough and calloused from eating the caterpillars, it sloughs off, and a new lining forms. Where pear psylla threaten his fruit, the backyard orchardist welcomes chickadees, kinglets, and nuthatches, which have ravenous appetites for the psylla. Pecan growers appreciate the tufted titmouse, which eats the pesky pecan nut casebearer.

Owls, especially the screech owl, may be the grove-owner's best friends, patrolling the orchard for mice, which often are more damaging to trees than bugs. The famous ornithologist, Edward Howe Forbush, noted many years ago in *A Natural History of American Birds of Eastern and Central North America* (New York, Bramhall House) that "while the owls were there, the mice did no damage in our young orchard, but two years later their box fell down and was not replaced for the next two years. The second winter mice girdled nearly all our apple trees. The next year a number of boxes were erected. The owls returned and we had no trouble from mice thereafter."

To have enough of nature's variety to effect some semblance of balance in the grove, naturalists know that areas of wild habitat near the fruit and other food trees are necessary. Most such areas have long been bulldozed or burned away from the fringes of commercial orchards, while birds like owls are illegally killed by ignorant and blood-lusting hunters. Having destroyed the environment in which biological controls of pests work, the modern orchardist shrugs and says such controls won't work. But the backyard grove-owner embarks on the long and seemingly impossible task of restoring that earlier environment. In many cases he must start with the soil itself. He first tries to obtain virgin land for his grove—land that has not been farmed, such as an old woodlot—since the makings of a natural environment exist there already, at least in the soil. If he cannot obtain such a piece of land, he takes what soil he has and begins to return to it the organic matter, nutrients, and the almost infinite variety of microorganisms that once kept plants healthy and vigorous and grew trees in such dense stands and sizes as to strain our belief today.

Then he begins to duplicate other natural conditions in and around his food trees. If brushy and unkempt natural areas in the grove are impractical (as on a suburban lot), he will grow a hedge around his trees or property that not only lures birds and insects but effects a fuel-conserving windbreak, too. In place of the "ditch and quicksett of hazel hedge" prescribed around the fruit trees in medieval orchard leases, the homeowner today may grow autumn olive or a combination of bush cherry, wild plum, black haw viburnum, mulberry, and hazel. Or he may set about a more exacting task of establishing a trellis or hedge of apples. In the Southwest, he might plant a hedge of eucalyptus gum trees to draw the bees and protect the more tender fruit trees from wind.

Just as he seeks diversity in the animal and insect populations in his grove, the home orchardist endeavors to increase the variety of plant life. Solid blocks of one variety of trees are open invitations to population explosions of pest bugs. Thus, in the home grove there may be a maple for syrup growing between a pear and an apple. Some innovators in the home grove plant their fruit trees in clearings in woodlots or at woodland edges, with native nut trees interspersed among them, along with maples and oaks. If sunlight is sufficient, such fruit trees will produce crops 50% or more free of pest injury, just like the wild apples so often do without any spraying at all.

Although weeds and grasses occasionally may rob trees of some nutrients, the grove-owner is not too worried to see them grow up among the trees. By and by he will cut them down, or smother them over with mulch, or turn sheep in. He knows that in the fertile soil he builds up, more often than not, trees can get more nitrogen than they need, grow too fast, and winterkill. Thus, he lets the grass and weeds temporarily borrow that nitrogen. He seldom cultivates around his trees, either, because of erosion problems or because the long-held advantages of such cultivation can be obtained better by mulching or by the grazing of animals. He remembers, too, a passage from Joseph A. Cocannouer's book, *Weeds, Guardians of the Soil* (Old Greenwich, Conn., The Devin-Adair Company, 1950), telling of a California orchard that became unthrifty but revived after it was abandoned and weeds grew up in it. The orchard, Cocannouer wrote, produced best where the weeds were thickest.

But nothing is simple in ecology. Where the green peach aphid is a problem, the grove-owner will eliminate weeds scrupulously in favor of grass. Researchers have discovered that the green peach aphid, which is becoming resistant to chemicals like so many other pest bugs, uses broad-leaved weeds as host plants. Eliminate the weeds and the aphid population decreases, especially if aphid-infested tree prunings are not allowed to lie beneath the trees over winter.

Since the backyard grove-owner continually seeks more diversity in his grove plant life, he is not afraid to test old and seemingly unscientific practices such as companion planting. When he reads, for example, what Charles Estienne and John Liebault wrote in the middle 1500s (in *Maison Rustique*), that the apple tree was "verie subject to be eaten and spoyled of Pismires and little wormes, but the remedie is to set neere unto it the Sea-onion," he wants to try it. He may plant nasturtiums under apple trees to keep away aphids. If the ploy doesn't work, the nasturtiums are still pretty to look at, and the leaves are good to eat. He may grow chives or garlic there, too, to see if the old wives' tale that the former prevents scab and the latter aphids has any truth to it. Or he may, as I and others are doing, try planting pennyroyal, a known insect-repelling plant, under the fruit trees.

The grove-owner's concern—to restore the pristine diversity of life natural to a grove of trees—is a never-ending and lifelong challenge. Who can learn the total life of a grove of trees in a lifetime? Our most expert experts know only a little. The complexity outruns the most gifted horticulturist's ability to express it within a logical framework comprehensible to the human mind.

Here is a small tachinid fly parasitizing a gypsy moth. Along comes a spider to eat the tachinid fly (the same spider has also just eaten a bothersome grasshopper). The spider in turn is eaten by a wasp, long before the scientist has figured out if the spider is "good" or "bad." The wasp does not try to make such decisions. It takes any spider and any other insects it can get. The wasp also eats some fruit as it knocks off spiders. While science worries about the value of the wasp to us, a redstart, one of the most beautiful warblers, darts by and eats it. Redstarts have a weakness for wasps. But there are far too few redstarts, and the wasps build up huge populations, especially the ground wasps. Just when they become too numerous to live comfortably with man in his grove, along comes a skunk, which digs up the nest for its Sunday dinner. Just when the skunks become numerous enough to make men nervous, a great horned owl, one of the few animals unperturbed by the scent of skunks, swoops down and reduces the population.

This chain of events is but a very short segment—and a very oversimplified short segment at that—of the interconnected dining table of the tree grove. Into this infinitely complex and fragile relationship blunders man, the only creature capable of *intentionally* altering the biological linkage holding all life together. And he has the temerity to say, in the face of millions of years of proof to the contrary, that the "only" way food can be grown from trees for human sustenance is by altering the natural environment with laboratory chemicals.

To have a backyard grove is by definition to live in it. The home orchardist soon learns that there is no season in which his presence is not required among his trees, and if he has no working excuse to be there, he will make one up. Even in January, the cardinal will be singing in the grove, joining the song of the orchardist's saw. Dead trees or spent trees need to be cut down for firewood (none smells so sweet or burns much better than apple), for tool handles (none wears any better than hickory), for furniture (walnut and cherry rival any wood the world knows), for fence posts (mulberry will last for years), and for hundreds of other uses. Pruning must be attended to now in this slack season. And what better time, anyway, when the dark branches are easy to eye up and shape against the white snow?

As the days quicken into March, the sap rises in the maples. The first "fruit" of the year, maple syrup, is ready to harvest.

When weather warms up enough for bees to fly, the grafting season arrives. Begin, say the old-timers, when the hazel catkins start to lengthen.

Then it's hurry, hurry to get the work all done on time. Spray dormant oil. Plant seeds for seedlings to graft onto next year, or to see what fruit develops naturally. Transplant new trees. Pay a mind to the bees. Get the birdhouses cleaned out. Insert spreaders on young trees if necessary. Stake or tie up new bud shoots. Seek out and cut off caterpillar egg masses on cloudy days when looking upward will not pain the eyes. Sing a song as you work along. And if you don't find time in May and June just to dream under an apple tree, you have failed to enjoy the deeper achievements you've accomplished in your grove.

Although in the South harvest of tree foods may come and go sporadically throughout the year, July is the real beginning of the harvest for most grove-owners. In August the floodgates of the orchard cornucopia open fully. Despite earlier frosts and freezes, bugs and blights, and forecasts of doom and gloom, there is enough food from the trees almost every year for the humans who care for them, as well as plenty of wormy and scabby fruit for the animals, wild and domestic.

Busy as the season of harvest is, time must be allowed in August to bud a few trees that are difficult to graft in the spring.

Autumn is nut-gathering time. Study any culture—prehistoric American Indian, 15th-century England, 19th-century rural Ohio—and you will find that the nut-gathering season was always enshrined in festivity. And why not? What could be more pleasant than lovers gathering their winter supply of protein in the fine, winy days of October?

Also in the fall the cider press comes out of storage, is cleaned, and put to work. Copper kettles bubble with apple butter over outdoor fires. Fruit cellars are aired, then choked with apples. Strings of apple and peach slices hang drying in the attic. All these activities were once, and in some places still are, occasions for parties and neighborly rejoicing.

In November, the grove-owner may renew the mulch under his trees if he didn't get time to do it in summer. Or, if mice are a problem, he may pull the mulch away from the tree trunks to discourage the rodents from hiding there. But the shrewd grower of apricots, peaches, and pecans in the North will keep the mulch handy. He has learned that mulch will keep ground frozen around the trees longer into spring, thus delaying blossoming until the worst of the spring frosts has passed. Now is the time, too, to gather in persimmons before they all fall to the ground and become soiled.

December is the orchardist's cleaning month. He removes rotten fruit still hanging on trees or lying beneath them. He hopes that his chickens or livestock can help with the job. He puts away stakes, limb supports, and ladders. He cuts scions for spring grafting, labeling each carefully and packing them away in moist moss in a refrigerator or underground. This job would be better done in early spring, but what if choice or rare stock left to the weather's hazards should winterfreeze?

The year comes full circle, and it's time to get the saw out again and watch for the cardinal to cheer you through the January cold. A dram of good cider, or a little applejack, will help some, too.

Living in a grove of trees does not mean a grueling schedule of work as you might conclude from the paragraphs above. The secret to avoiding this is embedded in the diversity of life you establish in your grove. If you plant 50 apple trees of the same variety, then you are going to have to *work* to care for them properly and dispose of all those apples ripening at the same time. But if, instead, you plant one or two of each fruit and nut tree that you like, you will find that the bit of work you do with each variety or each type is finished before it gets tiring. For example, rather than trying to harvest cherries from five trees, be content with one, and when that is finished go on to the plum tree, and then to the peach, and then to a couple of apples. You spread out the work load, and you do not put all of your fruit into one basket, so to speak.

Variety is more than the spice of life. It is the key to life.

CHAPTER 2

WHAT TO PLANT WHERE

A time-honored way to start an orchard is to buy a bunch of trees to which nursery catalogs ascribe almost supernatural powers of fertility, plant them helter-skelter around the house, and then spend the next few years moving the ones that survive to other locations as the mood dictates. Another favorite method is to plant the trees carefully and studiously, then a year later move *yourself* to a different location. Neither method, I can vouch from experience, puts much fruit in your cellar. Until some small measure of wisdom came to me in my middle years when I realized the fruitlessness (oh, those puns) of wandering from place to place, I was a veritable Johnny Appleseed, planting fruit trees wherever I set my suitcase down long enough to get an order back from Stark Bro's.

The decision to start an orchard involves a decision to stay put. The first plant you want to get rooted in the earth is yourself. That's what makes home orchards so valuable; where they abound, they speak eloquently of a stable and responsible community, the first necessity of a healthy civilization and a happy culture. The decline in home orchards between 1930 and 1970 parallels almost exactly the increase in social mobility and the consequent deterioration of family life and local institutions. As a result, we claim a population of very important people who tell their psychiatrists they do not know who they are. Not having recognized the natural habitat of *Homo sapiens,* or having ignored it, they wander the country over, hoping to find identity in money, badges, awards, or "rooting" for equally rootless professional sport teams.

But having decided that wisdom might come to you while sitting under an apple tree (look what Newton discovered), your next step must be to face more mundane matters: how to go about establishing this "Edenic" grove of trees.

To grow an orchard requires plans, but trees are living things, not bridges or houses. One should not blueprint a home orchard and then follow the plan too literally like a bureaucrat with a new regulation. There are reams of general information to help you select your trees, but none will be as authoritative as your own experience in your own place. Your own peculiar combination of climate, soil, luck, and preference will not be quite like any other grower's, so be ready to change any plan you put on paper. Besides, if you have any imagination and curiosity at all, sooner or later—and usually sooner—you will throw advice and caution to the wind and plant a tree that is perfectly ridiculous for your locale. That's how new discoveries are made, sometimes. That's also the way so many nurseries stay in business.

The limiting factors as to which fruits, and which varieties of a given fruit, you can grow or cannot grow are mainly two: temperature and moisture. Both factors work in several different ways to limit your orchard selections. Regarding temperature, your main problem in the North is too much cold weather, and in the South your problem may be not enough cold weather for temperate trees to break dormancy. As for moisture, too much produces poor drainage in the soil and humidity in the air—a humidity that contributes directly to the danger of developing blights and other fungal diseases. Too little moisture, of course, means that nothing will grow. But given a choice, a very dry climate with adequate irrigation combined with a mild, but not too mild, winter provides the best environment for temperate zone fruit culture. That's why California, Oregon, and Washington produce so much tree fruit. To choose the proper fruits for your area, you need to consider certain climatic factors in great detail.

COLD HARDINESS

Do not be surprised if a plant advertised as being able to survive $-30°F$ temperatures winterkills for you at temperatures of no colder than $0°F$. The nurseryman hasn't lied to you; he just hasn't told the whole truth. Many factors influence cold hardiness of a plant. Temperature alone is seldom the culprit—given a plant that's normally adapted to the North. If a plant "hardens off" slowly in the fall (that is to say, if the weather grows colder very gradually and steadily), a plant can take severely cold weather in midwinter. That plant will be especially hardy after a dry fall or if not fertilized late in the year. Wet fall weather and/or applications of nitrogen fertilizer induce late fall growth. Lush, late growth due to either of these factors invariably produces winterkill.

Also, a winter during which the temperature fluctuates markedly or rapidly will often winterkill hardy plants. A warm February day, with the sun shining, can send the temperature of a fruit tree trunk soaring to 90°F when air temperatures are 40°F. Sap begins to stir in the tree. Then at night, if the temperature plunges to near zero, you get winterkill. Robert Frost was not being merely poetic when he wrote about his orchard: "Fear 50 above more than 50 below."

To complicate matters further, there is more than one kind of hardiness. A tree may be winter-hardy "in the wood"; that is, the tree itself is able to withstand cold northern winters, but it's not hardy "in the bud." Many peach trees can stand below-zero weather, but the fruit buds on them winterkill at such temperatures or in severe fluctuations of temperature. The tree doesn't die, but it doesn't produce fruit, either. The bark of some sweet cherry trees will split under the same conditions, and the tree will eventually deteriorate and die.

Growers also speak of blossom-hardiness. Mostly this is a matter of the time of blossoming. An apricot tree blooms very early and will therefore suffer blossomkill from spring frosts in more northerly areas and rarely produce much fruit. But the tree itself may well be winter-hardy.

My own young orchard proved these observations during 1977 and 1978. In 1977, we recorded the lowest temperatures in a century, yet following a dry fall with a very gradual descent into winter, my peach, nectarine, and apricot trees came through with flying colors. In 1978, during a winter that never got as cold as the coldest days of '77, terrible storms abruptly following mild, rainy weather killed the nectarine and peach trees, winterburned evergreens, and even killed back the branches of wild willows I had never seen harmed before.

Meteorologists have divided the country into zones of hardiness, and hardiness maps are available everywhere in nursery

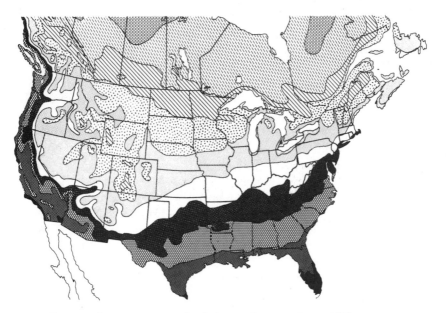

Range of average annual minimum temperatures (°F)

Zone

1	<50°		6	-10° to 0°
2	-50° to -40°		7	0° to 10°
3	-40° to -30°		8	10° to 20°
4	-30° to -20°		9	20° to 30°
5	-20° to -10°		10	30° to 40°

Illus. 2-1—United States Department of Agriculture (USDA) Map of Zones of Hardiness—In 1960, the USDA switched to a map that showed a range of ten possible hardiness zones, instead of nine zones traditional to gardening encyclopedias published before 1960.

catalogs and garden books to guide you in selecting trees. Without hesitation, I can tell you that these maps are all but useless, except as a *very* general guide.

First of all, there are two zone maps in use. If you own an older *Taylor's Encyclopedia of Gardening,* the zone map used there numbers the zones from 1 to 9, north to south. Since about 1960, the USDA has switched to a 1 to 10 numbering system, and this is the map to which nurserymen now allude when they say a certain fruit tree variety is hardy, say, from zones 5 to 7.

Furthermore, there are similar maps printed here and there that divide the country into zones according to the average date

15

of the last spring frost and the average date of the first fall frost. These maps may divide the country into only seven zones. *Organic Gardening* magazine, for example, has been using these maps in its regular "Garden Calendar" feature for years, relying on the zone numbers to designate when to do what in the garden. The beginner should not confuse these frost-date zones with the standard winter-hardiness zones referred to by nurserymen selling their stocks.

On the standard-hardiness zone map, no zones 1 or 2 appear in the United States but only appear in Canada and farther north. For all practical purposes, zones 1 and 2 are not suitable for tree fruit, anyway. Zone 3 is our coldest zone, in North Dakota, northern Minnesota, and northernmost parts of New England stretching on up into the milder parts of Canada. The warmest is zone 10, along the southern California coast and at the tips of both Texas and Florida. Between these lie the other zones, though they're not located in a steady, orderly north-to-south gradation.

Mountainsides and bodies of water produce their own microclimates independent of latitudinal location. From here in central Ohio, in zone 5, I can travel south to find a zone 6 area in the Ohio River Valley, but I can also travel north to a zone 6 around Lake Erie. The lake water moderates winter temperatures. Along the lake in Cleveland, Ohio, you are in the same hardiness zone as you would be in Santa Fe, New Mexico, even though you will get a good many more warm days and snowless weeks in Santa Fe.

The weakness of the hardiness map is that it can't tell you your own little microclimate conditions, nor can it tell you precisely the gradient range of hardiness you live in. Are you directly in the center of zone 5? Are you closer to zone 6 or zone 4? The USDA has tried to remedy this situation with a more detailed zone map that divides each zone into parts. Thus, you might learn from this map that you are in zone A5 or 5B. So you buy a peach tree that a catalog says is hardy "to zone 5." (Does that mean *in* zone 5 or only *up to* zone 5? No one wants to say.) So you then experience two winters back-to-back that are really zone 4 winters because the gods that make the weather do not care a hoot about zone maps.

Another thought to add caution to your selections: very often the hardiest varieties have the least quality. Experimental pears for the far north cannot be eaten out of hand with much pleasure so far. The Kieffer pear, which is an old, old variety, will

16

grow well both north and south, but for quality it leaves something to be desired.

In my own experience and capitalizing on the experience of others, the following list is about as close a general approximation of hardiness one can safely make:

1. For the coldest areas of fruit production (roughly zones 3 and 4): Crab apples, apple crabs, northern apples. Juneberries of the saskatoon type (*Amelanchier alnifolia*), heartier varieties of pears. Butternut. Sand cherry and cherry plum. Linden (Basswood). Sugar maple. Birch.

2. For the middle cold regions (roughly zones 4 and 5): All the preceding material plus most apples, pears, and sour cherries. Hickory, hazel, beechnut, black walnut. European-type plums. Hawthorns, most acorns except chinquapins. Very few peaches will make it—possibly Reliance and Prairie Dawn, but don't blame me whenever they winterkill. The same holds true for the hardiest nectarines and apricots. Red and black mulberries. Hackberry, black cherry, chokecherry.

3. Midway north and south (roughly zones 6 and 7): All the preceding material plus most peaches, nectarines, apricots, European hazels, oriental persimmons, northern-type pecans, hicans, chinquapins, the hardiest figs and almonds, Carpathian walnuts, English walnuts, sweet cherries, Japanese plums, American persimmon, papaw, and mulberries.

4. Mid-south between central and deep south (roughly zones 7 and 8): Most of the preceding material, but only low-chill apples and peaches; no butternut, beech, and rarely hickory. Papershell pecan. Figs, almonds, jujube.

5. Warmest areas, subtropical, tropical (roughly lower zones 8, 9, and 10): A few tropical-type apples, such as Granny Smith. Northern nut trees will not flourish here. Citrus—oranges and grapefruit are hardier than lemons and limes. Kumquats, satsumas, tangerines, and limequats. In zone 10 only, banana, date, guava, mango, olive, chayote, carambola, cherimoya, macadamia nut, carissa plum.

CHILL REQUIREMENTS

Temperature zone fruit have a chilling requirement—a certain number of hours of below 45°F temperature during dormancy without which the tree will not produce fruit abun-

17

dantly. In zones 7, 8, and 9, where the number of hours of colder weather diminishes, chilling requirements become a problem, and nurseries that sell trees—particularly peach trees—in this area usually list the chill requirements of each variety just as nurseries farther north list the hardiness limits. If you live in these zones and don't already know the number of degree hours below 45°F for your locality, a call to your local weather station or university research station will provide you with the information. Here's a general guide to chilling requirements of common temperature region fruit:

> Apple—800 to 1,500 hours, mostly 1,000 to 1,200 hours, though some apples introduced recently from South America and New Zealand have a requirement as low as 300 hours and can be grown in most of the South.
> Apricot—700 to 1,000 hours below 45°F.
> Cherry, sour—1,200 hours.
> Cherry, sweet—1,100 to 1,300 hours.
> Peach and Nectarine—500 to 1,200 hours, mostly 800 to 900 hours.
> Pear—900 to 1,500 hours.
> Plum, European—800 to 1,200 hours.
> Plum, Japanese—700 to 1,000 hours.

California, Georgia, and other states where chilling requirements are critical to peach production continue to develop varieties with low-chill characteristics. Among the better known ones at this writing are: Desertgold from California, which requires only 350 to 400 hours of chilling; Springcrest, from Georgia, which requires 650 hours, still comparatively low; Starking Delicious, Sunhigh (New Jersey), and Harvester (Louisiana) require 750 hours of chilling below 45°F. Needless to say, the low-chill peaches will be less hardy, and the high-chill peaches such as Reliance, Harbrite, and Harken (850 to 1,050 chilling hours required) will be the hardier peaches.

In states where considerable differences in climate exist between north and south regions, and where more-or-less temperature weather gives way to more-or-less tropical weather, state and Federal agricultural information centers make available exceedingly helpful maps to guide the peach and other fruit growers. Georgia is a good example. Horticulturists there divide the state roughly from north to south into five areas (mountain, limestone, piedmont, upper coastal, and lower coastal), and recommend trees for homeowners by area number.

But for citrus fruits, which are more tropical in nature than temperate, horticulturists use a different division of Georgia— into three zones, A, B, and C. Zone C is the northern half of Georgia where citrus will not grow. Zone B is roughly the region of area 4 on the map below, where citrus of some kinds will grow with some success if given adequate protection. Zone A, roughly area 5, is where citrus is best adapted in Georgia.

Horticultural areas

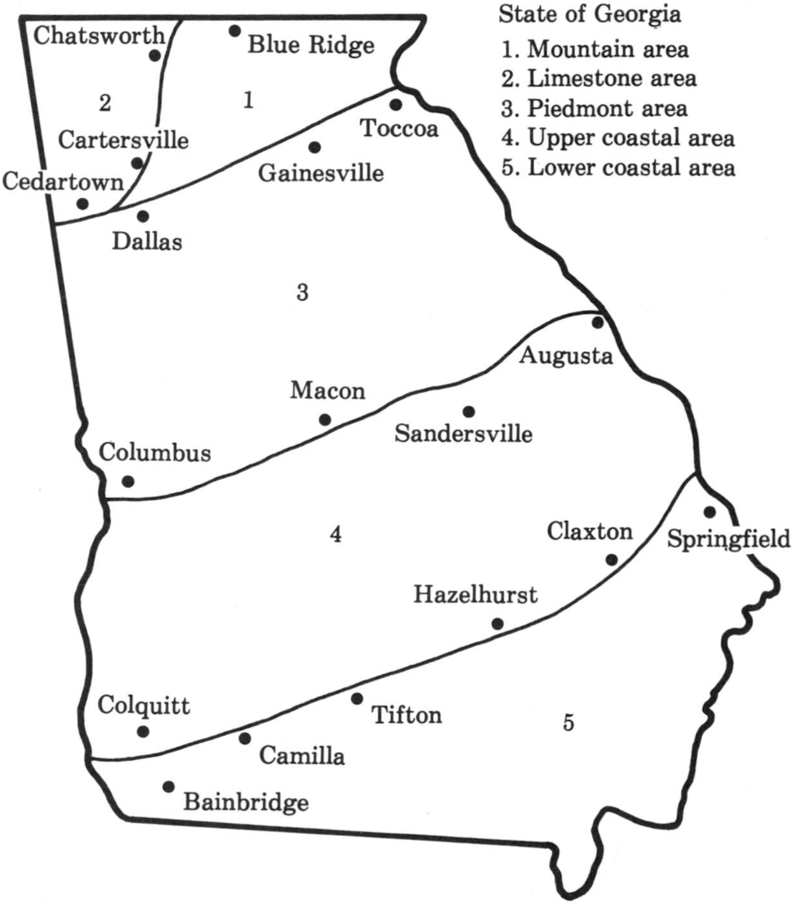

State of Georgia
1. Mountain area
2. Limestone area
3. Piedmont area
4. Upper coastal area
5. Lower coastal area

Chatsworth
Blue Ridge
2
1
Cartersville
Toccoa
Cedartown
Gainesville
Dallas
3
Augusta
Macon
Sandersville
Columbus
4
Claxton
Springfield
Hazelhurst
Colquitt
Tifton
5
Camilla
Bainbridge

Illus. 2-2—Map of Horticultural Areas in the State of Georgia— Horticulturists in Georgia divide their state into five areas according to an area's suitability for growing different tree varieties. The five areas are: (1) Mountain, (2) Limestone, (3) Piedmont, (4) Upper Coastal, and (5) Lower Coastal.

Table 2-1 **Fruit Varieties and the Hardiness Areas Where They Grow in Georgia**

Variety	Area
Apples	
Anna	4, 5
Detroit Red	1, 2, 3
Dorsett Golden *	4, 5
Ein Shemer	4, 5
Golden Delicious	1, 2, 3, 4
Mollies Delicious	3, 4
Ozark Gold	1, 2, 3
Paducah	1, 2
Priscilla	1, 2, 3
Red Delicious	1, 2, 3, 4
Redgold	1, 2, 3
Stayman	1, 2, 3
Yates	1, 2, 3, 4
Peaches	
Belle of Georgia	1, 2, 3
Dixired	1, 2, 3
Harvester	3, 4, 5
Jefferson	1, 2, 3
Junegold	4, 5
Maygold	4, 5
Redglobe	1, 2, 3
Redhaven	1, 2, 3
Redskin	1, 2, 3, 4
Springcrest	4, 5
Triogem	1, 2, 3
Pears	
Baldwin	4, 5
Carrick	1, 2, 3
Kieffer	all
Magness	1, 2, 3, 4
Moonglow	1, 2, 3, 4
Orient	all
Starking Delicious	1, 2, 3
Waite	1, 2, 3

Table 2-1—*Continued*

Variety	Area
Plums	
Bruce	all
Crimson	all
Frontier	1, 2, 3, 4
Methley	1, 2, 3, 4
Morris	1, 2, 3, 4
Ozark Premier	1, 2, 3, 4
Santa Rosa	1, 2, 3, 4
Satsuma	all

Types and varieties best adapted to Georgia are as follows:

Grapefruit—Coastal zone A only. Marsh and Redblush most frequently planted. Royal and Triumph, Ruby and Star Ruby are high-quality varieties.

Kumquats—Hardiest of citrus generally grown. Varieties: Marumi, Meiwa, and Nagami.

Lemons—Meyer is recommended.

Lime hybrids—Eustis, the limequat.

Satsuma—Most popular variety, Owari.

Sweet oranges—Zone A only. Dream Summerfield, and Washington navels for eating fresh; Hamlin for juice.

Tangerine—Clementine, and Dancy and Ponkan varieties.

Tangerine hybrids—Lee, Nova, Orlando, Osceola, Page, and Robinson. All require cross pollination for best fruiting.

Citrus on trifoliate orange (*Poncirus trifoliata*) rootstock increases hardiness considerably and is highly recommended by both backyard experimenters of the North American Fruit Explorers and by state horticulturists.

For papershell pecans, horticulturists use yet another division of Georgia as a grower's guide: above and below the fall line of the Georgia piedmont. Below that line, southern pecans can be grown commercially with success, while it's an iffy proposition above that line and suitable only for backyarders and hobbyists who do not depend on the crop for a living. Varieties recommended for homeowners who do not intend to raise pecans intensively with frequent spray programs, assiduous fertilization, close spacing, etc., are: Stuart, Desirable, Elliott, Farley, and Gloria Granda.

The more northern-type pecans, as distinguished from the papershell, can be grown in the northern part of Georgia and similar climates with comparative ease, except perhaps at high elevations. In fact, the northern pecan is surprisingly hardy, even in protected areas of the upper North. The Peruque variety is grown with fair success in northern Ohio, close to Lake Erie, by a hobbyist, Art Weaver. Doug Campbell, president of the Northern Nut Growers Association at this writing, grows pecans in Canada. (See the Appendix for addresses of organizations helpful to home orchardists.)

To see just how complicated the weather factors influencing tree-food production can become, study the northern pecan. The natural range of this pecan stretches up the Mississippi River Valley almost to northern Illinois and Iowa. Some horticulturists and archaeologists reason that the prehistoric Indians who built the mounds of the Midwest, and who were noted for their agricultural skills, may have selected pecans for hardiness over the centuries and planted them northward as their own culture advanced up the Mississippi and Ohio valleys. (The same explanation is applied to the papaw, a tropical fruit that grows wild as far north as Nebraska and Michigan.) Today, hardy varieties of northern pecans survive up into Canada.

The northern pecan not only needs 150 days of frost-free weather for a crop to mature; it also requires about 1,000 Cooling Degree days—a special measurement used by pecan researchers. One thousand Cooling Degree days is almost equivalent to an average July temperature of 75°F. So you can raise a crop of northern pecans in Ohio or Indiana, where the weather gets that hot in summer, but not necessarily in New England at the same latitude, because the East usually stays a little cooler during the average summer.

In the same vein, the pecan likes plenty of rain. Therefore, it will grow in eastern Kansas, but not in western Kansas without irrigation. You may conclude that Missouri should be a perfect place to grow northern pecans. But if you try it there at some of the higher mountain elevations, late spring frost will do you in.

Heat can be a limiting factor in fruit selection for your area in another way. The McIntosh apple, for example, is strictly a northern apple. You can grow it farther south, but where temperature exceeds 100°F for any appreciable length of time, the heat can almost cook a Mac right on the tree. It will not ripen nicely or put on what a commercial orchardist would call a good finish.

HUMIDITY TOLERANCE

In very humid weather, various fungal diseases, particularly brown rot on peaches, nectarines, and sweet cherries; leaf curl on peaches; scab on apples; fireblight on pears and apples, and black knot on plums, will make you wish you never heard the word orchard (mildew on apples and bacterial spot on peaches are lesser problems but irritating). Sulfur sprays and more toxic commercial fungicides can control some diseases sometimes, but down in a narrow deep valley in the humid East during a very wet spell in summer, you just can't grow nectarines profitably nohow. Nor will you stop fireblight in a susceptible pear in such weather—particularly if the tree has been fed amply with nitrogenous fertilizers—though you drown the tree in fungicide.

Resistant varieties and cultural practices that keep a tree from growing too fast are keys to organic blight control, or for that matter to chemical control. (See lists of resistant varieties in Table 2-2.) But if your grove of trees must grow in a very humid climate on a site not well ventilated by summer breezes, and you do not wish to spray some poison every week on your trees, you may wisely decide to quit trying to grow nectarines, sweet cherries, some plums, and some varieties of the other common fruits, even though they're hardy in your area.

I should perhaps make some exhaustive list of tree-fruit varieties that are hardy for particular regions or are somewhat resistant to particular diseases, but such lists are not really very useful. There are 22,000 known varieties of apples alone. The making of lists is endless and in the end becomes something like collecting postage stamps. Besides, the information on disease-resistance comes from commercial nurserymen and from the men who developed the variety. We can expect both sources to be enthusiastic about their varieties and emphasize greatly the fruits' strong points and not their weak ones. Only testing in your backyard will prove or disprove some of their claims regarding your particular situation.

What might be helpful is for me to set down from my notes and jottings the observations that backyard and professional

23

Table 2-2 Fruit Varieties and Their Resistance to Disease

Variety	Resistance	Disease
Apples		
Adanac	Resistant	Scab
Akane	Resistant	Scab
Prima	Immune	Scab
Priscilla	Immune	Scab
Red Baron	Resistant	Scab
Sir Prize	Immune	Scab
State Fair	Resistant	Scab
Transparent	Resistant	Scab

In my experience, yellow apples, even Yellow Delicious, are not as susceptible to scab as reds. But experience varies with area. Stark says its Earliblaze apple is resistant to scab and recommends it along with Starkspur Golden Delicious for organic growers. My Golden Delicious, growing beside a McIntosh heavily infected with scab during a sultry Philadelphia summer when we lived there, remained relatively free of the disease.

The Jonathan apple is particularly susceptible to mildew in the East.

Variety	Resistance	Disease
Nectarines		
Cavalier	Somewhat resistant	Brown rot
Cherokee	Somewhat resistant	Brown rot
Redchief	Somewhat resistant	Brown rot

Variety	Resistance	Disease
Peaches		
Biscoe	Somewhat resistant	Bacterial spot
Early White Giant	Somewhat resistant	Bacterial spot
Harbrite	Somewhat resistant	Bacterial spot
Harken	Somewhat resistant	Bacterial spot
Ranger	Somewhat resistant	Bacterial spot

Popular, long-cultured peaches such as Alberta, Belle of Georgia, and Redhaven have some brown-rot resistance.

Variety	Resistance	Disease
Pears		
Kieffer	Resistant	Fireblight
Lucious	Resistant	Fireblight
Magness	Resistant	Fireblight
Moonglow	Resistant	Fireblight
Seckel	Somewhat resistant	Fireblight

Bartlett, perhaps the most popular pear for eating, is one of the most susceptible to fireblight. As a rule of thumb, though exceptions exist,

Table 2-2—*Continued*

Variety	Resistance	Disease

Pears (*continued*)

the better tasting the variety, the more apt it is to be attacked by blights, bugs, and birds. This does not mean that low-quality fruit is more immune, however. For example, Kieffer pear is more immune, but Red Delicious apple, at which apple connoisseurs turn up their noses, is also quite disease-prone.

Plums

Greengage	Somewhat resistant	Brown rot
Ozark Premier	Somewhat resistant	Brown rot
Redheart	Somewhat resistant	Brown rot
Stanley	Somewhat resistant	Brown rot

As far as I know, no plum is particularly resistant to black knot.

Sweet Cherries

Stark Gold and other yellow varieties are somewhat resistant to brown rot. Sour cherries are much less affected by this disease.

orchardists whom I have visited and corresponded with have shared with me. Almost all of these notes are from contacts with my fellow members of the North American Fruit Explorers, who have always been most helpful and generous of their time and knowledge.

If you live in the coldest regions, you will be interested to know what Fred Ashworth, now deceased, grew in his orchards and nursery near Heuvelton, New York. Fred was a marvelous horticulturist and one of the most original thinkers I've ever had the privilege to know. He dedicated his life to the development of food plants for cold regions. He liked nothing better than to discover a tree fruit that would survive his climate. He was instrumental in the development of domestic blueberries and scab resistant, cold-hardy potatoes. He once sent me a list of the trees he grew and, at that time, he sold. Of the trees on his list, he marked the following as "northern hardy":

Apples—Alexander, Almata, Astrachan Crab, Atlas, Autumn Arctic, Bancroft, Beacon, Britemac, Carroll,

Chestnut, Cortland, Davey, Dodd Banana, Douglas Wormless, Duchess, Early McIntosh, Eastman Sweet, Fireside, Hadlock Reinette, Haralson, Honeygold, Iowa Snow, Irish Peach, Jenner Sweet, Jonamac, Joyce, McIntosh, Mandan, Manitoba, Mantet, Melba, Milton, Minnesota 1734, Newtosh, Niagara, Oriole, Ottawa, Puritan, Quinte, Red Astrachan, Redhook, Regent, Richardson, Royalty, St. Lawrence, Scott Winter, Sharon, Smokehouse, Spartan, Stone, Tydeman Red, Wealthy, Wellington, Wilson Juicy, Wolf River, and Yellow Transparent.

Beeches—Jenner Square.

Butternuts—Chamberlin, George Elmer.

Chestnuts, Native—Central Square.

Hazels—Dropmore Hazel, Skinner.

Hickory, Shagbark—Weschcke.

Pears—Golden Spice, Herman Last, Manning Miller, Southworth.

Plums, American—Dropmore Blue, Wessex.

Plums, European—Ewing, Todd.

Walnuts, Black—Bicentennial, Burns, Cochrane, Minnesota Native, Patten, Patterson, Weschcke.

Walnuts, Persian—Ashworth Carpathian, Himalaya Persian, Skukrud Carpathian.

Noteworthy, I think, is that Ashworth lists no cherries, peaches, nectarines, or apricots. However, he *could* have, if he wished, listed some sour cherries hardy for his area.

You cannot rush down to your favorite nursery and buy all of these varieties. If you're serious, join the North American Fruit Explorers (see the Appendix), then put your want lists in the organization's magazine, the *Pomona*.

Rootstock is another influence on a tree's ability to withstand cold and fluctuating temperatures. Ashworth used Dolgo crab, an exceedingly hardy tree, for rootstock on his apples, and Siberian pear for his pears. The typical backyarder will not, however, grow his own rootstock trees and graft varietal selections to them. Growing your own rootstock requires advanced propagation skills. If seedlings are used for rootstock, as is often done, the seedling tree is grown from seed and, in the tree's second year, cut off near the base and grafted onto the desired variety (see Chap. 6). You can purchase specific varietal trees used for rootstocks (such as Malling dwarfing stock) and, by a process called stooling, multiply each tree into many trees and graft desired varieties to them (see Chap. 6). Or if you have purchased a grafted tree with a desired rootstock on it, you can induce rooting of any sucker that comes up from it below the graft, cut it from the mother tree the second year, plant it on its own, and a year later, graft a desired variety to it. But this is a slow way to get new trees and seldom practical for the backyarder who wants only a few of each kind.

Growers are enthusiastic about a new dwarf rootstock for pears called Old Home-Farmingdale, which purportedly grows a hardier tree that's less susceptible to fireblight than the French quince commonly used for dwarfing pears.

Hardier rootstocks are now available for peaches (Nemaguard and Siberian C), and you can order trees with these rootstocks rather than the usual Halford or Lovell roots. Horticulturists are still arguing over whether these hardier stocks are necessarily better where winters are milder and trees are submitted to much freezing and thawing weather. But Halford and Lovell have demonstrated more endurance at least in some cases.

Some orchardists maintain that the Malling rootstocks, which are used to dwarf fruit trees, reduce hardiness in apples, but trials have not borne this out conclusively.

Finally, it is interesting to study Ashworth's apple varieties. Almost with exception, his hardier types have McIntosh, Duchess, Fameuse (Snow), or Wealthy varieties as one or both parents.

Harold Schroeder's orchard in northern New Jersey is interesting from several points of view. Though a commercial orchard, the varieties in it are mostly the older ones that are no longer marketed very much. Yet Schroeder has had little trouble selling all of his. (Advanced age has curtailed his activities considerably at this writing.) For purposes here, the orchard is interesting also because its location is an area where mountains are comparatively close to the ocean. Over a relatively small distance in miles, one moves quickly from zone 7 at the Jersey shore through zone 6 and into zone 5. Schroeder's orchard is therefore apt to have visited upon it all kinds of weather. He graciously sent me this amazing list of the apple trees growing in his orchard and also a list of the other fruit trees he grows (see Tables 2-3 and 2-4). He has never applied commercial fertilizer to his trees.

Because Schroeder's main interest is in experimentation

with apple varieties, he has kept detailed records of the ripening dates of his apple trees, which I've included in Table 2-3. Some trees with a date and the word "planted" next to them are too young to have ripened yet. Schroeder offered no ripening date for his other fruit trees in Table 2-4, possibly because of his concentration on apples.

Ashworth's and Schroeder's lists give an idea of the range of varieties that can be grown in a particular area. (For more information on what to plant where, see Part III, under chapters dealing with specific fruits and nuts.) You will, of course, have to make your own decision on varieties for your own area, and that takes good planning.

Table 2-3 Apple Varieties Grown by Harold Schroeder in Northern New Jersey

Variety	Average Ripening Date
Adams Pearmain	10/13
Arkansaw Black	11/1
Ashmead's Kernel	10/20
Baldwin	10/20
Barry	9/15
Belmont	10/1
Ben Davis	11/15
Benoni	8/5
Black Gilliflower	11/3
Black Oxford	10/25
Blenheim	9/20
Blue Pearmain	9/15
Bottle Greening	10/7
Bramley's Seedling	11/1
Bullock	10/16
Calville	10/27
Campfield	11/2
Chenango Strawberry	8/13
Cooper Lemon	10/10
Cortland	9/17
Cox Orange	9/24
Domine	10/5
Dyer	8/16
Early Harvest	7/25
Early Joe	8/20
Early McIntosh	8/1
Empire	10/8

Table 2-3—*Continued*

Variety	Average Ripening Date
Erwin Bauer	winter
Esopus Spitzenburg	10/18
Fall Pippin	9/24
Fall Wine	9/15
Fameuse	9/27
Franklin	9/25
Garden Royal	8/15
Gideon Sweet	9/7
Golden Delicious	10/27
Golden Russet (American)	11/5
Gould Sweet	9/15
Granny Smith	11/10
Gravenstein	8/20
Greasy Gate	10/5
Green Sweet	10/26
Grimes Golden	10/7
Hawley	8/20
Holiday	10/13
Holstein	planted 1971
Hubbardston	9/23
Idared	9/25
James Grieve	8/11
Jeffries	8/23
Jersey Black	9/26
Jewett Red	10/15
Jonagold	10/12
Jonathan	9/30
Kerry Pippin	8/18
Kidd's Orange Red	9/18
Knotty Russet	9/15
Lady	10/15
Lady Sweet	10/8
Lamb Abbey Pearmain	10/26
Late Strawberry	8/18
Leuthardt Russet	10/10
Lobo	8/26
Lodi	8/1
Lord's Seedling	8/18
Lowell	8/18
Lowland Raspberry	8/1
Lyman's Large Summer	8/4
McLellan	9/24
Macoun	10/10
Maiden Blush	9/3
Melon	8/18

Table 2–3—*Continued*

Variety	Average Ripening Date
Milton	8/25
Monroe	9/27
Mother	9/18
Muster	9/16
Mutsu	10/2
Newtown Spitzenburg	9/1
Northern Spy	10/6
Northern Sweet	9/15
Ohio Nonpareil	10/15
Opalescent	8/26
Orenco	9/5
Orleans Reinette	9/26
Ortley	10/1
Padleys Pippin	planted 1971
Patricia	9/20
Peck Pleasant	10/11
Pomme Grisé	11/1
Porter	9/5
Primate	8/13
Pumpkin Sweet	10/5
Quinte	8/11
Ralls	10/9
Rambo	10/6
Rambo Franc	8/22
Red Astrachan	7/21
Red Canada	10/21
Red Delicious	10/18
Red Gravenstein	8/20
Redhook	9/1
Red McIntosh	9/16
Red Spy	10/6
Rhode Island Greening	9/25
Ribston Pippin	10/2
Roman Stem	10/18
Ross Nonpareil	9/15
Roxbury Russet	10/15
St. Edmond's Russet	9/2
Secor	10/13
Smokehouse	9/22
Sops of Wine	8/7
Spigold	10/15
Spijon	10/25
Starkey	10/6
Starr	8/4
Stayman	10/23
Stearns	9/2

Table 2-3—*Continued*

Variety	Average Ripening Date
Summer Pearmain	8/19
Summer Rose	7/24
Sutton	10/10
Swaar	11/3
Sweet Bough	8/4
Tolman Sweet	10/11
Tompkins King	10/14
Twenty Ounce	9/11
Tydeman's Late Orange	10/13
Tydeman's Red	8/12
Vandevere	10/10
Wagener	9/16
Wealthy	8/25
Westfield	10/11
Williams Favorite	7/30
Winesap	10/30
Winter Banana	10/17
Winter Sweet Paradise	—
Wolf River	8/25
Yellow Bellflower	10/26
Yellow Newtown	10/27
Yellow Transparent	7/25
York Imperial	10/27
Young America	10/5

Table 2-4 Fruit and Nut Varieties Grown by Harold Schroeder in Northern New Jersey

Apricots

Alfred	Farmingdale

Cherries

Black Tartarian (sweet)	Montmorency (sour)
Emperor Francis (sweet)	Windsor (sour)

Nectarines

Newton	Surecrop
Rivers Orange	

Table 2–4—*Continued*

Peaches

Afterglow
Chenango
Eden
Fairhaven
Greensboro
Indian Blood Cling
Krummel October

NY-1456
Raritan Rose
Redhaven
Red Rose
Strawberry Free
Sunhigh

Pears

Bartlett
Beurre Dumont
Beurre Hardy
Bosc
Comice
Dana Hovey
Gorham
Josephine de Malins
Kieffer

Lawrence
NY-10274
Seckel
Sheldon
Snyder's Choice
Tyson
Vermont Beauty
Winter Nelis

Plums

Abundance
Beauty
De Montfort
French Damson
Greengage
Hall
Jefferson

Lombard
Mirabelle grosse
Mirabelle petite
NY-858
Santa Rosa
Stanley

Nuts

Chinese Chestnut: Kuling, Meiling, Seedling
Filbert: Barcelona, Cosford, DuChilly
Heartnut: Walters, Wright
Hican: Bixby, Burlington, Gerardi
Pecan: Busseron, Major
Persimmon: Garretson, Killen, Williams
Walnut, Black: Snyder, Sparrow
Walnut, Carpathian: Colby, Metcalfe

CHAPTER 3

PLANNING YOUR GROVE OF TREES

In planning your home orchard, try to weigh *all* of the purposes and advantages of various trees toward the comfort and health of your home environment. That's not easy. There's no neat, step-by-step procedure by which you can fashion a haven for a whole community of living things. Ecology does not proceed with linear, logical cause and effect, but by a dynamic implosion and explosion of interacting events only dimly understood.

You may achieve success sometimes not by action at all, but by inaction—that is, allowing nature to resolve the problem its way. For example, when we first moved to our homestead, my impulse was to remove the brush and weeds in the woodland so that it would look neat and parklike between the tall trees. So I mowed several times before I came to my senses and realized that I was clipping off the seedling trees by which the woods renewed itself, a renewal that guaranteed me a steady supply of fuel forever. Left alone, the seedlings grew thick and tall, blotted out the weeds and grass, and eventually thinned themselves into a productive stand of timber. Moral: The first consideration in developing your grove of trees is to consider considerably before doing anything.

Obviously the amount of time and space you have available for orchard care will influence your planning. Space is not, however, as important to your choice of trees as you might think.

A good degree of diversity and, therefore, a good degree of ecological quality can be achieved as well on half an acre as on 50 acres. The difference is more one of quantity than quality. The miniature grove will require a diversity of miniature trees, or diverse varieties grafted onto a few trees.

As for time, the orchardist who enjoys a grove of trees is limited only by the setting of the sun. He prefers being in his grove rather than pursuing other hobbies, games, or spare-time activities. He does not ask how little he can spare for his pastime, but how much.

On the other hand, growing backyard orchards and groves of food trees can be handled along with a full-time job without difficulty. The more natural method of caring for trees requires somewhat less time than conventional methods on the same size of orchard. To handle a 40-acre apple orchard or pecan grove commercially can be very much a full-time job, but a 40-acre homestead grove of trees can be adequately maintained in spare time. In the first case, you do everything you can to restrict nature within narrow limits for market profits, while in the latter the goal is to do as little as possible in favor of nature's own check and balance system.

EVALUATING CONVENTIONAL ORCHARD MANAGEMENT

With limitations of time, space, and climate in mind, the backyard orchardist should proceed in his planning with a questioning attitude toward the conventional platitudes of commercial orcharding. *Hardly anything most of us amateurs have heard about tree management is completely true.* Most of it is true, or at least "factual," only under modern, commercial situations. Rules of the factory orchard do not always apply in the home orchard, nor vice versa. Here are some of the usual remarks the home orchardist hears, and how he should respond:

1. "Seedling trees—those grown from seed—are worthless because they do not come true to the parent stock." Answer: A few fruit trees *do* come true from seed most of the time. The Dietz plum is one, and Lemon Free peach, usually. Any "heirloom" tree is quite capable of coming true from seed. An "heirloom" tree—a term used frequently by the North American

Fruit Explorers, who make a specialty of experimenting with seedlings—is an old variety of unknown genetic origin perpetuated from pioneer times in a given area. The pioneers planted trees from seed, adaptable ones survived, and the seeds were replanted. If the trees were self-fruitful (i.e., self-fertile—the tree needs no other variety for pollenation), seedlings coming relatively true from seed could evolve after several generations of inbreeding, as Dr. E. M. Meader, retired from the University of New Hampshire and a foremost breeder of new plant varieties, has often pointed out.

Seedlings often do produce poor quality fruit, and hence the five-year period growing them to bearing age might seem wasted. But if the seedling is hardy, you can graft on a good variety and have fruit in two years. What's more, extraordinarily good varieties might come from one of these seedlings if you're lucky, a variety fine for the home garden if not for the commercial market.

My own experience and those of other hobby orchardists have shown that seedlings produce reasonably good fruit often enough to justify a steady planting of a few at all times, if you have the space. The expectation of a real discovery adds much interest to orcharding.

Remember, too, that new strains of varieties come into being through genetic mutation. Many recent strains have come about this way, sometimes from the mutation of just a single tree branch. The cause of natural mutation is not understood, but mutation can be induced with cobalt irradiation (and other methods). A mutant, or "sport," as it is called by orchardists, is evaluated, and, if it's found to be superior to present stocks in some way, it's propagated by grafting into a new variety or patented strain.

It takes a sharp-eyed orchardist to spot a sport. It pays to be on the lookout. If a branch of one of your trees suddenly begins producing an apple redder than the others, or definitely different in shape, taste, maturity, or disease-resistance, you may be on to something. Sports are sometimes sold to nurseries for very high prices. For example, the original Red Delicious apple came from an unheralded seedling found near a yellow bellflower tree in a Peru, Iowa, orchard. That was in 1870. One of the most popular strains of Red Delicious today is Starkrimson, found by Roy Bisbee in his orchard at Hood River, Oregon, in 1951. It was a mutation. Stark Bro's paid $25,000 for it.

2. "Dwarf trees are the only size worthwhile planting today.

Standard trees are on their way out." Answer: That depends. Standard trees have some advantages over trees with dwarfing rootstock. In fact, only in apples are the dwarfing rootstock trees really satisfactory. In peaches, plums, cherries, apricots, etc., many horticulturists believe standard trees are better for home-owners. Rootstocks on standard trees are almost always strong-er, more adaptable to a wider range of soils, hardier, and more drought-resistant than dwarfing rootstocks. Dwarf trees usually bear earlier (but not always) and require less pruning. Dwarfs are easier to pick and spray, unless the standard tree is kept small, in which case the differences are minimal. You can keep a standard tree fairly small with intelligent pruning. Even in apples, skillful pruning can produce small standard trees. The smallest dwarfs usually require support, or the wind will make the trees wobble until the roots loosen, weakening the trees and even blowing them over.

You can order trees nowadays as you can order an automo-bile—with all sorts of optional features. The most popular dwarfing rootstock is East Malling 9, which produces a tree about 10 feet tall that needs to be staked or trellised. East Malling 9 is usually employed to develop hedgerows of trees rather than individually spaced trees; East Malling 26 grows to a slightly larger tree, one that takes up space of about 10 feet in diameter; East Malling 7 makes a tree about half the size of a standard tree, taking up space nearly 12 to 15 feet in diameter when mature; Malling-Merton 106 grows into a slightly larger tree than East Malling 7, and Malling-Merton 111 is a tree about 70% the size of a standard. Middle-size trees are called semi-dwarfs.

Refinements in dwarfing apple trees appear almost yearly. For example, some nurseries now engineer a tree that has seedling rootstock for sturdier anchorage. Size control is accom-plished by grafting a dwarfing interstem between the varietal graft and the rootstock. A second interstem of hardy trunk stock is then grafted between the dwarfing interstem and the root-stock to increase the overall hardiness of the tree. These advances are tremendously significant for commercial orchard-ing and may even be interesting to homeowners with difficult fruit-growing conditions. But for the typical homeowner, the cost and management time involved may be more than he can justify.

Orchardists also talk about spur-type trees to distinguish them from "standard" trees. A spur-type tree tends to produce short, fruiting branchlets or spurs all along the limbs rather than producing fruit mostly at the extremities of the limbs, as a standard tree does. Even without dwarfing rootstocks, spur trees are stockier and smaller than standard trees of the same variety. They usually require less pruning and, as smaller trees, produce more fruit than a nonspur tree of the same size.

The home orchardist, especially the homesteader with enough space, will find a spur tree on seedling (nondwarfing) rootstock to be a good choice. A spur-type tree on M 26 generally would be the next best selection because M 26 will adapt to a wide range of soils. The same tree on MM 111 will combine into a larger tree while still retaining the advantage of earlier bearing that dwarfing rootstocks induce. If you intend to pasture cattle where your trees grow, MM 111 is about the only dwarfing rootstock that will grow a tree tall enough to keep cows from eating the lower branches, and even then you will have to settle for the lowest scaffold branches being up higher than usual. (Sheep are better orchard grazers because they cannot reach very high.) For an orchard-pasture, a plain standard tree or a spur-type standard would be better. M 7 and M 106 dwarfing rootstocks are advisable to grow only on the best orchard soils.

3. "You have to prune hard and strictly by the book to get a good crop." Answer: Whose book? If you asked the five top professional orchardists how to prune your backyard tree, you'd most likely get five different sets of instructions. There is no one right way to prune a fruit tree, and a "prune-hard" formula can be a dangerous procedure for a backyarder, if not for a commercial orchardist. A tree's first five years or so are more for training than pruning, and excessive pruning at this time encourages vegetative growth but delays fruiting. Many horticultural experts therefore advise that on freestanding trees little pruning be done in earlier years (but of course not on artificially formed espaliers, cordons, and tree-walls). Start pruning to shape from ages five to ten.

In regard to what form that tree should be trained and pruned into, the central leader system is the method most often advocated today. But this method is advocated because it works best for commercial growers with medium- to high-density plantings of dwarf trees. The central leader system is not the only way to form a tree, nor is it necessarily the best way. The open vase form is usually better for the backyarder with semi-dwarf and standard trees, or at least the modified central leader system. These various forms will be explained in detail in the chapter on pruning.

4. "An orchard site must be tilled deeply and frequently for at least a year before the trees are planted." Answer: That is standard advice for anyone starting commercial orchards. You can find it in books 100 years old and in books one year old. The only trouble is, the advice is not necessarily essential and in some cases would be utterly disastrous.

I know it is not essential because I have been planting trees down through holes in sod for years and have rarely lost one. If the soil surface under the tree out to the dripline is mulched to prevent grass or weeds from growing there (or is hoed or tilled very shallowly), the tree will grow about as well as a tree planted in soil that is tilled for a year ahead of time. But don't expect a commercial orchardist to agree with that. His trees *will* grow a little more vigorously if the soil is deep-tilled, limed, fertilized, etc., a year ahead of time and that "little more" is important to him. But whatever extra growth such pre-preparation obtains will hardly be worth the cost to the homestead grower of a grove of trees to live in. What's more, deep tillage a year in advance cannot be practiced on steep hillsides, which are often eminently suited to tree culture. All the soil would wash off into the valley.

5. "Keep the orchard floor cultivated, or the sod will rob trees of water and fertility." Answer: Some commercial orchards will grow better, or crop better, anyway, with a dirt floor, particularly in dry regions or where soil will not erode. Peaches and almonds especially seem to prosper with this kind of culture. For reasons given above, the hillside orchard can hardly be kept cultivated. Nor is this method appealing to anyone who wishes to live in his grove of trees. He does not want to walk on mud or pick fallen fruit out of it. Besides, the cost in herbicides and mechanical cultivation for a bare orchard floor is surely not justified for the homesteader or backyarder. Better to mulch under the trees with old hay, straw, grass, and clover clippings, and a little manure. On very steep hills, you can't mulch, because water will wash away the mulch and then the soil under it. In such steep orchards, even the ground under the trees must be kept in sod.

6. "If you don't spray insecticides and fungicides on a regular professional weekly schedule, you might as well forget about raising fruit." Answer: Then why is it that I know personally of so many backyard fruit trees that produce without any spraying? For the backyarder, a combination of less toxic, so-called natural spray materials *a few* times a year with intelligent use of various biological and mechanical controls and

resistant varieties will suffice most of the time. Even commercially, orchardists are finding that a combination of cultural and biological controls have made it possible to decrease both the amount of spray material and the number of times the sprays need to be applied. The blanket use of poisons in the orchard is a crude and primitive form of insect and disease control that is already obsolete. Those very university and manufacturing concerns that have championed such practices in the past will be the loudest voices in their condemnation 20 years from now.

7. "You have to apply extra fertilizers to orchards just like you do any other crop if you want to get a high yield." Answer: I like to fertilize my trees, though I know the manure and wood ashes and bone meal are actually making the soil *too* rich around some of my trees—particularly too rich in nitrogen. Harold Schroeder in New Jersey has a large commercial orchard, described earlier, in which no extra fertilizer of any kind other than the clippings from the orchard grass has ever been applied to the trees. He believes and has fairly well demonstrated that skillful pruning produces better quality fruit without fertilizer. Dr. Elwood Fisher, in Virginia, grows hundreds of fruit trees as a hobby, and he uses no fertilizer, either, except grass clippings as mulch.

8. "You have to arrange your trees very assiduously into blocks in which pollenator varieties are spaced 'just so' next to the self-unfruitful varieties. Otherwise you will not get a crop." Answer: In large commercial orchards, especially where Red Delicious apples are grown in quantity (Red Delicious is self-unfruitful—that is, it needs another variety to pollenate it), the spacing of pollenating varieties requires careful planning. The idea is to use as few pollenators as possible in favor of the more marketable Red Delicious. Charts and planning diagrams to help the commercial orchardist accomplish this purpose look forbiddingly complicated to the backyarder. Then he hears that some professional orchardists are even grafting one branch of a good pollenating variety into every tree, and he throws up his hands in helplessness.

But there is no cause for panic. You need not strive for such perfect pollination. You don't really want your trees to bear that heavily. In a naturally managed grove of trees, an abundance of bees and other pollenating insects will do a fine job for you so long as the trees are reasonably close to each other. You do not have the commercial orchardist's problems. First he sprays to kill the bugs and, in doing so, kills the pollenating insects. So he scurries around to get good pollenation anyway, does so, and then must spray again to thin the fruit on the trees because it is too thick.

The rules you need to remember for home-fruit pollenation are quite simple.

Most apples are at least partially self-fruitful. The exceptions are: Red Delicious, Red Gravenstein, Rhode Island Greening, the Winesaps and Staymans, and Mutsu. There are probably a few more, but even these may be a little self-fruitful or may fruit when growing "alone" because some unknown wild apple tree or tree from a not-too-distant lot will pollenate it by virtue of bee or wind.

Horticulturists advise planting three different varieties of apples and pears if you want to be 100% sure of pollenating all the trees. In apples, a Golden Delicious tree is probably the easiest way to insure good pollenation. Golden Delicious is self-fruitful and pollenates all other varieties, as far as I know. Otherwise, the three-variety rule is the safest course to follow, if you plant self-unfruitful varieties.

Some plums are self-fruitful: Stanley, Greengage, Shropshire Damson, and many of the other old varieties (but not Yellow Egg), plus Italian, Blufre, and other prune plums. Fewer of the Japanese plums are self-fruitful, and not all will pollenate every other variety very well. Nurseries specify which varieties are self-fruitful.

I believe backyarders should stick with self-fruitful varieties. If you don't, you need two varieties for growing European plums and sometimes three with Japanese plums. Among Japanese plums, Methley and Santa Rosa are self-fruitful, but Methley won't necessarily pollenate Early Golden because of the difference in blooming dates. Make sure you find out from your nursery which varieties will pollenate which before you buy.

You must have two varieties of sweet cherries for pollenation, since none are adequately self-fruitful. (Stella, a new variety just on the market, is supposed to be self-fruitful). Most varieties will pollenate any other with some exceptions. Napoleon (sometimes called Royal Ann), Emperor Francis, and Bing will not cross-pollenate each other very well. There are a few other exceptions, but Vista, Vega, Sam, Valera, Ulster, Windsor, and many others pollenate all other varieties. Since varietal lists are unending, you should check your nursery catalog. Good catalogs include the necessary information. If you don't have room for two trees, graft two varieties on the same tree.

Sour cherries are self-fruitful, as are almost all peaches, apricots, and nectarines. Figs grown in the South and the East set fruit without pollenation. Smyrna-type western figs depend on a particular insect or on mechanical pollenation—a very special case beyond the usual skills of backyard growers.

Papaws and persimmons require two different trees for good pollenation. All citrus fruits are self-fruitful, except for the mandarin family, satsumas, and tangerines, all of which need cross pollenation.

Nut trees are generally self-fruitful and produce enough pollen for the wind to blow about so that insects aren't as necessary. But some growers, such as those in the pecan industry, believe cross pollenation between varieties produces a bigger and better quality crop. Having two varieties of the same nut tree is better but not necessary for the home-producer.

9. "Plant fruit trees on hillsides where they will enjoy good air drainage. Keep trees out of frost pockets." Answer: That is standard advice, printed and reprinted by every horticultural writer. What if you don't have any hillsides? What if you can't get a good flow of air through your orchard to keep temperatures just that little bit higher than they otherwise would be, and so prevent frost injury? Good air drainage is a practical consideration if you intend to make a good profit, but even then, quite successful orchards are maintained on level terrain, especially where large bodies of water or a naturally mild climate ameliorate cold weather. As for frost pockets, I would like for some frost-pocket hunter to point one out to me. Be honest now and tell me if you've ever seen a frost pocket hovering over the landscape. They hover mostly in horticultural libraries.

By definition, my creek bottom land, in a valley surrounded by hills, is a frost pocket. Cold air, flowing off the surrounding hills or settling out of the atmosphere, hovers there. I haven't planted fruit trees in that "frost pocket" only because it is too far away from the house, but I'm thoroughly convinced it rarely frosts any harder there than on the hills above. I have palpable proof, in fact, that one year frost killed tomatoes in the kitchen garden above the valley before it killed the ones planted down in the "frost pocket." Frost is not so easily categorized by pockets. There are different kinds of frost. Some that seem mild kill; some that seem severe do not kill.

Several miles from my place papaws grow down in a narrow valley that carries perfect credentials as a frost pocket. The papaw is a frost-tender tree that rarely survives anywhere in my

41

county. In fact, it is a tropical tree, but grows in the North because it doesn't know any better. How come it survives in this frost pocket?

I think low-lying areas that get labeled as frost pockets are bad for fruit and nuts because such low ground is often poorly drained, and very few, if any, food trees will grow in poorly drained soil. A deep, well-drained, creek-bottom loam will grow good crops of fruits and nuts, particularly black walnuts, hickory nuts, butternuts, and pecans, with little more injury to the trees than that of the same types of trees located above the valley. I'm sure there are deep mountain valleys and ravines where this is not so, but for the backyarder, any soil where the water drains well will suffice for family fruit and nut production. Worry about soil drainage rather than about air drainage. You can improve the former; there's not much you can do about the latter.

10. "Some trees prefer rich deep bottom land and some like light sandy upland soils. Plant trees on the sites they prefer naturally." Answer: Paul Stark, Sr., was once showing me around his family's orchards in the neighborhood of Stark Bro's Nurseries in Missouri. I asked him if there was anything special about the soil there that started the Starks growing fruit trees. He didn't hesitate. "No, I don't think there's anything special about the soil. The climate is more important. You can't do anything about that, but the soil you can always improve by adding the proper nutrients."

All my life I've heard how black walnut trees grow in river bottoms. Well, they grow pretty well on hilltops, too. When a nursery catalog describes a tree as one "that does best on a deep, well-drained loam," they are uttering a meaningless truism. Almost any tree will do best on a deep, well-drained loam. I have a hunch that a sand cherry or a beach plum would do better on a deep, well-drained loam if soil nutrients and acidity were favorable. I once found a wild apple tree growing out of a crack in solid rock. It bore many tasty apples, too. That's all I need to remember when some expert starts talking about preferred soils for food trees.

11. "It's foolish for older people to start an orchard. They'll never live to enjoy it." Answer: The best orchardists I know are all old men. They are all livelier, however, than many young men I meet. One fellow planted a pear orchard when he was 70. Twenty years later he was enjoying his pears while many of the people who had laughed at him were dead and gone. I sometimes think that old orchardists live long and healthy lives because they continue to plant trees to the end of their days.

CONSIDERATIONS "FOR THE BACKYARDER ONLY"

In addition to the foregoing considerations which pertain to the relationship (or lack of it) between commercial and backyard fruit production, the following tips are the ones you will want to think about that the commercial orchardist can forget. You are developing a grove of trees to live in and so, unlike the commercial orchardist, you are concerned about benefits from your trees other than the food they produce.

FOOD TREES FOR FUEL AND TOOL WOOD

Fuel wood is a fringe benefit of growing fruits and nuts because these woods are almost all excellent for heating. Hickory, oak, apple, and maple all make stove wood of high quality. Even mulberry and hawthorn are quite good, though they're small of trunk.

White oak, walnut, and mulberry make good fence posts. Black walnut and wild cherry are premier woods for fine furniture. Hickory makes good tool handles. Apple and hickory make aromatic smoke for fireplace burning and are first choices for smoking meat. All trees provide bean poles, garden stakes, clothesline props, even, on my place, livestock gates, a hay feeder, and a corncrib.

FOOD TREES AS SHADE

Maples and the taller nut trees are best for shading a house and lawn and may thereby reduce considerably (or altogether) your cost of air-conditioning. Maples, beeches, and hickories make a dense shade; oaks a medium-dense shade; walnuts and honey locusts a light, lacy shade. Grass will usually grow quite well under the latter two, but denser trees will have to have the limbs trimmed high to allow sunlight under the tree for grass maintenance.

Do not plant walnuts and hickories so close to the house that the falling nuts will bounce on the roof or against the windows. We once lived in a log cabin over which hovered a black walnut, and that's how we learned. Moreover, the squirrels worked on the nuts and dropped slivers of hulls on my wife's wash hanging on the line. White sheets adorned with brown stains do not a happy housewife make. Also, weird as it may sound, children playing under very tall specimens of these trees during the season when nuts fall are in danger. A black walnut with husk intact, falling from a height of 40 feet onto your head, is heavy enough to injure you. Don't plant them over children's play areas.

Mulberry trees grow tall enough to give good shade but are unsatisfactory around sidewalks and patios. The fallen fruit stains, but even worse, the kids will step on them and then walk into the house, staining the floors, too.

On the other hand, it's usually smart to plant cherry, or other trees the birds like, close to the house where children play, cats roam, and adults sit and chat. This activity scares away the birds, at least some of the time.

FOOD TREES FOR WINDBREAKS

In towns, the role of the windbreak is played by the houses themselves, which block the wind and ameliorate temperature to a degree that the urban dweller would find remarkable if he were suddenly transported on a windy January day to an open field in the country. In the country, the comfort index or wind-chill factor on the lee side of a woodlot on a breezy January day is astonishingly different than on the windy side. Even in towns and suburbs a windbreak of trees helps to cut heat loss from houses and, therefore, fuel costs. But in the country a good windbreak is essential, not only for saving fuel but for keeping

---

Illustrations 3-1, 3-2, and 3-3 were adapted from The Green Thumb, *a publication for home gardeners, published by the Department of Horticulture, University of Kentucky, Lexington, KY.*

Illus. 3-1—An Example of Trees as a Windbreak—This screen has been planted to make optimal use of the prevailing seasonal wind patterns at this location. In the winter, winds commonly come from the north and west, and are reduced in speed by the trees from 12 MPH to 3 MPH. In the summer, the breezes arrive most frequently from the south, and meet no obstacles to their natural cooling effect.

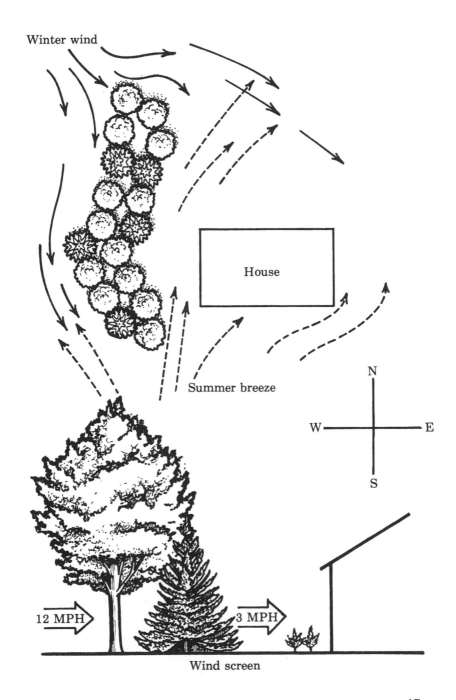

Winter wind

House

Summer breeze

N
W — E
S

12 MPH   3 MPH

Wind screen

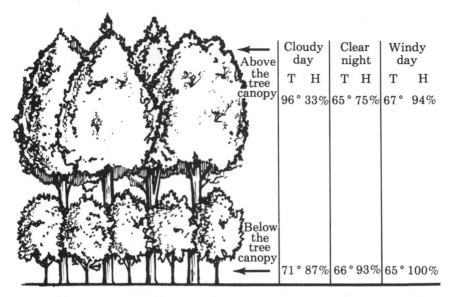

	Cloudy day		Clear night		Windy day	
← Above the tree canopy	T	H	T	H	T	H
	96°	33%	65°	75%	67°	94%
Below the tree canopy ←	71°	87%	66°	93%	65°	100%

Illus. 3-2—Differences in Temperature and Humidity Above and Below a Tree Canopy—Much cooler daytime temperatures under trees, compared to those in the open, are caused by more than the trees blocking the sun's rays. A tree canopy also increases humidity (air moisture) under it, which creates a cooler microclimate in the shade than possible without higher humidity. Conversely, as the sun goes down and temperatures in the open decrease, the humidity effected by the leaf canopy produces a slightly warmer microclimate under it, as anyone who has walked from a field into a woodlot on a late summer evening has experienced. A windy day tends to reduce the differences between shade and open areas.

winter an enjoyable time. It makes all the difference in the world if you can go to the barn in the morning protected from the wind.

Illustrations 3-1, 3-2, and 3-3 show some of the ways trees work to deflect winter winds and summer sunlight, and also how they let in cool summer breezes and warm winter sunlight. (In this example, the prevailing winter winds come from the west and northwest, and summer breezes come from the southwest.) The shade trees mentioned above handle the sun well enough, but for blocking the wind, evergreens are more effective.

Many kinds of evergreen seed cones contain edible (but small) seeds or nuts. In the East the Swiss stone pine, the lace-bark pine (*Pinus Bungeana*), Jeffrey's pine, and the Korean

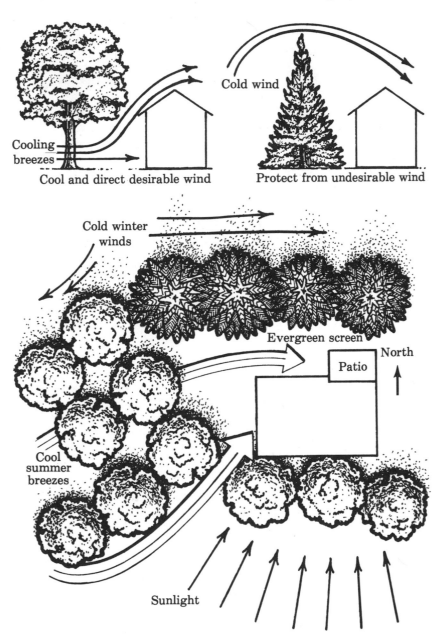

Illus. 3-3—Windbreaks Formed with Conifers and Deciduous Trees—This windbreak demonstrates the advantages of evergreens as north-side winter windbreaks, and of leafing trees as windbreaks for the rest of the house. In the summer, the leaves of the deciduous trees deflect the hot sunshine, while in the winter the sunlight warms the house through the leafless trees.

47

pine have a reputation for sizable nuts. The Swiss stone pine is a slow-growing tree, rather columnar in form, which makes it a desirable landscaping tree. The lace-bark pine is also a handsome ornamental. In the West, the piñon produces a larger nut that's more practical for eating.

Any tree that makes a dense hedge can be used for a windbreak. An orchard block of trees breaks the wind quite well, too. An L-shaped block of fruit trees in five or more rows to the north and west of the house, with a sixth dense hedgerow of autumn olive, hazelnut, beech, mulberry, or other food tree amenable to close trimming, would make a satisfactory homestead windbreak.

In our part of the North (corn belt), the ideal windbreak stretches from the southwest to the northwest of the house and barn. Our most severe blizzard winds actually come from the southwest, not the northwest, so the typical north-to-west Plains windbreak is not as effective all winter long as one protecting from the southwest, too. But complete protection means sacrificing some summer breezes, which also come from the southwest. However, I personally prefer fewer summer breezes in favor of blocking those keening southwest winds of winter and spring.

Wind protection helps your food trees, too, especially fruit trees. Hard winds push unstaked trees over on a slant, break fruit-laden limbs, winterburn branch tips, and loosen roots of dwarf trees in wet spring soils. Eucalyptus hedges protect citrus groves in Arizona and raise yields considerably. A century ago, English orchardists planted beech hedges around their garden orchards for wind protection. Pruned to grow densely, the beech was thought to block the wind almost as well as a solid wood fence. A beech hedge in the European manner (see Chap. 4) takes many years to develop, but nothing finer can be established as an orchard border or homestead windbreak. The beech provides food for man and wildlife, and the leaves linger over most of the winter.

FOOD TREES AND BEES

If you keep bees, position the beehives away from the prevailing winds, but where shade is available on hot summer days. Where the prevailing winds are westerly, as in most of the country, the beehives can be set at the southeast corner of the orchard, a comparatively warm and sunny spot in winter that's shaded in the afternoon in summertime. Very often on an ecologically balanced homestead wild bees will take over holes in woodland trees and from them will forage the abundant diversity of fruit and clover blossoms you provide. Bumblebees will also be attracted to such a homestead and will build their nests in the ground in brushy, undisturbed areas.

MICROCLIMATE VARIATIONS

If you notice microclimate variations at different places on your property, play them for all they're worth. An early-blooming apricot tree might do well on the north side of the garage where shade delays bloom during the critical frost period in early spring. An apple susceptible to mildew, or a nectarine to brown rot, might do all right on a breezy spot in the lawn, since good air circulation lessens fungal attacks.

FOOD TREE PLACEMENT AND THE GARDEN

Don't plant trees where they will eventually shade your vegetable garden. If space is at a premium and vegetables and trees have to be planted in adjacent areas, low dwarfs will be a good choice. It is the shade of the trees that hurts the vegetables more than the nutrients the trees take from the soil. You can always supply extra nutrition; you can't supply extra sunlight.

TREES AND YEARLY FOOD SUPPLY

Plant trees that will give a steady supply of food over as much of the year as possible. The longer you can stretch your harvesttime, the less you will have to store. Also, the more time over which you can spread your labor, the more work you can accomplish without straining yourself too much at any one time. This is one reason why maple sugar is an attractive enterprise for the homesteader—in March there's not much else to do except keep an eye on the lambing ewes. It's also more convenient (and comfortable) to "harvest" wood in the winter months.

Spreading out your available time is also why apples are such an attractive crop for spare-time workers. You can make

(*continued on page 52*)

49

Table 3-1 **Ripening Order of Common Fruits,
from Earliest to Latest,
in North Central States
(Adjust to your own region)**

Apples (beginning in July)

Early Harvest
Transparent
Lodi
Raritan
July Red
Quinte
Puritan
Jerseymac
Tydeman's Red
Akane
Gravenstein
Prima
Paulared
Ozark Gold
Wealthy
McIntosh
Mollie's Delicious
Cortland
Macoun
Grimes Golden

Spartan
Rhode Island Greening
Red Haralson
Honeygold
Empire
Priscilla
Jonathan
Northwest Greening
Red Delicious
Golden Delicious
Idared
Northern Spy
Mutsu
Rome Beauty
Stayman
Newtown Pippin
York
Arkansaw Black
Granny Smith

Peaches (beginning in July)

Harbinger
Springcrest
Desertgold
Candor
Garnet Beauty
Stark Early White Giant
Harbelle
Sunhaven
Reliance
Redhaven
Harken
Triogem
Harbrite

Sunhigh
Babygold #5
Glohaven
Suncrest
Madison
Cresthaven
Early Elberta
Elberta
Belle of Georgia
J. H. Hale
Rio-Oso-Gem
Monroe

Table 3-1—*Continued*

Pears (beginning in August)

Starkrimson	Seckel
Clapps Favorite	Anjou
Moonglow	Howell
Aurora	Bosc
Bartlett	Comice
Maxine	Kieffer

Plums (beginning in June)

Early Golden	Yellow Egg
Methley	Blufre
Earliblue	Italian
Shiro	Shropshire Damson
Ozark Premier	Valor
Burbank	Seneca
Formosa	Verity
Frontier	Vision
Mohawk	President
Stanley	

Sweet and Sour Cherries (beginning in June)

Vista	Ulster
Viva	Bing
Napoleon	Hedelfingen
Sam	Van
Schmidt's Biggareau	Stella
Rainier	Gold
Napoleon Royal Ann	Windsor
Venus	North Star (sour)
Emperor Francis	Montmorency (sour)
Valera	Meteor (sour)

Table 3-2 **Storage Periods for Common Apple Varieties (from Canada Department of Agriculture, Publication 1260)**

| | Months | |
	Normal	Maximum
Cortland	3–4	5
Delicious	3–4	6
Golden Delicious	3–4	6
Gravenstein	0–1	3
Grimes Golden	2–3	4
Jonathan	2–3	4
McIntosh	2–4	4–5
Northern Spy	4–5	6
Rhode Island Greening	3–4	6
Rome Beauty	4–5	6–7
Stayman Winesap	4–5	5–6
Wealthy	0–1	3
Winesap	5–7	8
Yellow Newton	5–6	8
York	4–5	5–6

cider until Thanksgiving, even in central northern areas. In fact, you can make cider all winter long from stored apples. Cider made in cooler fall or winter weather keeps better, ages more slowly, makes better vinegar (in my opinion), and sometimes if the cider barrel sits out in freezing weather the cider turns into a surprisingly champagnelike drink, as we found out by accident.

In planning your fruit supply, it helps to know early varieties from late ones, so you can plant for a continuing supply. Earlier, I listed Harold Schroeder's apples with dates of ripening. In Table 3-1 is a more general list of various fruits ranked roughly by dates of maturity. There are some that overlap; the list should not be used as a precise guide.

YIELDS OF FOOD TREES

Grow more fruit than you can use. Since diversity is a condition for ecological food production, and since a steady supply of fruit over a long season is more desirable to the homesteader than a glut at any one time, you will find that in attaining these goals, in good years, you will have much more fruit and nuts than you need. That's good. In bad years you will get enough. In plentiful times you have some to sell. In all years, the wildlife will not go hungry.

Here are a few general statistics on fruit production per tree. So much variability exists, due to a tree's age and condition, the annual weather, and other environmental influences, that you should not lean on statistics. What's more, production per tree is not as revealing a figure as production per square foot or per acre. It is possible to put 600 very small dwarf trees on an acre (or even many more than that in the special, ultra-high density plantings in commercial orchards). To get 1,000 bushels of apples per acre, each of these little trees would need to fruit 1⅔ bushels. In a planting of mature standard trees, you could get 48 trees per acre at the most, each of which would have to produce more than 20 bushels of apples to get 1,000 bushels per acre. That's possible, but you better figure your standard apple tree at something like a 10-bushel yield. Generally speaking, the denser the stand, the more the yield. In a hedgerow orchard, dwarf trees set 4 feet apart in the row with 11 feet between rows comes to 792 trees per acre with an expected yield of around 1,600 bushels per acre. In a backyard situation, a 50-foot hedgerow of these trees—about 12 trees—could mean a yield of 48 to 50 bushels of apples. That's a lot of apples for a family. In that same space two standard trees could be planted, and they would spread out a good deal more in width than the hedgerow and not produce that many apples. Nevertheless, the two standard trees, perhaps each grafted to half a dozen varieties, would require less overall labor and management than the hedgerow, while producing 20 bushels of fruit, more or less.

Three bushels is a nice yield for the semidwarf tree; expect a bushel or less from the smallest apple dwarfs with typical backyard care.

A standard pear tree will yield three bushels of fruit, often more. Figure roughly the same for peaches and nectarines, remembering that they all can do better (or worse).

For plums and apricots, figure two bushels per tree. The latter won't average that yield over the years in the North because of frost injury but in a good year might produce better than that. A medium-size cherry tree is good for a bushel or more—figure half for the birds.

A pecan tree ten years old should produce about 50 pounds of nuts. A big old hickory or black walnut tree not crowded by other forest trees can be counted on for a bushel of nuts (hulled). The hickories usually produce well only every other year.

We get 3 gallons of cider per bushel of apples, and 20 to 25 quarts of applesauce from a bushel's worth. By the time you add back cider and sugar (or honey) to the applesauce to make apple butter, a quart of applesauce makes about a quart of apple butter. How much apple butter, plum butter, peach preserves, cherry preserves, frozen and canned fruit of all kinds, dried and fresh fruits, cider, and other fruit juices your family will eat is yours to calculate. We have found that a family will eat as much as a family has time and energy to process and preserve. Homemade is just that much better.

A last word about spacing. You can put your trees as far apart as you wish, if you have the space. Or you can squeeze dwarfs into 6 × 14-foot spacings. Or you can train single cordons into rows or walls with plants just a couple of feet apart. Your inclination is your guide, relative to the amount of space available. For most busy homesteaders, trees spaced comparatively far apart will be easier to take care of. If you are planting a more or less conventional orchard block, you'd do well to keep standard trees on about a 30 × 40-foot spacing, though that is more room than they are allowed in commercial orchards. Pecan and other large nut trees require a space of 70 to 80 feet in diameter when they're 50 years old—that's only seven trees to the acre. In a grove, commercial growers plant much thicker, then thin them out as the trees grow larger.

For the commercial grower, very complex spacing arrangements have been worked out for every variety and every rootstock, but the homesteader need not worry about following these management procedures. Give the trees more room than they need. Mix the varieties and the types. Putting a nut tree between two apples, or separating a row of peaches from a row of nectarines with a row of persimmons and papaws, might just foil the spread of bugs and disease a little.

With all these cautions and uncautions in mind, study the homestead layouts in the next chapter. These plans are all actual homesteads of various sizes, not hypothetical ones. We'll discuss them, including both advantages and disadvantages. You're likely to find ideas you can use, and pitfalls you can avoid.

CHAPTER 4

MAKING
A TREE PLAN
AND
KEEPING
RECORDS

I don't like to use the word "landscaping" to describe the homestead plans that follow. They *are* landscape plans, but not within the framework nor in the proprietary fashion that professional landscape architects formulate their designs and lay down their infallible rules of beauty and taste. Landscaping, as pursued by America's better-homes-and-garden class, is half common sense and half fad. Its principal goal seems to be status, achieved through whatever is conceived to be the current, most fashionable style for the house-beautiful.

Landscaping, as the term is used here, has a different connotation. It seeks beauty in ecological balance, in diverse communities of living things that share the same piece of earth, in the integration of the unnumbered parts of the biological chain into an organic whole. It is, in the current sense of the word, "holistic" landscaping.

A good example of the difference in the two concepts of landscaping is the American invention, the large bluegrass lawn. From the modern landscaper's point of view, the large lawn is the principal medium—tool, so to speak—by which space around the American home is arranged to achieve beauty. The lawn allows the homeowner to keep (he hopes) the exterior of his home as neat and prim as the interior. The lawn is but an extension of the living-room rug. The more perfect the lawn grass, the better it apes the advantages of the rug; uniformity in color, texture, height, and growth enables it to be completely controlled. In other words, the lawn is perfect when it most closely resembles a nonliving piece of furniture. It is only a matter of time before Astroturf will start replacing grass in suburbia.

Believers in holistic landscaping see the large lawn as impractical and wasteful, taking up space that could be used better for food, fiber, and shade plants, and demanding a heavy cost in upkeep: fertilizer, herbicide, mowing, rolling, thatching, gasoline, oil, steel, time. Instead, lawns should give way to food trees and garden plots wherever possible, says the holistic landscaper. Lawns should only provide a place to walk between the more beneficial plantings, or as a means of holding soil in place wherever necessary.

The suburbanite's large, pure stand of bluegrass, sometimes whole acres of it, is a clear example of monoculture in action. Being contrary to nature, it is constantly beset by problems, just as any other system of agricultural monoculture. The executive's bluegrass sward swings from one crisis to another: brown from drought to mildewed from oversprinkling; too thin to too thick; too many weeds to too many fungal or insect attacks. Chemical after chemical is proposed to make the grass act like a rug, all to no avail. Just when lawn experts finally seem to have found the right "improved" grasses and chemical mixes for success, along comes a new danger, annual bluegrass. Annual bluegrass requires the same treatment that regular bluegrass requires to grow well, and so there is no way to get rid of one without harming the other. But annual bluegrass will crowd out regular bluegrass, then die and turn brown in late summer. No socially brainwashed American can endure a brown lawn.

But if men cannot learn to bend to nature with their lawns, how can we expect them to do so on a farm where profit, and not just status, is at stake?

Perhaps I pose the question needlessly. Perhaps we will be forced to begin holistic landscaping because the alternatives are too costly. For example, all of the landscaping plans that follow more or less embrace holistic ideas, yet the owners of these homesites do not use words like holistic, have never really thought about the wastefulness of lawns, and are not particularly concerned about ecology. They have arrived at their homestead designs out of a desire to raise more of their own food, enjoy their home, and achieve more self-sufficiency. They have arrived naturally at a more natural life, and that is perhaps the best or only way to get there.

TREE PLANS FOR VARIOUS SIZES OF HOMESITES

A QUARTER-ACRE HOMESITE TREE PLAN

This quarter-acre homestead (Illus. 4-1) in a small village proves that you can give up lawn in favor of food trees and raise surprising quantities of fruits and vegetables without detracting from the attractiveness of the yard. There are, however, a lot of lawn edges to keep neat. These can be managed easily with a mechanical edger. Note that the trees are all food producers. Even the maples can be tapped for syrup, though two trees will produce enough annually for only a few pancake breakfasts. The maples shade the house nicely from the summer sun, and the hickory is far enough from the house so that the nuts won't bounce on the roof or against the windows. The grape arbor under the maples will probably not do well—mine in a similar situation did not. The quince tree in the backyard corner is okay, but a mulberry, Juneberry, or chokecherry might be more valuable to lure the birds away from the tiny garden that's full of more tasty fruits. But the fruit plantings, even the dwarf cherry and the small peach, could be protected with netting. The fruit trees on the north side of the house might benefit from the shade of the house by a delay of growth during spring frosts. Certainly the wind protection provided by the house will shield the trees from southwest storm winds.

From the standpoint of saving heating fuel by deflecting cold winds, the yew hedge in front—on the west side of the lot—breaks the wind as well as any hedge, and yew grows well in

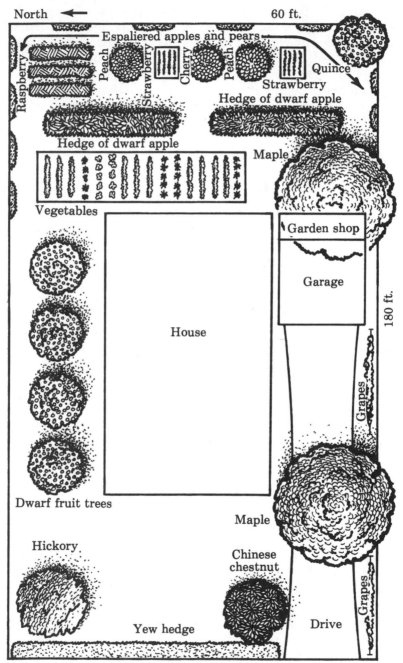

North ←   60 ft.

Espaliered apples and pears

Raspberry

Peach

Strawberry

Cherry

Strawberry

Peach

Quince

Hedge of dwarf apple

Hedge of dwarf apple

Vegetables

Maple

Garden shop

Garage

180 ft.

House

Grapes

Dwarf fruit trees

Maple

Hickory

Chinese chestnut

Grapes

Yew hedge

Drive

Illus. 4-1—A Quarter-Acre Homesite Tree Plan.

partial shade. But a yew hedge bears no edible parts. Hedging is hardly necessary directly on the north side of the house because a neighboring house blocks the north wind there. But a howling northwest wind can hone in against the house in full force under the hickory tree. It was no surprise to learn that the bedroom in the northwest corner of the house is the hardest room to keep warm. The yew hedge might be continued under the hickory tree. Where sunlight is adequate along the rest of the north side, a hedge pruned to grow dense, perhaps of beech or some kind of dense bush fruit acclimated to the area, might enhance wind protection and increase food production, too.

AN ACRE HOMESITE TREE PLAN

People don't sit on porches and watch the world go by like they used to do. The owners of the homestead in Illustration 4-2 are an exception. They believe the entertainment value of porch-watching beats most of television. Because the east side of the house faces the road, the east porch makes a nice, protected rocking chair space in spring and fall, though it lacks enough summer breezes in the hottest weather. At that time, the patio on the west side, with its superb shading from the maples, makes a cool, private place for summer cookouts.

Note that the cherry trees are next to the patio, but not so close that the fruit might fall on the stones. Having the center of human activity near the cherry trees will deter birds a little, as I've mentioned. By feeding the family cat beneath the cherry trees, it should be encouraged to linger there. Robins will then worry so much about the cat that they will eat only half as many cherries. These particular cherry varieties are sweet cherries. In most cases you need two trees for pollenation. Having two plums and three apples and three pears, all different varieties, insures good pollenation. The peach is self-fertile, so it doesn't need a partner.

I like the double run behind the chicken coop. By turning the hens first into one run and then into the other, alternating every two to three weeks, the runs do not get a chance to be trampled and eaten down into a bare messy soil. The mulberry tree overhanging one of the runs is fine, but it would be better located if it were planted in the middle of the two lots so that the chickens could eat all of the mulberries and benefit from all of the shade, instead of just a portion of both.

The empty space north of the chicken coop is for "expansion." The owner plans to extend his garden into that area or to use it for grain, alfalfa, or perhaps more fruit as his needs and

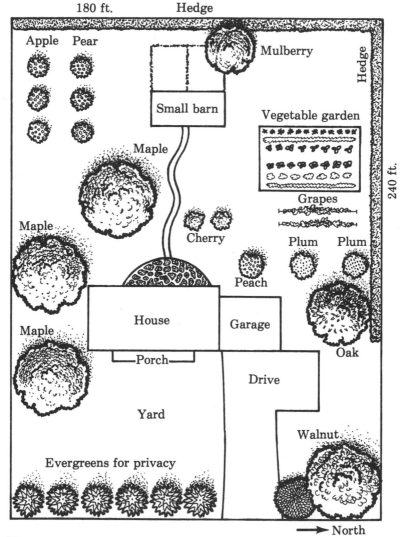

Illus. 4-2—An Acre Homesite Tree Plan.

skills increase. The hedge around part of the property is of caragana, a common hedge plant. It is very neat and eye-catching but, unfortunately, it's without any food value.

A 2-ACRE TREE PLAN

This grove of trees (Illus. 4-3) was our home for nearly ten years, so I can speak of it with intimacy. It was not an ideal grove of food trees, but it certainly was a diverse one. What enhanced this grove ecologically far more than I can describe in words or show with the landscape plan was the way it was surrounded by other homestead groves of trees much like it, the total effect being an almost wild woodland of great botanical variety, with the house in its midst almost, it seemed, as an afterthought. Behind us were about 6 acres of brushy woodland full of wild fruits and nuts. On either side of us were about a dozen homesites just like ours. I saw more wildlife in a month on this half-suburban, half-woodland area than I saw in a year living in a rural area of Minnesota.

The ash in the front yard made a nice shade tree, but had it not been there, I certainly wouldn't have planted it. It seeded little ash trees all over the lot, worse than any weed. The seedlings are difficult to cut or pull out. And the tree added little food value to the homestead (ash can be tapped for syrup, but it isn't as practical as maple or birch), though in a woodlot situation it provides excellent fuel for the stove and wood for tools. A nut tree would be better use of the yard space in this situation.

Two peach trees, four apple trees, four cherry trees, three pears, and a crab apple kept us in fruit through the year. The sweet cherries, except for the yellow one, suffered badly from brown rot, the McIntosh apple from scab, and the peach trees, which were already badly infected when we bought the place, from borers. The sour cherry, the yellow sweet cherry, the Alberta peach, the Golden Delicious apple, and the Seckel pear were more dependable. I liked my multiflora hedge that bordered the south and north sides of the property. It had to be severely pruned each winter, but it gave wind protection, privacy, and bird shelter. Intermingled with honeysuckle and bittersweet, the hedge provided food for the birds, too. Contrary to what other homeowners say, I had no trouble keeping the hedge within bounds.

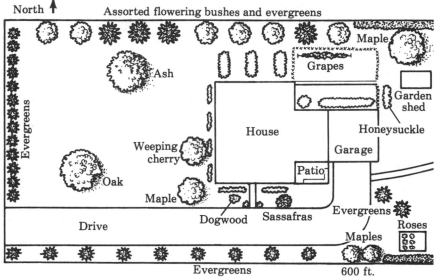

North ↑ Assorted flowering bushes and evergreens

Maple

Ash

Grapes

Garden shed

Evergreens

House

Honeysuckle

Weeping cherry

Garage

Oak

Patio

Maple

Dogwood Sassafras Evergreens

Roses

Drive

Maples

Evergreens 600 ft.

Illus. 4-3—A 2-Acre Tree Plan.

A TREE PLAN FOR 3½ ACRES

This homestead (Illus. 4-4) incorporates domestic animals into a grove of trees on a limited scale without unsightliness. Two small, attractive barns house horses and laying hens respectively. An outdoor, permanent, slat-floored pen concealed by trees houses a fattening hog in summer, and a small coop hidden behind the pine grove shelters summer-fattening broilers.

In the south pasture, the owners have a small grove of sugar maple because of their fondness for maple syrup. Fruit trees flank the house on the north hillside to take advantage of air drainage down the hill, some north shade to delay blossoming, and protection from stormy southwest winds. The disadvantage is that winter snow piles deeply on the hillside and must be tramped down around the tree trunks to keep rabbits from chewing on the lower limbs. Another reason for tramping down the snow is that the crusting snowdrifts are capable of piling up around small trees and then, as they melt, breaking down the limbs with their weight.

The pine grove makes a fine windbreak for the house to the northwest, but there is little protection from the critical west

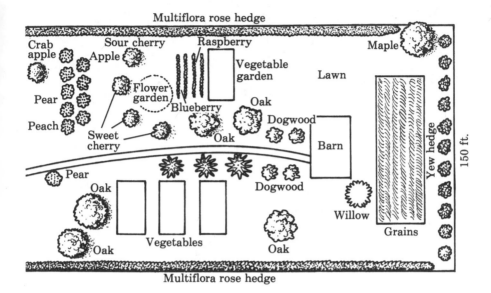

Multiflora rose hedge

Crab apple
Sour cherry
Apple
Raspberry
Maple
Vegetable garden
Lawn
Pear
Flower garden
Peach
Blueberry
Oak
Dogwood
Sweet cherry
Oak
Barn
Pear
Oak
Dogwood
Willow
Vegetables
Grains
Oak
Oak
Yew hedge
150 ft.

Multiflora rose hedge

and southwest directions. Lack of wind protection to the west is somewhat alleviated by the design of the house. It is set into an east-facing hill, and the whole first floor is below ground level and easy to heat. In the terrible blizzard of 1978, the wind carried snow across the open fields to the west and dumped it literally on the house, burying it to the roofline on the west side and providing almost perfect insulation.

Yard trees are bur oak, of which acorns in alternate years yield heavily enough to make considerable hog feed; thornless honey locust, a tree that J. Russell Smith in his *Tree Crops* believes to be a practical source of protein feed for animals and humans; maple; and assorted nonfood trees. The owners have started nut trees, including a Carpathian walnut with seed from a tree with proven hardiness in the area. The owners also planted birch trees (though not with the idea of making syrup or birch beer) when they first moved to their home and, as is the case almost universally, disease and insects killed the trees in about 15 years. The beauty of the white-barked birches is too much a temptation for homeowners, even when they know that growing the tree outside of its natural range is a very poor investment.

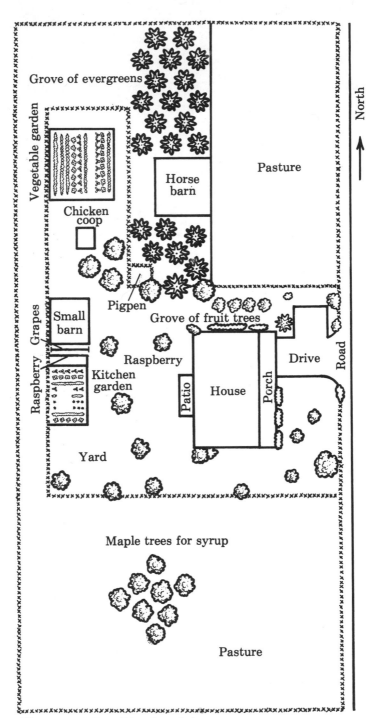

Labels within the illustration:

Grove of evergreens

Vegetable garden

Pasture

North

Horse barn

Chicken coop

Pigpen

Grove of fruit trees

Small barn

Grapes

Raspberry

Raspberry

Kitchen garden

Drive

Road

Patio

House

Porch

Yard

Maple trees for syrup

Pasture

Illus. 4-4—A Tree Plan for 3¹/₂ Acres.

A 5-ACRE TRACT TREE PLAN

This 5-acre tract (Illus. 4-5) is owned by a professed tree-lover and, as he freely admits, if even half of the trees grow that he has started, his house will be surrounded by a veritable jungle 25 years from now.

Both husband and wife are avid bird-watchers, and their landscaping reflects their interest. First of all, water is plentiful. Both the creek and the half-acre pond lure the birds and other wildlife. Both south and north sides of the property are flanked by autumn olive hedge, of which the berries draw birds and the blossoms lure bees. The back of the property is an old sheep pasture through which the creek winds. Trees are now reseeding with remarkable speed and variety in the pasture naturally from the woods adjacent to the property. The owner exercises only a "weeding out" role, choosing the nicest and the widest diversity of trees and mowing between them to keep other seedlings from overcrowding. The farthest reaches of the property along the creek are allowed to grow with complete natural abandon.

The result is one area where small trees, mostly walnut but with some wild cherry, hickory, and ash, grow without competition from brush. Another area is almost completely overgrown with brush through which the trees are just now beginning to emerge. Much of the brush is multiflora rose from an old hedge that had once bordered the sheep pasture. Its thorny limbs have taken over parts of the pasture, but already trees are fighting through and up. In about 15 years unpastured and unmolested brushland like this will revert to trees of which the shade will then kill out the multiflora rose. In the meantime, the brush, weeds, and new tree growth provide a cornucopia of food and impenetrable protection for birds.

On other sections of the property, where the owners like to walk, they grubbed out all of the multiflora. I've come to believe that this bramble, about which there has been so much controversy, both pro and con, grows with much more vigor in some areas than in others, or at least that some different strains spread much more vigorously. My own multiflora hedge was fairly easy to control, and Gene Poirot, the famous ecological farmer from Missouri, insists that multiflora is easy to manage. But Wendell Berry, the Kentucky farmer and writer, considers it one of his worst weeds.

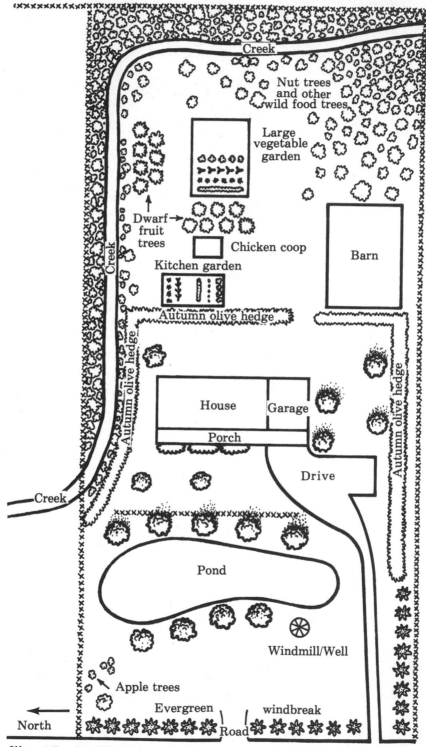

Illus. 4-5—A 5-Acre Tract Tree Plan.

Closer to the house, and spotted elsewhere around the property, are fruit trees, though most of them are grouped toward the middle of the property as shown on the plan. Most grow on a north-facing slope. Also spotted around the property are beech, maple, hackberry, and many other trees. The owner hopes eventually to grow at least one of every species that's hardy in his climate.

Birdlife has increased dramatically with the pond and with increased tree growth. Record bird counts for the county have been made without leaving the property. Drawback: The owners find it increasingly difficult to grow sweet corn—the birds eat the sprouting seed.

A 10-ACRE TREE PLAN

Just as the former plan is an example of a tree grove that fulfills most of a family's food needs amid thriving wildlife, this plan (Illus. 4-6) is a good attempt to combine a family's needs with intensive market-gardening while still preserving ecological balance and diversity. The owner believes that even 10 acres can contribute significant sideline income for a family if all of the land is used in an efficient manner.

In this case, the homesteader chose apples as the main cash crop. While the orchard trees are growing, he plants the land between them with grains. In another portion of his land, he has set out walnut trees in rows, the land between given to sweet corn, squash, and pumpkin crops for commercial marketing. (Trees the size of walnuts should be set no closer than 40 feet between rows.) He is establishing a windbreak hedgerow along the entire southern, western, and northern borders of his property, experimenting with various wild fruit and nut trees, plus evergreens. In addition, the family keeps bees to pollenate the fruit trees and raises a few hogs and chickens for family food, and occasionally a steer for extra meat. A small pond for swimming, fishing, and ducks completes the ecological circle on this small farm. To the south a small hardwood woodlot provides fuel for the wood stoves, plus shade and a little pasture for a pony and steer. Altogether this little farm is an amazing example of what you can do with a small amount of acreage—if you want to work at it.

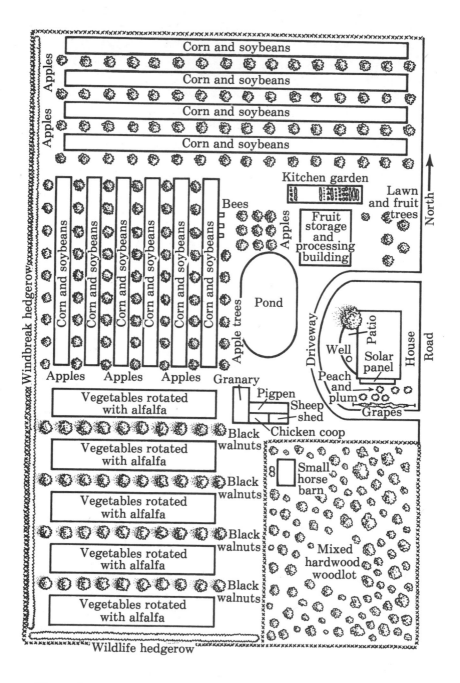

Illus. 4-6—A 10-Acre Tree Plan.

LOGSDON'S
22-ACRE HOMESTEAD

This homesite (Illus. 4-7) is our own 22 acres. Like the other examples, some of the trees shown are small and do not yet serve the purpose they were planted for. For example, the hawthorn hedge on the west side of the property behind the woodlot is still quite small, and the red cedar trees along the eastern border, just planted this spring, are barely alive as I write this during another dry summer.

When we bought our place, it contained about 6 acres of pastured woodlot, 14 acres of cultivated land, and a bit of sheep pasture along the creek. Out of this we hope to fashion a completely self-sustaining food and fuel resource for our family, plus eventually a little sideline income from our surplus. When we came here, we gave ourselves ten years to get on target, and after five years, that "ten year plan" seems to have been a wise allowance. From what we have learned so far, I feel confident that in ten years we shall know exactly what we can do for self-sufficiency and extra income, and what is not practical for us to do in this area.

As the plan shows, in front of the woodlot we have planted and are planting every conceivable type of fruit, with emphasis on raspberries and grapes, since we think (so far) that we can grow these two fruits dependably enough to market. Around the berries, grapes, and fruit trees, I planted autumn olive on the west side, backed by two rows of red and Austrian pine to serve as a hedge-windbreak. Three rows of pines on the west half of the north boundary will stop northwest winds (I hope). Along the rest of the north side, I planted a hodgepodge of trees and bushes that have not grown well. Much of my lack of success along this stretch I blame on my own negligence. I planted the trees down through sod, hurriedly, and did not mulch around them. Dry weather has taken its toll. Meanwhile, my knowledge grows. Instead of the nonnative evergreens, chestnuts, and European filberts I have tried to grow there, I am now planting native oaks that hold their leaves all winter and which are amenable to some pruning. I hope to fashion them into a hedge not unlike the beech hedges of Europe, but it will take years. In the meantime, however, as they grow they will form an attractive screen for privacy along the road, even in winter.

Among the orchard trees and along the south side of the fruit plantings, I am establishing as much wild fruit as possible:

69

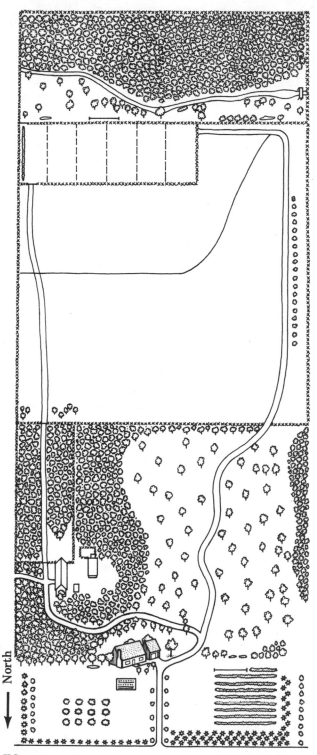

*Illus. 4-7—
Logsdon's
22-Acre
Homestead.*

North

chokecherries, wild black cherries, elderberries, persimmons, papaws, mulberries, hackberries, Juneberries, dogwoods— anything that produces fruit of interest to birds, if not to us.

In the woodlot, the trees are reseeding themselves now that livestock no longer graze there. As I mentioned before, I made the mistake the first year of mowing the woodlot floor with the notion of making my woods look like a park. I was mowing off the trees that would be my family's firewood 40 years from now. Also, when allowed to grow, these young trees would stop the cold winter winds from blasting through the sparse woods against the house and barn, particularly on the open west side of the woods.

After just three years of not mowing, many oak, maple, hickory, and ash trees have sprung up. The woods don't *look* neat and comely; instead, they are more like a thicket. Yet in a few years the young trees will crowd each other, some will die out, and the woods will open up again, becoming easy to walk through and free of brush under the trees, the way a properly managed forest should be.

I introduced hazels on the west side of the woods. The hazels are natives, transplants from just a couple of miles away. What wild crabs and wild apples I found growing along the woods' edge I have encouraged as much as possible, though if you let hardwoods in, they will eventually shoulder the wild fruits out. I also planted a few pine and spruce along the west side. They survived transplanting well in that rich woods' dirt, but the hardwoods will crowd them out, too, if nature has her way in this locale. In various, more or less open, spots in the woods I have planted other kinds of trees: walnut, beech, gum, sourwood, yellowwood, and sycamore. I had no special reason for planting these trees except to add to the diversity of plant life.

I tend to favor the natural inclination of the woods to revert to our climax hardwoods: hickory, maple, ash, and, above all, oak. This is what nature wants to do, and it could not be served better for my purposes. As I inventory our future needs, fuel wood looms high on my list of priorities. Fuel bills are soaring much higher for us than food. Because of the costs to heat our home by the grace of our public utilities, in "retirement" time I might be forced to move into some kind of economy apartment simply because I won't be able to pay fuel bills here. As for social security, part of my social security I see for my old age is the wood that I can cut and the food that I can grow.

If I can maintain a sustaining woodlot, wood will be a better source of heat for me at this location than solar, wind, or other alternative sources of power. At least that's the conclusion I've come to. My neighbor has heated his home with wood from an 8- to 10-acre woodlot all of his long life with no difficulties. So why can't we do it, too?

A hardwood forest managed properly produces about a cord of wood per acre per year without diminishing the woodlot. Oak, ash, and hickory are superior fuel woods that grow splendidly on my soil and in this climate. To get 8 acres (8 cords of wood will heat a small, well-insulated house for a winter), I am planting the back 2 acres, formerly sheep pasture, to hardwoods to go along with the 6 acres near the house. Actually, I have not had to do much seeding because a huge ash tree already there has scattered its seeds and, without the sheep there to eat them, the seedlings are growing up everywhere. Honey locusts are growing rapidly, too—they're considered weed trees in a pasture, but they also make good fuel wood. So I've planted only a few oaks and maples on the hilly ground above the creek, and black walnuts in the richer soil next to the creek. With some of the ash trees and honey locust already near the thinning size, we will be able to start relying on the back two acres for fuel in less than ten years.

If all goes well, the main woodlot will come on to self-sustaining production by that time. The young trees, kept so long from growing by grazing cattle and, then, by my thoughtless mowing, will begin to contribute to overall fuel production with their thinnings. Assured that plenty of younger trees are coming on to replace them, I will also be able to start cutting mature trees. A time will come (I hope) when a systematic harvest of ten mature trees per year will be possible without diminishing the woodlot. And at that point the large energy industries can get wealthy on someone else's sweat, not mine.

The main lessons I have learned so far in landscape renovation—to give my efforts a fancy name—are two. I've already mentioned the first: Don't start cutting down or clearing brush, etc., until you know for sure what you need to cut or clear. Mowing those seedling trees was one example. Another was cutting out the natural hedge that grew along the north edge of the woods when we started clearing a place for the house. The hedge seemed to me to be composed of just another ragged bunch of bushes, so I hacked and grubbed them out. I left a few—out of exhaustion, not perception. They bore dainty white flowers, which turned into blue and white berries that the birds loved. The foliage turns from an attractive dark green to red in the fall. The plant was a wild species of dogwood which, I have learned since, makes an attractive wildlife hedge.

I did learn, too, so there's hope for us all. This year as I flailed into another thicket, the better to destroy it, I noticed a small shrub with attractive green leaves similar to apple or pear leaves in the midst of the poison ivy and briers. I carefully cleared the brush around it and left it to grow. My reward? Later in summer the bush bore small, blue berries quite good to taste. I don't know the identity of the bush yet, but it appears to be a strain of *Amelanchier*—serviceberry—which is quite rare in this area.

The other important lesson I've learned in starting a grove of trees to live in is that native species will grow better for me than plants purchased from afar. What's more, a careful, knowing search of the surrounding area yields a much greater variety *and quality* of fruits and nuts for man and wildlife than I expected to find—perhaps as good as many of the lavishly described (and priced) exotics in mail-order catalogs.

The wild apple trees and wild plums I have started in my orchard are healthier than purchased trees, and the fruit is of satisfactory quality. I have learned that some wild cherries are much sweeter than others, some wild grapes are far less offensively pungent or foxy in taste than others, and that some wild plums are almost equal to domestic varieties in flavor. The better ones, acclimated to both climate and insects of this area, make dependable food with less care than regular orchard trees require.

So far I have resisted planting trees on a considerable, 8-acre space because I need pasture. I could perhaps plant this acreage to black walnut trees on 40 × 40-foot spacings, as some farmers are doing in Missouri (more on this later), and still use it for pasture of for making hay. So far, though, I've been content to establish a grass-legume graze, part of which I cut hay from. This pasture supports two cows and their offspring, several sheep, and a horse for about seven months during the year. If you've had to buy hay these days, you know that seven months of pasturage is a very good return on the land. Also, it requires very little labor on my part.

The lower end of the pasture is fenced off for my grain-alfalfa plots. Though not shown on the plan, I will eventually plant a row of trees inside the fence where the cattle can't get them. There will be nut trees and, I hope, acclimated Persian walnuts if I can find satisfactory varieties.

As I mentioned, the back 2 acres along the creek are now growing hardwood trees. We are experimenting with a low, temporary dam in the creek to hold enough water to provide more fish than the few meals we can get from the creek's natural production. The area is very much a bird haven right now, and we continue to add birdhouses, particularly bluebird houses. I fear we are also making a haven for woodchucks, muskrats, rabbits, and deer, all of which can play havoc with our small plots of grain and beans. So far, though, problems have been minor.

Our lanes, other than the one from the public road to the house, are not graveled and so are usable for truck or tractor for only about half the year, May to late November, and when the ground is frozen solid in winter. With careful planning, a homesteader can get all of his hauling completed in the dry months. If he has a team of horses and a sled, he can do the heaviest hauling (such as of wood) in the winter.

You can add about a month's usefulness to dirt lanes by laying them out on high ground or wherever the soil drains faster. To find where the soil firms up quicker in spring in a woodlot, you have to live with it a full year. Our lanes follow such areas as much as possible. Avoid making permanent lanes straight up or down a hill—they will surely rut and wash out, even in a woods. In general, don't run pickup trucks or similar machinery through your woodland any more than you have to. Tires are hard on forest land. Horses are much better, but walk whenever possible. In thawing time, homesteaders are often tempted to work their horses in the woods simply because the animals won't get stuck. At this time of year, horse hooves trampling the soil can cause much harm and mischief.

AN 80-ACRE WOODLOT

The following plans have been adapted from a USDA Forest Service brochure, "Managing Woodlands for Wildlife." I add them here to demonstrate the wide variety of "tree groves" that can be shaped to homestead ideals and ideas. In Illustration 4–8, this tract is a typical 80-acre woodlot in eastern hardwood country showing how the trees can be divided into 2- to 5-acre tracts, then harvested systematically by using both clearcut and selective cutting methods to increase wildlife while still profiting from the lumber.

With this example, the Forest Service would advise as a first timber harvest selectively cutting units 1, 6, 11, and 19. Then clearcut the area where the pond is to be built, where the road is to be laid out, and those areas which are to be planted to conifers. Then regenerate units 10 and 15 by the even-aged cutting method (cutting all trees of the same age regardless of size). After the pond is built, the conifers are planted, the trees

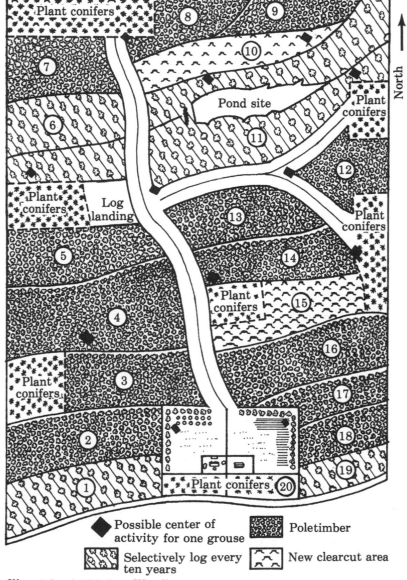

Illus. 4-8—An 80-Acre Woodlot.

are removed from the road and log-landing areas and these areas are seeded to grasses or legumes, and no harvesting (except, of course, for firewood) is done until about ten years have elapsed. Starting then and continuing every ten years, units 1, 6, 11, and

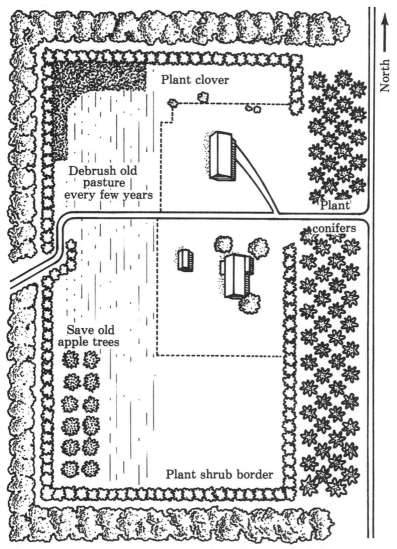

Illus. 4-9—An Abandoned Farmstead—A closer view of the farmhouse and yard on the 80-acre woodlot shows that wildlife has been encouraged to inhabit the area by the owner, who has allowed high brush to grow for cover and allowed the old apple trees and clover to grow for the animal food.

19 are selectively cut again. Units 4, 13, and 17 are regenerated by even-aged cutting at the end of the first ten-year period. Then every ten years, two or three units that do not adjoin tracts that were even-aged cut ten years previously are regenerated by even-aged cutting.

After two or three cuts (20 or 30 years), hardwoods are established on about 75% of the land and conifers on 25%. Even-aged units comprise 70% of the harvest, selective cutting 25%, and permanent openings about 5% of the land. This type of management keeps a forest rather evenly balanced in the ages of its trees—about 50% sawtimber, 25% poletimber, and 25% seedling-saplings. This admixture is best for continuous marketing and for wildlife, particularly grouse.

Section 20 of the plan, enlarged in Illustration 4–9, is of special interest to homesteaders, who often buy tracts of wooded and brushy land like this. Section 20 is abandoned agricultural land, and the plan shows what you can do to enhance it for wildlife (and perhaps for a bit of livestock, too). The old pasture growing up in brush is cut off with a heavy rotary mower, a job that will have to be repeated every few years if no grazing is done (for wildlife, of course, it's better not to graze at all). The old apple orchard is saved because apples are a favorite wildlife food, too. The clover provides good wildlife forage and an attraction for bugs, which young grouse, turkey, and other birds eat. Rather than allowing it to revert to woodland, debrushing the pasture periodically keeps it in the bushy stage and provides a variety of food and cover. The shrub border—autumn olive is one of the best—offers handy cover and escape for birds and small mammals. And the conifers in front provide privacy, not only for you but for wildlife using your improved habitat.

AN 1830 FARM IN OHIO

This landscaping plan (Illus. 4-10) is of a farmstead of about 1830. I add the plan here, which I took from an old history of Wyandot County, Ohio, as something of a curiosity. First of all, in 1830, Ohio was barely emerging from the wilderness, and the horticulturist is usually surprised to find such sophisticated planting of gardens and trees in land so recently occupied only by Indians.

I think it is curious that this farmer planted black locust trees in his yard. Black locust groves were often planted for use as fence posts. The trees are also good bee trees and are quite attractive in early summer bloom. Still, one wonders if there were other reasons that would prompt planting them in the front lawn. Perhaps it was the fashion of the time.

Note how the apple orchard and pasture are combined.

Certainly an unusual feature of this farmstead, and fairly unusual for the country it was located in, is the spring-fed stream that disappears into a sinkhole behind the house. The plan gives no indication of what happened to the water, but you can be sure it was troughed off to the barn, perhaps running constantly through the barn via pipe from the sinkhole.

Why the sycamore over the springhouse? Probably only because the tree was there first.

Note the osage orange hedge; 1830 is a very early date for use of osage orange this far east, where it is not native. The arborvitae hedge indicates to me that the owner was probably a wealthy farmer.

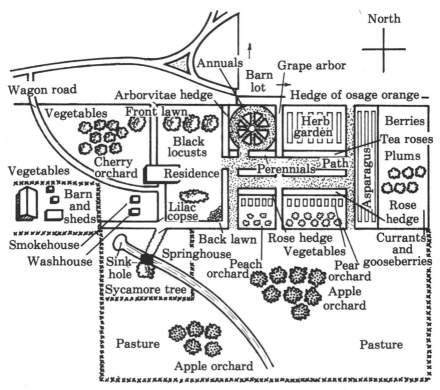

Illus. 4-10—An 1830 Farm in Ohio.

MAKING
YOUR OWN PLAN

There are at least two good reasons you should draw a plan or map of your property. Not only will it help you make plans for the future, but it becomes a record of what you have planted. When a veteran tree-planter first told me to keep a detailed map of where I planted what, I laughed. What, me forget? I could remember every tree I ever touched.

So I thought, and so I was so arrogantly wrong. The more trees you plant and the older you get, the less you can remember for sure. Trees die and are replaced. Identifying tags fall off. Without an accurate map you will be in trouble in five years, believe me.

A farm need not have as precise a map or plan as a half-acre plot, but in either case, the more detailed and accurate your plan, the more useful it will be. On, say, a 5-acre homestead, you may want to sketch a general layout and then divide the acreage into four or more enlarged, detailed sections. With a larger farm, you can divide into detailed sections by field. On a small homestead (if not on the large as well), each tree that is of a special, important variety should be assigned a number if there is not enough room on the plan to identify each specific variety. The numbers can then be listed below the map with the proper tree name. As we have seen, fields and tracts of forest can also be numbered so that rotations and harvestings proceed in systematic order.

More than one map may be advisable for the home landscape—one to show the plantings, another to show placement of the sewer, drain tiles, utility lines, the septic tank, and so forth. The latter map will not concern us here except to point out that, where irrigation is desirable, you may want to plan outdoor water lines to handle it conveniently. Also, you should be aware that the Environmental Protection Agency (EPA) and other engineers are experimenting with home septic systems that reuse the treated effluent for underground irrigation of orchards. (More on this later.)

If you use graph paper it's simple to draw your landscape map to scale. Let each tiny square of your graph paper represent a certain number of feet, the fewest possible while still getting your map on the size of paper you have. You can tape together four or more standard sheets if you want to make a *really*

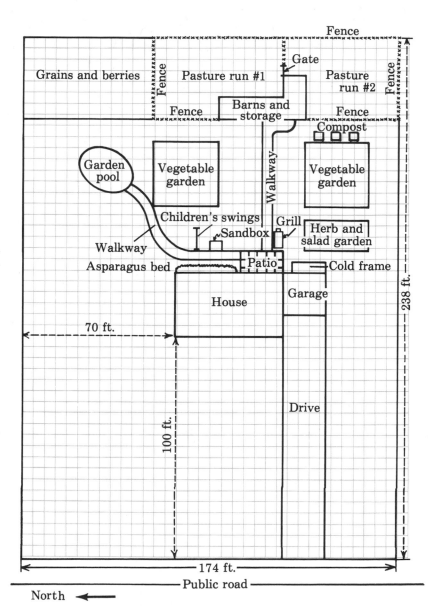

Illus. 4-11—Example of Drawing a Tree Plan—Each square in this example equals 5 feet per side, or 25 square feet. Boundaries have been drawn in, as well as permanent features, such as houses, walls, and existing garden plots.

detailed map. If each square of the graph can equal a foot, you can scale your map down with ease—20 feet equals 20 squares. But if you use graph paper like my example in Illustration 4-11, you can get only about a quarter-acre on an 8½ × 11-inch sheet of paper at a scale of 1 square per foot. So in my example of a lot not quite 1 acre in size, I use a scale of 1 square equals 5 feet per side or 25 square feet.

Measure your boundary lines accurately, or look up the information from your deed. Then draw the boundaries on the graph paper. In Illustration 4-11, the lot size is 238 × 174 feet, so it fits nicely on the page at a scale of 5 feet per square. Give orientation of the directions (show which way is north with an arrow) and on what side public roads or streets are situated. Next, locate your house and other buildings accurately on the map. You need to know the distance that one corner of your house stands from two adjoining boundary lines. Measure and position the house on the map accordingly, and do the same with any other buildings. Once you have one corner properly positioned, if you know the dimensions of the building you can easily draw them in. Use a ruler for neatness.

Next, draw in walls, fences, walks, driveways, the outdoor grill, compost bins, birdbaths, yard lights, the kids' sandbox, and any other more or less permanent installations, after measuring as accurately as you can their positions from two boundaries. (See Illus. 4-11.)

Existing trees can then be drawn on the map. (See Illus. 4-12.) On smaller lots, measure the position of each tree from two boundaries. On larger homesteads, the positioning might be by groups of trees, or close approximations of the positions of single trees, to avoid interminable measuring. But, where space is limited, it is important to know about how much room each planned tree or those trees in early stages of growth will take up at maturity. Aiding in this calculation is the most important function of the map. It prevents you from overcrowding your trees, the most common failing of do-it-yourself landscapers. If you deliberately plant too thickly, the plan helps you determine upon a systematic thinning procedure as the trees grow.

You can draw in trees you plan to establish later, but these should be readily recognizable from the trees already planted. You might use a second map or plan, or draw in future trees with a different color of erasable pen or pencil. Always use erasable markers for cases such as when you move a tree, or one dies, and you replace it with another.

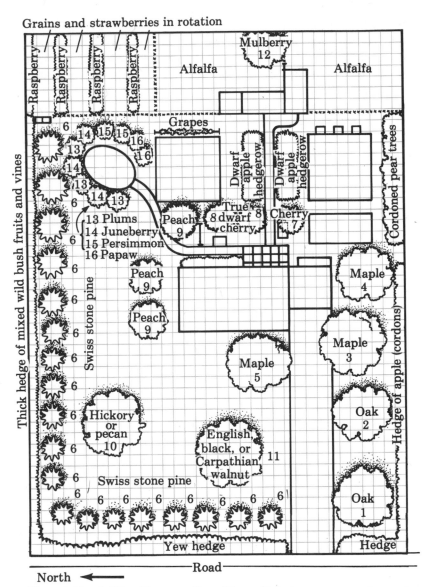

Grains and strawberries in rotation

Raspberry | Raspberry | Raspberry | Raspberry

Mulberry 12

Alfalfa

Alfalfa

Thick hedge of mixed wild bush fruits and vines

Grapes

6
14 15 15
16
13 16
14
13
6 14 13

13 Plums
14 Juneberry
15 Persimmon
16 Papaw

Swiss stone pine

Dwarf apple hedgerow

Dwarf apple hedgerow

Cordoned pear trees

Peach 9

True dwarf cherry 8

8

Cherry 7

6

6

6 Peach 9

Maple 4

6

6 Peach 9

Maple 3

6

6

Maple 5

Oak 2

6 Hickory or pecan 10

English, black, or Carpathian walnut 11

6

6 Swiss stone pine

Oak 1

6

6 6 6 6 6 6 6 6

Hedge of apple (cordons)

Yew hedge

Hedge

Road

North ←

Illus. 4-12—Adding Trees to Your Plan—Existing trees are drawn in first, then the trees that will be planted in the future. All trees should be identified on the map in some way, for future reference. In this plan the trees have been labeled and numbered.

If you view your work with trees as a serious contribution to society (which it is, even if you're too modest to admit it), you should keep a record book of your trees. Each tree number cannot only be identified by name, but pertinent information about the tree's place of origin, history, yield, and disease-resistance or susceptibility can be kept. This information is particularly important if you graft, grow seedling trees, hybridize, or select quality trees from the wild. Because tree work necessarily spans more than one person's lifetime, you will want to pass your grove on to someone who cares. That someone will find your record book worth its weight in gold.

CHAPTER 5

LANDSCAPING WITH ORNAMENTAL FOOD TREES

Many homeowners have gotten into the habit of looking at their lawns for the dilettantish fashionableness of a turn-of-the-century estate owner. Instead of filling the ground around their homes with useful trees and gardens, they plant ornamentals and lawns merely as decorations for the house. They wish to have a lustrous green rug of grass, bushes sculpted into artificial shapes, and trees that bloom profusely but do not fruit. Landscaping becomes nature imitating art, the absurdity of the fashion outweighed only by the cost to achieve it.

Landscape architects imbued with the idea of nature imitating art create formulae based on appearance only for landscaping correctness. Rules proliferate about the supposed proper proportion of tree and bush height to house and door. We are expected to accept the mathematics of these proportions as natural law. More importance is attached to shape and form than to light and water. Trees are described not in terms of usefulness but as art forms: ovoid, globose, pyramidal, columnar. A globose body of literature springs up to discuss the appropriateness of one shape over another for this particular site or that. Horticultural departments of state universities find it necessary to "serve the people" by conducting extensive programs to breed trees yet more ovoid and columnar, globose and pyramidal. Budgets, supported by taxes, also tend to grow more globose and pyramidal.

Emphasis centers on novelty, and the results are predictable. About the only columnar tree the ordinary taxpayer can afford is the Lombardy poplar, as unsatisfactory and short-lived a tree as was ever sold. It lasts 15 years, then falls down on your neighbor's grape arbor. The wood will not even burn unless you dry it for three years, and then it gives off no heat, only a foul odor.

Novelty brings us the ubiquitous white-barked silver birch tree that invariably dies quickly from borer attacks when planted outside its normal range, and that even when alive becomes so infested with birch leaf miner as to require constant spraying with toxic chemicals. A Purdue extension entomologist warned recently in a news bulletin that white birch, silver maple, and European mountain ash should be avoided (he spoke for Indiana, but tree growers in a far wider area can profitably heed his warning) because "they are almost certain to die from borer attack within a few years after transplanting."

Novelty. Why is a locust with yellow "sunburst" leaves prettier than one with green leaves? Is it really more satisfying to the eye to have a crimson maple with leaves that remain red all through the growing season than to have a common sugar maple with greenish yellow blossoms in spring, green leaves in summer, and orange red leaves in the fall? The latter has a far greater sugar content in its sap and wood of more value. James and Louise Bush-Brown, in their classic *America's Garden Book* (New York, Scribner's, 1958), called the sugar maple "unsurpassed as a shade tree for broad lawns or as a forest tree." And anyone can have all the sugar maples desired, for free, simply by gathering seeds in the forest or along the streets and planting them.

One other common family of trees might surpass the sugar maple in both beauty and usefulness, and that is the oak, particularly the white-oak group. The white oak sports pink-to-scarlet fall foliage, then often maintains its dead brown leaves attractively long into winter. It is a permanent tree like the sugar maple, lasting for centuries. It grows *slowly,* and this is an advantage, not a disadvantage as so many new homeowners seem to think. Fast-growing trees are invariably short-lived and are forever outgrowing the space allotted to them or demanding

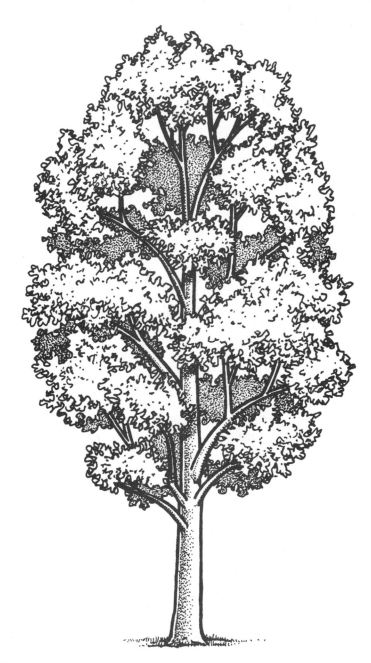

Illus. 5-1—A Young White Oak.

pruning. What's more, a young white oak is an attractive ornamental, lustrous green in early summer, often glowing maroon in the fall. And until it reaches about 20 feet in height it grows quite a bit faster than you would think. After that it seems to grow slower, but at that height it already begins to serve as shade. The added advantage of white oak is that it provides a practical source of protein for animals and birds, and for humans if a survival food is ever needed. Whole cultures have lived on acorn protein (see Chap. 18).

Oaks and sugar maples have traditionally been good choices of trees to minimize insect problems. Honey locust (except for some of the thornless, podless strains in certain climates), sweet gum, and linden are especially insect resistant and beautiful. Honey locust is another excellent potential source of protein (see Chap. 18). Linden is one of the best bee trees for honey in the East. Sweet gum, though not directly a food tree, is the source of storax, used in perfumes and medicines. The wood is also widely used in furniture, and the tree is unsurpassed for red leaf colors in the fall.

But *your* choice of trees depends upon your climate and environment. Sweet gum does not prosper in the North, nor do sugar maples in the South. Learn your native food trees and plant them first.

Foresters divide the country into regions according to the characteristic communities of trees that naturally grow and maintain themselves there more or less permanently if not disturbed. These communities of trees are called forest associations. Some maps of forest associations, like the one presented in Illustration 5-2, are very general. More complex but accurate mappings will show as many as 97 different forest associations in the eastern United States alone. But even a general map gives you a grasp of the necessary lesson the ecological planter of a grove of trees must keep in mind: Go with the proven winners in your climate and soil.

If, for example, your home is in the Southwest, in the juniper-piñon forest association, then junipers and piñon pines should figure prominently in your "food-landscaping" plans. Both kinds of trees produce useful food and fuel. The Indians built a culture on them (see Chap. 18). Moreover, when protected from the encroachments of civilization, natural stands of juniper and piñon develop an almost parklike beauty that you can duplicate around your home.

The surest way to select the right landscaping trees for your

(continued on page 90)

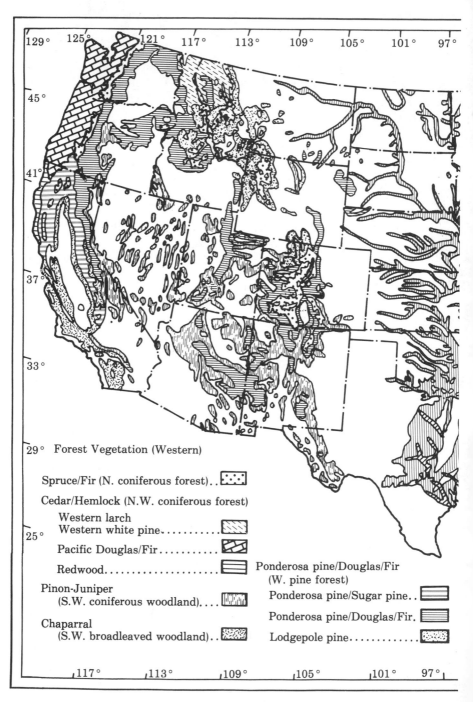

Illus. 5-2—A Map of Forest Associations in the United States—This
map from the USDA 1949 Yearbook of Agriculture is a very general

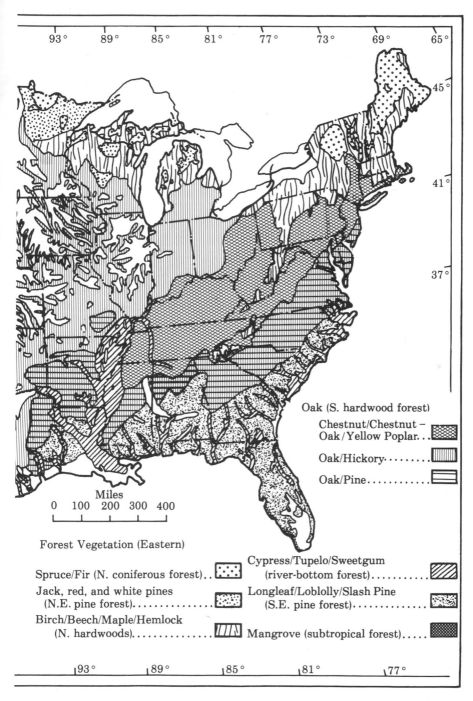

93° 89° 85° 81° 77° 73° 69° 65°

45°

41°

37°

Oak (S. hardwood forest)
Chestnut/Chestnut –
Oak / Yellow Poplar...
Oak/Hickory.........
Oak/Pine...........

Miles
0   100   200   300   400

Forest Vegetation (Eastern)

Spruce/Fir (N. coniferous forest)..

Jack, red, and white pines
(N.E. pine forest)...............

Birch/Beech/Maple/Hemlock
(N. hardwoods)...............

Cypress/Tupelo/Sweetgum
(river-bottom forest)..........

Longleaf/Loblolly/Slash Pine
(S.E. pine forest).............

Mangrove (subtropical forest).....

93°   89°   85°   81°   77°

example of a division of the country according to the trees that are naturally characteristic to a community.

89

grove is the simplest. Walk in woodland as close as possible to where you live and see what's growing there. Ideally, a remnant of virgin forest is the best kind of woodland to study, if you can find one, but any well-kept farm woodlot where trees have been harvested selectively as they mature is adequate. If the land was once cleared for farming, the new forest on it may not yet represent the stable climax community of trees native to the area. An abandoned field first grows back to weed trees, scrub growth, and thorns before the climax trees grow up and shade them out. These pioneer trees may have a place in developing your grove, but you can hardly get an accurate picture of your true forest association until the woodland is 50 to 100 years old.

For instance, I study the trees growing in two small acreages of more or less virgin timber, one in the southern part of my county on heavy, poorly drained soil, and the other in the northern part, on lighter, hilly ground. In addition, I note carefully the pioneer trees that grow around the sunny edges of these woodlots and along open fence rows nearby.

In both the northern and southern woodlots, the predominate species are oaks and hickories, just as the forest association map shows for our region. On the hilly light tract, sugar maple and beech are the next most frequently seen trees, while in the lowland soil, walnuts and white ash occur more often, with red maples common on the wet soil. Large and small black cherry trees occur occasionally in both forests.

Along the edges of the woodlots, redbud and dogwood grow in partial shade (reaching out for more light), plus hazels, hackberries, and an assortment of small, nonfood trees and shrubs. Where the forest is creeping out into old pastures, hawthorns, honey locusts, and walnuts grow, and the grass is surprisingly lush under the latter two trees. In the fence rows where sunlight is plentiful, honey locust and wild cherries grow, along with crab apples, hawthorns, wild plums, hazels, pin oaks, white oaks and wild apples. Of these trees, only the wild cherry grows as well in forest shade.

These few food trees alone can give all the landscaping beauty the imaginative homeowner desires, especially when you include their domesticated and improved strains. The fence rows tell me that cherry, apple, and plum are the fruit acclimated to my climate and soil and will make the most dependable fruit trees in an orchard. Black walnut and honey locust will grow well as lawn trees because as pasture trees they grow vigorously, improving the grass under them (see Chaps. 17 and 18 for reasons why this is so).

The oaks, maples, and other nut trees easily planted from seed provide enough variety in color, shape, and size to produce a stunning landscape. Shingle oak (often called northern live oak) keeps green leaves even into November in the North, then brown leaves all winter. The smooth-barked beeches hold tan leaves most of the winter. The hickories turn gorgeous yellow in the fall.

In the partial sun at the edges of the grove, I plant redbud and dogwood, taking a cue from nature. Both will grow from seeds of wildlings. Cornelian cherry (*Cornus mas*), a dogwood, has large and very edible berries. Though not a wild strain, it will grow well along woods' edges where it can get at least a half day's sun. Persimmons and papaws do well in this locale, too, and both are extremely attractive ornamentals if you wish to display them more prominently on the lawn. If the exotic intrigues you, the huge, tropicallike leaves of the papaw and its purple spring blossoms are hard to beat.

The apple, cherry, and plum families that I'm partial to for dependable fruit are also very decorative trees. As I write this, on November 7 here in northern Ohio, I look out the window at Winesap and Yellow Transparent apple trees still green, at a Stanley plum in bright orange yellow dress, and a Montmorency cherry extremely attractive in green, with branch tips orange. The only tree in the orchard with a prettier fall color this late in the year is an apricot, still golden yellow. Wild plums beyond the domestic trees have been a bright orange since October. All, of course, bloom profusely in spring. Blue plums, red cherries, red and yellow apples—what more could a landscapist ask?

Another fruit tree not recognized enough for fall coloring is the old-fashioned winter pear, one of which grows on nearly every old farmstead in this neighborhood. I suppose they are Kieffer pears, not much for eating until January and even then best when canned. In late fall, these trees glow in the sunlight with the most pronounced coppery orange color imaginable. And in spring, each is a shower of splendid white blossoms.

Fall coloring varies from tree to tree in the same species and from year to year in the same tree. This past fall the ashes (the most drab of all trees in my opinion; late to turn green and early to lose leaves) held their purplish fall color longer and brighter than usual. But the maples were duller than usual. Certain wild cherries, most of which normally fade to a drab yellow, sparkled with a warm orange, holding the hue until mid-November.

Flowering crabs are, of course, among the most acceptable of landscaping trees. Some, however, have better-tasting fruit than others (see Chap. 13). The best for eating are the large old-fashioned crabs used to make spiced crab apples, but these look more like regular apple trees from a landscaping point of view. Wild crabs, or native crabs gone wild, vary in taste and beauty. In eastern Pennsylvania north of Philadelphia, in abandoned fields between subdivisions, a most varied assortment of red, orange, and yellow crabs flourishes. Most of the fruit goes to waste, although it often tastes like miniature Golden Delicious or Red Delicious apples.

Hawthorns and southern "mayhaws" are attractive lawn trees, often with fairly good fruit. Even wild hawthorns, the dreaded "white thorn" weed of our area, are most attractive—a cloud of white blossoms in spring, a burst of red berries in fall, and an attractive silvery gray bark all winter long. If only they did not spread so horribly over pasture fields.

So-called contorted forms of hazels, such as *Corylus avellana* 'Contorta,' grow twisted and curled branches. Hence comes their popular nickname, "Henry Lauder's Walking Stick." Other strains of *C. avellana* bear yellow-tinged leaves and some even purplish red leaves. Though they do not produce nuts as abundantly as regular hazels, they do produce some for a family's needs.

Weeping forms of mulberry make beautiful and unusual lawn trees. There's one on the grounds of the grade school I attended, which seemed an old tree when I was there. Today it is hardly any taller (about 18 feet), still gracefully weeping, and with fairly good berries. They tasted better, though, 40 years ago when we were forbidden to eat them.

I recently visited a Persian walnut grove in northern Ohio (very unusual to grow there, even close to the moderating temperature influence of Lake Erie) and came home convinced that here was the best food-shade tree of all where it is hardy. The lustrous green leaves hold late into the year. September in this grove seemed more like June. The owner said that the trees cool his home so well that air-conditioning is unnecessary.

Another walnut, the Japanese heartnut, hardy to warmer parts of zone 5 (but just barely), has large tropical leaves and distinctive catkins as much as 12 inches long. In addition, with its tiny, pink-tipped blossoms, the tree is an ornamental gem.

Nuts are excellent eating, too, when frost doesn't catch the early-blooming flowers.

When in the South, I stand in awe and wonder at the beauty of date, banana, fig, orange, lemon, and lime trees. But the home folks seem accustomed to this Eden-like array of fruit. I even think that the turpentine "orchards" of longleaf and slash pine offer beautiful natural landscaping when the trees are in thin stands and cattle graze between them. But an orange grove? That beauty I could never get used to.

Everyone wants a few evergreens around the house. Why not grow ones with food value? The piñons are often used in the West and should be used more—the nuts are delicious, although the trees normally do not produce them every year. In the East, Italian stone pine and Swiss stone pine can provide the same service. I have a friend who gathers pinecones from the ground under Italian stone pines on the lawns of the Department of Agriculture Library at Beltsville, Maryland. (Who says the USDA doesn't help the people?) He even has a tree of his own started from one of the nut-seeds he gathered. He hopes eventually to have a protective evergreen hedge of them around his garden. He gathers the cones when they fall, dries them until the seeds shake out readily, then stores the seeds in jars. He cracks them only a few at a time as needed, because the kernels will turn rancid quickly after cracking unless they're frozen, he says.

A much-prized and unusual ornamental tree, the lace-bark pine (*Pinus Bungeana*), sports a unique, mottled bark pattern. It also produces edible nuts. Many other pines produce edible nuts large enough to gather (see Chap. 18).

Birch trees, including gray birch and especially sweet birch, are popular ornamentals and can be tapped for syrup just like maples (see Chap. 20). Sassafras, used for teas and root beer, has striking orange foliage in the fall. The carob, in its California range, is a good street-side tree, its beans used to make carob candy and other foods. The Chinese chestnut, a good nutbearer, is particularly handsome when in full bloom. The eucalyptus, from which comes eucalyptol oil, is beautiful in all seasons and an excellent choice for a windy location.

Summing up, you will find that in choosing ornamentals, the trees that provide food are also among the most useful and most beautiful for landscaping.

CHAPTER 6

PLANTING AND PROPAGATING TREES

I lay aside the books that propose to tell me how to plant fruit and nut trees, and with my mind full of their instructions, I walk through my tree groves. I observe trees in all stages of growth, in every normal type of environment: trees that have stood for over a hundred years in the leaf mold of their ancestors; trees that have newly sprung up in abandoned pasture fields; trees gaining a foothold in fence rows; trees that I have planted from seed; trees that I have planted from roots; trees that I have planted from nurseries. I see walnut trees coming up unbidden in an old pasture that without any care at all have put on 3 feet of growth in their second and third years. I see walnut trees I have planted dwindle and die. I see peach trees I set out with infinite care struggle to stay alive, but I see peach trees I slapped hurriedly in the ground in defiance of all right ways prosper vigorously. I see mysteries that no doubt can be explained, or at least explained *away,* but I do not see any steadfastly correct set of rules for planting trees. It is of the nature of trees to grow where they are acclimated to grow, and the closer we can mimic that natural grace, the easier will be our task of planting. It is as simple as that, yet evidently the lesson is more complicated than a man will readily grasp. My failures with trees all point to one factor: I too often have approached tree culture from an overly man-centered and technical point of view.

On an empty lot in our town grows the largest apple tree I have ever seen. It is at least 50 feet tall and over 3 feet in diameter in the trunk. No one knows how old the tree is, but surely a guess of 100 years would not miss by much. No doubt it grew from a seedling, perhaps a Johnny Appleseed seedling, for he roamed this area. I doubt if the tree has ever been cared for "properly"—I know it has not been sprayed or pruned in 30 years. Yet invariably in the fall it is loaded with large yellow apples, at least half of which are unblemished by insect or disease. Many of the apples grow so high our ladders will not reach. The tree is so thick with branches and water sprouts that we cannot climb up it. A wonder.

I walk every day in the grove of trees I live in, but only after four years did I notice the wild apple tree along the edge of the woods, crowded by brush. It has five small trunks coming out of the ground and looks like some errant wild crab apple rather than an apple tree. I discovered it when, much to my surprise, I looked up into the topmost branches and found nice apples hanging there. The tree violates every rule of proper apple tree culture. But men do not make the rules by which trees grow.

Trees propagate themselves by seeding, by sprouts from spreading roots, or occasionally from branches that bend down to the earth and root. Birds and animals help by scattering the seed, usually after eating it. The eating helps by softening the seed coat so that it can germinate more easily and by passing out of the animal's body with a bit of manure to supply nutrients for the new plant. Man has helped unconsciously, too, by haphazardly dropping seeds after eating fruit in the open.

Unhindered, trees will spread quite rapidly in humid climates wherever there are enough old trees to supply abundant seed. Recently I bought a small woodlot, the back portion of which had been heavily grazed pasture, devoid of trees just ten years ago. Shortly after getting the land, I took a sack of black walnuts there intending to plant them. To my surprise, almost all of the previously empty land was coming up in walnut and ash seedlings, a few of the trees already of bearing age. Instead of having to plant trees, all I need to do is "referee"—decide which should grow and which should be thinned. And the trees will thin themselves, too, if only I will be patient.

PLANTING
TREES FROM SEED

As I said earlier, planting fruit trees from seed is not a generally recommended practice because there is no guarantee that the seed will produce a tree like the parent. But as we have seen, it can produce such a tree or even a better one. In any case, there are more good reasons to learn how to grow fruit trees (and certainly nut trees) from seed than there are good reasons not to. Planting seeds is a far easier, far cheaper, and often an excellent way to get rootstocks upon which to graft either named varieties or that old wild tree you have found to be good for your purposes.

Books and instructions on planting tree seeds have always confused and discouraged me with their detailed complexity about "seed coat dormancy," "internal dormancy," and the need for "stratification" to break these dormancies, and maybe also "scarification." But all you really need to know is that some tree seeds need to be planted in the fall or stored over winter in the refrigerator so that they are subjected to the cold that breaks dormancy, while other seeds can be collected and stored like vegetable seed and planted in the spring. All fruit and nut trees of the north temperate region need cold stimulation to germinate (at least 32° to 41°F for about two to three months). Warm weather nuts and fruits, such as citrus, do not. Citrus seeds will sprout right inside the fruit on the table, given enough time. Cold treatment to break dormancy is called stratification when seeds are stimulated by storing them under sand or compost in a nursery bed over the winter, or when they are stored in the refrigerator.

"Scarification" is a word many beginners confuse with stratification. Scarifying a seed merely means to rub the seed coat thin with an abrasive, or cut away part of the coat with a knife, to weaken the coat so that moisture and temperature changes can soften it more quickly and hasten its germination.

The homestead grower is better served by planting his seeds in the fall. Both seed coat dormancy and internal dormancy can be broken by fall planting, though seeds with both kinds of dormancy may take two years to germinate. Planting seeds where you want the tree to grow has always seemed to be better than nursery planting and subsequent transplanting. I usually plant three seeds or more at the spot where I want a tree and cut away all but one if they all grow.

It is better not to let fruit seeds dry out too much before planting them. Cherry seeds and, in fact, most of the stone fruits ought to be dry to the touch, but not completely dry. The way to do that is to plant them within a few days after separating them from the ripe fruit. If the seed must be stored, a cool, slightly moist environment is best. Apple seeds will take cool, dry storage for a while. I once allowed peach seeds to dry out too much and they still germinated. Papaw and persimmon seeds should be kept moist and planted as soon as possible after harvesting. Persimmon has double dormancy and may take two years to germinate. You never know. I've had them come up the first year, the second year, and not at all.

By far the easiest way to start apple seedlings is to throw the pomace left from pressing the apples for cider onto a layer of mulch and forget them. Next spring literally thousands of the little seedlings will germinate, and if you move them at that time to where you want a tree to grow, they suffer little transplanting shock. I just drop a handful of pomace where I want a tree and cover it with a shovelful of mulch. In the spring I destroy all but the healthiest seedling that comes up. I recommend this "procedure" for all fruit. When you have seeded a bunch of cherries for a pie, throw the seeds on a mulch bed and forget them until the next spring. Do this for peaches, too, though they may germinate better if planted under a couple of inches of mulch or one inch of soil.

Nuts germinate in nature in leaf mold, where they fall or where squirrels bury them. You can grow them that way, too, but if squirrels or chipmunks are a nuisance, you may wish to store the nuts in the refrigerator or in the garage over winter. I put hazelnuts in the deep freeze once and got better germination than those stored in the refrigerator. If you decide to stratify nuts under a layer of sand, you may need to protect them from rodents by pegging a piece of hardware cloth down over the sand.

Another way to protect from squirrels is to plant the nut inside a beer or soft drink can full of dirt. Cut out the bottom of the can, then cut a cross in the top and bend the sharp points so they point upward—enough to let out the germinating sprout in the spring but not enough to encourage squirrels in fall and winter.

Black walnuts can be planted hull and all, but usually I plant dehulled ones. They're easier to carry. In soft forest loam, you can push the nut into the ground sufficiently with your foot, but in old pastures, along fences and lanes, etc., I carry a short-handled shovel in one hand, slip open the soil or sod, bend the shovel forward, and with my other hand drop a nut into the hole made by the shovel. The same with hickories, acorns, and other nuts. But I only just cover them with soil. English walnut, particularly, should be just barely covered.

Seeds that have very hard coats, such as honey locust, redbud, some persimmons, jujube, Digger pine, and Swiss stone pine, can be put into boiling water and allowed to cool gradually for 12 hours, but this method is not necessarily any more effective than fall planting.

Commercial nurseries and professional propagators may use the hot water treatment on fruit tree seeds, too, to induce faster, surer germination. The old way of doing this is quite complex, and practical only for a large number of seeds. Without going into detail, since the method hardly applies to homesteaders or homeowners, air-dried seed in sacks is dipped into water at 165°F for about ten seconds, allowed to cool for half an hour, dipped again, and then stored wet but aerated at about 36°F. In about two months apple seeds will start to germinate and then can be planted outdoors. Stone fruits take about three months before being ready to sow.

Some acorns, especially white oak acorns, do not possess the protection of dormancy and sprout in the moist leaf mold right after they fall in autumn. These seemingly fragile sprouts are susceptible to winterkill then, but they have a remarkable toughness. I have often noticed bedraggled, frozen, and apparently dead little seedling sprouts send up new seedling leaves in the spring from the root put down the previous fall. If you dig up this little seedling before the taproot starts growing fast—as it soon will—the little oak can be transplanted with success. Otherwise, oaks and most of the nut trees are extremely difficult to move after they have grown for a full year. Filberts are an exception. They are shallow rooted and spread by root suckering, and they transplant easily.

PROPAGATING FROM SPROUTS

Sprout generation is characteristic not only of hazels but also of hickory, persimmon, papaw, and most common fruits. Sprouting can easily be induced with many fruits. Cut the shallow root of an apple tree and it will often send up a shoot. Natural sprouts, such as the ones that come up around hickories, persimmons, or papaws, are extremely difficult to transplant because when they are small enough to move, very few roots have

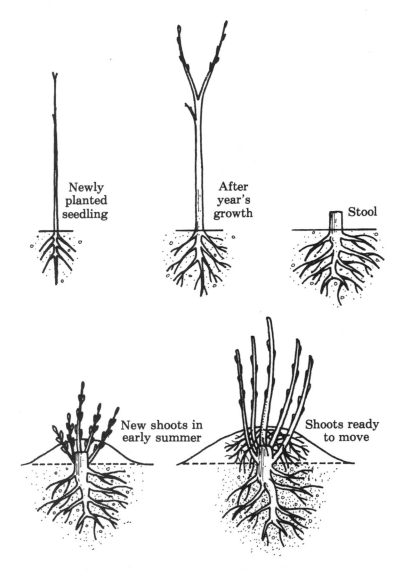

Illus. 6-1—Stooling Fruit Trees' Rootstock—To stool fruit trees, first cut the trunk of the tree flush to the ground. After the stump has sent up sprouts, mound soil around them. After they've developed their roots, the sprouts are ready to be dug up and replanted.

developed. Dig one up, and all you have is a piece of the mother tree root to which the sprout is attached.

Induced sprouting on fruit trees, called stooling, is, among other things, simple and practical. Though stooling is more often thought of as a commercial orchard technique, it's an excellent way to increase your supply of dwarfing rootstock. Allow the dwarfing rootstock to grow (or, in the case of apples, you can purchase Malling trees and plant them) until the trunk is about ¾ inch in diameter. Then cut it off even with the ground. The resulting stump will send up numerous sprouts that will develop their own roots during that year if soil is mounded up around them in the middle of July. Carefully dig them up and replant them the following spring. Allow another season of growth so that they develop good root systems. Then you can graft on a variety to make your own dwarf tree. Quince, for dwarfing pear trees, can be multiplied by stooling, too.

If a dwarf tree you've purchased dies or is winterkilled back to the graft union, don't give up on it completely if you want dwarfing rootstock. The root may not be dead, and if it grows up below the graft union you can cut the dead tree off and graft anew onto the rootstock sprout, or increase it by stooling. In some cases you may even be able to cut back a seedling or a grafted tree (staying above the graft union, of course) and induce sprouting of that variety. Then, by mounding up dirt around the sprouts or stools, you can increase the variety or the seedling by having it develop its own roots. If the seedling is one of a kind, however, I would never try this. If no sprouts come up and the tree dies, you've lost that ball game.

Fruit trees sometimes can be increased by rooting cuttings, but you need almost a controlled atmosphere and a mister. Rooting cuttings planted in a glass container or under plastic may work, but fruit trees seldom root easily, and the cutting may mold or mildew before anything happens.

Pinning branches down to the earth (layering) will induce rooting and sprout growth. The way this is usually done is to plant a tree at a 45° angle, then peg the tree down flat in a slight depression in the earth. Before its buds swell, the tree is covered with an inch or so of soil or peat and sand. Another inch of soil is placed around the young shoots when they come up but before their leaves unfurl and open. More layers are added two or three times during the first weeks of the growing season. When the shoots have grown 4 inches above these added layers, more dirt is layered after intervals of a few weeks until 8 inches of dirt cover the bases of the shoots. The process is called etiolation and is successful only by adhering closely to this elaborate method.

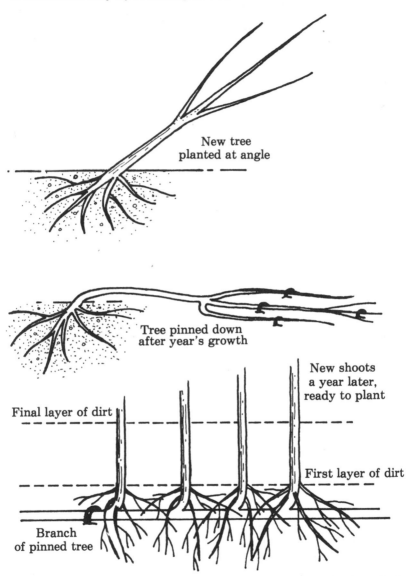

Illus. 6-2—Etiolation of a Fruit Tree—To induce layering in a fruit tree, the tree is planted at a 45° angle, then pegged down in a prepared depression in the earth. Before its buds swell, the tree is covered with an inch of soil, or peat and sand. As shoots come up, layers of earth are placed around them periodically until 8 inches of soil cover the base of the shoots.

101

PLANTING
NURSERY-GROWN TREES

Ordering fruit trees from nurseries is, in the beginning at least, the best way to get started provided you get good healthy trees from good healthy nurseries in the varieties best suited for backyard and homestead production. Most of us continue ordering from nurseries as our groves grow along, but you may decide to maintain your own tree nursery, from which you will sell or set out stock. Or, you may discover wild or neighborhood seedlings that you wish to move to your grove. No matter how you obtain your nursery-size trees, you'll find that growing them successfully depends upon mulch.

You can dig a very elaborate hole for the tree and fill in around the carefully placed and pruned roots with the best soil and rotted compost. Or you can hurriedly set the tree out between spring showers or in the dark before going to bed. The tree will usually grow just about as well in the second case as in the first case if you mulch the soil surface around the tree adequately. Six inches of mulch cover a multitude of planting sins. Even watering the tree every day is not as effective as mulch (unless you really soak the ground with many gallons of water). In clay soils watering with a few bucketfuls per tree per day does little more than harden the soil surface into a plaster cast. Then the soil cracks open and dries out the roots faster than if you had not watered them at all. Of course, you should not overwater, either, especially with some of the dwarfing rootstocks.

Do not put fertilizer in the planting hole with the tree—neither manure nor chemicals. Spread the roots of the tree out in the bottom of the planting hole, sort of in a circle. I like to set the tree on a ball of earth in the hole so that when I push earth back in the hole to fill it, the soil does not mash the roots all together. Compact the soil firmly but gently around the tree, taking care that the trunk is not left leaning to one side or the other.

How deep should the tree be set? The normal rule is to plant at the same depth the tree was growing before if it is an ungrafted tree. With grafted trees, opinions vary. Some dwarfing rootstocks tend to produce lots of sprouts around the trunk of the tree, and keeping them trimmed off can be a major job in a large orchard. Malling 7, 7a, and 26, desirable rootstocks in other ways, are particularly prone to root sprouts. Some nurseries have

102

begun grafting the variety *high* on the rootstock trunk (10 to 15 inches above the crown), so that the grower can plant the tree deeper. Another advantage of planting dwarf rootstocks deeply is that the resulting larger root mass anchors the tree better. Sometimes deep planting inhibits rootstock sprouting; sometimes it doesn't. But if you buy a high-grafted tree, the intention of the nurseryman is that you set the tree deeper in the soil than usual. If you want the *variety* to have a chance to root, plant with the graft union at or below ground level. This is seldom done, but it can be a way to give a weakly rooted dwarf a better bracing. But if the variety above the graft roots, the tree may not remain a dwarf in growth.

It is not a bad idea to stake all newly planted fruit trees. This can be very simply done with a slanted stake, bracing the tree against the force of the prevailing wind (which is almost always from the west in the United States so that your slanting stake should be positioned on the east side of the tree). You can also stake the tree on the west side by using a wire line looped around the trunk that is then attached to an upright post. A rubber tube on the wire prevents the bark from abrading, as the wind pushes the tree from the stake. If you don't stake your trees, many of them, particularly peach, nectarines, and apricots, will start leaning toward the east as they grow. Apple trees on Malling 9 rootstock should be braced even more securely so that they can't wobble in the wind. Malling 9 is a weak rootstock, and trees on it are invariably trained by being tied to some kind of trellis if they are not staked. Trellising is better.

Trees that come bare-rooted from reputable mail-order nurseries are always accompanied by detailed and excellent planting guidelines. Directions don't always mention a trick I've found beneficial, however. I unwrap the trees and set them in a bucket of water for a couple of hours before planting. If the trees have been stressed by a lack of water in shipment, they will take up water in the bucket, and you will not have to water them in the planting hole.

For surface mulch around the tree, just about any organic matter will do: leaves, cardboard, straw, hay, grass clippings, stable manure. If the latter, it ought to be mixed well with bedding so as not to be too rich, and it's better, of course, if it's well rotted. Do not pile the mulch up around the little tree trunk. Trees have been killed that way, particularly if the mulch is manure. It's best to leave a small area around the crown of the tree open to the sky.

103

In very dry, hot summers, additional water can be applied to the trees without harm. The mulch will prevent surface crusting and cracking. But a little water is not going to help the tree much. It makes you feel better, but the mulch is what will save the tree.

Transplanting trees with long taproots is often a losing proposition, which is why I have recommended planting seeds for nut trees and oaks as well as papaws and persimmons. However, Carl Whitcomb, a horticulturist at Oklahoma State University, recently announced success with a rather novel method for moving trees that grow long taproots. He plants seeds in cardboard cartons containing a porous soil mixture and places the cartons, with the bottoms and tops removed, onto a raised mesh wire support. The seeds germinate and send their taproots down through the soil in the cartons. When the roots reach the mesh wire, exposure to air causes their tips to die. This in turn encourages growth of heavy fibrous lateral roots that fill the carton in two to three months. The trees must then be transferred to larger containers, or they must be planted at their intended sites, where they will grow more roots rapidly. For a growing medium, Whitcomb uses a mixture of peat and perlite one to one, or two parts of ground pine bark to one part of peat, along with fertilizer. A good compost and topsoil mixture should work as well.

There are mechanical tree planters on the market that make tree planting a snap, or at least no more than a twist of the wrist. Pulled by a tractor, the mechanical planter opens a trench, you thrust the tree into the trench (and if you're good at it you'll get the roots spread out decently as you thrust), the planter closes the trench, and two big wheels compact soil around the tree. For setting large numbers of trees, as in a windbreak, hedgerow, or reforestation project, mechanical planters are fine, and you can often borrow or rent one from your local office of the Soil Conservation Service (SCS). (The machine is too expensive for a home grower to justify owning, at least $2,000.)

Smaller trees and seedlings can be planted fairly fast by hand, however. I don't like the usual spade or dibble-stick method that the forestry people tell us to use when planting large numbers of very small seedlings. The method works, and given the necessity of planting many trees in a short length of time, it may be the only practical way. But when you jam a seedling down behind the planting spade the roots often get compressed, pointing straight down. The little tree wobbles in the wind (if it is a conifer, it is top-heavy, anyway), and the roots dry out. Also the little tree, so set, can easily heave from frost after the first winter, right out of the ground in the clay soils of an old pasture field.

In the typical home situation, the owner of a grove of trees probably never has to plant more than 50 little seedling trees a day (if he's smart, he's planted seeds, anyway). If you take your time to dig a little hole with your shovel, place the tree in it on a ball of earth the size of your fist, and spread out the fragile, fine roots, you will get a better survival rate. If it's a nice spring day, who wants to be in a hurry, anyway?

Nematodes may be a problem, especially when planting trees in an old orchard or in old citrus groves. According to USDA research, soils nurtured with large amounts of organic matter have overcome root-knot nematode. Also, research shows that the old organic folklore of using marigolds to combat nematodes works. Plant them *thickly* a year ahead of planting the tree. I know of an orchardist who plants all kinds of flowers around his fruit trees anyway, so if you don't want to admit you are hoping to ward off nematodes, just tell everybody you like to see marigolds blooming in your grove.

GRAFTING

In my opinion, grafting is an absolutely necessary skill for the serious producer of home tree foods. Without at least knowing how to make a few of the easy grafts, an orchardist is only half an orchardist—at ten times the cost. Scions of desirable fruit and nut varieties are much more easily available at a very low cost compared to trees, and some of the varieties you most likely will want are available only in scion material.

Grafting enables you to do many things that keep a nongrafting orchardist hamstrung. There's no limit to the number of varieties and fruits you can cram into a small space, for one thing. A score of varieties can be grafted onto one tree (though three or four offer the best results), and the ones that do well can be increased by grafting them onto other trees. You can make your own dwarf trees. You can "collect" rare or exotic trees and propagate them in your yard. Wild trees of merit yield scions for your orchard—some rare old apple varieties have been found and saved in this manner by hobby grafters.

To combine a bad pun and a shopworn cliché, there are more kinds of grafts than you can shake a stick at. Once a tree-lover learns how basically simple it is to transfer one tree to another, he usually gets carried away with the infinite possibilities that his newfound skill presents to him. He has a vision of making a fruit tree do everything except pick up its roots and follow him around the yard. The grafter can multiply any variety endlessly, even the rarest. He can make a tree with a number of different apple varieties on it. He can grow pears on hawthorn, serviceberries on mountain ash, pecans on hickory, and many more weird combinations. He can make his own dwarf trees easily. He can repair a decaying tree trunk and make it strong again. He can grow branches together to make living braces. He can begin to invent new and wildly complicated grafting cuts and, like a surgeon, enjoy describing them in ways that make them sound very difficult.

Grafters are similar to surgeons in more than one way. They like to use surgeons' scalpels for grafting and are not altogether displeased to be referred to as tree surgeons. Their pride in their craft is commendable, but it has the negative result of making the rest of us believe that grafting is a difficult and esoteric art, just as we are convinced that surgery is way beyond our feeble skills. Actually, anyone who is knowledgeable and skilled at butchering can be trained in six months to perform many surgical operations, but only surgeons know that, and they aren't telling. In the same way, albeit on a much more mundane plane, you can learn how to graft in about 15 minutes, something grafters find hard to admit unless cornered.

Grafting is so easy it sometimes happens naturally. Two branches of a tree cross and rub against each other until the bark wears away, exposing the cambium layer of growing tissue between bark and wood. If the cambium layers of both branches remain in solid contact with each other for a growing season or even part of a growing season, a graft union can form, and the two branches will grow together into a stout bond.

Hundreds of clever variations on this basic theme of cambial contact have been invented and used with success, so long as the grafting is between two "compatible" trees—usually trees closely related—and so long as the grafter attends to the details closely. (See chapters on individual tree species.) But you need to master only two or three grafts to cover most situations—actually, the splice graft described below alone will suffice for most homestead grove-owners. After learning these, you can go on to others if you wish, or contrive your own. *The Grafter's Handbook* (New York, Oxford University Press, 4th ed., 1979) is a good text to study, but there are many other books, too.

BUD GRAFTING OR BUDDING

One of the most common kinds of grafting, especially for placing varieties on seedling or dwarfing rootstock, is budding. Almost all grafted fruit trees you buy from northern nurseries have been budded. The transfer involves just one bud, not a length of stem (scion), with a piece of bark attached to it. Budding is done in late summer, usually August, when the bark can be easily pried free of the wood—in grafting parlance, when the bark slips. Budding of pears and some apples can be done in late July, and, actually, grafters have been known to bud even earlier. Grafters of nut trees have even tried budding in spring on dormant wood, but such exceptional cases need not concern you at the beginning. Budding is more a northern practice because farther south the little bud may start to grow right after budding instead of staying dormant until the following spring, and that tender growth is likely to winterkill. Budding is the preferred method for peaches and nectarines, which are harder to graft by the splice method described later.

The bud to be grafted must be dormant, that is, not growing. It is usually cut, in the case of fruit trees, from a branch of the current year's growth, not out toward the end of the branch where the buds might still be too green in August, nor down at the base of the branch where they might be too old. The best buds are in the center of the branch. The branch is often cut off the tree and taken to the tree to be grafted. Such a branch is referred to as a bud stick; its diameter will be roughly that of a pencil up to the thickness of a finger.

In shield budding, the bud is cut off the bud stick in the shape shown in Illustration 6-3. Be sure to use a flat leaf bud at the base of the leaf's stem (axil of the leaf), not a rounded blossom bud. Leave the stem of the leaf on the bud shield, since you will need it for a handle when inserting the bud. Note that the bud shield is cut below the bud about ½ inch, just deep enough to catch a sliver of wood under the bud, then tapering back out about 2 inches above the bud. Part of the top of the "shield" (that's the shape of the bark you have cut out) will have to be cut off later.

Make an incision in the form of a T in the bark of the little tree to be budded. Use a very sharp knife so that you cut clean edges. (You should make this incision before cutting your bud shield so that you can immediately insert the shield into the incision before the bud has a chance to dry out.) Tip the edges of the incision outward with the point of your knife so that the bud can be slipped in more easily. Notice that the bark pries free of the wood easily. Now, holding the bud shield by the "handle," slide it as gently as you can into the incision from the top. You

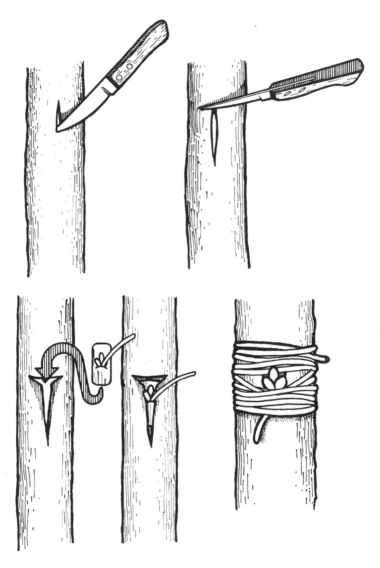

Illus. 6-3—Shield Budding—Cut a T in the bark of the tree, and work the flaps of the bark slightly back from the trunk to accept the bud. Once the bud has been carefully slipped into the T, cut off any of the shield that doesn't fit the T in the tree. Wrap with rubber grafting strips.

should try to get at least an inch's worth of shield length under the bark. The top of the bud shield will stick up above the horizontal cut of the T and has to be cut off so that it fits perfectly under that cut. But you may want to cut off the top of the shield a little higher at first so that you can place your knife blade flat on the top of the shield and press it down firmly, seating the shield solidly in the incision. Then cut off the top again so that it fits exactly under the horizontal cut of the T.

Next, tie the shield firmly, binding the bark tight against the shield. Rubber grafting strips are best; the old-fashioned raffia is harder to find now. Freezer tape works okay, too. Start tying at the top first. Do not bind over the bud, but around it as close as you can get.

With a little practice, you should get 60% to 90% takes. Some beginning budders put two or three buds on a tree to insure that at least one takes. If all take in the spring, cut off all but one. Some budders believe that a bud on the north (shady) side of the trunk will take more often. I sometimes wind a strip of bread-wrapper over a bud graft, tight above and below the bud but loose right over it, to keep it from drying out the first week or so. But in very hot weather, such a mini-greenhouse effect might be too hot for the bud.

If time must elapse between cutting the bud stick and doing the budding, you can keep the bud stick for a week or more moist and cool in a plastic bag in a refrigerator. If you collect budwood on a trip, you can preserve it that way until you get home. All good orchardists and tree-lovers carry plastic bags with them when traveling—you never know when you might meet an interesting seed or scion.

In spring, when the bud starts to grow, cut off the stock tree above it to force the vigor of the plant into the new bud. The bud will grow as the trunk of your new tree. Allow some growth (3 to 4 inches) to occur on the tree before cutting back to the bud. This enables the tree to begin growing, and you can see if your bud has taken. If it hasn't, and you've already cut the tree back, you'll have little left for that season. As pointed out previously, if you bud high on the rootstock trunk (6 to 8 inches), you can plant the tree deeper than usual and still keep the varietal trunk far enough above the soil surface so that it will not make its own roots, which can happen if the trunk is in contact with soil. On the other hand, some tree growers have budded low and planted so the varietal trunk *is* in contact with the soil. If roots form, it gives the tree extra bracing, especially if some of the weaker

109

Malling rootstock is used for dwarfing. Also, you can then possibly propagate the variety by stooling, just as you would propagate rootstock. This is not often done, but it is one way to increase a variety without grafting.

The shield bud is the most common budding method used, but there are others, called patch or chip budding, that you might find handy when working with larger trees. In this type of

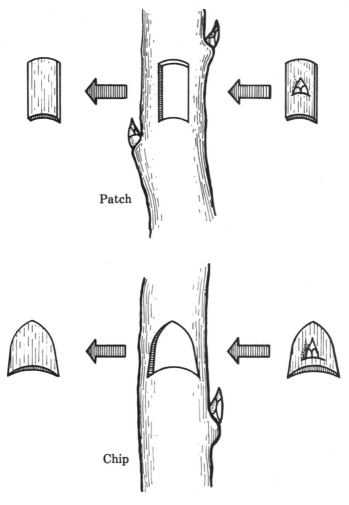

Patch

Chip

Illus. 6-4—Patch or Chip Budding—These variations on shield budding work well when grafting onto larger trees.

graft, a patch or chip of bark with a bud in the center is taken from one tree and placed where an identically sized patch of bark has been removed from another tree. Special knives with twin blades facilitate patch budding by enabling you always to get a perfect fit, at least on two sides. Some grafters make special four-sided patch knives with four razor blades so that by pressing the blades into the bark, they cut exactly the same-size patch every time.

SPLICING SCIONWOOD

In regular grafting, a scion is used instead of a bud. A scion is a piece of young, vigorous, wooded stem with (usually) two buds on it. Scions are usually about 5 inches long, though they can be shorter. They are cut square across on the top, and they're cut on a slant at the bottom to fit the slant cut of the stock tree.

Many grafters tell me that the condition of the stock is more important than the condition of the scion. A poor scion on healthy vigorous stock might take, but if the stock is weak, old, or unhealthy, not even the best scion will take on it.

Scionwood must be kept dormant until grafting time in spring. I like to cut my scionwood in March, about a month before trees start breaking dormancy, and store it in a cool, moist place. That might be underground wrapped in plastic, or in the refrigerator, also in plastic. One year I stored some in a snowdrift. Sometimes I store scions under a pile of leaves. But storage must be cold enough so the buds don't start growing.

I usually cut my scions from branches that have to be pruned. You can cut scionwood all winter, as far as that goes, and this is necessary if you are selling or trading in scionwood and need to have a supply, or perhaps have found what you are looking for on a winter trip. But my opinion (and many agree) is that the longer the scionwood can be kept on the tree, the better. However, if the scion tree is not a very hardy variety and you fear it will winterkill, cut scions in early winter and store them. Some growers dip the scions in a mixture of 80% paraffin and 20% beeswax, the same sort of wax they use for sealing certain kinds of grafts. Art Weaver, the nut grower in northern Ohio who specializes in northern-grown Carpathian walnuts, says that if you add food coloring to this protective dip, the scions take better when grafted. Any color will do, but most use green. Why that helps, no one is sure.

Scionwood should be fairly young wood, a year old for the best results. The best comes from trees three to five years old, or from older trees that have been cut back promoting your vigorous growth. I like it ⅜ to ½ inch in diameter, but scionwood a little larger or smaller is okay, too.

THE WHIP AND TONGUE GRAFT

When grafting two stems or branches, or small trunks of the same size, the whip and tongue graft, a variation of the simple splice graft, is used most often. The whip and tongue is not hard to master. The first one that I made took. As one nurseryman says: "If you can whittle, you can graft."

In using the whip and tongue to graft a variety to a seedling, the trunk of the seedling has to be cut off at a point at which the diameter is the same, or nearly so, as that of the scion. Cut a slant in the stock and a matching slant on the scion so that when spliced together the two appear as one. Sometimes you have to recut the slant in the scion to match up the two perfectly. Use a very sharp pocketknife or, if you can get one, a surgeon's scalpel with replaceable blades. I use one of those knives frequently seen in hardware stores now, the kind that has replaceable blades. The blades are very sharp and come in various sizes, all a little too large for grafting but adequate enough.

Next, cut the "tongue" into the slanted faces of both stock and scion. Cut in only a little way, and then turn the knife slightly and cut parallel to the slant. If you cut straight in too far, the scion will often split. The scion may also split if you make the turn too forcibly. Practice makes perfect. Some force is necessary along with a slight sawing, wiggling action of the knife, but don't cut yourself. Remember, if you can whittle, you can graft. You must start the tongue cuts a little high toward the long end of the slants so that when you slip the scion tongue into the stock tongue, there is room to slide it home in perfect alignment. I realize that sounds complicated, but do a few practice grafts. You will see that the joining is really quite simple, and the better the fit, the surer the graft.

You will now learn the reason for the tongues. If you let go of the graft, it holds in position by itself, leaving both your hands free for tying and wrapping. The extra strength that the tongues impart to the graft will usually keep it from breaking over if a bird sits on it before the graft union bonds together. I often tie the graft by simply wrapping freezer tape around the union tightly, but not over the buds on the scion, of course. To get a better percentage of takes, I sometimes wrap bread-wrapper or some similar plastic around the tape, or loop a plastic sack over the scion and fasten the sack closed below the graft union with a rubber band. The sack forms a little greenhouse that keeps the

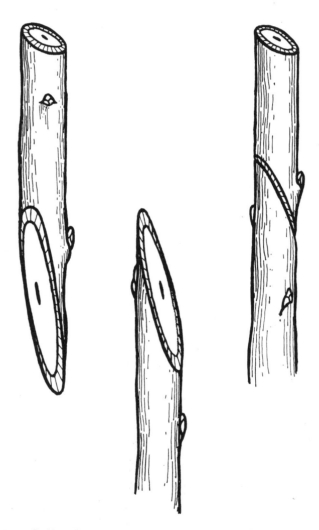

Illus. 6-5—Splice Graft—The basic splice graft depends upon the scion and stock being cut with matching angles, which cause greater contact to assure good growth.

graft from drying out, just as with the budwood, mentioned previously. If the weather turns hot, though, the graft inside the plastic may get too hot, and the plastic should be loosened or taken off.

Other grafters tie the graft, first with rubber budding strips, and then wrap plastic and/or freezer tape around it. Either way you do not need to seal with wax, which is why I like this graft best of all.

You can graft onto a seedling tree the scion of a dwarf stock and, after it grows a year, graft on your variety to the dwarfing

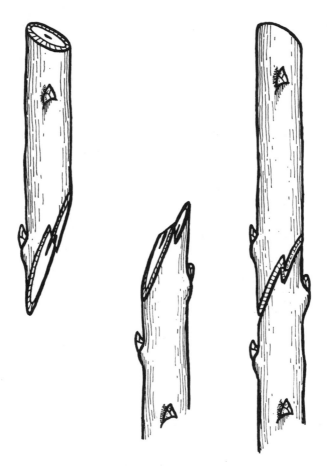

Illus. 6-6—Whip and Tongue Graft—The most frequently used variation of splice graft, the tongue holds the scion in place by itself, freeing the hands to tie the graft.

interstem. Professional grafters can do both splices at the same time and have both take. Either way, a tree dwarfed with dwarfing interstem rather than dwarf roots seems to be a more satisfactory tree, especially in situations where the dwarfing rootstock is weak or has not adapted to a particular soil as well as seedling roots.

The whip and tongue graft is especially suitable for grafting a variety, or several varieties, on small- to medium-size established trees. Once a tree reaches four or five years of age, almost any number of whip and tongue grafts can be made on it, though it is never wise to rework a whole tree at once. Find a branch close to the trunk that is the same size as your scion. After grafting, cut away any competing branches that are in the vicinity of the graft.

Even on large trees, the whip and tongue graft can be employed. Use low sprouts on the trunk, and later cut off the bigger branches above. Cutting back the tree will push the grafts with great vigor. When using this graft, or the side grafts described below, on an old tree, it's best to graft to younger wood. If there is none, cut back an old branch so that it makes new sprouts, and graft onto them.

THE CLEFT GRAFT AND SIDE GRAFTS

Normally, older, established trees are grafted by placing scions into a split in the sawed-off face of a large limb. It is possible, but difficult, to wrap a cleft graft with tape tight enough to keep out air adequately, so cleft grafts are usually sealed with grafting wax. I don't like to mess with wax, so I don't make cleft grafts.

The side cleft graft is popular with some orchardists and is easy. It has the advantage of being as versatile as the whip and tongue since it can be grafted onto stock ranging from only a little larger than the scion up to about any size. The scion is cut into a wedge much like that for cleft grafting, but one side of the wedge is longer than the other. The longer side fits against the stock. Make a cut in the stock at an acute angle of about 20° from the lay of the stock and deep enough to accept the scion's wedge. Bend it out a little bit as you cut and, when you insert the scion, bend the stock (if it is slender enough to bend) to open the incision better. Seat the scion as solidly in the cut as you can, then carefully tape the whole thing in and around, or seal with wax. Allow only one bud on the scion to grow. After it starts well, cut back the stock above the graft halfway to help draw up sap to the graft. Later, cut back all of the stock above the graft. Of course, on large- or even medium-size trees, this would not be necessary unless you're grafting the whole tree over. Then it is

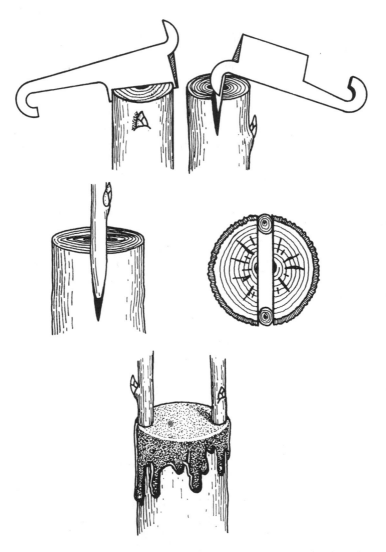

Illus. 6-7—Cleft Graft—Older trees are grafted using a cleft graft. Scions are placed into a split limb on the tree and then are sealed with wax.

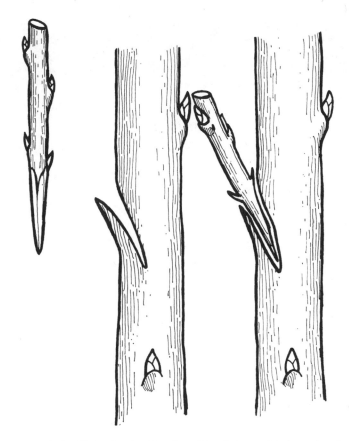

Illus. 6-8—Side Cleft Graft—In the side cleft graft, the scion is cut into a wedge, with one long face, and a shorter face. The scion is then placed against a cut into the side of the tree and taped or sealed with wax.

customary to leave up to half of the branches alone and graft them the following year.

A more sophisticated side graft, called the bark graft by its practitioners, is used often for nut trees. Art Weaver generously showed me how he does it when grafting Carpathian walnut scions on black walnut stock. The scion, about 5 inches in length with a ⅜-inch diameter (or larger), is sliced in half lengthwise from a point an inch or so below the buds to the bottom of the scion. This gives a flat surface to the scion for the 2 inches or so of stem below the buds. Lay this flat-end side down on the branch or trunk where you intend to graft it, and carefully trace

117

Photo 6-1—Bark Grafting—The variety grafted to the side of this tree has taken hold and is growing well. Side bark grafting is a particularly good method for use with nut trees. Rodale Press photograph.

its outline on the bark with your knife. Next, cut the lines you have traced just through the bark on the sides and on the front—but not at the back. Lift this flap of bark up, and set your scion in place on the wood. The fit should be as perfect as you can get it. Now lower the bark flap back on top of the scion. If you cut an angle into the very end of the scion where the bark is still attached to the tree, then the bark will fit down over the scion much better. Then nail down the bark and scion to the stock with a small tack or brad. Then seal the graft with wax or wrap tightly with tape. Weaver says tape works just as well as wax. Weaver grafts when the leaves on the stock walnut trees are halfway out. He grafts pecans to hickories the same way.

BENCH GRAFTING

Bench grafting is done inside. Seedling trees or stooled sprouts are dug, brought to the grafting room, and the grafting is done in relative comfort. Commercial nurseries bench graft when grafting large quantities of trees, but some of the techniques might be handy sometime for the home orchardist to know about.

Leslie Wilmoth, in Kentucky, was the first nurseryman to bench graft nut trees in quantity successfully. He gave me a detailed description of how he does it. The seedling trees are lifted in early spring—black walnut stock for all the walnuts, and pecan for the hickories, hicans, and pecans. The mud is washed off the roots, and the trees are held in cold storage in sawdust until grafting season starts, about April 25. The seedlings are one- and two-year-old black walnuts, and two- and three-year-old pecans. (The latter grow more slowly.) The trunks ought to be at least ¼ inch in diameter to graft, and preferably ⅜ of an inch or more.

Scions of the same size are selected, since the whip and tongue graft is used. Scions are cut from young, vigorous trees or vigorous wood on old trees. They should be solid and supple, not hollow and pithy. Wilmoth tries to graft at about an inch above the crown of the seedling but, for a good fit, will go a little higher or lower to where scion and stock are precisely the same size. He ties the graft with rubber strips and immediately puts the newly grafted tree into a large tank of sawdust at a slight angle, burying the whole tree except for one top bud.

The moisture content of the sawdust is critical to the success of the graft. When squeezed, the sawdust should not dampen the hand, but it should feel moist. Wilmoth uses a soil moisture meter to check the sawdust. The meter must only barely register a moisture content—in the lowest range on your meter scale. (The ranges of meter scales vary, so check your own for the lowest.) He mixes perlite into sawdust that is too wet to bring the moisture content down. The perlite, an artificial growing medium available at garden stores, absorbs the excess moisture.

The temperature of the sawdust must be kept between 75° and 80°F. A plastic cover is kept over the tank for controlled humidity, but condensation must not drip onto the newly growing buds, or it will kill them. The trees usually start growing in about a week, but poorly developed buds may not break for 20 days. After growth starts, the trees are moved back to the nursery and are removed from the tank after growth has reached 2 inches. Newly set out trees are quite tender, so if a late frost threatens, cover them. Partial shade won't hurt at first, either.

When grafting trees, *always* tag any varieties you want to remember. Don't trust your memory. Buy some aluminum tags and use them. Wire them loosely onto the grafted variety to prevent girdling the growing tree.

CHAPTER 7

THE ART
OF PRUNING

Two quotations, both from unimpeachable sources, help show the difficulty of discussing pruning over a typewriter rather than out in the orchard. The first is from Lewis Hill's good book, *Fruits and Berries for the Home Garden,* the second from the excellent instructions in the Hilltop Orchards & Nurseries, Inc., catalog, written by horticulturist Don R. Heinicke.

For the first few years—in fact until the fruit trees begin to bear—they need very little pruning. . . . But as your little tree grows, all you'll need to do is correct any bad crotches, keep a strong central trunk (leader), and keep it from getting too wide or too leggy. . . . After the tree begins to bear fruit, however, you'll want to prune more heavily and prune each year. . . .

. . . Where constructive training is used, any undesirable shoot is removed or modified when it is a one-year-old. As a result, the tree is never pruned heavily after *(emphasis added) the first 2 or 3 years. As the tree comes into bearing, pruning is reduced rather than increased as it would be with corrective pruning. . . .*

Obviously, the two methods are somewhat contradictory. Neither, though, is easily disproven. The second method will likely be preferred by commercial orchardists, the first method

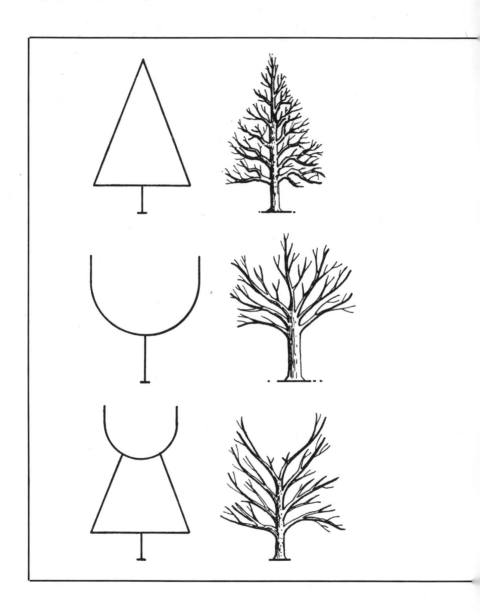

by backyarders. The second method is based on heading back
side branches in a somewhat sophisticated manner required in a
high-density orchard. The method demands a certain skill that
the first does not, and also a good deal more time, at least in the
early years.

PRUNING FOR THREE POPULAR TREE SHAPES

Central Leader Form

Standard apple and pear trees generally have this habit of growth. Dwarf apple on Malling 9 can usually be pruned to this form as can dwarf pear on quince rootstock. Most nut trees grow naturally to this shape. Commercial growers consider this shape ideal for high-density orchards of dwarf apple trees. Easy to harvest and spray, and all portions of the tree get sunlight.

Open Center Form

Peaches, nectarines, and sour cherries can be grown to this form. Some apples, such as the Cortland, can be grown this way naturally, too. Most plums, sweet cherries, apricots, and almonds (in their domesticated species) can be pruned to this shape.

Modified Central Leader Form

As you can see, this tree form (also known as modified open center) starts out as a central leader system, then heads out into a high open center. Sometimes the tree wants to do the opposite—head low into an open center and then one of the scaffold branches straightens up and dominates so much as to become a central leader. In either case, this is the type of tree you most generally get with today's dwarfing and semidwarfing rootstock, especially with East Malling 1, 2, 4, 7, and other apple rootstock. This form is difficult to prune for the novice, since in essence, the tree seems to be shapeless—it is neither one nor the other classic form, and varies markedly in pattern from species to species. The best you can do is prune out weak crotch branches and keep the tree from getting too bushy.

But what makes me sigh, in a mournful sort of way, is the assumption both of those passages makes—that every tree *can* be trained to a central leader and therefore develop into a perfect Christmas-tree shape for better light distribution, easy harvesting, spraying, and bug monitoring.

'Tain't so. Some trees will not form a well-defined central leader (in all fairness, Hill goes on to point this out, and Heinicke is assuming that his readers know he is talking about apples and pears that will usually form a central leader). Some trees, such as peaches and sour cherries, will even resist the modified central leader shape (sometimes called delayed open center) much employed with semidwarf trees—a central leader halfway up that then branches into several leaders of more or less equal height. Peaches and sour cherries and some varieties of other fruits can be grown to the open center form, a form that resembles a cup shape or a vase shape rather than a Christmas-tree shape, or to a modified central leader if the leader is left intact.

The point is that there is no "law" of pruning, no scientific right way to control a tree's growth, except the overall rule: Approach each tree individually, and prune it in a way that enhances the natural form it wants to take. Pruning is more an art than a science. It is an act of cooperation or compromise between what you want the tree to do and what it wants to do.

The most artful form of pruning may be none at all. This is the somewhat radical opinion of Masanobu Fukuoka, the Japanese farmer who describes in his book, *The One-Straw Revolution,* his own orchard-management methods inspired by a philosophy and an experience similar to that advanced in this book. Fukuoka eschews all pruning in his citrus orchard, where his trees grow helter-skelter *amid other food and forest trees.* He writes:

If a tree is planted carefully and allowed to follow its natural form from the beginning, there is no need for pruning or sprays of any kind. . . .

If a single new bud is snipped off a fruit tree with a pair of scissors, that may bring about disorder which cannot be undone. When growing according to the natural form, branches spread alternately from the trunk and the leaves receive sunlight uniformly. If this sequence is disrupted the branches come into conflict, lie one upon another, and become tangled, and the leaves wither in the places where the sun cannot penetrate. Insect damage develops. Then if the tree is not pruned the following year, more withered branches will appear.

In other words, according to Fukuoka, pruning is only necessary when man starts tampering with the tree.

While his theory may not be literally true for American situations, there may be more to it than there appears to be at first. Apple trees that I have grown from seed grow in a natural central leader form with good, wide branch angles. They require no constructive or corrective pruning. Wild apple trees I have observed also (but not always) grow without needing pruning other than what takes place naturally from lack of sunlight. With adequate sunlight, nut trees in the wild grow remarkably well-proportioned limbs without pruning. The only trees that grow so perversely for me that they need constant attention in the form of pruning are trees grafted to other, different root-stocks, especially dwarfing rootstocks. Invariably they want to grow upward in a pronounced fashion, whereas natural seedlings will spread out in a more graceful attitude. The dwarfed trees also want to bunch branches much too closely along the central leader, and the side branches often make bad crotch angles and then try to outgrow and subdue the main trunk, something the seedling rarely does.

An apple orchard that has been pruned for many years and then abandoned will grow into a jungle of sprouts. A wild apple, never pruned, more likely will not, unless some natural or unnatural violence occurs. Fence-row trees sometimes grow dense with water sprouts because of the high concentrations of nitrogen fertilizer applied to the field next to them. Fukuoka's tampering theory cannot be lightly dismissed, and the owner of a grove of trees to live in might do well to emulate him as much as possible. The grove-owner at least ought to have as his first guiding rule the advice of Harold B. Tukey in his book *Dwarfed Fruit Trees* (New York, Macmillan, 1964): "Prune as little as possible."

Where space is at a premium, and dwarf or semidwarf trees are utilized, some pruning will almost always be necessary. In that case, the question even before "How?" is "When?" As you might expect, there is much disagreement on this question, too. Some prune in the late fall, others in late winter. Trees pruned in fall or early winter, say the latter, are more susceptible to winterkill. Some growers even prune in late summer when leaves are still on the trees but growth has ceased. At that time, they say, heavy pruning will not induce vigorous vegetative growth the following year. Some say not to prune in early spring when the sap is running or else the trees will bleed excessively. Others say the bleeding doesn't do any significant harm. Most pruners, however, prune in late winter or spring before buds begin to swell. Some additional light pruning may be done in summer. Summer pruning seems to sap the tree's vigor a little and in fact is employed for that reason in special cases. Normally you'll want to prune when the tree is dormant, toward the end of winter in the North; earlier, if you want to, in the South. Or you can, without too much fear, follow the old orchardists' wry advice: Prune when your pruning knife is sharp.

If you know how to use a pruning knife without cutting your finger, you can thin out branches *flush* to the trunk or main branch in a proper manner, allowing the tree to callous over the cut quickly. Most of us still use pruning shears, not yet having graduated to the knife, and the typical pruning shears will not really cut as close as the ideal. Nevertheless, cut as close as you can so as not to leave a stub, which can die and rot back into the trunk, providing a handy entrance for disease. On larger limbs, use a pruning saw to make flush cuts. Limb-loppers do not cut close enough to the trunk.

GENERAL PRUNING GUIDELINES

Whereas your goals and the nature of the tree itself will determine to a great extent how you will prune, there are some cause-and-effect relationships that can guide your work:

1. If you cut a branch partway back (called heading back), the buds behind the cut will grow more than they would have otherwise, develop more branchlets and spurs, and therefore thicken the growth. This kind of heading back can easily be overdone on normal, freestanding trees. If in doubt, don't. Heading will also stiffen a branch, so if its crotch angle is too acute, head with caution. Otherwise, bending the branch down afterward will be more difficult.

2. Where two branches of about equal length form a Y, the one cut back the least will grow the most, thus avoiding a weak Y crotch.

3. In heading back a branch, always make a cut just above an outward-pointing bud, preferably a bud on the lower side of the branch. In this way you encourage low, spreading growth with less use of spreaders and tie-down weights.

4. When heading back a central leader, cut back to a bud so that there is no dead stub left when the top bud grows out as a

(*continued on page 132*)

PRUNING TIPS

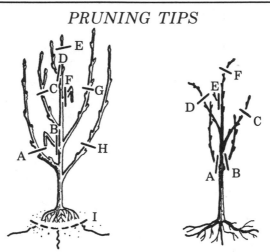

At left is shown the way a nice two-year-old nursery tree typically will look when you order it through the mail. First you do the obvious. Prune back broken roots. Prune off D, which, with E, is making a weak Y crotch instead of a strong leader. Cut back leader E just a little. Thin out broken branches B and F. Head back C and G, A and H, to balance the branches into the beginning of the Christmas-tree central leader form. If A and H are less than a foot from the ground, you might consider thinning them out completely, especially if the root system is sparse. On the other hand, some growers I know who mulch trees lavishly would thin out D, F, and B, but barely tip back the other branches, since their philosophy says that a tree well mulched will grow faster if not decapitated as severely as is customary.

Above to the right is a little peach tree pruned to branches when set out, balancing top growth with sparse root growth.

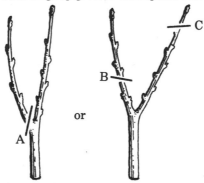

Very often you get this kind of Y leader tip. There are two ways of handling it. Thin one out completely, or if you want a branch at that point, head one back severely to an outside bud and tip back the other just a little. C will grow much faster than B and preserve its dominance as central leader.

PRUNING TIPS—Continued

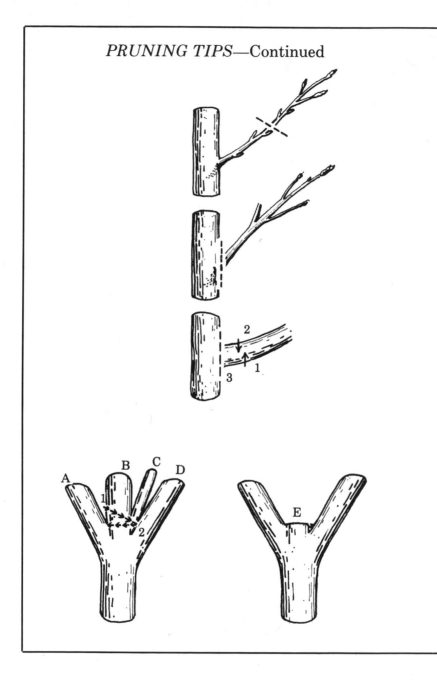

When heading back a branch, try to cut to a bud on the underside of the branch that points outward. Cut about ⅛ inch above the bud—not too close to avoid injuring it, not so far away that an ugly dead stem butt remains.

When thinning out a branch, cut it flush with the trunk. Don't leave a stub, or it can die and rot back into the tree.

When thinning out a heavy branch, make cut 1 first, then cut 2, so that the branch doesn't split back or peel off the bark of the trunk when it falls. Then, with the heavy part of the branch amputated, make a third cut flush with the trunk. Use a tree saw for the optimum flush cut.

Here's a difficult situation you often face with open center and modified central leader trees. B and C should come out (or A, C, and D should have been pruned off a year or two earlier), but it is difficult even with a saw to make a good flush cut. Saw through 1 as indicated first. Then you can work your saw in close enough to make cut 2, so that the finished job looks something like E.

You might argue that A, C, and D should be removed even at this late date. Probably not, unless the tree is heading decidedly too low. To remove A, C, and D will sap the tree too much at this point and remove too much fruiting wood all at once. E is a better solution, since the tree obviously wants to open up now. More often than not, especially on low-headed semidwarf trees, the pruner is content to cut out only C, thereby leaving a crowded, weak-crotched tree.

THE INFLUENCE OF ANGLE ON THE GROWTH OF SIDE BRANCHES

When the scaffold branch grows too vertically, the crotch is weak, the lower part of the branch is unbearing, and the branch competes too much with the central leader.

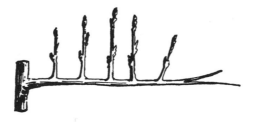

When a branch is bent too much into a horizontal position, branch development tends to be sprouty, overly vigorous, and vertical, interfering with branches above. This growth habit is used to advantage in forming espaliers and other artificial forms but diminishes tip growth and fruiting on conventional freestanding trees.

Arching a branch will induce the most vigorous growth at the highest point of the arch. This trick can be used to advantage in forming arched cordons, arches palmettes, and other sophisticated artificial shapes, but it only causes problems in normal trees.

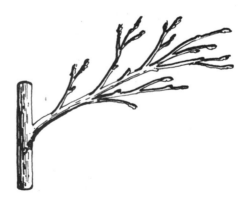

When the branch is at the proper angle, 45° to 60° from the trunk, the branch develops balanced growth and requires the least pruning.

new leader. (In special cases, a stub or snag is left temporarily.)

5. In training branches to a proper horizontal position, a crotch angle somewhere between 45° and 60° is best. If the angle is more acute than that, the branch will develop too fast at the end in relation to the section nearer the trunk. If the branch is tied down to level position, the shoots nearer the trunk will grow too fast compared to the end shoots. If the branch is bent and tied in an arch, vigorous shoots will grow straight up from the middle (highest point) of the limb and end growth will slacken too much. These principles are used extensively in shaping espaliers and other artificial forms. The general rule is that shoots will grow fastest from that part of a limb that is highest in altitude.

6. Pruning tends to delay fruiting. Exception: Skillful heading back on *dwarf* trees can induce fruit budding on spurs close to the trunk so long as a careful balance between vegetative growth and fruiting growth is maintained. This technique applies mostly to summer pruning in the Lorette manner and related European systems.

7. On dwarf trees, keep the lower scaffold branches low. If you trim off lower branches, you can easily get a tree that is too leggy for its ultimate height. Also, the weight of the crop should be controlled, or it may topple the weak-rooted tree. On paper, a low heading of 18 to 24 inches seems too low, but for a dwarf tree, that's about right. Don't be in a hurry to cut lower limbs from a semidwarf, either, unless you live where snowdrifts get heavy enough to weight and break them down, or where you intend to graze sheep. Even then, go slow. I have made the mistake on apple trees of cutting too many vigorous lower branches off too soon, which slows the growth of the tree.

8. You only begin to understand pruning after you have lived with a few trees from their planting to their heavy fruiting years. Then you know what you should have done. If you can outlive your orchard, the second time around you'll really know how to prune. Since not many of us are that lucky or healthy, the old-timers' advice is about as good as any: "Keep a tree just open enough so a robin can fly through it without touching its wings."

ESPALIERING

I hesitate to discuss the more advanced practices of artistic pruning used in the formation of espaliers. In most cases in the

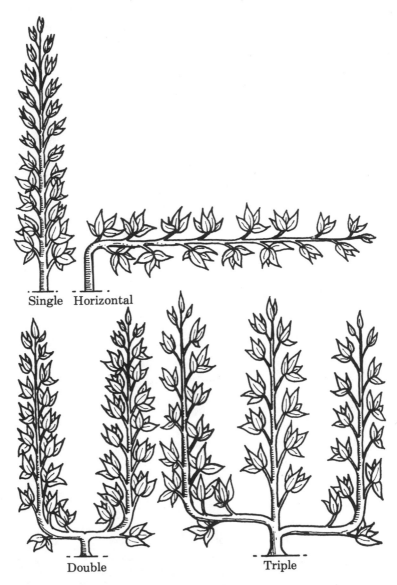

Single   Horizontal

Double   Triple

Illus. 7-1—Cordons for Apples and Pears—Once the basic pruning steps are understood, one can easily see how any shape can be achieved by tying the cordons to trellises.

133

United States, homeowners and homesteaders interested in establishing a grove of trees to live in will have enough lot space or acreage for the tree diversity necessary to maintain ecological balance. With the use of available dwarf trees and conventional pruning, sufficient diversity can be attained with even an acre or less. By grafting several varieties on each tree, most space problems occurring on even a half-acre can be overcome.

But what about even less space? Can you maintain sufficient ecological diversity on less than a quarter-acre, for example? The answer is that Europeans and Orientals do it all the time, using pruning and training methods that severely restrict tree growth. Usually the goal has not been ecological diversity, however, but artistic beauty and a small but varied supply of the very highest quality fruit. This is accomplished with espaliers that can be shaped almost any way. Gardeners in Europe are skilled enough to shape trees even into the letters of their names. The art of espaliering has never taken hold in the United States—Americans aren't that patient as a rule. The intricate forms of espaliering require, moreover, a poorer soil, or some artificial method, such as root pruning or resetting the tree, to keep the tree from growing vigorously. Trees usually grow too vigorously in the United States for severe forms of espaliers.

For these reasons, I doubt most Americans will find the striking kind of success in espaliering that you see so beautifully executed in small English gardens. Indeed, this kind of severe restriction of fruit tree growth is more akin to bonsai than to nurturing a grove of trees, and would-be practitioners should understand that. Finally, one must question whether the grower of a grove of trees to live in really has enough time to practice espaliering and the sophisticated types of summer pruning it demands. I think not.

There's a rather extensive nomenclature connected with the practice of espaliering. Harold Tukey's book, which I've referred to, has a good short treatment of the subject, but if you really want to immerse yourself, find a 19th-century book on espaliers. I have found Thomas Rivers' *Miniature Fruit Garden* (New York, Orange Judd & Co., 1866) awesome in its detail.

Some of the techniques of espaliering can be adapted to the American situation in at least one practical way. Dr. Elwood Fisher, an apple and apricot collector in Virginia, grows hundreds of trees on less than half an acre around his home with his adaptation of one form of espalier, the single vertical cordon. He assures me that if a person tends the trees on a regular

SHAPING THE VERTICAL CORDON

Shaping the vertical cordon on this grafted tree begins at one year of growth and proceeds through to the fourth year. The drawings are purposefully oversimplified to show the basic pattern. If the side branches were allowed to grow farther out, they would form a pyramidal bush tree. If allowed to grow yet a little broader, the result would be a rather typical dwarf, central leader tree. Vertical cordons, or slanted, horizontal, double, or triple cordons work best with apples and pears and only on the most dwarfing rootstock—Malling 9 for apples, quince for pears. Height is arrested at about 7 feet.

Sometimes, to force the central leader straight up on cordons, a snag of a previous leader is left on the tree to which the new leader is tied. (See detail.) After the new leader grows erect, the snag is cut off.

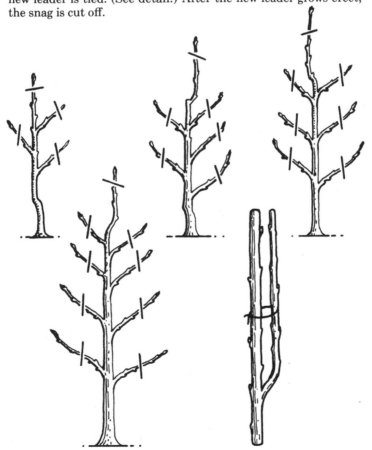

schedule, the time spent is not inordinate and the results are practical for his rather unique purposes—to preserve large numbers of old and rare fruit tree varieties in limited space. The single vertical cordon that Dr. Fisher described to us at the annual meeting of the North American Fruit Explorers in 1976 is but one of many once popular forms of espaliers. Among the expert pruners, the single vertical cordon is something different from the slender-spindle tree shape, or the pyramidal tree, but for practical purposes here, these shapes are all essentially the same; that is, very small, very slender, or upright trees on which very little branching is allowed to force fruit production on short spurs along the central trunk. These forms differ from a central leader dwarf apple tree (Malling 9) only in size. They are very small; indeed, they're bushes, not trees, no more than 2 feet wide and 7 feet high. They can be spaced as close as 13 inches apart, though Dr. Fisher says that about 20 inches is better. He grows such bush-trees as a trellised tree wall all around the boundary of his property.

To keep the cordon from growing too fast, soil of only moderate fertility helps. Certainly you would not apply nitrogen fertilizer, and other nutrients you would use only sparingly. As I have mentioned, sometimes roots are pruned annually on alternate sides of the tree to control growth, but this is a very touchy practice when years of trial and error may be necessary for success. Both winter and summer pruning must be done, and there are several methods. In winter, Dr. Fisher cuts back all branches to three buds. The bud nearest the stem, if not too vigorous, will form a fruiting bud (the experts call that bud a fruit dard); the middle bud may form a fruit dard or a vegetative shoot (or leaf bud); the outer bud will always be a vegetative shoot. Then in summer the new growth must be pinched back constantly, except for leader shoots. When the shoots grow to about 4 inches in length, pinch back to four buds. Then, when the secondary shoot grows about six leaves, pinch it back to two buds. Keep doing that all summer. Wait until late summer, after the tree has stopped growing, to pinch back the leader. Pinch the leader back to about nine buds.

This method is very similar to that described by Rivers in 1866, and which I assume was, and is, common knowledge among better gardeners in Europe. One practice often alluded to is that of cutting notches about "half an inch wide and nearly as deep," according to Rivers (but shallower than that, according to more recent American authors), either below or above a bud to make it

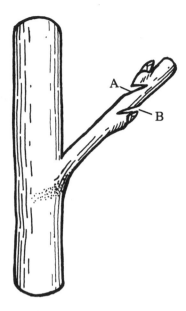

*Illus. 7-2—Methods for Suppressing and Encouraging Tree Growth—
To suppress vegetative growth on a tree branch, nick the branch below
a new bud as in example A. To encourage the bud's growth, nick the
branch above, or past the bud, as in B.*

a fruit bud or a leaf bud. If the notch is cut above the bud, it
forms a leaf or shoot; if below the bud, it forms a fruiting spur.
Sometimes the effect can be obtained with a simple incision cut
into and across the bark but without removing any bark tissue,
says Dr. Fisher. This practice is referred to as "nicking." Either
way, what seems to happen is that the flow of nitrogen and
carbohydrates to the bud is altered from normal. If the cut is
below the bud, nitrogen coming up the tree to the bud is blocked,
but carbohydrates coming down are not, a condition that favors
fruit-spur development. With the cut above the bud, the opposite nutrient condition prevails, and the imbalance of nitrogen
favors vegetative growth.

Cutting a strip of bark about ⅜ inch in width from around a
limb will suppress growth, too. Sometimes the bark ring is
complete; more often it is in a spiral shape, or two half rings, so
that there is no complete cutoff of the vascular bundles. (Ringing
a tree can kill it, especially if done late in the year.) In ringing
bark to suppress growth, the bark is cut out early in the growing

season so that the cut heals and hardens before freezing weather. The cut must always be wrapped immediately (adhesive tape will do) to prevent infection. Tying a wire around a branch also suppresses the flow of nutrients to the growing wood somewhat. I assume that the folk practice of pounding nails into a tree to produce fruit may occasionally work because it partially blocks the upward flow of nitrogen.

Peaches and all trees that grow in the open center form will not adapt to cordons very well. They can be shaped into fans for training against walls. As Abraham Lincoln was quoted when forced to say something nice concerning a matter he was doubtful about: "For people who like that sort of thing, this is the very sort of thing they will like."

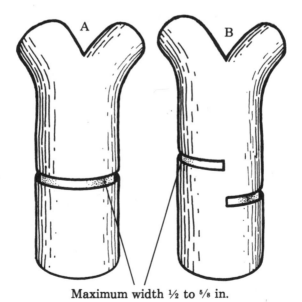

Maximum width ½ to ⅝ in.

Illus. 7-3—Ringing Bark to Suppress Growth Vigor—Stripping a ring of bark from a tree will suppress the growth as well. The narrower the ring is, the shorter is the time of effect. A complete ring as shown on tree A is safer. In either case, the exposed area should be wrapped immediately after ringing.

138

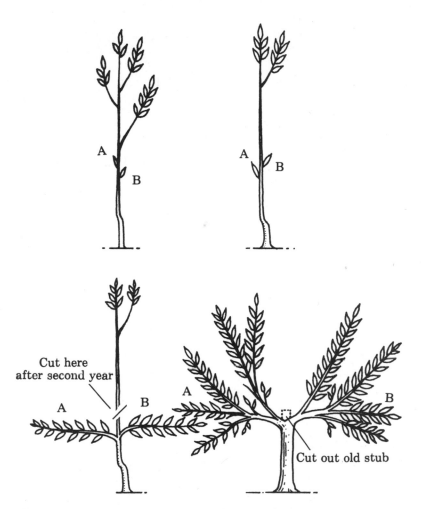

Illus. 7-4—The Fan Shape for Peaches and Other Stone Fruits—In the fan shape, all new branches develop from two original horizontal branches. The central leader is cut from the tree after the second year of growth.

For apples and pears on dwarfing rootstock, the training of cordons on trellises can be extended to the palmette form quite easily. In fact, palmettes are easier to shape in general, since scaffold branches are allowed to grow longer, as they are wont to do. The design and training method is that typically employed in the basic hedgerow method in intensively planted apple

139

orchards (see Illus. 7-5). The scaffold branches of palmettes can be trained in a horizontal mode, or more commonly (and more satisfactorily) at about a 45° angle in what is called the oblique palmette. Whereas a cordon may take up 2 to 4 feet of space on the trellis, an oblique palmette usually fills 8 feet along the wires after four years of training. But the width or thickness of the hedge should be maintained at about 1½ to 2 feet.

To train a tree to the four-wire trellis, head back the newly transplanted tree 18 to 24 inches (depending on the overall height of the tree) to encourage branching of low scaffolds. Tie the headed leader loosely to the bottom wire. As shoots develop in summer, bend and tie to the wire any good scaffold branch that wants to grow out away from the wire. If such a branch is not needed, cut it out completely at the end of the first growing season or in mid-August. Tie branches chosen for scaffolds to the wires at about a 45° angle from the central leader. Head back all terminals, including the central leader. At the end of the second year, repeat the pruning and training. In general, head back a leader about 4 inches above where you want side shoots for new scaffold branches to grow out. Vigorous side growth on scaffolds is cut back to three leaves (or as described earlier for cordons).

There is some leeway in all this, and only the art and the skill of experience can be your guide. For example, some shoots from the central leader will grow in the wrong places and may

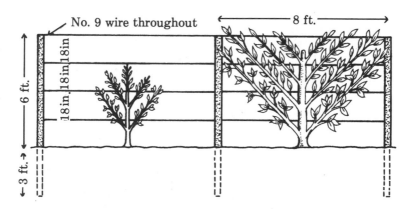

Illus. 7-5—The Palmette Form for Apples and Pears on Trellises— Apples and pears from dwarfing rootstock train well to the palmette shape on trellises. The left side of the trellis shows a tree after a year's trained growth, and the right side shows a tree after four years of training and pruning.

have to be bent to a wire. Bending and arching can induce fruiting spurs, too, just as can cutting back in mid-August. The key is to try to fill up all the space on the trellis before full fruiting occurs. The hard part is to keep the lower portions of the palmette fruiting; the inclination of the tree will be to fruit up and away.

THINNING FRUIT

Just as much espaliering is done for art's sake, the laborious task of hand-thinning dwarf trees is done principally to develop extra-large fruits to win prizes at fairs. If you like to grow tomatoes on stakes and religiously prune away every unwanted sucker, then you may want to grow apples on cordons and religiously prune out extra apples so that only one remains for every 6 inches of space on fruiting wood. But pruning can go too far. I had a peach tree that once produced only one fruit. The peach was as large as a softball and no doubt I could have won a blue ribbon at the county fair with it. Big deal.

Apples and peaches will thin themselves to some extent (called the June drop), and that usually suffices for busy people. If only a few trees are being maintained, supporting overladen limbs with wooden props is easier than trying to hand-thin the fruit. Commercial growers feel that they must resort to chemical thinners to keep trees from overbearing, particularly when over-bearing seems to aggravate the alternate-bearing habit, as in pecans. But thinning is hardly a problem for the owner of a grove of trees to live in, and certainly not one to justify the expense or hazards of chemical thinning. The home grove-owner should thin only to assure that his fruit is of good size and quality.

CHAPTER 8

ORCHARD FERTILITY

In the early 1960s, soil conservationists and state extension personnel in the Spokane, Washington, area began a novel program to halt serious soil erosion in dryland (unirrigated) orchards. Instead of the traditional clean cultivation under which the apple trees were managed, the experimenters substituted mulch. In the early years, they applied 6 inches of straw; later they used sawdust and shredded bark that were readily available in the area, and spread the material 12 inches thick. Even in the first trials results were so unbelievably beneficial that the soil conservationists hesitated to report them. Trees that previously had not been producing salable apples at all because of poor eroded soil sported high-quality fruit after the very first year of mulching. The mulch stopped erosion completely. Moisture content in the soil under the mulch stayed three times higher even in the driest part of the year.

As the years progressed, more advantages were noted. (A totally unforeseen benefit in insect control will be described in a later chapter.) Production kept increasing in mulched sections of the commercial orchards until it surpassed production in the unmulched sections. In 1977, during the severest drought in Washington history, the mulched orchards produced a fair crop; the unmulched, none at all. The mulch adequately controlled weeds without cultivation or herbicides. And, wonder of wonders, no additional fertilizer was found necessary. Growers at first reasoned that the decaying mulch would tie up soil

142

nitrogen, so they applied extra nitrogen for the trees. Terminal growth spurted as much as 4 feet a season, where only about 18 inches was desirable. So they quit fertilizing. The trees grew adequately. So long as the mulch was simply layered on top of the soil and not incorporated into it, ample nitrogen was available for the trees as the mulch rotted to humus.

Despite the advantages, mulch orcharding hasn't yet been adopted by most dryland orchardists. The reasons, as usual, are all "economical." The initial application of mulch 12 inches thick can cost in excess of $500 an acre, including the transportation of sawdust and bark to the orchard. Although after that the amount of mulch and number of applications are far less (the mulch rots at a rate of about an inch a year and the per-year cost of maintaining the mulch is more like $100 per acre), that initial cost and the charge in machinery represent a sizable investment. The investment must be paid before the advantages in lower management costs are realized. In the short-term view, an orchardist can "afford" heavy soil erosion, heavy fertilizer applications, heavy herbicide and insecticide spraying; he cannot "afford" a mulch system that would in the long term avoid all three costs.

In more humid areas where clovers can be maintained between the trees, mulching for fertility need not cover the entire orchard floor, but only under the trees, and then perhaps only in the early years of the trees' growth. Some clovers, however, especially red clover, are the favorite food of certain leafhoppers that transmit a disease from chokecherries to peaches. Thus, growing clover among peach trees may not be a good idea.

Harold Schroeder, whom I mentioned earlier, never fertilized his fruit trees after they began to bear. He felt that the combination of grass clippings from mowing the orchard and judicious pruning gave him a higher-quality apple to sell, albeit not quite as many. Applying extra fertilizer, particularly nitrogen, in his estimation led only to greater danger of problems, such as blight diseases and winterkill.

THE BEST LAND FOR ORGANIC GROVES

Those who wish to establish an ecologically clean grove of trees to live in start, in most cases, with two strikes against them.

The soil that they hope will nurture the tree through its early critical years has been raped by erosion and compaction from intensive farming, saturated by chemicals into an imbalance of nutrients, microorganisms, and mycorrhizal fungi, or bulldozed away to make a proper contour for a housing development. What's more, the proper natural environment around the new orchard usually has been altered extensively so that birds, animals, insects, and beneficial fungi that prey on orchard pests are not present in suitable numbers to control the pests. In this modern situation, the grove-owner is years away from "natural" orchard management, and if he is surrounded by heavy spray-and-pray farming, he may never completely attain his goal of nontoxic, self-renewing fertility.

Therefore, the best place to start a grove of trees to live in is on land never disturbed by agriculture or industry, particularly a well-drained, established natural woodland. Here the mulch is already present in the form of falling leaves, a thick layer of rotting organic matter that supports soil microorganisms in proper equilibrium. Seedlings planted on woodland rather than on old cultivated land invariably survive better, as I mentioned previously. I believe this is mainly because of the healthy status of mycorrhizal fungi in such soil that, in symbiotic partnership with root hairs, enhances nutrient uptake by the plant. Science does not know yet the exact mechanics of this uptake process, but when soils have been fumigated, the beneficial fungi are killed along with certain soil pests; new trees grow much better there if the soil is inoculated with endomycorrhizal fungi. Nature would gradually repopulate fumigated soil with the beneficial fungi herself, but it takes longer—and who knows how long, if ever, it would take for the virgin state to be achieved?

High levels of phosphorus also can suppress the beneficial activity of the fungi, as quite obviously can fungicides. Dr. J. W. Gerdemann, plant pathologist at the University of Illinois, who has graciously answered my questions about endomycorrhizal fungi, would not say that insecticides and herbicides are harmful to them, but only that the effect of these chemicals has not been studied. However he did say, regarding fertility, that "some crops such as citrus and peach are so dependent on mycorrhizal fungi for obtaining adequate amounts of nutrients that it is doubtful that optimum growth can be obtained by substituting high-fertility levels for mycorrhiza."

Substituting high-fertility levels for a naturally balanced soil is exactly what the commercial orchardist feels compelled to do. He establishes a new orchard site by first deep-tilling to break up the compaction endemic to all heavily farmed American soils (except for the most sandy ones). Then he submits the field, if he is wise, to a year or two of green manuring, during which he also limes the field to a pH of around 6.5 (depending on what fruit he plans to grow). Then perhaps having achieved some resemblance of improved soil again, he fertilizes it heavily *and* fumigates it for nematodes. The fumigation suppresses, at least temporarily, the mycorrhizal fungi that, in a healthy soil, could help the orchardist avoid heavy fertilizer applications. But to the orchardist, the nematodes seem to be the worst problem. And why is that? Why are harmful nematodes a characteristic problem in old, chemically managed orchards? Since such nematodes are not harmful in a woodland situation, one can only conclude that there's some failing in the artificial-orchard environment.

In any event, if you feel it is necessary to prepare an orchard site the way commercial growers do to get *maximum* growth of young trees (I believe striving for maximum growth only leads to more problems), there's another way to clean up nematodes. Plant the site to a *dense* stand of marigolds. Scientists say that this old folklore practice really works. The marigolds exude a substance from their roots that drives away various species of nematodes, including the more harmful ones. Then when you plant the trees, mulch them. Research done in various places, particularly in India, has demonstrated that rotting organic matter protects against nematodes. Curiously, growers of woody ornamentals are finding their potted plants to be virtually free of soil-borne diseases, such as those caused by phytophthora fungi, when the plants are grown in composted bark rather than in sterilized peat moss.

If you are fortunate enough to have a well-drained woodlot that has never been plowed (or if you single-mindedly set out to acquire one as a major goal in life, which is what I did), the only "fertilizer" you will have to apply to your trees is sunlight. In making over the woodlot to the trees you want, or nurturing the desirable ones already there, you must make sure each tree gets adequate sunlight for its proper growth—what a forester would call "releasing" a tree from the shade of taller trees. In nature, the smaller fruit trees grow along the edge of the woodlot away from the shade of larger nut and forest trees. Plant accordingly. You can plant little oaks and maples in the shade of large ones and they will grow slowly, biding their time until the giants fall, and then shoot up to take their places. But fruit trees will not do in the shade. Wild fruit trees along the woods' edge should be allowed to remain; cut away any brush that could grow into larger trees that eventually would shut off the sunlight to the fruit trees. If the fruit on these trees (wild apple, plum, haw, crab, peach, hazel, etc.) is not tasty enough to suit you, you can graft on better varieties. Where I have successfully grafted in this manner, and I am only now learning how, growth of the graft has been excellent. That's why I feel certain that with such soil, no fertilization other than the natural mulch of falling leaves is necessary for plenty of good fruit.

Virgin pastureland, particularly if it has not been grazed too much, is the next best place to start a grove. One has only to observe the amazing growth of walnut seedlings on a bluegrass pasture sod to be convinced. Fruit trees on such sites can be helped by mulch, however, to keep grass from competing with them. Some pasture soils, after years of overgrazing, are in almost as poor shape as heavily farmed soils. Old apple trees in such pastures will often rejuvenate remarkably if mulched with manure. On two occasions I have observed this rejuvenation. One such abandoned old apple tree was near dead and unproductive until the new farmer put sheep in the pasture again. They congregated under the tree, it being the only shade around. The sheep, as sheep will do, bared the ground under the tree of grass and covered the soil with manure, which their hooves ground to a dusty mulch. The very next year the tree showed a remarkable recovery and bore a large crop of apples without either spraying or pruning.

From the standpoint of ecology, the next best place to establish your grove of trees is in the residential part of a town or city, especially in old neighborhoods where the trees, gardens, and plantings resemble to some extent a modified forest situation with a wide variety of plants. In such situations, the amount of spraying done is usually (but not necessarily) far less than in a heavily cultivated agricultural district. Also, there is a wider variety of established plants, along with parks or brushy land waiting for "development," in which a surprising amount of animal, bird, and insect life abounds. Unfortunately, some suburbanites, interested only in an artificially neat appearance to their homes, use more chemicals per acre than farmers do and with far less justification. But suburban areas peopled by grove-owners interested in an ecological environment could indeed provide one of the best environments of all for a grove of trees to live in.

In such backyard situations, if not elsewhere, mulching can supply most of the nutrition needed by a fruit or nut tree. The type of mulch you use is mostly a matter of preference or availability, since any kind of organic matter will work. Dr. Elwood Fisher in Virginia mulches his apple and apricot trees with cardboard overlaid with leaves. Robert Kurle, near Chicago, who collects and grows all manner of unusual fruit varieties, relies almost entirely on leaves. Penn State researchers have demonstrated good results from using old hay. On poor ground, I like to use strawy manure. Les Wilmoth, who owns a small nursery in Kentucky, says tobacco stems are the best if you can get them. Grass clippings are a favorite of many, especially clippings with a large proportion of clover in them.

BENEFITS OF MULCH

What does mulch do? First of all, as we have seen, it subdues weeds and grass under the tree that would compete for available nutrients and water. At the same time it conserves moisture during periods of drought. These two benefits are the main reason young trees survive better when mulched than when not mulched. The mulch also begins slowly, and sometimes speedily, to release nutrients to the tree. Straw, for instance, can give a tree a quick shot (though only a small one) of potash, which readily leaches out of the straw when it is rained on. The mulch also begins to decay and, as it does, both nitrogen and potash become available to the tree.

Here are several cautions about mulching: Do not pile mulch, especially manure, deeply against the trunks of the trees. Leave a little space between trunk and mulch. Do not try to mulch trees on *very* steep hillsides, or headwaters will wash away the mulch and erode the soil. Establish sod in such critical places.

Nitrogen (N) and potash (K) are what a fruit tree (and all plants) needs most of. Phosphorus (P) requirements are necessary but smaller. Decaying organic matter with an NPK ratio averaging something such as 2% N, .5% P, and 1% K is the right balance for a fruit tree in usual situations. The overall amount of these nutrients in mulch is small and is available only over a

147

period of time. A chemical grower might find this slow-release characteristic objectionable, but it results in growth just as favorable as with chemicals more enriched with NPK.

If the mulch is not giving the tree enough of the important nutrients, which include calcium and magnesium in addition to nitrogen, phosphorus, and potash, other more-or-less natural, slow-release fertilizers will prove adequate. Wood ashes are an excellent source of additional potash, and they also contain high amounts of calcium. Manure is good for both nitrogen and potash. In situations where calcium and magnesium are both needed, dolomitic limestone can supply them. Very often on good soil a cover crop of white clover in the orchard, clipped occasionally, can provide the necessary nitrogen and potash for the trees. Any additional fertilizer applied to the clover or sod will also benefit the trees. Bone meal or rock phosphate can supply additional phosphorus, if needed.

The importance of a *balanced* nitrogen-potash supply for trees (and all plants) can hardly be overemphasized. The controversial argument of organic growers, that proper organic fertilization gives plants resistance to disease and insects, has been ridiculed by conventional science for years. (In an earlier book, I questioned the notion myself.) But there is a steady increase in startling announcements from conventional science that a balanced fertility program may indeed keep plants healthier and more resistant to bugs and disease, not just help them to grow faster or yield higher. For example, the Potash Institute published in 1977 a detailed review of extant research on the effect of potash on plant health (*Potassium and Plant Health,* Research Topic No. 3, Potash Institute, Bern, Switzerland, 1977, ed. by S. Perrenoud). Potash was found in most cases to improve plant health by providing resistance to both insect pests and fungal diseases. Reductions in nematode and viral infections were accomplished in less than half the tests, but fungal disease decreased in 71% of the tests, and insect damage decreased 60%. Potassium in pot trials reduced the intensity of powdery mildew in apples, and in field trials of scab in apples and brown rot in apricots. Perhaps more interesting to organic fruit growers, in most trials aphids, mites, and scale-pest activity were depressed by applications of potassium to potash-poor soils.

No specific conclusions can be drawn from the data, as the Potash Institute admits. But unquestionably the evidence leads to some very significant general conclusions. "There can be little doubt that with very few exceptions, potassium has generally an effect in reducing the damage that crops suffer through pest and disease," the study concludes cautiously, and then in a later paragraph, repeats in a stronger voice: "This survey has shown beyond reasonable doubt that provided the fertilizers used are correctly balanced, and the nitrogen-potassium relationship is of overriding importance, ... fertilizers ... more often than not improve plant health." Results from the research reviewed indicate that "nutrient balance is particularly important in the context of plant health. The widely accepted view that excessive use of nitrogen is damaging to plant health is due not so much to the deleterious effect of nitrogen *per se,* as to the fact that 'excessive' use of nitrogen implies a lack of balance. Similarly the general opinion that potassium favors plant health appears most often to be due to the fact that it has an ability to counteract the unfavorable effects of nitrogen."

Be aware that the Potash Institute is interested in selling more potash, not less, and that it hopes its findings lead to a justification or even the necessity for using more potash to balance the large amounts of nitrogen that commercial growers feel they must use. Nevertheless, these conclusions fit well—fit much better—in organic cultural practices because the N-K balance is more closely maintained in decaying organic materials that organic growers use for fertilizer. The findings certainly support observations I now have been forced to admit after ten years of very heavy mulch gardening: the plants *do* resist insect and fungal attacks, and even viral and bacterial attacks.

NUTRITIONAL DISORDERS OF TREES

Where land has been abused, or perhaps is naturally deficient in some trace element, some nutritional deficiencies may occur. These deficiencies often look like fungal diseases, though they also can look like insect damage, hail damage, etc. In fact, some of the more common types of nutrient deficiencies are actually alluded to as diseases. In addition to deficiencies of the nutrients already mentioned, shortages of manganese, zinc, boron, copper, iron, and others may show up. But on normally good soils under good natural fertility programs, suspect some blight or insect infestation rather than the following nutritional disorders, which occur in normal situations only infrequently. Diagnosing nutritional disorders by the color or condition of the leaves of the trees is most difficult even for experts and should be substantiated by a leaf analysis when there is doubt.

1. *Little Leaf* or *Rosette* is a condition referred to by fruit and nut growers when the whorls of leaves at the tips of the branches remain small, bunched, often mottled, and eventually turn yellowish or whitish. The condition is caused by zinc deficiency. Suspect it on alkaline soils in drought conditions. Little leaf affects the whole apple-pear-hawthorn-Juneberry-crab family, all the stone fruits, and nuts, especially walnut. Applying zinc, or any trace element, is not for amateurs. Follow directions explicitly and consult an extension horticulturist or other tree expert. Zinc sulfate is often used as a foliar spray or just before bud break in the spring, though the sulfur may not be desirable because it can kill beneficial bugs if not beneficial fungi. Zinc is rarely if ever deficient in soils fertilized well with animal manure. The diagnostic difficulty with little leaf is that the same symptoms may also indicate iron, magnesium, or manganese deficiency, especially in stone fruits and nuts.

Malcolm C. Shurtleff, in his technical work *How to Control Plant Diseases in Home and Garden* (Ames, Iowa, Iowa State University Press, 1962), gives an interesting remedy for zinc deficiency very much like old folklore remedies for iron and copper deficiencies. To correct zinc deficiency in walnuts, he says, drive strips of 18- to 20-gauge galvanized sheet metal into the main trunk or limbs of the tree at 2-inch intervals. The strips should measure about 2 inches long and about ¾ inch wide. Insert in horizontal bands around the tree parallel to the grain of the wood. Six bands per tree trunk or limb should be inserted. On trees larger than 10 inches in diameter, drive the strips into the limbs, not the trunks. Headless, galvanized nails can be used in place of the strips by substituting five or six nails for each strip. This sounds very much like old-timers I listened to as a boy telling how they made pear trees bear again by pounding nails of steel or copper into the trees. On the other hand, old-timers also drove copper nails into the trunk to kill a tree. Also, deep cuts in the cambium layer of the trunk could provide an entry point for disease.

2. *Internal Cork* or *Dieback Disease*—Dieback is a word orchardists use rather carelessly to describe any number of bad situations in the orchard, but internal cork is a specific problem in apples and pears caused by insufficient boron in the soil and a calcium deficiency. Brown corky spots develop in the flesh of the fruit. Borax powder can be sprinkled around the tree, or a boric

acid spray can be used, but consult a tree doctor for sure. A little too much boron can be disastrous, also. Its safest application is on the ground.

3. *Leaf Scorch* may be a deficiency of potash or calcium, not likely to occur in a well-managed, mulched orchard. Leaves on the margins turn brown and shrivel at the height of the growing season. Growth is stunted, and fruit is of a poor quality. You can get the same symptoms from drought, high, persistent winds, or from a combination of the two.

Photo 8-1—Dieback of a Norway Spruce. USDA photograph.

4. *Mouse Ear* is really another name for little leaf, but it refers more specifically to manganese deficiency in nut trees. Manganese sulfate spray may be prescribed, 2 to 4 pounds per mature tree as a soil additive, or in a spray of 1 to 2% mix. Better to use a chelated or other form of manganese, if possible, to avoid the sulfate.

5. *Fireblight* is not a nutritional problem. Horticulturists have found that an *over*supply of nitrogen and late heavy pruning induce vigorous growth of blossoms and young shoot-tips that are the entry points of this fearsome bacterial disease. I do not know why, nor do I claim a connection, but my mulched, natural orchard was the only orchard I know of in our county to escape the fireblight epidemic in the spring of 1979.

Many commercial orchardists who use chemical fertilizers are leaning more and more toward slow-release fertilizers, which have advantages especially when drip irrigation is used. You should remember that all organic fertilizers are slow-release kinds. Mulch itself is a slow-release fertilizer. If you need extra nitrogen, blood meal, soybean meal, and cottonseed meal are slow-releasers. Rock phosphate and bone meal release phosphorus slowly. Granite dust and greensand are very slow-release forms of potash, so slow as to be rather ineffective except where a very high content of organic matter is breaking down to humus in the soil. For trees you expect to live for 40 to 100 or more years, those safer, slower builders of balanced fertility will repay your efforts far better in the long run. Art Weaver, who accomplished the improbable feat of raising Persian walnuts in northern Ohio, managed his grove almost totally with a mulching system, hauling in ton after ton of old hay straw and manure to his 2 acres of trees. The only fertility problem he encountered was a slight manganese deficiency, which was able to be remedied with a foliar spray.

HUMAN WASTE AS FERTILIZER

Human wastes, a "problem" now that human populations have reached such proportions that we are in conflict with nature even in our natural functions, can be an asset to the owner of a grove of trees. Human manure makes good tree fertilizer, especially on young, nonbearing trees where there is no chance of disease organisms coming into contact with fruit or nuts. On bearing trees, chances of such infection are nonexistent, unless you would allow fruit to fall on fresh manure and then eat it without washing, something just about anyone would avoid doing. I know of gardeners and homesteaders who use their own families' excrement around their trees, but they are slow to talk about it because of supercilious snickers and strained looks from those who think their wastes disappear from the face of the earth when they flush the toilet. Though composted manure is preferred, some even use fresh, covering it with sawdust or some other less "offensive" organic material to control flies or odors, if any.

The EPA in Ohio is working on an ingenious system for using septic tank effluent to fertilize trees. Their idea is to provide a septic system in which *all* the effluent would be permanently disposed of on the homesite. As septic systems go now, percolation through clay soils continues satisfactorily only for a few years. In most cases, the effluent from rural homes then runs merrily down through field tile into a creek or oozes up in the backyard. The practicality of using effluent for fertilizer is evident to most people who own septic tanks. As Erma Bombeck has observed in her book of the same title, the grass is always greener over the septic tank. In an alfalfa field I pass occasionally, I can easily trace the course of a sewage-carrying drain tile from a mobile-home community to a creek, because in the dry part of the summer the alfalfa over the tile stands a good foot taller and several shades greener than the rest of the field. A network of such tile through the field would double the yield at zero cost in fertilizer from now until forever. Instead, the greater portion of the nutrients passing through the tile goes right on into the creek, causing pollution.

The EPA design (see Illus. 8-1 and 8-2) is much more elaborate and costly, befitting the bureaucracy, but the alfalfa example shows just how simple and beneficial such an idea would be to a grove of trees planted above an effluent drain tile that allowed the liquid to leach out into the surrounding soil. The EPA plan calls for evergreen trees, because they transpire all year long, as Bob Manson, who graciously provided the plans to me from EPA regional headquarters in Bowling Green, Ohio, pointed out. Since even medium-size trees can use up hundreds of gallons of water per day through transpiration, a grove would take up a very significant portion of daily household effluent and prolong the life of the leach bed and trenches indefinitely.

153

In addition, EPA designed the septic drain system as two separate systems. The effluent runs through half the system for awhile and then alternately through the other half through valves in a distribution or splitter box. Thus one-half of the system works while the other half is rejuvenating itself. Though more expensive, such a system in the right kind of soil would last indefinitely. To assure long life, the system has cleanout pits designed into it at strategic intervals along the tile lines.

Using evergreens has the advantage of continuing the transpiration of water through the winter when deciduous trees are leafless. In the Deep South, citrus would work as well. The northern grove-owner might intersperse nut-bearing evergreens with more conventional fruits and nuts to gain the best of both alternatives.

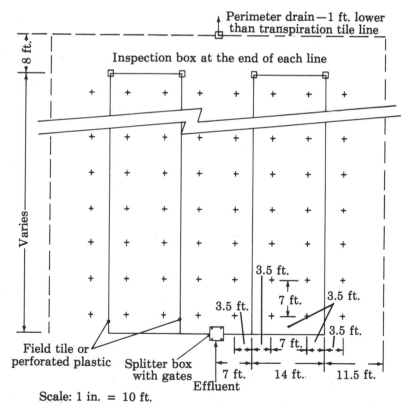

Scale: 1 in. = 10 ft.

Illus. 8-1—EPA Tree Transpiration Layout, Bowling Green, Ohio— Scotch or Austrian pines on 7-foot centers can each handle 25 gallons of effluent flow per day. Initially, every tree requires a 50-square-foot area. The tile lines are laid in a fairly level position.

Manson says the system is reliable only for individual homes and other small waste sources, not for industrial sites or food service installations where large amounts of greasy wastes must be disposed of. He cautions that the system will not be feasible where the soil surface is subject to flooding. He also says the system works "a lot better" with an aerobic, stabilized effluent and a small filter to remove solids prior to disposal.

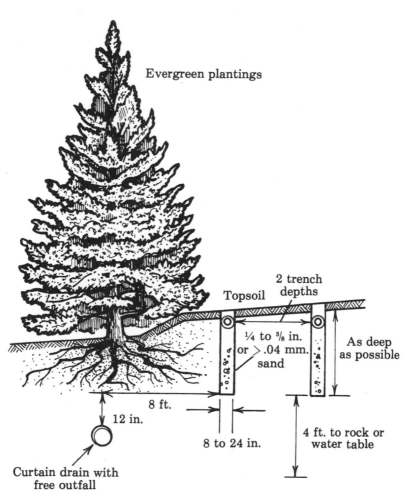

Illus. 8-2—Side View of On-Lot Disposal—Cleanout pits have been placed at regular intervals at the end of each tile line in order to assure the system a long life.

155

The main objection is cost, but for the grove-owner the cost may well be justified because of the lifelong "free" fertilizer and irrigation to the trees.

Using your own sewage or sludge has this advantage over city sludge: usually no heavy metals or polychlorinated biphenyls (PCBs) to worry about. Nevertheless, city sludge can also be a good fertilizer for groves and orchards as long as you can get a reliable analysis of every load you apply *before* you apply it. I would not apply it during the fruiting season since some of the liquid could spray up onto the fruit. Composted sludge is always preferable since harmful organisms are seldom present in it. Just as rural people must someday start paying the full cost of their waste disposal rather than getting a free ride by sending the effluent down the nearest tile line, so urban dwellers will someday certainly have to pay their fair share of the full cost of processing their wastes into a safe material for land application. As it is now, much cheap land application of uncomposted sewage is being done, and it's the farmer who takes the risks of contaminating the soil with heavy metals and PCB-type hazardous wastes. But the risk comes home eventually to haunt the urban dweller and consumer.

WATER

Water is seldom considered a "fertilizer," but actually water (along with air and sunlight) produces most of the plant growth, while minerals are a comparatively minor (but necessary) addition. Too much water is just as bad as too little. In fact, most food trees will do better in a slightly dry environment than in one slightly too wet.

I do not foolishly wish to brand *all* irrigation as being ecologically destructive. I suppose using Columbia River water on its way to the sea, for example, can hardly be considered wasteful or destructive of water. Yet modest irrigation projects almost always lead to rapacious and wasteful irrigation and, hence, to a life-style built on an artificial basis that comes tumbling down when extra water is suddenly unavailable. Also, irrigation is enormously expensive and in places where it seems to be the most necessary—the driest and most remote areas from water—it is the most expensive. Irrigation agriculture leads to a new set of agricultural problems, the chief of which today is a gradual buildup of salt in the soil that in turn demands more irrigation water to flush out, which in turn builds up more salt.

Thousands of acres of the once fertile San Joaquin Valley have now been abandoned to salt due to this kind of cycle.

Where a wetness problem is caused by poorly drained soils, some kind of artificial drainage is necessary, usually tile drainage. Reshaping the soil surface so that water will drain away rather than stand on the ground may alleviate some overly wet conditions, but the addition of tile in heavy clay soils is almost always necessary, too. Tile-ditching engineers or the Soil Conservation Service (SCS) office in your area should be consulted, since every site has its own peculiar problems of soil type, soil depth, and slope. Normally you can expect a 4-inch tile line to drain the soil sufficiently 25 feet on either side of it, if laid 2 to 3 feet deep. Tighter soils might require lines closer together, and looser soils might need lines farther apart. It usually takes a year or two for a new tile line to start draining the soil around and above it at maximum efficiency.

Some form of irrigation is used in commercial orchards in nearly all parts of the United States, dry and humid, but home grove-owners should approach the practice cautiously. Studies in Ohio indicate that sprinkle irrigation of conventional orchards in humid eastern climates doesn't pay. But in dense plantings of dwarf trees, demand for water and nutrients becomes more intense, and the various forms of drip- and trickle-irrigation systems do become profitable with proper management. Recent experiments, however, demonstrate that only with slow-release fertilizers is drip irrigation in high-density orchards profitable. Since the organic matter associated with mulch orcharding releases nutrients very slowly, we can logically conclude that drip irrigation is "right" for mulched trees in a hedgerow system. But in normal years, mulching will supply (or conserve) all the extra moisture a fruit or nut tree needs in a typically humid climate.

The example at the beginning of this chapter demonstrates that even in western dryland orchards, where rainfall averages just a little over 20 inches a year, mostly as winter snow, mulching can conserve enough moisture to grow a fruit crop even in a drought year. Soil moisture stayed consistently higher in the mulched Greenbluff orchards near Spokane than in unmulched orchards, and it remained surprisingly high in the mulched orchards even during the summer. Soil conservation technicians believe that they observed a phenomenon in the mulched orchards that went beyond mere moisture conservation. SCS technician Judd Milton told me this:

157

The mulch would be so moist under the surface on the driest summer days you could almost wring water out of it. Because of the mulch the trees' fine feeder roots grew right up to the soil surface and fed on that moisture. We think the water comes from the dense fogs we get on the bluffs in summer. The fog condenses on the mulch and is absorbed into it. Our tests showed an accumulation of moisture under the mulch equivalent to a good spring rain.

If the SCS is correct, what is happening in the orchards is the same natural phenomenon ancient man in Europe learned to harness. The dew ponds of England and Europe were built on mountaintop fortresses to catch and hold water from dew that condensed on huge piles of rocks stacked up for that purpose. Historical records indicate that during English droughts, the dew ponds did not dry up as did the lowland ponds that normally were relied on for cattle water. Anyone who has walked through a cornfield that is dripping with dew on a foggy August morning has no trouble grasping the engineering theory behind a dew pond or a mulched orchard on a foggy bluff.

In Arizona, Papago Indians still harvest fruit from desert peach trees up to a century old. So dry is the soil in which the trees grow that wind will blow away the sand and expose the tree roots if farmers aren't careful to pile protective brush around the trees when necessary. Gary Nabhan, who studies native American agricultural methods in the dry land of the Southwest at the University of Arizona, tells me the Indians know where the water table is high enough to support the growth of these trees by the type of vegetation growing naturally there. Nabhan, like almost every thoughtful observer of the arid Southwest, believes that at the frightful rate groundwater is being used for irrigation, industry, and recreation, it will become too scarce to use for modern methods to irrigate farming, necessitating a return finally to the floodwater farming methods of ancient Indian civilizations.[1]

In this method, the Indians learned how to control runoff water when it did fall, funneling it through ditches and dikes from wide "catchment" areas into small fields or holding basins, to be drawn off later for crops. Nabhan says a catch basin 4 times

---

1. *Gary Paul Nabhan, "The Ecology of Floodwater Farming in Arid Southwestern North America,"* Agro-Ecosystems *5, no. 3 (July 1, 1979), pp. 245–55.*

the size of the field will produce enough water for sorghum near Tucson, but basins from 15 to 27 times the size of the cultivated fields are used by Hopi Indians in the Great Basin Desert.

This method of floodwater or runoff farming is being perfected for orchards in Israel, too. The Israelis have demonstrated that even with an average rainfall of only 5 inches per year, unirrigated orchards can be practical if ancient methods of runoff agriculture are employed. For many years scientists believed that changing weather patterns in places like the Negev Desert were responsible for turning once productive farmland into sparse rangelands. But closer study in recent years revealed that biblical farmers built catchments that collected rainwater when it did fall, and carried it from the expansive hillsides down to smaller, cultivated areas. The ruins of these ancient hillside catchments are still visible. When the Israelis rebuilt one, it effectively funneled rainfall to an orchard below, which received as a result not 5 inches of water per year, but 30 inches, making the production of fruit and olives practical. Further experiments showed that a small catchment basin around each tree could produce the same effect with even less water loss.

Another method of harnessing runoff water is to plant trees on terraces where water that runs off hillsides can be trapped and held or slowed in its journey downhill. The water then seeps into the root areas of the trees. For example, in reforesting hilly areas, tree growers have found that, by plowing furrows parallel to the slope of hills so that the plow throws the furrow downhill, a shallow ditch is formed in which planted seedlings survive much better. Such furrows must be laid out carefully, however, because if they have any appreciable downward grade of their own they may quickly turn into gullies.

Where some form of additional water is necessary for food production, the wise grove-owner will think first of diverting runoff water from a stream or river, either with a catchment or, where the land will hold the water, with a pond. With a pond, the grove-owner enhances the ecology rather than detracts from it and helps keep the watershed he lives in from flooding by storing water that would otherwise rush quickly into the valleys after heavy rains. If pumping groundwater is the only course of action, use drip-irrigation under mulch, and you will need only a small portion of the water that's usually involved in sprinkle- or flood-irrigation, much of which evaporates before the plant can use it, anyway.

BROAD ASPECTS
OF FERTILITY
IN THE HOME GROVE

The foregoing comments and suggestions about soil enrichment for healthy tree growth have been offered as if trees were just like any cultivated crop in their needs. That approach has its advantages, including an understanding of the role of individual plant nutrients, but it does not adequately convey the full meaning of tree fertility. The whole is greater than the sum of its parts.

A permanent grove of trees is *not* like a cultivated field crop, and the differences become more profound and pronounced with the passage of time. A grove of trees managed properly, which is to say managed to mimic the natural woodland grove (or managed *as* a natural woodland grove), in a thousand years hence will contain a richer soil that produces more super-nutritive food than it does today. A field cultivated annually to corn and soybeans for a thousand years will have no topsoil left at all unless it is one of those rare places so level that the soil does not wash away, and so moist it does not blow away. Even such a level, moist field can be maintained in fertility only by tremendous outlays for fertilizers and, if the current trend continues, in a thousand years it will be so compacted by heavy machinery and so toxified with pesticides as to be virtually useless for the production of nutritional food.

On the other hand, the grove is essentially self-fertilizing. The leaves fall to build rich topsoil through the interplay of soil microorganisms and humus. Tree roots feed on the nutrients released in the topsoil and also plunge deep into the earth for minerals and water. The minerals find their way, via the leaves, back to the topsoil. Silviculturists say that woodland can actually raise the water level, and, of course, woodland acts as a reservoir of moisture as rain soaks and holds in the deep, permeable, humus-ladened soil beneath the trees. While the trees produce their food and nourish a whole food chain of plants and animals under and around them, there is a net gain in fertility; in cultivated fields there is almost always a net loss. On a steep mountain field, the net loss of fertility may be readily apparent in a generation or two. On gentler, deep-loam slopes it may take a couple of centuries. But the end is the same.

In nearly every instance, trees can produce more food than grain. Corn yields something like 5 tons of grain per acre on good soil in a good year. Honey locust trees with proper management produce 15 to 20 tons of pods and seeds, far richer in nutrients, particularly proteins, than corn, points out J. Sholto Douglas and Robert A. de J. Hart in their book *Forest Farming*. Heaven only knows what kind of production we could get from trees like honey locust if they had enjoyed the kind of varietal improvement we have worked into corn. The honey locust is, furthermore, a legume and can fix nitrogen in the soil. Being fine-leaved, it could be double-cropped with pasture grass or a limited interplanting of small fruits. Douglas and Hart list yields for other tree crops: carob (also a legume and a close relative of honey locust), 18 to 20 tons per acre; mulberries, 8 to 10; persimmons, 5 to 7; walnuts, 10 to 15; oaks, 10 to 12; pecans, 9 to 11; olives, 3 to 4; hazelnuts, 9 to 12; dates, 4 to 7; apples, 7 tons.

While producing crops, protecting the soil, preserving moisture, exuding oxygen, cooling summer air, tempering winter winds—in short, supporting a stable population of man and animals—the trees are never lost, even in death. The wood can then be used as fuel, the ash returned to the soil as fertilizer. Or the wood can be used for an endless array of useful items, such as shelter, tools, furniture, and so forth. No material, and certainly no renewable resource, can be adapted to as many uses as wood.

Why, then, do "advanced" civilizations destroy their forests in favor of cultivated crops? One reason is that trees are so useful (and therefore lucrative) as wood that the temptation to cut them down for profit is irresistible. Solomon, supposedly a wise man, employed 70,000 men to cut down the Cedars of Lebanon, an act that geologists and soil conservationists can now show destroyed the food production resources of that region forever after. The tropical forests of South America are now similarly being destroyed even though science knows the loss is irreplaceable. The destruction proceeds with full governmental condonation because governments can be just as greedy as individuals.

Once the trees are cut down, man often plants annual crops because he can't wait even five years for another crop of trees to start bearing. Even if the land is not cultivatable, he rarely will plant trees because it is more difficult to harvest food from trees than from low-growing plants. We cannot climb as agilely as other primates anymore. If man were challenged to make a machine to harvest, for example, honey locust pods, he could do it. But corn is easier to make a machine for, just as it is easier and faster to breed corn for better varieties.

Another reason agriculture rather than silviculture has become the "mother of all the arts" is that population always seems to increase one step ahead of increasing food production. More food equals more babies, and in this sense improved agricultural technology causes future overpopulation even as it relieves some of the present population. Trees in the short run cannot increase food supply as fast as the population increases, so "advanced" civilizations cut down the trees upon the assumption that cultivated crops will meet the demand for more food faster. When the soil can be mined no longer with the most clever of technologies, a decline may occur.

A state of emergency exists in any human community from the very moment it can no longer live comfortably without consuming nature around it faster than nature can replace the loss. One of its first signs is the wholesale destruction of forests in favor of cultivation. The plow is indeed the symbol of agriculture as "mother of all the arts," but it is also a monument to the tragedy of the human condition. We forsake the trees of our primal ancestry and the evolutionary environment that nourished us into human consciousness. We do not recognize who and what we are. We put our hands to plows dreaming of a land flowing in milk and honey—a land that the plow can only ultimately destroy.

PART II
PEST CONTROL

CHAPTER 9

A GENERAL PHILOSOPHY OF ORGANIC PEST CONTROL

For the purposes of both the commercial orchard and the home grove, a "pest" might be defined as any animal (including passing motorists and small boys), insect, fungus, bacterium, or virus that reduces marketable yields below profitable levels. But the commercial orchardist and home orchardist have different definitions for the words, "marketable" and "profitable." For the typical commercial orchard that faces debts at exorbitant interest rates, a profitable level of production over a fair return for labor and management means keeping the amount of unmarketable fruit below at least 5% of the total crop and, ideally, below 1%. But a home orchardist need not be under such stringent economic pressure, and he can "market" blemished fruit profitably that the commercial grower usually cannot.

Badly damaged fruit in the home grove will feed domestic and wild animals. Perhaps a third of the crop can be used so, "profitably." For instance, according to F. B. Morrison's classic *Feeds and Feeding* (Reston, Va., Reston Publishers, 2d ed., 1979), the bible of the livestock-feed industry, apple pomace has nearly as much nutritional value for cows as silage. Another third of the crop, the slight-to-medium damaged fruit, can go for jams, jellies, and pies—after all, you have to cut the apple up and core it, anyhow, at which time offending wormy parts can be discarded. Out of this portion of the crop comes cider for home use and perhaps vinegar, usually with surplus to sell. That leaves the last third of the crop, with little or no damage, for eating or marketing fresh. A standard tree yielding 12 bushels of apples, of which 4 are market-fresh, represents a "profit" well worth the time to the home grove-owner, though hardly enough for the commercial grower to run a successful business.

Can you raise even a third of your crop blemish-free without heavy and continuous spray schedules? The answer depends on whom you ask. Important studies in Nova Scotia, mentioned frequently in this book, suggest on the basis of a five-year experiment in which no insecticides at all were used that as much as half a crop can be marketed fresh without spraying in that area. But at Purdue, in a three-year test on high-density plantings, insect damage was as high as 95% when no insecticides or fungicides were used. In the latter case no conscious biological-control methods were employed. Had there been some, and had there been a couple of well-timed organic sprays, one might reasonably expect at least a third of the crop to be market-fresh, especially if disease-resistant varieties were used.

Because of his different economic outlook, the homeowner might profit from dividing pests into categories: (1) serious, (2) harmful to fruit, and (3) minor. The serious pests are those that kill the tree. The ones harmful to fruit only the orchardist can live with; the minor ones in a good biological program will remain minor. Scab is an example of the first category since in many cases it will kill trees if left uncontrolled. Apple maggot and codling moth are examples of the second. They can ruin lots of fruit, but they won't kill the tree. Mites are an example of the third. Even most chemical growers admit now that mites would not be a problem in a biologically controlled orchard, as I'll explain later.

A HISTORY OF CHEMICAL PEST CONTROL

Commercial growers will brand this approach to pest control as a naive form of naturalism, I'm sure, since there was a time when I would have thought so myself. Therefore, just a bit of history of chemical orchard management is in order. As far as I know, no complete, objective history of this kind has been written yet. It would be too embarrassing to the agrichemical industry. Whatever good intentions chemists in the field have had, their work is a chronicle of blunders, as one chemical after another used to solve one problem only led to other problems. What little history I give here I preface with remarks by entomologist A. D. Pickett, a pioneer in biological pest control long before this term came into popular usage. In the mid-1940s, he and his colleagues at the Kentville Research Station in Nova Scotia began the kind of work that we now refer to as "integrated pest management." Pickett could look back in 1950 to a half-century of chemical spraying and predict with startling accuracy what would happen if agriculture persisted in depending totally on chemicals for pest control. Here's what he wrote in *The Canadian Entomologist* in March, 1949:

> *Man can only hope to mitigate the insect problem; he cannot eliminate it in an open environment. . . . Those who feel that insecticides alone can be depended on to control all insect pests are not at all daunted when, for instance, the application of DDT to apple trees, while practically eliminating the codling moth, induces the buildup of tremendous populations of mites, wooly aphids, or red-banded leaf rollers. They would solve the problem by adding another chemical and possibly another application or two of spray. New machinery and techniques for the application of chemicals are developed and so we are carried from crisis to crisis, always hoping that the newest chemical or technique is the final requirement. And it must be remembered, and this is vital, that as this goes on the expense increases. . . .*
>
> *. . . It could happen that posterity will condemn the present generation as despoilers on account of the indiscriminate dissemination of poisons.*
>
> *The methods used in many cases in testing the effects of various agricultural chemicals on soils leaves much to be desired. . . . In other words, the present methods used by investigators in testing agricultural chemicals are entirely too empirical and should be regarded with acute skepticism. This applies not only to the work of the scientific staffs of industrial organizations, but to that of governmental officers as well.*
>
> *There are a number of reasons, most of them economic, why this policy has been allowed to develop as it has. There are many incentives established and various pressures exerted to induce the carrying on of insecticide testing but there is little to*

encourage long-term ecological studies of the changes in the complex biological relationships that may be brought about by the application of spray chemicals. The results of such work are so slow in coming to light that the problem is side-tracked because no organization is behind it and only the primary producer stands to profit immediately from any progress in this field. The farmer should be interested in this line of approach but for the most part he too is subjected to economic pressures to get immediate results and the problems are mostly too abstruse for him to comprehend fully.

. . . In spite of the fact that the following statement is likely to be criticized, the writer is of the opinion that the tendency to prescribe mathematical formulae to explain complex biological phenomena is very often premature and tends to suppress rather than stimulate the elucidation of ecological phenomena.

. . . It may well be that in the long run an insecticide which kills 50% of the pest insect and none of its predators or parasites may be far more valuable than one which kills 95% but at the same time eliminates its natural enemies.

. . . It must be recognized that each individual orchard with its environment is a dynamic biological community within which the various components fluctuate according to the various pressures involved and no two orchards are directly comparable. There may be a tendency toward similarity if conditions and treatments have been approximately the same over a period of time and a state of equilibrium has been approached. It is unlikely that a state of complete equilibrium will ever become established. It is not possible to make direct comparisons when so many variables are involved and it is for this reason that statistical methods may fail to have significance and attempts to use them lead to misinterpretation and frustration. It would appear that there is still plenty of scope for the sometimes despised observational methods of the old-time naturalist.

If in attempting to control our insect pests we are simply trading off one group of pests for another group of the future, then the only damage will be the relative costs of the control measures and the degree to which control of those new pests can be attained. There may be, however, inherent in our present policies, the danger of creating agricultural and nutritional problems with such far-reaching results that we cannot simply return to some previous stage and start over again.

167

... Agricultural practices are the conscious attempts of man, who is himself a factor in the biotic community, to so alter the interactions of the factors in his environment that he may bring about advantages favorable to himself in his competition with other species. There must be recognition of the fact that he is a part of the whole and when he wishes to alter the normal functioning of the component parts, he must realize that although he can single these parts out for study, he cannot, in the natural community, alter one factor without disturbing many others.

Finally, the writer believes we should accept as a fundamental concept the proposition that crops should be grown primarily for the purpose of satisfying man's food requirements and not as a means of making particular human activities commercially profitable regardless of the overall effect on human welfare.

Pickett and his philosophy were ignored, and the chemical approach continued to dominate food production for another 30 years. Reviewed briefly in chronological retrospect, events proved that Pickett's fears were justified. The first systematic use of insecticides in America was the application of Paris green to control Colorado potato beetle, which suddenly developed into a scourge after the Civil War when large acreages of potatoes were planted. The beetle, which hitherto had eked out a living on wild plants of the Solanaceae family, such as horse nettle, quickly overpopulated. Despite every chemical thrown at it for 100 years, the beetle still flourishes. Interestingly, here is what T. B. Terry, writing in his book *Our Farming* (Philadelphia, The Farmer Company, 1893), says about controlling potato beetles on his farm long before anyone dreamed of the notion of "organic farming":

When the beetles first came, we were obliged to use poison ... but soon I began to consider the injury to vines even when not killed and that some vines must be eaten to get the poison, and the risk of having poison washed off by a shower ... and that I must put it on myself if I wanted to be certain no vines were killed by careless spraying, and that living in the midst of a dozen acres of poisoned tops, with the wind blowing, might not give us the purest air possible, and that sooner or later some accident might happen from having poison about the place, and that the beetles were not nearly so numerous as at first, and that I believed we could manage so as to pick them by hand successfully. And we have for a dozen years. When we went at it rightly, it was not a very large job. We have kept twenty-four acres clean for two years, eighteen acres for two years, and about a dozen other years. . . . If raising 100 acres, I should never think of using poison . . . I am no crank on this subject, but have simply made it a matter of business. I might say quite a few potatoes are grown about here and all fight bugs as I do, so far as I know.

Whatever region, orchard, or pest one chooses to trace the chemical control of, the pattern of stumbling "from one crisis to another," as Pickett puts it, is about the same. If we look at the eastern apple orchard as one example, the first sprays used were fungicides, and this was after apples had been grown quite successfully for over a century on the subsistence pioneer farms without any spraying at all. Apples were a staple food and drink in colonial America, and per capita consumption was higher than today because apples were one of the few dependable fruits the more northerly colonists could grow. Pickett says that before the turn of the 20th century, insects were not a serious problem despite occasional outbreaks. Spraying in 1900 was simple. Writes John Williams Streeter (*The Fat of the Land*, New York, Macmillan, 1904): "I bought a spraying-pump for $13 . . . and we were ready to make the first attack on fungus disease with the Bordeaux mixture. . . . Another vigorous spraying with the same mixture when the buds were swelling, another when the flower petals were falling, and still another when the fruit was large as peas, the last two . . . with Paris green added . . . and the fight against apple enemies was ended for that year."

Bordeaux mixture was the standard fungicide around 1900. According to folk history, the first use of Bordeaux in France was not as a fungicide, but to discourage the peasants from stealing grapes. Since in natural environments fungi invariably hold each other in check, one might theorize that the first use upset the balance between "pest" and "beneficial" fungi. The initial effect must have been favorable to the grapes, but the long-term effect may have been to make a fungicide necessary from then on to maintain the artificial situation.

In about 1910, lime sulfur began to replace Bordeaux to reduce russeting in fruit aggravated by using the copper-based chemical. The use of sulfur precipitated a series of serious pest outbreaks, but it was not until the 1940s that the connection

169

between the outbreaks and sulfur was definitely established. The sulfur was killing the predators and parasites of the harmful insects. Had the fledgling apple industry mounted a campaign to show that russeting was beautiful or at least totally harmonious with good fruit quality, untold thousands of dollars in time, money, and research could have been saved. Fruit connoisseurs say that some of the old, heavily russeted varieties (such as Ashmead's Kernel, which one apple variety collector describes as having the appearance of an Idaho potato) have excellent taste and often good disease resistance. For example, Grimes Golden fell out of favor partly because of its inclination to russeting. But Grimes Golden is one of the few highly praised dessert apples that's fairly resistant to scab.

Sulfur won the day and shortly thereafter, lead arsenate came along to kill the burgeoning bugs. Lime sulfur eventually gave way to modified sulfur and elemental sulfur sprays. The most immediate serious problem that arose was an outbreak of eye-spotted budworm, so severe that the use of lime sulfur dust (and copper-lime dust) had to be discontinued. The dusts were killing the predators of the budworm.

In the 1930s, oystershell scale and other scale insects became dominant and serious pests in eastern orchards. Sulfur was lethal to their predators, as the researchers at Kentville discovered. All they had to do was convince growers to stop spraying sulfur and the oystershell scale subsided dramatically. Pickett wryly commented in one of his reports on this first major biological-control victory: "Had the staff of our laboratory developed an insecticide that would control the oystershell scale as effectively as these mere changes . . . that allowed nature to take its course, they would have been assured of a place in entomological history" (*The Canadian Entomologist,* December, 1953, p. 477).

Meanwhile, the use of lead arsenate was indirectly helping the codling moth to major pest status from its position as a minor pest at the turn of the century. DDT arrived on the scene to avert another crisis. DDT killed codling moth like nothing previously used. Parathion and other deadly broad-spectrum poisons were also very effective, but more expensive, and were not used as extensively until DDT was restricted.

When DDT, parathion, and all the rest of the broad-spectrum killers came into general use, there occurred an immediate and dramatic upsurge in another pest hitherto of only minor importance: mites, particularly European red mites. The

170

Nova Scotians halted DDT and parathion applications in test orchards, and there was a dramatic decrease in mite injury. After a decade of study, the researchers could conclude and state flatly that the broad-spectrum insecticides then in use killed the predators of mites and caused the mite problem. What's more, when predator mites (mites that prey on mites) were allowed to do their job unhindered by spraying, mite pests were not a problem. "We would get into trouble with mites only when we were spraying to control some other pest with a material that harmed mite predators," Dr. A. W. McPhee, an entomologist in Nova Scotia, told me.

The buildup of harmful mites following the introduction of DDT was a nearly universal experience, not just limited to the orchard. Where DDT was mist-blown in towns to control mosquitoes, the buildup of spider mites in gardens was enormous, notes Cynthia Westcott in her popular *The Gardener's Bug Book* (New York, Doubleday, 1973). The frightful part of all this history is that there was not a voluntary movement by the chemical industry to stop DDT (any more than there is to stop parathion today) even when its short-term harmful effects were known, regardless of their ignorance of long-term residual buildup in living creatures. Periodically DDT defenders still praise the chemical because it kills some bugs effectively and because it is cheap. Farmers like cheap, effective products even when the "cheap" products force them to buy more sprays that aren't so cheap.

Since the 1960s, the chemical approach has emphasized poisons specific to particular insects rather than broad-spectrum sprays, even though these newer sprays are often more dangerous to the applicator. Specific miticides were the first on the market. Where spraying codling moth kills mite predators, the orchardist can now spray a specific miticide that harms the "bad" mites more than the "good" mites, bringing down the population of the former while the latter is recovering from the codling-moth spray. Again, the farmer pays more, not less, with this approach to bug control.

The problem with potent and specific chemicals is the pests' demonstrated ability to become immune to them. Immunity is now the most immediate control problem in chemical orchards, and the potential effects could be the most disastrous suffered yet. To control immune bugs means stronger and stronger poisons, until a time might be reached when a bug not only resists the most potent sprays but resists them at a point in the life history of its environment at which natural controls have been destroyed beyond quick recall. It is this spectre that is finally impressing the agriprofit mentality, especially after its disastrous experience controlling pink bollworm, or trying to, with a chemical program that precipitated an extremely costly outbreak of tobacco budworm in the Southwest. The pure chemical approach ultimately is not profitable for anyone.

A perfect, current example of how orchard-pest management is coming full circle—*must* come full circle—is the plight of Northwestern pear growers. In trying to control pear psylla with toxic poisons, they have succeeded only in developing psylla that for all practical purposes are immune to the organophosphate sprays that have killed off the psylla parasites and predators. I quote directly from a USDA bulletin out of Oakland, California, of February 8, 1980: "Pessimists say the Northwest pear industry will disappear within five years, while optimists say within ten years, unless something is done to control pear psylla . . . "

And what now, finally, is the USDA suggesting as the answer? Ladybug beetles—a suggestion the USDA laughed at ten years ago. Currently, growers are gaining some control by using synthetic pyrethroids, which are related to the old botanical insecticide pyrethrum. Pear psylla have already become resistant to synthetic pyrethroids, however. But as Deke Deitrick, who operates an insectary in California, tells me, in an orchard *without* a long history of heavy chemical spraying, where predators and parasites (including ladybugs) of pear psylla are present in good environmental balance, you can get fairly adequate control with water and dormant oil alone if the spray is applied precisely as the adult psylla emerge to lay eggs in the spring, a time entomologists can now accurately predict for any orchard.

Meanwhile, codling moth and apple maggot seem to be gaining on us, even with effective, more or less specific (but still very environmentally dangerous) sprays like Imidan. Apple maggot has no known effective predators (unless you count livestock that eat fallen apples), and so eludes, for the time being, effective biological control.

Codling moth has plenty of predators, although none of them seem to depend on it as a sole food source. They prey upon other bugs as well; hence, biological control appears to be difficult. A male sterilization program in British Columbia worked but was considered too expensive and so was dropped for the time being. Pheromone scents that confuse the moths out of their normal mating patterns are being tried. Pheromones for mating disruption are very expensive, however, as are most new experimental techniques. This method is being used with mixed results, and the present mass-distribution technology may leave the orchard covered with millions of plastic micro-fibers that contain the pheromones. Viral infections for moth control are being tested as well. So far, the best biological control of codling moth over a long period of time was obtained in Nova Scotia by a combination of a number of controls. Since codling moth has only one generation per season in Nova Scotia, control is easier there than farther south, and the same methods may not necessarily be as effective elsewhere. But as an example of the kind of biological approach home grove-owners must pursue, the experiment is worthy of wider attention.

The approach underscores the extremely complex life systems a natural orchardist must understand (however dimly), and why a book such as this one, which attempts to deal ecologically with an environmental problem, presents such difficulties in organization. In the old days a writer was content merely to treat pests under logical categories: insects, fungal diseases, bacterial diseases, animal pests, and so forth. But the truth is, all of these various characters in the ecological theater of life interrelate in more ways than we know. One cannot speak of a particular insect without immediately mentioning a score of others and apologizing for not citing as yet unrecognized ones. I suspect this is why ecology seems so fearful to proponents of the conventional scientific approach. It transcends the compartmentalization of our little human minds.

NOVA SCOTIAN INTEGRATED PEST MANAGEMENT

Somewhat by trial and error, the Nova Scotians perfected a four-pronged control system for codling moth. One of their earliest discoveries was the significant contribution that woodpeckers, particularly hairy and downy woodpeckers, make to codling-moth control. Ater a study that ran through most of the 1950s, in as many as 70 commercial orchards, C. R. MacLelland found that woodpeckers reduced the overwintering larval population by 52% on the average and that "woodpeckers frequently reduced the pest population in orchards to a level where other natural control agents were able to prevent the succeeding generation from damaging the fruit to an uneconomical degree" (*The Canadian Entomologist*, January, 1958, pp. 18–22).

"Frequently" is, of course, not good enough for a commercial orchardist, nor is an average of 52% control (though it might be adequate in a home-grove situation). What's more, orchards

Illus. 9-1—Hairy Woodpecker—One of the main predators of codling moth (overwintering larvae) is the hairy woodpecker. Nova Scotian orchardists depend upon this bird to control codling moth, along with abandoning the use of sulfur and arsenicals, which kill other predators of codling moth. The orchardists have also used the botanical spray ryania and sex pheromone traps to control codling moth.

in modern times are hardly ever established with the idea of leaving adjacent woodland for woodpeckers. The typical commercial orchard point of view is that woodland is evil and therein lurk the "bad" bugs, though backyard homeowners' apple trees isolated along the edges of woodlots are seldom severely affected by bugs. So researchers sought other biological controls. Abandoning sulfur and arsenicals greatly improved predator and parasite control of codling moth, but this second step was not as effective as it had been for oystershell scale. What the researchers needed was a spray, mild enough not to harm the predators too much, but specific enough to stop some codling-moth activity.

The best solution they found was an old botanical insecticide, ryania. "Along with a well-managed biological program, two or three sprays of this mild insecticide gave us good economical control," A. W. McPhee reported. (Unfortunately, ryania is almost impossible to buy in North America at the present time.)

A fourth step in the control method was discovered somewhat more recently, when in 1974 sex pheromone traps were introduced into the orchards to monitor insect populations. Researchers discovered that the traps *themselves* added to overall control *in an orchard already in a biological-control program.* MacLelland reported (*The Canadian Entomologist,* December, 1977):

> *Under insecticide-free conditions, captures in sex phero-mone traps were associated with significant pest suppression. The traps, by not interfering with other suppressing factors, acted as additional, effective predators. They were more successful in orchards where only mildly toxic insecticides were used than in orchards where broadly toxic insecticides were used.*

Codling moth remains a serious pest in Nova Scotia as elsewhere, and some spraying remains necessary, though rarely the "last-ditch methods of using broad-spectrum insecticides," says McPhee. Unfortunately growers no longer use ryania (except dedicated organic growers) as their selective codling moth spray. Ryania is expensive, doesn't kill fast or completely enough in a chemically managed orchard, and won't control apple maggot. The botanical, however, gives every evidence of being an adequate, selective spray for codling moth in a biologically managed grove of trees.

Nor were the Nova Scotian test orchards ever free of all toxic chemicals, it should be emphasized. Fungicide sprays have always been used, or the trees would simply die from scab. Some of the fungicides now in use are, or seem to be, less ecologically offensive than former ones—Captan and Polyram are fairly easy on beneficial mites, anyway—but all can affect the balance of soil microorganisms adversely. Moreover, scab is developing strains resistant to some fungicides, and, true to the century-long pattern, stronger ones such as Cyprex are brought into the battle. The correct approach to scab is in the development of immune varieties, which are now just beginning to be distributed (more on these later). It will be interesting, and I predict satisfying, to the ecologically concerned when sophisticated biological-control methods can be practiced in an orchard in which little or no fungicide needs to be applied. I would not be surprised at all if a connection were found between heavy fungicidal spraying and the increase in virulence of the bacterium that causes fireblight.

As I have already pointed out, a discussion of individual pests carries with it a certain amount of unreality according to the true picture of pest control because no pests act individually, but in relation to each other. Before going on to such a discussion of individual pests, a few lessons from history and from the Nova Scotian experience seem in order:

—You cannot eliminate (kill) one organism without affecting others, and the effect historically has almost always been cumulatively counterproductive.

—An effect that may begin as ecologically destructive inevitably becomes financially destructive as well. This is the lesson so difficult to learn. Farmers believe in the short-term gain that the chemical salesmen offer, and thereby accept a long-term loss.

—The greater the area under biological and integrated pest control, the more effective that control can be. The Kentville experiments produced substantial evidence that when one orchard under biological-control methods is surrounded by heavily sprayed orchards, it has less of a chance of attaining optimum good effects from biological management. If true, a potentially explosive social and political problem could arise over the violation of property rights as interpreted by farmers of varying persuasions. Chemical farmers will blame pest outbreaks on unsprayed orchards; biological farmers will blame them on sprayed orchards. This is already happening, of course, but the legal problems are beyond the scope of this book. Suffice it to say here that it seems that the more growers who can be convinced to retreat from total reliance on toxic chemicals, the more effective the overall program will become. Instead of a few people establishing groves of trees isolated from the concentration of chemical orchards, perhaps the future could bring the whole landscape of human habitation into a pleasant grove of food trees to live in and from. And that vision is the dream I have.

If no one tries to follow such visions, what is the alternative? If we do not change, how much longer will it be practical to grow tree fruits at all? As things stand now, here is the current (1978–79) "correct" way to control pests in Georgia peach orchards, as given by the *Georgia Peach Spray Guide*. The schedule, suggested by University of Georgia horticulturists, demands as many as 15 to 20 spray applications in a year's time, depending on how often rain washes off an application. Here's the list:

1. Several dormant sprays of Ferbam or lime sulfur, and of superior oil (for leaf curl, brown rot, scales, mites).
2. One or often two applications at blossom time of Benlate and Captan (for blossom blight).
3. A petal-fall spray of sulfur plus either parathion, Guthion, Imidan, Thiodan, or Penncap-M (for brown rot, plum curculio, and catfacing insects).
4. Shuck-fall or first cover spray of Benlate and sulfur, plus either parathion, Guthion, Imidan, Thiodan, or Penncap-M (for brown rot, scab, plum curculio, and catfacing insects).
5. Second cover spray same as above, which should be repeated, at least the fungicides, if heavy rain occurs.
6. A mite spray, if they are a problem, with Kelthane, Trition, Tedion, or Plictran.
7. Third cover spray 12 to 14 days after the second cover spray, same as second.
8. A fourth cover spray, 14 days after third, of sulfur or Captan (for brown rot and scab).
9. A spray six weeks before harvest of sulfur or Captan, plus parathion, Guthion, Imidan, or Penncap-M (for brown rot, oriental fruit moth, and plum curculio).
10. A spray four weeks before harvest, same as above.
11. A spray two weeks before harvest of Captan plus

Botran, or Benlate plus Captan, plus either parathion, Imidan, or Penncap-M (for brown rot, rhizopus rot, oriental fruit moth, plum curculio, catfacing insects).

12. A spray seven days before harvest of Captan or Captan and Botran (for brown rot and rhizopus rot).

13. A spray one day before harvest of Benlate and Captan, or Botran and Captan (for rots).

14. A post-harvest treatment of fruit, Benlate and Botran (for rots).

15. Two sprays after harvest a month apart of Thiodan or Lorsban (for peach tree borer control).

16. During the season and after harvest, one or two applications of Diazinon (for white peach scale).

17. If necessary, additions of Cyprex, plus Captan or zinc sulfate in all cover sprays (for bacterial spot).

Is the product that comes from this type of chemical orcharding worth the effort? I have not been able to buy a good Georgia peach for the last eight years in supermarkets—or a good peach from *anywhere*. The peaches are picked green, are hard, splotched with brown rotting places, and are nearly tasteless. What is the use of it all? On top of all that, according to the fruit-growing magazines and industry leaders, the peach business in the Southeast is in financial trouble. Little wonder. What is ecologically destructive inevitably becomes financially destructive.

CHAPTER 10

ANIMAL PESTS AND ANIMAL FRIENDS

In orchard-pest control, bugs and blights get more attention, but for the backyard grove-owner, animals, especially certain birds, usually destroy more tree fruit, and their control is more elusive. No one has found a really effective way to keep squirrels out of nut groves or robins out of cherry trees, although for the latter there is a chemical now touted as being effective. (After reading the cautionary provisions in the directions for the chemical's use, I would have to be very hungry for cherries before I'd buy some from an orchard where I know it has been used.) Most animal-control methods listed below are only partially effective, thank heavens. If we *could* eradicate squirrels and robins, we would probably do it, and the result of that would be worse than the loss of fruit. Besides, I have learned, after an uncounted number of cusswords, that if I try hard enough I can get my share of the grove's bounty. Events average out in nature. If in one year you lose a tree's whole crop, the next year you're likely to get enough to last two years.

ANIMAL AND BIRD PESTS
DEER

Deer in some areas have reached population levels beyond the food supply of the wild environment around them. In parts of northern Pennsylvania, deer wander around as bold as cows and eat everything that has a root on the other end. Hunters, who go forth from their urban enclaves to the "wilderness" once a year to shoot at anything that does not have a root on the other end, are glad for all of these deer. Country-folk would be glad for all of these hunters if only they would shoot deer instead of everything else, including each other.

Overpopulations of deer are very destructive to small fruit trees in winter. Fencing is about the only effective defense, other than improving the shooting skills of hunters. Some researchers claim success with concoctions containing Tabasco sauce, and with creosote. Growers who use creosote tie rags soaked in the stuff to stakes next to the fruit trees. Felt strips on lath stakes at about half the height of the dwarf trees seem to do the trick. Drive the stakes in about 4 inches away from the tree trunk and lean them out a little; otherwise, the creosote fumes might burn bark or leaves.

Repellents don't work consistently for most growers. The Department of Natural Resources in Michigan has tried chemicals, scare guns, lion scent, bone tar oil, and bags of human hair tied to the trees, and found all "rather unsuccessful in keeping deer out of orchards."

Henry Hartman, a New Jersey nurseryman, at a recent annual meeting of the Northern Nut Growers Association (NNGA), described a method using mothballs to discourage deer attacks. He cuts off a 6-inch length of flexible plastic tubing, heats one end and clamps that end in a vise to close and seal it. Then he fills the tube with mothball crystals and closes the other end with a round piece of window screen cut to fit and held in place by a sort of wooden washer that also fits tightly in the end of the tube. He hangs the tubes in the young trees at deer-nose level, with the sealed end up and the screened end down so that rain cannot get in. A tube will remain effective for two years, he said. He cautioned that the tubes should be hung so that the wind does not slap them around and tear the plastic. He hangs them with nylon string and winds the string around the top several times before tying to the tree so that the tube doesn't sway much in the breeze. There are two kinds of mothballs—one

180

type made of naphthalene and the other made of paradichloro-
benzene, which is a chlorinated hydrocarbon as is DDT. This
latter type should not be used.

Penn State University has devised an electric fence that
researchers there say will keep out deer, but at least one Pennsylvania homesteader told me the fence did not work for him. A
woven wire fence needs to be very tall, 9 feet, anyway, and
therefore will be very expensive except for the smallest enclo-
sures. Small fruit trees, which deer harm the most, can be
enclosed in wire cages. Charles Kinsey of the Minnesota Department of Natural Resources has designed an electric fence barrier
that he says is effective except when there's snow on the ground.
He advises constructing a single-wire electric fence about 4 feet
off the ground to which flaps of aluminum foil are affixed by
using adhesive tape to hold them to the wire. The flaps should
measure 3 × 4 inches. The adhesive is applied to the underside
of the wire, sticky side up, and the aluminum stuck to it with the
4-inch length across the wire. Peanut butter is smeared to the
backing of the adhesive tape. Deer, attracted by the smell, touch
the aluminum flap with their noses and get the shock of their
lives. One such experience is sufficient to keep them away from
the fenced area from then on, says Kinsey.

Deer will injure lower branches of larger fruit trees, too.
Wild apple trees usually do not have low branches because deer
eat them off. This is why, if I had ample space, I would plant
only standard-size trees in deer country, just as if I planned to
graze cows in the orchard. Then you can invite the deer into your
grove after the trees grow up, let them eat the cull apples, and
then fill your larder with venison.

Orchardists are loath to shoot deer, even where the animals
are so overpopulating that they cause great damage and are in
danger of winter starvation. Even when an orchardist is not so
sensitive to the beauty of this wild beast, he may have to go
through a lot of red tape to shoot deer out of season to protect his
orchard. Nevertheless, "harvesting" deer in this fashion is a
most logical and necessary procedure, it seems to me, and not
the least reason why natural orchards are "profitable" to the
home grove-owner.

On the other hand, the mere presence of deer does not
necessarily mean danger to your trees. I have occasionally met
deer on my morning path to the barn and yet, so far, I have never
had a tree injured. But if deer become too numerous here, I
would not hesitate to kill and butcher one as I do my own
domestic animals.

RABBITS

Rabbits are the second most destructive animal to trees (and the most destructive to vegetables). In winter and early spring, when there is a shortage of wild foods and an abundance of rabbits, the bunnies chew the bark of fruit trees greedily, both trunks and any low branches they can reach from the ground or snow surface. Wrapping the young trunks with some commercial tree-guard product or a homemade substitute (I use old window screening) to a height of 2 feet and keeping the snow tramped down around the trees are usually adequate defenses, although a determined rabbit can usually find a way to gnaw the trunk crown at the bottom of the wrapping material. A simple chicken wire fence, 2 feet tall, will keep rabbits away from trees effectively, if wrapping the trunk is ineffective.

Some growers paint tree trunks with a coat of latex exterior white paint to which they may or may not add a commercial animal repellent or insecticide. The white coating with arsenate of lead added repels rabbits and mice, one grower tells me, but he thought perhaps less-toxic additives might work as well. The main reason for the white coating, of course, is to protect tender tree trunks from winter sunscald.

As for the old folklore remedies against rabbits, after extensive experimentation the University of Illinois found that none of them, including Tabasco sauce, red pepper, creosote, or blood, would keep rabbits from eating cabbages, even when the rabbits were fed pellets on the side. I think that will prove true also of hungry rabbits tempted in early spring by the tender bark of young fruit trees.

MICE

Various members of the vole family have become serious pests of apple orchards in some regions. In fact, the Interior Department says that mice are more destructive in agriculture than birds. Since mice also eat cocoons of harmful insect species, they are not totally harmful. In a more or less natural environment such as my trees grow in, they may do no harm at all—or so is my experience. Mice are preyed upon by both hawks and owls where nature is free to take her course. Mice are less harmful in an orchard with a weedy, grassy floor since various plants can supply them with the food nutrients they seek, instead of apple roots and trunks. Mulch will encourage mice, however, and in orchards where they are a problem, the mulch should be pulled back away from the trees in winter. A mulch of gravel, on the other hand, will protect tree roots because the mice cannot tunnel through the loose gravel easily.

Illus. 10-1—Animal and Bird Pests.

Commercial growers have relied on endrin to poison mice, but this chemical is so harmful environmentally that it is being phased out by the EPA. Somewhat more specific poisons are replacing endrin (that is, chemicals with less chance of accidentally poisoning other birds and mammals), but these seem to be safe for other wildlife only if special, hand-placed feeders are used. Small grove-owners can do this hand-placing, but it is not usually economical in large commercial orchards.

In my experience, mice are a problem for commercial orchards, not natural groves. An orchard floor of various weeds and grasses, and back-up support from owls, hawks, foxes, cats, etc., will keep mice under control. Commercial growers disbelieve this, but as I have already mentioned in Chapter 1, Edward Howe Forbush's observations add evidence to the organic viewpoint. Organic gardeners vouch that house cats kept around backyard fruit trees keep the mice at bay.

SQUIRRELS

For nut growers, especially small grove-owners, squirrels are almost an insolvable problem. This is especially true in suburban areas where laws protect the squirrels, even when the rodents are in violent overpopulation and fend off starvation only by eating maple buds (and thus ruining these trees, too). Squirrels love hazelnuts, pecans, and Persian walnuts, and they'll go out of their way in search of these nuts in areas where such trees are uncommon. But they will eat all nuts. They will eat mulberries, too—which is fine if that keeps them from eating your good nuts—plus many other garden berries and vegetables. But I must repeat my observations, though commercial growers smirk. I look out my window at squirrels playing in the oaks every morning, and the rodents have not yet bothered any of my domestic food plants because their population is in balance with their environment.

Currently, we allow hunters to harvest the squirrels in our woodlot. Hunters never get all of them, and if they did threaten to do so, I would stop the hunting. A few squirrels are beneficial, since they plant nut trees and never demand even the minimum wage for their work. I always make sure a few hollow trees remain uncut in the woodlot so that the squirrels have a place in which to raise next year's brood. Those nests of leaves you see squirrels build in treetops are not overwintering homes.

Both fox squirrels and gray squirrels are good meat animals

for the table. The smaller red squirrel is almost totally pestiferous without much redeeming quality. They sometimes even try to drive out the more desirable squirrel species.

In towns, ordinances usually forbid shooting squirrels, so population control takes devious and hypocritical methods. The animals must be poisoned or trapped and killed secretly. I don't know how many suburbanites have told me they kill squirrels, "but for God's sake don't publish that or the neighbors will rise in wrath." This attitude is ridiculous. The same people who eat flesh meat every day, who do not flinch over the fact that traffic deaths kill thousands of humans every year, "rise in wrath" at the notion of killing and eating those cute fuzzy tails only out of a peculiar kind of modern ignorance. Having too many squirrels is as dangerous as having too many rats.

I don't advocate it, but squirrels (or mice) can be effectively poisoned with peanut butter for bait into which is mixed a fast-acting poison such as zinc phosphide. Dabs of peanut butter and rodenticide are wrapped in little bags of clear plastic film, then buried just under the dirt around nut trees, or placed in the crotches of trees. Needless to say, there are obvious risks involved. Such poisoning practices must be child-proof, and how do you guarantee that in a grove of trees where people live? In an isolated setting, the bait might seem safe in an inaccessible tree crotch or buried underground, but not from pet cats and dogs, or from birds. And if a cat or dog eats a mouse or squirrel poisoned with zinc phosphide or similar rodenticide, it too can be poisoned. It's much better, I think, to manage the squirrels toward a stable population, and eat the surplus squirrels.

Cage trapping is not always effective against squirrels. I have seen squirrels enter a Havahart trap, grab the bait, and get back out before the trap doors fall. No matter how craftily I set the trap's trigger, the squirrels reacted faster. The larger traps, with slightly more distance between bait and door, work better than the medium-size ones that look just right for squirrels. Once you have a live squirrel in your trap, you still have to kill the rodent. To take it to the country and free it is simply visiting your problem on someone else and is almost as cruel a fate to the animal as killing it. Squirrels already populate in full measure all the areas in the country where squirrels can live. Introducing yet another into what you think is an empty area only means that the squirrel will be driven out by the natives, or contribute to overpopulation in that area. Drop the trap, animal and all, into a barrel of water and drown it. Then butcher and eat it. Or, if that repels you, at least let your dog or cat eat it. Someone is sure to respond that if the rodent has certain kinds of parasitic worms, the pet eating it can become infected. This is true, but pets will get worms, anyway.

RACCOONS AND GROUNDHOGS

Coons and woodchucks are not usually troublesome to tree fruit because they are too busy over in your corn patch and garden. They do, however, savor a good persimmon as much as humans do, and if you grow choice varieties you may lose some. Tie your dog under the tree, or wrap the lower trunk with a piece of tin so that the animals can't climb.

ROBINS AND OTHER FRUIT-LOVING BIRDS

Scare devices to keep birds out of fruit trees have one thing in common: none of them work very well. I have tested, or have observed being tested, scores of stratagems to scare birds: shiny objects waving in the breeze; whirligigs; scarecrows; hoses entwined in tree branches to simulate snakes; fake owls; various contrivances made with tin cans that, when swaying in the wind, make eerie scraping noises; radios playing ungodly loud rock music; records of bird cries of alarm; barbaric exploding cannons. Birds don't scare easy for long.

Since all birds, even robins, do at least as much good in the orchard as harm, don't blow your top and grab the shotgun until you at least assess the true amount of damage. After many years of growing a few cherry trees and cursing birds along the way, I have to admit that seldom have the birds eaten all of the crop. They occasionally have eaten all of my dark red and black sweet cherries. The sour cherries they invade with a vengeance when the fruit is barely ripe, then lose interest when the cherries are truly ripe and leave us all we want. They work at yellow sweet cherries so unenthusiastically that we can pick all we want. Friends of ours have a huge, old, yellow sweet cherry tree from which they eat, bake, can, and freeze more than enough, while at the same time the tree harbors a delightful variety of songbirds, all of which get their fill, too.

Netting is the only practical protection I know of, and that isn't very practical on larger trees. Fortunately for those areas where birds seem to be an especially bad problem, the fruit industry is developing compact-size sweet cherry trees that are easier to enclose in netting. Compact Lambert, Compact Stella, and Garden Bing are already being offered for sale, and by the time you read this, these and others should be readily available.

The best way to deal with birds is to shower them with bountifulness—offer them a choice of many fruits. This will dull their gluttonous appetites for your best fruits. Ideally, the home grove of trees should include as bird food, primarily, but also as survival insurance food for you, at least the following: mulberry, chokecherry, wild black cherry, Juneberry (or serviceberry), hawthorn, crab, wild plum, sumac, and oaks. Elderberry bushes are excellent. Birds like juniper, holly, and dogwood, too. Black haw viburnum is good (as much for wild animals as birds), and cornelian cherry, a type of dogwood, is excellent and pretty good eating for humans, too. Autumn olive is excellent, but it seems to be showing signs of becoming a spreading, persistent weed worse than multiflora rose. Where they grow, bayberry, beach plum, buffalo berry, saskatoon, and sand cherry are good choices. Mulberry and the various types of Juneberry and saskatoon trees are about the only ones that fruit early enough to help protect the cherry crop.

The real payoff for growing a wide variety of wild as well as domestic fruit is not, however, in persuading birds not to eat your cherries, apples, and peaches, but in luring to your grove as wide a variety of birdlife as possible. All birds, even the greediest fruit-eaters (robins), and even the gross destroyers of other birds (take a bow, starlings), eat many insects, the total effect of which is unknown. But there is a large body of data that suggests that if bird power were used purposefully in agriculture, which it seldom has been, many insect problems could be reduced to levels that would be considered tolerable.

BENEFICIAL BIRDS AND ANIMALS

Don't overlook domestic birds and animals in your pest-control practices, especially with an eye to that fruit going to waste. You can raise most delectable hams on wormy, fallen acorns. Chickens, turkeys, geese, sheep, cows, horses, and pigs will clean up fallen fruit and thereby control pests such as plum curculio. Geese will help control grassy weeds. Sheep will rid

Illus. 10-2—Animal and Bird Friends.

your orchard of poison ivy. Turkeys love grasshoppers. Sheep make mowing all but unnecessary and pay you back in excellent manure. But if your sheep can't get a balanced diet, they will gnaw the trunks of your trees sometimes, necessitating your wrapping the trunks. Cows will clean up all fallen apples for you but will also ruin limbs on dwarf trees. Livestock are compatible only with standard-size trees.

OWLS

Owls, except for the snowy owl which eats mostly other birds, are probably the most beneficial grove creatures you can have. The barn owl, barred owl, short-eared owl, long-eared owl, and screech owl are particularly helpful by preying mostly on the wild rodent population, especially mice, rats, gophers, and squirrels, and by eating quantities of insects. The screech owl is the most practical to attempt to lure to your grove. It is a rather common owl, and it accepts a man-made nest box, eats insects as well as mice, remains all winter long, catches English sparrows in winter if the snow is too deep for good mouse hunting, and likes to inhabit barns where it helps control rats and mice. According to directions in old books on birds,[1] a nest box for a screech owl ought to have a floor that's about 8 inches square, with the entrance about 9 to 12 inches above the floor. The entrance hole should measure 3 inches in diameter. Place the box in a high, secluded corner of a barn or in a tree 10 to 30 feet off the ground.

For a barn owl, the box needs a floor measurement of about 10 × 18 inches, and should be about 18 inches tall. The entrance hole should be 6 inches in diameter and positioned about 4 inches above the floor (I think higher positioning would be better), and the nest should be at least 12 feet off the ground. Shoffner (see footnote 1) reported that under the nest of one pair of barn owls the skeletons of 3,000 mice were counted.

If you allow a few dying and/or hollow trees to remain standing in your grove, owls may take up residence in them, and they will treat you with their deliciously mysterious hootings at night. Teach your children to love, not fear, the seemingly spooky owl. Unfortunately, owl hunting is still deemed an

---

1. *One book I find most useful is* The Bird Book *by Charles P. Shoffner (New York: Frederick A. Stokes Company, 1932). Shoffner was an editor of* Farm Journal *magazine in the early days when that publication was a leading crusader for the preservation of wild birds for crop protection. My, how times change.*

upright sport among some country people who rationalize that owls eat chickens and songbirds, which is not really true. The great horned owl is especially maligned in this way. The bird is almost entirely beneficial. I once kept track of the food a mother great horned owl brought to her young. Rats were far and away her favorite prey. Of birds, the owl brought in a couple of blue jays, a robber of other bird nests, and one cardinal. For all the rats she killed, I wouldn't begrudge her the cardinal. Great horned owls are one of the few species of animals that prey on skunks, checking population explosions of that animal.

WOODPECKERS

Woodpeckers, as already mentioned, help control codling moth. They like to nest in tree hollows, though they will take to nest boxes, too. The best houses for woodpeckers are pieces of hollow branches or logs, plugged top and bottom and fastened to trees. The downy woodpecker needs about a 4-inch-diameter (or square) cavity, the hairy woodpecker a 6-inch cavity. The entrance hole for the downy should be 1¼ inches, and for the hairy, 1½ inches. Red-headed woodpeckers like a cavity the size of the hairy's nest or larger, but the entrance hole should be 2 inches in diameter. This is large enough for a starling, and such boxes will often be taken over by this rather undesirable bird. But if a red-head takes up residence, it will defend its nest successfully from starlings, which is not true of some other birds. Red-heads do not mind living close to humans and will join you in the orchard without hesitation. In late summer, ours bring their young to the garden and the fruit trees where they seem to be trying to teach the fledglings how to find insects, amid a loud clamor that sounds to me like bird-cussing.

The flicker is a most beneficial member of the woodpecker family because it feeds largely on ants. Ants seem to be enemies to many of the natural predators of harmful fruit aphids. No ants, fewer aphids. Flickers need fairly large hollows to nest in. They will sometimes nest in boxes, which need to be nearly as large as the ones described for screech owls. Flickers will take no sass from starlings, either.

BLUEBIRDS AND WRENS

Bluebirds and wrens are two extremely beneficial birds in the orchard because they are voracious insect eaters, without

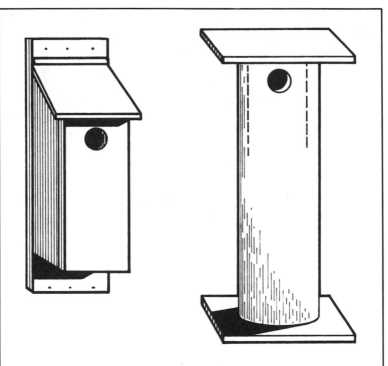

TWO BIRDHOUSE DESIGNS

The house at left is the common bluebird house design, but it can be used for any box-nesting bird, so long as the dimensions are increased or decreased according to the bird's specific qualifications (see text).

The nest box on the right is the one I prefer because I'm lazy. Hollow pieces of branches are quickly converted into birdhouses by closing both ends, if necessary, with scrap blocks of wood, and drilling in an entrance hole at the top. Then, attach the house to a tree or post. Log houses lure most birds better than the man-made box and do not attract English sparrows as well. Make the entrance hole at least 12 inches above the floor of the nest, even for bluebirds, though the usual directions call for only 8 inches. The reason for this is that bluebirds will build the nest up inside high enough in an 8-inch house to allow raccoons and starlings to reach in and kill them.

When you can afford to, put all bluebird houses on a flanged ¾-inch (or larger) galvanized steel pipe that's anchored solidly into the ground. Grease the pipe and no cat, coon, squirrel, or even snake can get to the birds.

consuming any fruit. Both are fairly easy to attract, and both like the environment of an orchard. Bluebirds will take naturally to holes in old apple trees if given a chance. Wrens are the easiest to attract because they are more numerous, have little fear of man, and their entrance holes need to be only a ⅞-inch diameter, small enough to keep out English sparrows, which often ruin bluebird nests. Place a wren nest near bushy cover, a bluebird's nest on a post out in the open. Bluebird entrance holes are often 1½ inches in diameter, but English sparrows can get in that size of hole. Some birders, contrary to the accepted design, claim that a hole 1⅛ to 1¼ inches is large enough for bluebirds but keep sparrows out. Since I have measured natural nests of bluebirds where the entrance hole was smaller than 1½ inches, I'm inclined to agree, although I have not experimented with smaller holes yet myself.

Some bluebird house plans I've seen in books and magazines are, unfortunately, death traps. Not enough depth is allowed between the entrance hole and the floor and so a starling can stick its scoundrel's head into the entrance hole and kill the baby birds. This is not so much a problem with wrens, who will usually fill the box with sticks and put the nest cavity below or behind the sticks where the starling cannot spear the young. But bluebirds build an open nest inside the box. Typical plans for bluebird houses call for about 8 inches between the entrance hole toward the top front of the box and the floor. This 8 inches would be safe enough, except that the bluebirds often build up the nest so that the young or eggs are really within 2 to 4 inches of the entrance hole. Raccoons, squirrels, blue jays, and starlings can reach them. When building bluebird houses, allow 12 inches between entrance and floor, with a 6½-inch-square cavity. As with woodpeckers, the best and cheapest houses are pieces of hollow branches or small logs, the bottoms and tops sawed off square and plugged with pieces of 1-inch board if necessary. A perch is unnecessary.

When placing bluebird houses on posts, a height of about 5 feet seems best. Use a metal post, or sheath a wood post with tin so that coons and cats cannot climb it.

KINGBIRDS

In earlier times when orchardists learned a little ecology through traditions handed down from one generation to another, much effort was made to lure kingbirds to nest near the fruit trees. The kingbird eats little or no fruit itself, but it is such a ferocious guardian of its nesting territory that it will drive off even robins who venture near. Some beekeepers worry about kingbirds, which like to eat bees. But they eat mostly drones, say ornithologists. Kingbirds live along the same fence row where my beehive sits, and no harm has come to the bees yet.

CUCKOOS

Both the yellow-billed cuckoo and the black-billed cuckoo make fine orchard birds because they eat various types of hairy webworms and tent caterpillars that other birds cannot swallow. But if you build your house in your tree grove (which is a proper thing to do), you may inadvertently present a serious problem to your cuckoos. If our experience is typical, more than any other bird cuckoos will fly head-on at full speed into double-sash windows and die of broken necks. When the sun is at a high angle, Thermopane windows reflect tree branches almost as well as mirrors—at least to a cuckoo—and the birds cannot seem to adjust to this. Other species seem to be able to pull up short at the last second, or, in the case of robins and cardinals, fight their image in the window all day long. But storm windows kill cuckoos. Drapes inside the windows are not much help—in fact, when the light is right, they make the window reflect the tree branches and skylight even better. If the windows open, you can keep them slightly ajar during the day (June seems to be the only month we have cuckoo trouble), which breaks up the reflection. A blanket or piece of cardboard over the outside window on sunny days will also work.

The best solution to the whole problem of birds banging on windows (and if you live in the woods, it *is* a problem) would be real, old-fashioned shutters. Because of the need to conserve heating fuel, shutters that close on winter nights will (or should) come back into fashion since there is no more effective way to keep heat from escaping from windows. Shutters are quite attractive, too. In summer they could be closed or half-closed on sunny, early summer days and save both cuckoos and windows. And save you from going batty when a robin decides to battle for his territorial imperative with his image.

BARN SWALLOWS AND OTHER BIRDS

The barn swallow, a most beautiful bird, is a great bug catcher that eats little fruit. It builds its mud nests on low rafters in old barns. English sparrows will try to take over their nests, but not always with success. Nevertheless, trap or shoot English sparrows whenever you can. They do not eat fruit, but they drive off bluebirds as well as barn swallows.

Black-capped chickadees, vireos, orioles, warblers, flycatchers, tanagers, quail, and goldfinches are also great helps in pest control among the trees. But about all you can do to attract them is to provide a great variety of plant food, ground cover, and nearby woodland and hope these birds will find your grove hospitable. In any case, keep fresh water available at all times.

Do not be dissuaded from setting out birdhouses and providing natural bird habitats by the worldly wise commercial orchardist and his advisers. They will tell you that the benefits are not worth the effort. But you will be repaid in exactly the amount of time you put into it. In fact, that is the main drawback to bird management. Experimentation shows it takes as much time, if done effectively, as spraying takes. No agriculturist in modern times can take the risk of spending $15,000 on bird management rather than on a sprayer, and so the wild grove approach to tree food production never gets a fair trial. Yet, where experiments in bird management have been undertaken, results are surprisingly good. In *Birds in Our Lives*, a government publication published in 1966, Philip B. Dowden and Robert T. Mitchell, in a chapter loaded with statistical evidence on the effective control of bugs by birds, report:

Many investigations are being made in Europe as to the effect of birds on the numbers of forest insects. Scientists compare conditions in forests, where birdhouses have been erected to attract birds, with conditions in forests where such attraction is lacking. One such study was near Steckby-on-the-Elbe, where infestations of the pine looper moth have occurred.

Regular samplings for pine looper moths over 33 years indicated that infestations of the pest remained low and little damage occurred in "attracted" forests, as compared with "unattracted" forests. Only one or two birdboxes to the acre were erected in the "attracted" forests. Most of the observations in Europe, though, indicate that many more birdboxes than that are needed for best results.

In another example, University of California entomologists experimented somewhat successfully with birdboxes in forests heavily infested with lodgepole needle miner. But the authors note—and I suggest this might be the crux of the matter—"the erection, care, and maintenance of boxes on a large scale is expensive. . . . Although the use of boxes may prove beneficial in natural woodlands, the labor necessary to operate them in large areas will likely preclude their widespread use in the United States." Perhaps true, but their use in small groves cared for by interested homeowners who live there and can tend the birdhouses as a form of recreation seems to me entirely practical.

Another example of when and how birds can be useful in bug control comes from celery fields in Florida, as reported in the previously mentioned survey. Federal entomologists learned that the palm warbler, tree swallow, and red-winged blackbird kept the celery leaf tier under control *in isolated fields and in fields adjoining woodlands.* But in solidly planted fields where there was no protective habitat for birds nor wild fruit to draw them, the fewer number of birds could not and did not control the bug. The same authors point out that the black-capped chickadees, ruby-crowned kinglets, gold-crowned kinglets, and red-breasted nuthatches prey heavily on pear psylla. "It may be worthwhile there to erect birdboxes to attract more birds," they suggest.

I have learned that kinglets can't be attracted by boxes like the other birds I mentioned, but they dearly love piles of brush along the edges of woodlots. They and other small birds feel safe from cats and other predators in such surroundings. I never burn brush piles anymore, though from the standpoint of human-inspired "neatness" they look ugly and brand a woodlotter as "lazy."

Ornithological records indicate that birds eat enormous numbers of bugs and bug eggs. A yellow-billed cuckoo can down over 2,000 webworms at a feeding; a flicker, 5,000 ants; a red-winged blackbird, 28 cutworms; a yellow throat, 3,500 aphids an hour. Cuckoos have been observed polishing off 150 cotton worms at a sitting. Some 41 cotton boll weevils were found in the stomach of a Bullock's oriole, and 91 May beetles in the stomach of a common nighthawk. When we look at some of our major bug pests today we can get a hint of why they are pests. At least 66 different species of birds feed on cotton boll weevil, but how many of them will you find in a poison-saturated cotton field on the endlessly plowed acres of the denuded Mississippi Delta? Some 50 species feed on alfalfa weevil, but you will wait a long time to see them all in a modern alfalfa field in the Midwest—

there aren't that many alfalfa fields left anymore, anyway. Some 205 species eat wireworms, but if you stand in an Illinois cornfield for three years you will not see 205 species of birds eating wireworms. Chemicals saturate the ground to kill the worms, but the worms remain worse than ever, while the birds disappear.

However, it would be wrong to overrate the birds' usefulness in insect control. The same bird that eats aphids may eat the syrphid flies that also eat the aphids. Birds are one of a community of controllers, none of which dare become too effective or else the whole system collapses. When I walk among my trees in the morning, hand-picking a few bugs as I go, I like to muse about a totally unscientific mathematical assumption. I figure that adverse weather controls 10% of the insects on the average. Spraying oil and perhaps a treatment or two with some biological insecticide, such as *Bacillus thuringiensis*, takes care of 25%, perhaps. Insect predators and parasites account for another 20%; birds, 15%; and my hand-picking, 5%. That leaves 25% to botch my trees and fruit, a little, but also to give a continuing food source to my community of helpers. The figures may not be accurate, but when I add everything up at the end of the year, there is food going to waste around here.

CHAPTER 11

INSECT PESTS AND INSECT FRIENDS

The problem of pear psylla is just another example of the growing evidence that you can't control a pest with chemicals alone, with no regard for biological diversity of pest and predator in nature. I can show you a pear orchard that is next to woodland up the valley here that has been neglected for three years—not sprayed with anything. The pear trees are healthy. When I looked at them last summer they did not need spraying. There was an invasion of bugs, all kinds of bugs, out of that woodland into the orchard. The air was full of them. I could identify a dozen species preying on pear psylla.

Paul Lanphere, organic orchardist in Washington, from a conversation with the author.

A detailed entomological life history of all the bugs that relate to your grove of trees would take several large volumes at least and still not tell you all of the interrelationships between the insects and other life forms that you need to know to produce tree fruits without heavy spraying. Even those scientists brave enough to call themselves ecologists admit that they do not know all of these relationships and perhaps know a few of them only imperfectly. The best I hope to do here is to discuss those insects most likely to give you problems and those most likely to give you pleasure and even help you solve the problems, together with other methods that are useful in dealing with insects destructive to your trees.

INSECT PESTS

APHIDS

From the standpoint of the grove-owner, aphids, or plant lice, as they are often called, are bad news. From the standpoint of nature, aphids are wondrous creatures, almost perfect food forms. Aphids are amazingly prolific and therefore insure an adequate and essential supply of food for a large number of other life forms. What's more, they perform this service usually without fatally harming the plant species they live on.

To accomplish this feat, aphids demonstrate unbelievable adaptability. There is a species for nearly every plant family. Overwintering fertilized eggs hatch in the spring, and subsequent generations are born live to females without fertilization. Few aphid species are literally host-specific—that is, they do not depend entirely on one plant for their entire life cycle. Instead, they live on one plant species for part of their lives and on another entirely different plant species during another part of their life cycle. This characteristic complicates chemical control (or any control) exceedingly. Moreover, most species overwinter as eggs, although a very few overwinter as nymphs. It is as if nature foresaw the chemical strategy that man would devise and produced the aphid to confound it.

Rosy apple aphid, wooly apple aphid, and green apple aphid are mainly pests of apples, but they feed on pear, hawthorn, mountain ash, and other related trees, too. As adults you can tell them apart by color, although the young are all green and difficult to identify specifically. The rosy apple aphid is reddish or pinkish; the wooly apple aphid is brownish, appearing in little white masses that look like fluffs of cotton (but not to be confused with cottony cushion scale, described below, or spittle bugs); the green apple aphid is greenish, as the name indicates.

The traditional botanical insecticide to control aphids is nicotine. A strong tea from tobacco or tobacco dust (available from organic gardening stores) is currently preferred over nicotine sulfate because the sulfur in the latter may be harmful to beneficial organisms, particularly to predators of scales. Neither the tea nor the sulfate mix is very effective, but that's not a harsh criticism because a spray has to be deadly indeed to control a bug that may go through six or more generations in a year, perhaps developing greater immunity to the spray in any given generation. The "old reliable" chemical, malathion, never gave me effective control of aphids, either. During warm weather, when the many predators of aphids become active, I do not believe spraying aphids in the backyard grove is worth the harm possibly done. For example, an introduced parasite, *Aphelinus mali,* effectively controls wooly apple aphid. But if you spray a broad-spectrum poison such as methoxychlor, which is still considered a "safe" backyard spray by some, the experts say you will kill this parasite. However, in cool weather, early in the spring and late in the fall, aphid predators are not active enough to control the pest, at which time one of the safer botanicals

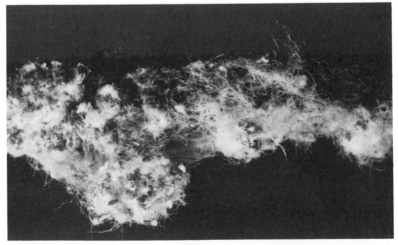

Photo 11-1—Wooly Apple Aphid Infestation—The appearance of what looks like fluffs of cotton on tree branches signifies an attack by wooly apple aphids. Photograph by John Colwell from Grant Heilman.

199

(that is, nonresidual and biodegradable) might be in order. But remember, also, these early and late cool periods are when migrating birds are most active against aphids.

I listened to a natural orchardist from Vermont, Dr. Eugene Carpovitch, give an interesting talk at the University of Maryland a few years ago. He said that he'd had success against aphids by dipping infested branch tips in a ryania solution. He mixed four heaping tablespoons of ryania into a gallon jar of water, then dipped the branch ends in the jar. He believes the method is a practical control for groves of a few backyard trees, especially smaller ones. And it is smaller, younger trees that seem to suffer most from aphid attacks, in my experience. Dwarf trees and young trees produce lusher sucker growth than standard trees, especially when heavily fertilized with nitrogen, and the resultant succulent growth is attractive to aphids.

Dr. Carpovitch spoke of another interesting method of aphid control. Ants like the honeydew that aphids secrete and therefore protect aphids from predators. Dr. Carpovitch reasoned that if he could keep ants off the trees, he could control the aphids better. Of the several methods he's tried, the most effective is to wrap a band of kraft paper about 4 inches wide around the tree trunk and coat it with Bird Tanglefoot (available from garden stores). On old tree trunks, you can smear the sticky material right onto the tree. Either way, the ants can't get up the tree.

Many aphids overwinter in crevices in the bark. A good soaking oil spray in early spring when the tree is dormant will kill many of them. Some careful backyard growers scrape the loose bark off their trees to expose the eggs or knock them off, a practice that can be effective if used along with an oil spray.

The rosy apple aphid uses the narrow-leaf plantain (what we call buckhorn) as a host plant in summer. If you have this weed in your orchard, July mowings may help to control the aphid. Buckhorn is hard to keep down with mowing, as we all know. Where possible, grazing is much more effective. Livestock love the nutritious weed, which is why you don't see it in pastures that have been grazed for a few years.

Ladybug beetles and larvae, the larvae of lacewings (called aphid lions), the adults of some lacewings, the larvae of syrphid flies, and a number of parasitic wasps of the Braconid family all prey heavily on aphids. The aphid lion lifts an aphid off a leaf, sucks the juices out of it, and tosses the skeleton away, not unlike a man quaffing a can of beer. A ladybug larva can eat between 200 and 500 aphids as it grows to maturity; the adult beetle downs up to 50 or 60 a day. The larvae of syrphid flies eat an aphid a minute for several days without stopping for so much as a good belch. The adult syrphids, flashing their rainbow colors of metallic blue, red, and yellow as they hover around blossoms, help pollenation, too. When they are present, I would not spray even rotenone or pyrethrum, though these products are helpful in aphid control. The idea of dipping branch ends in botanical insecticides has that added appeal—dipping may not harm beetles, lacewings, and flies that much. However, dipping an aphid-infested shoot tip in a botanical insecticide solution would probably be fatal to the syrphid and cecidomyiid larvae (midges) who live in and prey on the aphids. Cecidomyiids have been identified in recent research (1980) to be the most effective predator in green aphid control.

Nasturtiums and garlic have been named in folklore as plants to grow under fruit trees to ward off aphids, but I've not yet seen either used this way successfully. Some claim garlic juice makes a good aphid spray, but others deny it. Since pennyroyal and certain other mints have known qualities as bug repellents, I'm planting the former under some of my trees this year. I'm not hopeful, but nothing ventured, nothing gained.

Last, but not least, study your trees for resistance to aphids. Some varieties are less susceptible than others. The old Winter Majetin has known resistance to wooly aphid, and scientists are looking for others.

The black cherry aphid attacks both sweet and sour cherries, but sweet cherries much more so. It is the only aphid that has been a serious problem for me, and then only on one black sweet cherry. It is a blackish colored aphid, quite large as aphids go, and exudes lots of honeydew. The honeydew spawns a sooty mold that harms the trees more than the aphids themselves do (see Sooty Mold in Chap. 12).

The black peach aphid infests both roots and terminal shoots of peach, almonds, apricots, and plums. If you are using moth crystals around tree trunks for borer control, you will help solve this problem, too, by hindering the movement of aphids from root to branch. Controlling ants with Tanglefoot will help, too.

The green peach aphid is actually more harmful to vegetables than fruit trees despite its name. It is a vector (or carrier) of mosaic diseases and other viral diseases that attack the Solanaceae (potato-tomato) family. This aphid is pale green with three dark lines on the back. (You almost need a magnifying glass to identify aphids.) It hatches out from black eggs on the bark of the tree when peaches bloom. Early, thorough dormant spray is helpful. Scrape off loose bark first.

Many, many other aphids can be troublesome at certain times or in certain places. The leaf curl plum aphid uses plum and prune as winter hosts and, in warmer climates, can cause plum leaves to curl tightly and stunt growth. Dormant oil is the best control. Mealy plum aphid is a pale green aphid with a powderlike coating that infests apple, apricot, peach, and plum occasionally, curling leaves and encouraging sooty mold in the wake of its exuded honeydew. It winters as eggs on twigs and can be controlled with dormant oil. Rusty plum aphid is common in the East on plums. Hawthorn aphid attacks the whole apple-pear-quince family and uses clover as a summer host. Walnut aphid can be particularly troublesome on English walnut in the West. A parasitical braconid wasp introduced from Europe promises to give some control.

Sometimes just a strong spray of water can wash off aphids and thereby provide effective control of wingless specimens. Westcott, in her *The Gardener's Bug Book,* which is certainly not an organic publication, suggests this control in some cases, such as for white pine aphid on small pines.

BORERS

Just as there is an aphid for every plant species, so there is a borer for almost every kind of tree. Among fruit and nut trees, the peach tree borer, which attacks most members of the stone fruit family, is the worst problem. The white, brown-headed, inch-long borer is difficult to control without a regular, heavy spray schedule. Invariably it infects and nearly ruins a tree before the novice backyarder detects it. What finally appears as a small hole oozing frass and gum reveals, upon being cut open, a riddled inner bark from which the borers have eaten the life-essential cambium layer away. There is nothing left to do except cut away all infected bark, cover with roofing tar or tree wound paint, wrap with burlap, and hope the tree will recover. Reinfection will occur almost always, and continuous vigilance is necessary to keep borers out.

The lesser peach tree borer is almost as bad as its larger cousin, at least in the South, but confines its activities more often to the higher crotches of the trees and, so, does not kill the

Photo 11-2—Adult Peach Tree Borer, Female. USDA photograph.

Photo 11-3—Peach Tree Borer Larvae. USDA photograph.

tree as the greater peach tree borer can. The lesser borer prefers bad-angled crotches that usually develop lesions into which the borer can more readily tunnel.

The flatheaded apple tree borer is a fairly wide-ranging pest of many trees, including fruit trees and maples. The shot-hole borer is common throughout the United States. The maple borer is sometimes troublesome in the Northeast, and a mulberry borer can sometimes be a headache in the South. Since borers can kill trees, you have to control them or be prepared to lose specimens. Fortunately, none of the other borers seems to be as damaging as the peach tree borer, although in your location you may experience an exception to that statement. Whatever the species, the treatment is the same for all.

All those carefully worded directions for poking out borers with a length of wire make grist for articles but are worthless unless you catch the borer shortly after he has tunneled into the tree. You might just as well try poking a groundhog in his hole with a 2 × 4 as try to thread a wire through borer holes in hope of smashing the worm. Prevention is the only way. Place a ring of naphthalene mothball crystals around the tree, just under the soil surface, then pile soil around the trunk about 3 inches deep. This will discourage the blue black female, with her characteristic orange band around the abdomen, from laying her eggs.

Other growers paint wood creosote on the trunks, from about 2 feet high down to as low on the crown as possible. Wood creosote comes from wood tar, and if you have an airtight wood stove, you know about wood creosote. The creosote you buy as a wood preservative is made from coal tar, and the fumes from that could damage green wood. With all of the wood stoves in use, you should have no trouble getting a supply of wood creosote with which to fight peach tree borer. Steep the wood creosote in a can of water for a month, and then apply the cinder-browned water mixture to the base of the tree and around the crown of the roots. Another effective control is to apply a 12-inch band of Tanglefoot around the bottom of the trunk a week or two before the borer begins laying eggs. Along with placing a ring of naphthalene mothballs about an inch away from the base of the trunk, this might be the best solution.

Wrapping the trunk is some help, but the borers are liable to tunnel into the upper roots and then on up into the trunk. It also makes spotting the worm hole difficult or impossible, should the borers get in under the bark in spite of wrapping.

Whatever control you use, you need to know the emergence dates and egg-laying time of the borer moths to combat them effectively. The moths begin laying eggs about July 1 in the North, and sooner in the South, followed by a later generation down there. The eggs hatch in about ten days, the borers bore into the tree where they live safely through the winter, finish feeding in the spring, and then pupate in the soil.

In 1978, a breakthrough was reported in controlling tree borers that is still too new to be adapted to the backyard. Scientists have been able to reproduce sex attractants of some borer moths and can use these pheromones in traps to lure the moths to their capture. Work has been going along full pace at the Ohio Agricultural Research and Development Center in Wooster, Ohio. The purpose of the traps is to help commercial growers monitor the moth life cycle so they know precisely when to spray. But since the traps do catch moths effectively, one can logically deduce that at least in backyard situations they can be used directly to control the borers—a system the scientists call "mass-trapping." "Perhaps," says the Ohio report, "enough pheromone traps can be used in a given area to capture all male moths before they can inseminate females."

Consult your local or state Cooperative Extension Service. Some traps are commercially available at this time.

CURCULIOS

The plum curculio is a snout beetle, or weevil, and is a major pest of stone fruits, and sometimes apple, pear, and quince trees. The beetle is humpbacked, brown, and ¼ inch long with a telltale snout. It becomes active in spring when the weather warms up, just in time to eat both blossoms and newly forming leaves on plum trees. Females lay eggs in young fruit, making a characteristic crescent-shaped mark on the fruit where they insert their eggs. The larvae do enough injury to cause the fruit

Photo 11-4—Adult Plum Curculios. Photograph by Grant Heilman.

to drop off. Then the larvae go into the ground and pupate. From middle sections of the United States on south, two generations can occur, while in the North there is only one, so the problem generally increases the further south one tries to grow stone fruits.

Curculios are sort of like opossums: disturb them and they roll over and play dead. Place a light-colored piece of plastic or old sheet under the tree and rap or shake the branches soundly. (Old-timers drove a large spike into the tree and struck the spike to jar the tree.) If present, curculios will drop off as if stunned. When many of them fall off, then, by chemical wisdom, you are supposed to haul out the sprayer. But since you have just demonstrated to yourself an effective way to capture curculios, instead rap on the tree a few more times, fold up your plastic or sheet, and dump the contents into a fire or a can of used oil. Be sure you have your sheet in place before you jar the tree even the slightest bit, or the curculios will drop before you're ready. Repeat this practice twice a day for a week right before and after the bloom period. This method of control is traditional and still advised for the backyarder even by universities who habitually go along with the poison-power crowd.

Among the other species of curculios, the apple curculio is a main pest that is similar to the plum curculio but does not make the crescent-shaped mark on the fruit. Curculio larvae often infest some of the fruit that falls at the "June drop," and it is

Photo 11-5—Plum Curculio Larvae on a Plum. USDA photograph.

essential if curculio is a problem to clean up all fallen fruit as soon as possible. Scrupulously followed, this stratagem breaks the curculio's life cycle. Horses and livestock can be of immense help in keeping the fruit cleaned up, but a surer way is to grind the fallen fruit in a hammer mill and feed it as pomace. Or compost it. Chickens will eat some fruit and will also scratch around in the mulch under the trees and find some of the worms that have already left the fallen fruit.

Curculios like to overwinter in hedgerows and woodland next to orchards, but the advantages of such plantings far outweigh the disadvantages.

FRUIT FLIES
AND THEIR MAGGOTS

Apple maggot, the maggot of the apple fruit fly, is a serious pest in apples and related fruits. For the grove-owner it is even more pestiferous than the codling moth because an apple maggot will tunnel all through an apple, ruining most of it, while a codling moth makes just one route out, leaving three-quarters of the apple still available for use.

Chemical control with materials such as Imidan is effective but tedious and never ending. Fortunately for the backyarder, trapping methods have been worked out that seem to control the pest effectively. "Sticky traps" were originally used simply as monitoring devices to catch emerging flying insects as a tip-off for the best time to spray. But backyard experimenters and innovative scientists learned that the traps themselves could significantly cut down on pest populations if enough of them were hung in the trees, a job seemingly too time-consuming to do in a large commercial orchard. Yellow rectangles of cardboard attract the flies of apple maggot (also aphids and other bugs). With a coating of Tree Tanglefoot, the boards catch the flies landing on them. Ron Prokopy at the University of Massachusetts learned that red balls covered with the sticky Tanglefoot were more effective. According to his research, six red spheres hung per mature tree gave 95% control of apple maggot (Ronald J. Prokopy, "Wooden Apples Lure Costly Pest," in *Frontiers of Plant Science,* Connecticut Agricultural Experiment Station, 1967).

Various natural orchardists have experimented with everything from croquet balls to realistic plastic fruits coated with

Photo 11-6—Apple Maggots. Photograph by Grant Heilman.

Tanglefoot. Effectiveness of color seems to vary. Red and even blue seem to work, and plastic oranges have been occasionally as effective as plastic red apples.

The little worms you find in sour cherries are usually the maggots of the cherry fruit fly. One worm per cherry. If you do not see the maggot, you eat the cherry with relish and get a bit of protein as a bonus. Very civilized Americans fill with revulsion at the idea, but the truth is the worm doesn't hurt you nor do you taste it. You get a stomachache from eating too many cherries, not too many worms.

In Germany, orchardists have controlled the cherry fruit fly successfully by using flat, sticky, yellow panels similar to the apple maggot traps. Rotenone is fairly effective, if sprayed when the fruit flies are getting ready to lay eggs. I am not too enthusiastic about spraying even this botanical. Cherry fruit flies can emerge more or less continuously for a month and so you would have to spray more or less continuously. Is it worth it? Some years cherry maggots are bad and some years they are not. Infestation may vary from tree to tree, backyard to backyard. Since we have to pit all of the sour cherries we use first, wormy

Photo 11-7—Apple Fruit Flies. USDA photograph.

fruit can be discarded in the process. And everyone I know who picks cherries understands this. As I seed, quite often I can flick the worm out while saving the cherry, which is frequently still in quite edible shape. You can tell a cherry with a worm in it because when you pop out the seed, the cherry will make a noise that sounds almost exactly like a kiss. That may seem like a silly detail, but after you have seeded several thousand cherries, you can just listen for that sound in your speedy seeding work instead of having to examine each fruit carefully as you seed it.

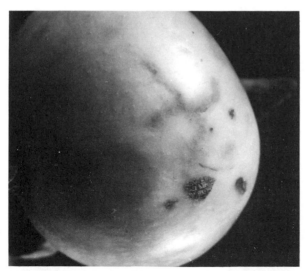

Photo 11-8—Maggot Damage to an Apple. Photograph by Grant Heilman.

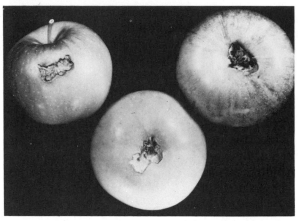

Photo 11-9—Damage to Apples by a Red-Banded Leaf Roller. USDA photograph.

LEAF ROLLERS

Leaf rollers, especially the red-banded leaf roller and the fruit-tree leaf roller are difficult to spray with anything because they roll up the leaves in a bit of web and remain safe and sound inside, where they eat the new tip growth as fast as it appears. The red-banded leaf roller has been making my trees quite unsightly for the last two springs, while I fuss and fume. But the first generation disappeared, and so far a second generation has not put in a noticeable appearance. (The fruit-tree leaf rollers have only one generation per year, but the red-banded can have two or more.) Some fruit is always ruined by the little worms' work, but after they are gone the tree leafs out and seems no worse for the attack. In fact, I believe that some leaf roller injury acts as a form of tip pruning that may not be all bad. I handpick a great many leaf rollers each spring.

MITES

Most of the mites injurious to fruit trees, and the mites that eat the harmful mites, are very small, barely visible to the naked eye. You can tell the presence of the harmful ones by the condition of the leaves—dry, curled slightly upward, and a telltale coppery cast (called bronzing) to their undersides. If the coppery cast is not there and the leaves look reasonably healthy even in hot, dry weather, you can be fairly sure that you have a good supply of beneficial mites taking care of the bad guys.

Mites will control each other if you can avoid spraying material that kills the beneficial mites. A closer look at the predators of mites gives a good insight into the complexities and promise of natural insect control. In 1972, Robert P. Holdsworth published a study, *Major Predators of European Red Mite on Apple in Ohio* (Research Circular 192, Ohio Agricultural Research and Development Center, Wooster, Ohio). "During a six-year period," says Holdsworth in his introduction, "it has been shown by experiment and by actual trial in commercial orchards that the European red mite is consistently controlled by its predators, unless the predators are destroyed by spray chemicals."

Holdsworth lists and describes the major predators: the yellow mites, the minute pirate bug, the black hunter thrips, the black ladybug, the green lacewing, and several plant bugs. Yellow mites are the most effective control of red mites, but what Holdsworth learned was that yellow mites alone could not stop red mite injury, nor could the other predatory bugs without yellow mites. It took all of them. The yellow mites build up slowly, almost too slowly, before they reach numbers significant enough to hold the harmful mites under control. But while they are building, other predatory bugs get their licks in.

Of these larger predators, the minute pirate bug is particularly valuable because it is active early in the season when the yellow mite population hasn't built up yet. It attacks rosy apple

Photo 11-10—Pear Leaf Blister Mite Infestation on an Apple Tree. USDA photograph.

211

aphids and other apple aphids, too. It is only $\frac{1}{16}$ inch long, with buff on the back except for a white outer part of the wing, when mature. The black hunter thrips is the same size, but long and narrow in shape. Unlike the other predators, the black hunter seems to subsist well even when red mite populations are low. The black ladybug has a black shell and yellow feet. Its back is covered with yellow hairs, but it is the black shell that you notice. The larvae are bristly and brownish in color. Like other ladybugs eating aphids, this one can build up population fairly quickly in response to a mite population buildup. The aphid lion larvae of lacewings are well-known consumers of aphids, but they like mites, too. Aphid lions look like miniature alligators ($\frac{1}{4}$ inch long) with hornlike mandibles protruding from the sides of their heads.

As Holdsworth points out, predatory insects are native to woodlands. They readily fly into orchards and become established. "A grower, therefore, needs to do nothing to attract predators into his orchard," says Holdsworth. Well, that's not quite true. He can provide woodland, or preserve it. In the Midwest, that is rapidly becoming a very crucial thing to do.

Steve Page, an orchardist in Maine who combines chemical and natural controls in his commercial operation, says that he uses mites as a sort of indicator of mismanagement. If too many of the harmful ones are present, it means the orchard is being oversprayed. (Page puts out "The Spraysaver Apple Calendar" [Northwind Nursery, Washington, ME 04574], an excellent guide for chemical orchardists who want to taper off heavy spraying schedules of the more toxic chemicals.)

The chemical industry has made much of its newer miticide sprays that are more specific; that is, they kill harmful mites while affecting beneficial insects less. Certainly these chemicals are safer than broad-spectrum sprays that kill indiscriminately. But it should be pointed out that there is a very old spray that is also specific and far safer than the miticides: dormant oil.

Superior oil, the high grade of dormant oil commonly used, is harmless to yellow mites and other predators of bad mites. An application of superior oil with a viscosity rating of 60 to 70, which can be sprayed even at the early bud-break stage of spring apple growth, is best for mite eggs. This oil is still heavy enough to smother the eggs but does not hurt the opening buds.

Speaking of a good, soaking, dormant oil spray, it can hardly be overemphasized that in spraying oil, you have to cover all parts of the tree for the oil to work effectively. When I first bought a sprayer I somehow had an unconscious notion that it was a magic wand and that if I went through the motions of pumping spray around the trees, I was taking care of whatever insects or disease were going to harm my fruit. (I painfully realize now that I had absolutely no idea of what I was actually spraying for, except for some hazy idea of keeping fruit from "getting wormy.") But especially with dormant oil, the spray must come into contact and cover the eggs or insects for which it is intended. Dormant oil kills more by asphyxiation than by poisoning. You need to spray all sides of the trunk and branches.

Red spider mite is one of the many spider mites and the most harmful to a variety of plants. A hard blast of water from a hose will knock enough out of the tree to give some control. In my experience, red spider mite is more troublesome on evergreens than on other trees.

MOTHS

The larva of the codling moth is now considered the worst pest of apples. It is a good example of the long-run failure of chemicals. The best chemical controls, DDT especially, are too harmful to the rest of the environment. New chemicals such as Imidan work, but codling moth continues to be a problem. Ryania, an old botanical, is hard to get. It is hard to get because it is expensive and so orchardists don't demand it. The saddest part of the matter to me is that before spraying was instituted, codling moth was only a minor problem, which means there were fewer wormy apples on the tree. Why was the consumer allowed to believe in the first place that he or she could buy a bushel of apples 100% wormless? All of us who were brought up to eat apples are accustomed to handling the larva of a codling moth in an apple. This worm seldom ruins more than a small bit of the apple. It tunnels out from the core usually in a rather straight line. We always cut apples in two, or break them in two, if there is a worm hole, toss the worm out and slice away the hole or eat around it. *It is no big deal.* There is every reason to believe that there are plenty of consumers smart enough to know this and willing to buy apples of which some are wormy, because these apples would be much cheaper (and the money paid for them would remain with the grower, not be passed on to the chemical industry).

Because humans no longer understand nature, and have been educated to deny it, the apple industry must keep spraying or try to find nonchemical controls that are going to raise the

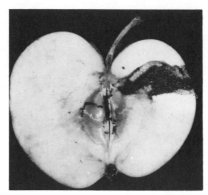

Photo 11-11—Codling Moth's Effect on an Apple. USDA photograph.

price of apples even higher. For example, scientists and growers in British Columbia recently completed a highly successful test, controlling codling moth in 800 acres of orchard with a male moth sterilization program. Moths are sterilized with gamma radiation, then set loose in large numbers. Matings do not result in fertile eggs, so no larvae are produced. If the program were continued, codling moth could be adequately controlled in certain, somewhat isolated areas just as screwworm in cattle have been all but eliminated in the Southwest. But the expense is high and orchardists with a cheaper chemical alternative—which is more costly in the long run—have refused to finance the program for a second year. In a letter to me, Harold Madsen, research scientist at the Summerland, British Columbia, station, writes: "We have estimated the cost of the sterility program to be in excess of $100 per acre compared to a chemical program of around $30 per acre. As a result, we have been forced to abandon the program even though the control was excellent."

So once more, here's evidence that nontoxic pest control in fruit trees is not a biological problem but an economic problem. In this case, the problem is sad to bear because that $70 per acre is not all that much to an apple grower—it amounts to only pennies per bushel of apples. If I know orchardists, it is not the money they are objecting to, but to the increase in management time that a sterility program demands of them. Nevertheless, if history repeats itself, the chemical codling moth program will finally collapse, and growers will have to spend more time in the orchard, anyway, whatever biological program they adopt. In the meantime, they are content to spend $30 per acre (and rising) to further destroy the orchard environment. Dr. M. D. Proverbs, an entomologist at the Summerland station, reported that one of the side benefits of not spraying for codling moth was that "few orchards required sprays for other pests, as predators and parasites held spider mites, rust mites, and aphids well below treatment level." In some orchards the only spraying done was a regular dormant oil treatment for scale and mite eggs, and one petal-fall treatment for leaf roller control. Farther south, leaf rollers have two or three generations a year, and treatments later in the season may be necessary.

A sterile male program is an example of a nonchemical method that works on large-scale orcharding districts but hardly as well, or at least with even much more expense, in backyard trees. Backyard growers, at least for now, are too scattered and their susceptible trees are not grown in dense enough blocks to make the distribution of the male moths practical. But there are other methods that the small grower can use. The use of sex pheromone traps is helpful, some organic orchardists tell me. Others are looking at virus disease and are working closely with scientists on how to implement it against codling moth. O. F. Thostenson, an organic orchardist in British Columbia, writes that he has had limited success with *Bacillus thuringiensis*. "It works well against leaf rollers and other foliage-eating pests, but codling moth apparently does not eat enough of it to be seriously affected. A food source for codling moth has been developed at Wenatchee Research Station in Washington State. . . . We hope to test it out and if it works we will be applying it with BT (*Bacillus thuringiensis*) and see if that brings any additional control."

Gypsy moth is not normally thought of as an orchard pest, but it certainly is a pest to the whole grove of food trees, at least in the eastern part of the country. Gypsy moth larvae like oak, an important tree in your grove, and also hickory, maple, and sassafras, to name a few. It will attack apple and cherry, too. *B. thuringiensis* (trade names: Biotrol, Dipel, and Thurcide) is effective but expensive. No spraying of large grove trees such as oaks and maples is very practical—backyard spray rigs won't begin to reach. Data so far indicate that severe population explosions of gypsy moth are beyond any control of an individual property owner. Nor does widespread spraying seem to be the answer. The large populations seem to collapse of natural causes, anyway. In the meantime, scientists are working with viruses

215

and hormones in an effort to find a safe control. The European ground beetle seems to be an effective predator.

Oriental fruit moth attacks peaches mostly, but sometimes quince, apple, pear, apricot, plum, and cherry. When you see the tips of your peach tree die back and blacken, suspect oriental fruit moth larvae (although similar-looking dieback symptoms might be caused by nutritional disorders), particularly if the dieback affects only occasional branch tips rather than all of them. The first generation feeds on plant material, and the second attacks fruit and twigs. The larvae bore into the peach

Photo 11-12—Adult Male Gypsy Moth. USDA photograph.

Photo 11-13—Gypsy Moth Caterpillars. USDA photograph.

through the stem, and you may not suspect their presence until you open the ripe peach, of which the inside is usually ruined by then. More often, though, the peach drops to the ground before it matures.

Photo 11-14—Gypsy Moth Damage to a Tree. Rodale Press photograph.

In locations where peach trees don't produce a crop every year because of adverse weather (such as here in northern Ohio) the oriental fruit moth is not a problem because it rarely has a chance to get established. (I knew there was something good about our climate.) In *Organic Plant Protection* (Emmaus, Pa., Rodale Press, 1976), growing strawberries near peach trees is suggested as a control because the same wasp (*Macrocentrus ancylivorus*) that parasitizes the strawberry leaf roller also preys on oriental fruit moth. Also, a Trichogramma wasp parasitizes the moths' eggs. Lacewings eat the larvae and field mice eat their cocoons.

Since pupae overwinter in the soil around the trees, the practice of cultivating peach orchards gives some control. Cultivate only very shallowly—4 inches at the most; 2 is better. Peach rootlets are often close to the soil surface.

Clean up fallen fruit. Do not let dried, rotten peaches (mummies) hang on the tree or lie on the ground over winter.

Photo 11-15—Damage to Branch by Oriental Fruit Moth Larvae. USDA photograph.

PSYLLA

The psyllid looks much like an aphid and sucks plant juices the same way. Psylla hop around rather than crawl, however. The pear psyllid is currently the worst pest of the family. In addition to sucking the juice, it secretes honeydew, which can cause mold on leaves and blackening of the fruit. Bartlett and Anjou are especially susceptible. Pear psylla are becoming resistant to organophosphates, and growers are using synthetic pyrethroids with some effect, as already mentioned in Chapter 9. Dormant oil and cold water timed exactly when female psylla are emerging to lay eggs is the safest control for backyards. In commercial pear-growing regions in the West, the time of emergence can be obtained from insectaries and from scientists at universities. Entomologists have learned how to examine eggs in a captured female to determine exactly when she will fly out to the branch tips and lay them. But egg laying by pear psylla as a cue for oil-spray application is both effective and simple for the backyard orchardist. It generally begins about one week before bud burst. The tiny, yellow eggs are quite visible on the small twigs usually clustered around the buds.

SAWFLIES

The European apple sawfly is sometimes a pest in eastern apple orchards. An effective backyard control is the sticky trap. Cardboard rectangles painted *white* (yellow for aphids and fruit flies) and coated with Tanglefoot do the trick. Steve Page, the orchardist mentioned earlier, says four such traps per tree do the job.

The red pine sawfly and the European pine sawfly may attack edible pines (Italian stone pine and Swiss stone pine) in addition to their regular fare of ornamental pines. Rotenone helps. A nurseryman and Christmas-tree grower near my place tells me that he never has to spray pines anymore. Since the trees have grown up, robins nest in his groves in unusual numbers, and he thinks they control sawfly insects.

SCALE

Cottony cushion scale used to be a major threat to citrus and other plants in warm climates. A ladybug called vedalia was introduced and became one of the first really effective biological-

Photo 11-16—Cottony Cushion Scale on an Orange Tree. USDA photograph.

control programs. If you see masses of little white "cushions" on your citrus trees and they have tiny red eggs inside, find an insectary in your area and order some vedalia ladybugs—fast.

Black scale, California red scale, purple scale, Florida red scale, and olive scale are all serious pests in warm climates. Oil is the safest spray since it will smother eggs and does little harm to predators, of which the scales have many. Incidentally, black scale has the distinction of becoming immune to cyanide, which once was the standard control. Don't let anyone tell you a bug can't get immune to almost any poison.

Scale insects always surprise new backyard fruit growers. When I inherited some fruit trees that came with the first home I bought, I was so ignorant that I thought the peculiarly rough, mottled surface of the peach trees was the bark. The "bark" turned out to be the dead outer shells of millions of scale insects. But I didn't catch on until the next spring when the rough, mottled "bark" began to swell a little and move up to the branch tips. The old gardener across the road educated me about my problem. Sure enough, that "bark" was soft and slimy, now, and alive, even though the individual scale insects never seemed to move.

I grabbed the all-purpose spray off the shelf in the garage where a previous owner had left it and sprayed. I didn't know it then, but all-purpose sprays are the worst you can use because, as the name suggests, they usually contain poisons that kill all bugs. However, it didn't faze the scale. I was also spraying sulfur at the time, not realizing that sulfur kills the predators of scale insects. The more I sprayed, the more the scale proliferated. In desperation I soaked a rag in oil and wiped the scales off every branch by hand. Fortunately, I had only two rather small peach trees.

The neighbor said my scourge was San Jose scale, but since it attacked only the peaches and not the apples, I'm not sure it was. In hindsight, I believe it was oystershell scale, though at the time, fresh from the corn belt, I did not know what an oyster shell looked like, let alone the scale.

A good, soaking, dormant oil spray is the safest protection against scale. Don't use sulfur as a fungicide. And weird as it sounds, wiping branches with an oil rag works. But don't touch leaves. The oil might kill them.

WEEVILS

Pecan weevil is a pest of both hickory and pecan, and a fairly serious one for both. In wild stands of hickory and native pecan, the weevil infestation varies from year to year, and from tree to tree in any year. The alternate-bearing habit of these wild nut trees acts as a control of the weevil, but not a very effective one. The weevil has adjusted its life cycle to alternate bearing: Some of the current larvae pupate in one year and some in two, so even if the current generation should starve to death for lack of nuts to eat, enough would remain to carry on in the next year. Nevertheless, alternate bearing helps control the insect and, as repugnant as it sounds to the domestic pecan growers' good sense, it might be a trait not to be bred out of pecans. Nuts store very well when frozen. Might it not make a little sense to harvest every other year and store half the crop for sale in the off year, rather than mount expensive spray campaigns along with even more expensive management programs to make the pecan bear every year? Economics most likely rule out such impractical ideas, but not for the home grove-owner. We only get hickory nuts every other year, but we can easily crack and freeze enough for the off year.

Commercial pecan growers use several sprays to control pecan weevil, such as Torak, Zolone, and Supracide—a whole litany of computer-compounded nonwords. But spraying is not the answer for the home grove-owner, even if he wants to spray. You'd need a helicopter to spray a big old hickory or native northern pecan. Southern researchers have devised an effective nonchemical control trap that works better. The trap was perfected for commercial growers to help them ascertain when

Photo 11-17—Adult Pecan Weevil. USDA photograph.

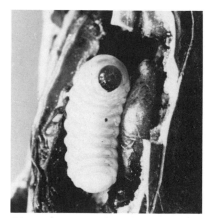

Photo 11-18—Pecan Weevil Larva. USDA photograph.

the weevils are flying—the best time to spray. But the traps can be fairly effective controls themselves in the backyard situation.

Weevils pupate in the soil under the trees. Some emerging adult weevils crawl up the tree trunk and some fly up to the branches directly from the ground. Therefore, two kinds of traps are necessary. For the flying weevils, the Cooperative Extension Service of the University of Georgia at Athens has issued a bulletin (Leaflet 26) that describes the trap built by researchers S. G. Folles and J. A. Payne. The trap is in the shape of an inverted funnel formed of lath frame covered with screen. There is a small inverted plastic funnel at the top of the tepee-shaped

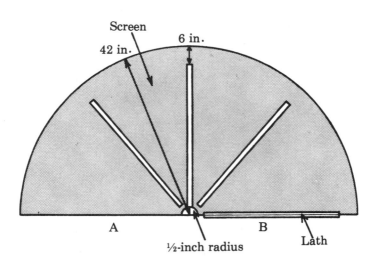

Illus. 11-1—Trap for Weevils—Flying weevils and other pupating pests will fly up the cone into the collecting jar. The more traps, the better the control, and once the traps are built, they're easy to place and convenient to store by stacking.

structure, with an inverted glass jar fastened above the funnel. Weevils emerging from the soil inside the "tepee" fly up into the jar and cannot escape.

Materials for the trap include a 7-foot length of 42-inch-wide aluminum screen, four 32-inch laths, a 3-ounce plastic funnel with a ½-pint fruit jar and lid ring. Cut the screen to form a semicircle with a 42-inch radius. Cut a ½-inch radius semicircle in the middle of the straight side of the screen. Staple the four lengths of lath to the screen so that the ends are 6 inches from the 42-inch semicircle. Then overlap sides A and B (see Illus. 11-1) and staple to the same side of the lath to form a cone. Place the funnel in the inside of the point of the cone and embed the screen in the funnel base by heating the plastic with an electric soldering iron. Glue the lid ring to both screen and funnel with cellulose nitrate glue so that the jar can be screwed on upside down. Make sure there are no holes for weevils to escape through around the edge of the funnel or the lid ring. The trap can be anchored by piling soil on the 6 inches of screen that flare out beyond the end of the lath. The laths and funnel give the necessary support to prevent the cone from sagging to one side, which might block weevils from entering the jar.

The more traps you set under the tree the better, of course, but the researchers say set them no closer than 4 feet from the trunk nor farther away than 12 feet. You might figure out an easier way to build a trap of this kind. This design works well for trapping other kinds of bugs, too.

For weevils that crawl up the tree trunk, a band of Tanglefoot will work. The band should be no narrower than 3 inches and certainly no wider than 12 inches.

Some pecan authorities say a backyard grower can jar the limbs and thereby knock weevils off onto a sheet, a method similar to that used for plum curculio. This method would apply to smaller domestic trees, I assume. You can't jar the large hickories and pecans farther north unless you hit them with a bulldozer.

HICKORY SHUCKWORM

Hickories and pecans are bothered by the hickory shuckworm, also. The worm primarily eats the outer husk, but the first generation also destroys the infant nuts before the shell is hardened. Later generations, working in the husks, may deform the nuts. The problem is more critical with commercial growers

*Photo 11-19—Hickory Shuck-
worm. USDA photograph.*

in that the shuckworm may ruin the cosmetic appearance of the
nut for sale to finicky consumers.

The home grove-owner can effectively control shuckworm,
say pecan authorities, by scrupulously raking up all shucks and
burning them. That can be a time-consuming job, but if you are
dealing with only a couple of trees, not impractical.

WALNUT HUSK FLY

The larva of the walnut husk fly eats the husk of walnuts
but does not directly harm the nut. Often English walnut
producers feel they have to spray the husk fly for purely
cosmetic reasons. The worms make streaks on the outer surface
of the shell and consumers then resist buying them, though the
nuts are usually perfectly all right. Real heavy infestations
impede proper development of the nut, however, and may cause
a slight off flavor. The home grove-owner nevertheless can
ignore the husk fly.

WEBWORMS

Tent caterpillars and other hairy worms that gather into
clusters in the trees are easily controlled by burning. I have
noticed that some writers criticize this method, but I find it fast
and effective. A long stick with a rag, soaked in coal oil, tied to
the end of it can be set afire and then briefly held under the web
of worms. Some small harm is done to the tree in the vicinity of
your flaming torch, but the injury is negligible if you use
common sense.

Photo 11-20—Webworms. Rodale Press photograph.

JAPANESE BEETLES

Japanese beetles may become a problem in fruit and nut trees, although at our first homestead in eastern Pennsylvania they did little damage despite dense populations. They were too busy eating other plants, I guess. Milky spore disease, available from good garden stores or by mail through advertisements in garden publications, is a standard treatment. Traps help, and much experimentation is being done with beetle traps.

Japanese beetles seem to be worse as they invade a new area, as they are now doing in Ohio. In the East, where the beetle has been endemic for many years, I never saw it cause the kind of damage it is causing currently around Wooster, Ohio. Beetles like sod. They are much worse where there are large expanses of well-kept lawn than where the soil is continuously cultivated.

To counterattack the Japanese beetle outbreak in the Wooster area, Dr. T. L. Ladd, entomologist at the USDA's Japanese Beetle Research Lab in Wooster, has successfully used extracts from neem seeds. The neem tree is found in India where its seeds have long been used as an insect repellent. The neem extracts appear to be, according to Dr. Ladd's reports, "out-

Photo 11-21—Japanese Beetle Larva, Pupa, and Young Adult. Photograph by Grant Heilman.

Photo 11-22—Adult Japanese Beetles' Destruction on Apples. USDA photograph.

standing deterrents" when applied to leaves of soybeans and sassafras. Some beetles starved to death rather than consume the treated foliage.

PEAR SLUG

This soft-bodied larva of a black and yellow sawfly is an example of an insect very easily controlled by chemicals, but in an unsprayed orchard like mine, they can become a pain in the neck. These very dark green, slimy "slugs" appear on pear leaves at about the time the trees are fully leaved, first as tiny blobs that grow eventually to about ½ inch long. They skeletonize the leaves and can cause considerable damage in some years. I handpick them, but I believe that any harsh botanical would kill them. Pear slugs also attack quince, cherry, and plum, though not in my orchard. One pear tree, a wild seedling of Kieffer, I presume, is unaffected. Pear slugs are less damaging on larger trees and do not seem to produce large population outbreaks.

NEMATODES

Nematodes are not a problem on fertile soils rich in organic matter, especially any virgin woodland soils. But old orchard sites, especially in the South, often have serious root-knot nematode infestations, particularly peach and citrus orchards. Scientists have now discovered a biological control for root knot at work in California. The "parasite" is a fungus, a new species that scientists have named *Dactylella oviparasitica*. The fungus penetrates the egg clumps of root-knot nematode clustered on the root and destroys them. Sometimes the fungus grows right inside the female nematode and causes egg production to cease. Graham R. Stirling, Michael V. McKenry, and Ron Mankau at the Department of Nematology, University of California, Riverside, reporting on this discovery in 1978, stated: "We hypothesize that on hosts such as Lovell peach where root-knot nematodes produce relatively small egg masses, parasitism by *D. oviparasitica* can substantially reduce nematode populations. On hosts such as grape, parasitism is generally insufficient. . . unless environmental conditions favor the parasite or are unsuitable for the nematode."

BENEFICIAL INSECTS

WASPS

Wasps are important predators of many insects. Fortunately or unfortunately, the large stinger types prey on spiders as well as aphids, grasshoppers, and flies, and so both wasp and spider are an unknown quantity in the suppression of harmful bugs: do they eat more or less of them than of beneficial bugs? The most beneficial wasps, or perhaps I should say the totally

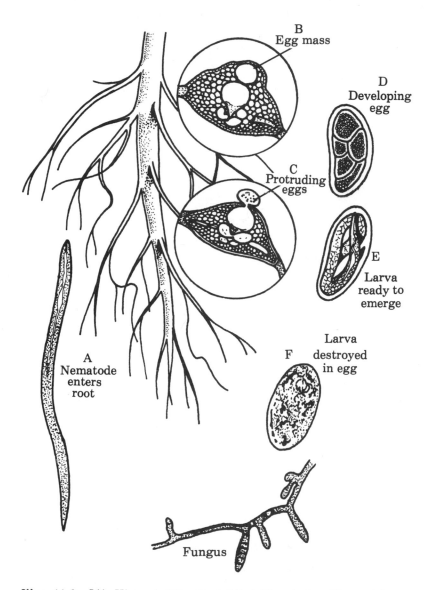

Illus. 11-2—Life History of the Root-Knot Nematode—The root-knot nematode (A) enters the root of a plant during its second larval stage. If unimpeded, the adult female within the galled root lays eggs (B) that protrude into the soil (C). A single egg (D) will develop into a larva (E), which will emerge to begin the cycle over (A). Fungus can invade the developing egg (F), however, to parasitize the egg and kill the embryo. Note: Elements of drawing not to scale.

beneficial wasps, are the very tiny ones that most of us have never seen, even though they exert greater influence over insect populations than the large, stinging wasps. Larvae of the these tiny Trichogramma wasps feed on many pest bugs and can now be purchased from many mail-order seed houses. Some Torymidae wasps feed on insects that attack seeds and plant tissue. Tiphiidae wasps of some species attack Japanese beetles. Thysanidae wasps attack whitefly and scale, though some attack the parasites of aphids. Some Pelecinidae wasps also feed on Japanese beetles. The ichneumon wasps are extremely beneficial, parasitizing a variety of pest caterpillars and sawflies. Braconid wasps are extremely beneficial in that they not only prey upon aphids; they also prey upon the larvae of many moths and flies. The Eulophidae family of wasps parasitizes certain crop pests but also parasitizes other parasites of crop pests. We tamper with this exceedingly complex system at our own risk.

SPIDERS

Entomologists do not think spiders play a very important role in controlling harmful bugs, since most spiders feed indiscriminately on any bug that they can catch, good or bad. Also, most spiders do not really seem to start their bug-catching campaigns in earnest until late in the growing season, when the die is already cast as far as protecting the current fruit or nut crop goes. I wonder, though, how many entomologists have walked through groves of food trees that have not been habitually treated with chemicals. The quantity of spiders and webs in my groves in September can be a shock to an observer

Photo 11-23—Spider and Web in an Orchard. Rodale Press photograph.

used to seeing only sprayed orchards. And in meadows adjacent to or under the grove trees, the spider population in the fall is nothing less than phenomenal. In early morning dew, before any grazing animal is afoot, the ground can be seen to be literally covered with spiderwebs. I have a hunch spiders influence bug populations more than we think if conditions are right for them. I also have a hunch that mowing lawns has destroyed most of the beneficial spider population in the suburbs, not to mention almost the entire toad population, which is one of nature's most effect agents in controlling bugs.

BEES

The honeybee is certainly one of the most beneficial insects in the world, and the most desirable, if not essential, insect in your grove of food trees. If you keep a bit of sheltered woodland in your grove complete with the hollow trees where squirrels, woodpeckers, and other creatures have made homes, sooner or later a swarm of bees will settle into one of the holes and you will have a beehive without any work at all.

But you are missing out on one of the chief benefits of your tree grove if you do not have a regular hive of bees from which you can draw off at least enough honey for your own use. I don't know if beekeepers will appreciate my saying this in print, but if you keep only one hive and take away only enough honey for your own family, you don't have to follow *all* of those rigorous rules the books pontificate about. Books on beekeeping are usually predicated on the idea of producing honey for profit, which demands that you follow all those rules. But economic conditions change everyday, while the bees go on making honey the way they did thousands of years ago. Bees are really much like other livestock. I have found that if they have all they need to eat (plenty of honey), are warm enough in winter and cool enough in summer, have access to water and plenty of "grazing," and are not overcrowded, they do just fine. If they do get overcrowded and swarm, that's only bad news if you are in the honey business, and not necessarily even then. A swarm means that you can get another hive started if you want to.

If you work with bees in this casual manner for a few years, *then* you are ready to start increasing your hives and going into business, if you want to.

There are many bees that help pollenate your trees. There are small ones, which I cannot identify, that will work earlier in

231

the year when it is too cool for honeybees. In a letter to me, experimental fruit grower Robert Kurle, who has forgotten more about tree fruits than I'll ever know, says that he believes these small bees, which he doesn't identify, either, are more of a factor in the success or failure of early-blooming apricots than are late frosts. "I think frost is sometimes blamed for lack of apricots when in fact it is the lack of these small wild bees. Apricots are really hardier than we think."

Another innovative tree grower I know attracts a certain large, pollenating bee that's active in cool weather to fly to his early-blooming papaw trees by placing the carcasses of dead animals under the trees. I pass that along in the interest of folklore, if not science.

Scientists are studying a number of "non-apis bees" that may be potentially good pollinators and that can be used, better than honeybees, with chemicals. One of the more grievous problems with chemicals is that their careless use has caused the slaughter of honeybees. One "non-apis bee" that seems promising is *Osmia lignaria*, a bluish black bee that's a little larger than a honeybee. *O. lignaria* will work in colder weather than that in which honeybees work. Also, *O. lignaria* seldom sting and are present in the orchard for only about 30 days during the spring blooming season, and so are not killed by toxic sprays used after pollenation time. At the Agricultural Research Station at Logan, Utah, researchers learned that they could lure *O. lignaria* to the orchards by making nests for them. The nests are simple holes drilled into planks. Using beams of redwood (or even pieces of Styrofoam), 4 × 10 inches and any length, the researchers drilled 9-millimeter holes nearly all the way through the 10-inch width; 30 holes per beam worked best. The beams were placed near a supply of mud that the female bees use in their nests. After the females sealed their eggs in the beams, the beams were stored away. The only rule seems to be a storage temperature no warmer than 40°F through the winter. Warmer temperatures can trigger the bees to hatch at the wrong time.

When spring came the beams were put in the orchard and the newly hatched bees soon emerged and flew among the blossoms. Information on these bees can be obtained by writing the BEE Biology and Systematics Lab, USDA Agricultural Research Service, NRB Building, Utah State University, Logan, UT 84322.

Obviously, *O. lignaria* will be of limited use in most home groves and certainly not a replacement for the honeybee. *O. lig-*

232

naria won't be present when you need it for late-blooming trees, raspberries, melons, etc. Where the bee is native, it may be of supplemental help. But honeybees do 90% of the pollenation in most orchards, with help from bumblebees, solitary bees, and others, and most honey-loving home grove-owners will want to keep it that way.

FLIES

Most of us are inclined to think of all flies as pests. Many, however, are beneficial, and some are extremely beneficial for controlling pest bugs. Tachinid flies are as a family (1,300 species parasitic on other insects) the most beneficial. They look like houseflies but are very bristly. Syrphid flies (sometimes called flowerflies), mentioned earlier, comprise another large family, most of whose members are highly beneficial, especially in controlling aphids. Aphid flies (Chamaemyiidae family) also prey on aphids, scale, and mealybugs. Bee flies (Bombyliidae) are parasites of caterpillars, grubs, and grasshopper eggs. Robber flies (Asilidae) are mostly beneficial, preying on many insects.

Photo 11-24—Syrphid Fly Larva Feeding on Aphids. USDA photograph.

BEETLES

Ladybug beetles (also called ladybirds or just ladybugs) in some instances have proven extremely effective in controlling pest bugs, such as vedalia's effect on cottony cushion scale, already mentioned. But introducing common ladybug beetles into gardens and orchards as a sort of general control measure is not always so effective. Listening to what other gardeners tell me, and observing on my own, I believe that if you have to introduce ladybugs, something is out of balance in your grove's environment. The beetles may simply fly away to what must appear to be greener pastures elsewhere. Or die. On the other hand, if ladybugs already have found the environment conducive, you don't need to introduce more. Where native ladybug populations are healthy and vigorous, they seem to work marvelously well. The only disadvantage I see is that they usually take some time to build up enough numbers to be effective in stopping an aphid outbreak, during which time some harm may be done to the plants. But patience pays off. One year, aphids attacked our oak trees so fiercely that honeydew covered cars parked under them. After about a month we began seeing ladybugs everywhere, and the following spring hordes of them were skittering about, especially around the bases of the trees—as thick as box elder bugs can get. We noticed no more aphids that year nor in succeeding years up to the present. Another species of ladybug flocks into our cane sorghum patch each summer and erases thick clusters of aphids there.

There are many species of ladybugs. The most common is the convergent ladybug, with a red-to-pink back, dotted with 12 black spots. On the thorax between the head and the back are

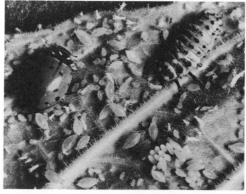

Photo 11-25—Adult Ladybug and Larva Preying on Aphids. USDA photograph.

two white lines that almost meet in a V. The two-spotted ladybug has red forewings and 2 black spots. The transverse ladybug is sometimes plain red, but usually has 3 elongated black spots across the back. The twice-stabbed ladybug has a black back with two red spots, hence the name. The thirteen-spotted ladybug is like the convergent beetle with one more spot. A variation of the black ladybug mentioned earlier has a pinkish abdomen offsetting its shiny black back. It controls black scale in California. Most ladybugs eat scale as well as aphids and mealybugs; the twice-stabbed is, like the black, more of a scale eater. Some ladybug larvae look about like mealybugs—another reason not to spray with *any* material unless you know what you're doing. Other families of ladybugs prey on spider mites. They are very small and black, and do not look like ladybugs as we customarily think of them. That is also true of the Scymnus family of ladybugs, slightly smaller than common ladybugs and brown, black, or mottled in color.

Every good grove-owner should carry an inexpensive magnifying glass to view insects with. My daughter made a leather case for mine, and I can slip it on my belt, where the glass is always handy. You will see some sights, believe me. The dramas of the insect world—and its magnificent beauties—have not yet been all recorded, in my opinion. Have you ever watched ants herding their "flocks" of aphids around and fighting off ladybug beetles who come to eat them?

The ground beetle family is almost entirely beneficial, but some of the members look so ferocious and mean-jawed that ignorant humans often kill them. These beetles are mostly large and often beautiful. *Calosoma scrutator* (popularly called the fiery hunter) is green and loves tent caterpillars, but if you try to pick it up without gloves it may secrete a caustic fluid that burns the skin. The European ground beetle (*C. sycophanta*) almost glows with a metallic green-blue-gold sheen. Over an inch long, this beauty has been imported to help control gypsy moth, which it helps to do in Europe quite effectively.

Literally hundreds of other beetles prey on pest insects; some prey on insects indiscriminately, and some are pests themselves preying on other pests. It is good to learn to recognize soldier beetles, tiger beetles, and rove beetles (an illustrated complete book on insects is a necessary tool for grove management) because they are beneficial even if they do not exert significant influence on pest bug populations.

PRAYING MANTIS

The praying, or preying, mantis (take your pick) is the best known of all beneficial insects because of its large size and easy identity. I have doubts about its reputation as an effective biological-control tool—the praying mantis will eat harmful and beneficial bugs, including its own kind, and it is easily caught by birds. Nevertheless, in my groves protected from toxic sprays I am seeing a prodigious increase in its numbers. I counted seven egg masses on just one small hawthorn tree last winter. The grove-owner who fosters a good environment for insects might consider gathering some of his praying mantis egg clusters for sale. You can spot them easily in winter—tan clumps on tree or bush limbs, somewhat resembling cocoons, but having more the consistency of hardened foam.

Photo 11-26—Praying Mantis. Rodale Press photograph.

LACEWING AND FIREFLY

The goldeneye green lacewing and the brown lacewing are important predators of pest bugs, especially of aphids and mealybugs. The adults have large, lacy, transparent wings that

Photo 11-27—Aphid Lion (Larva of Lacewing). USDA photograph.

Photo 11-28—Adult Lacewing. USDA photograph.

extend well behind the skinny green or brown body. Lacewings are poor fliers and, thus, might be thought of as easy prey for predators. Lacewings emit a nasty odor, however, that protects them from birds and other enemies. Their larvae are called aphid lions and have been described earlier.

The firefly's larvae feed on slugs and snails and are therefore of much more benefit to the garden than to the orchard. But I mention them because of their beauty as adults. Beauty should not be the least of reasons for not using toxic chemicals in your grove. Is there not a profit in beauty worth the extra dollars for the protection of fireflies? When a person has lived his life, and dying, looks back over the happy times and the sad, what is it then that he understands was the real profit? Is not beauty more valuable than money? For those who might think so, I list in addition to the firefly the following insects, which can provide the kind of pleasure money can't buy.

237

INSECTS FOR BEAUTY

The luna moth is a large, delicately green moth whose larvae feed on black walnut and hickory leaves but not to any harmful degree. This moth has long, narrow, striking tails trailing out from each wing and a purple band on the front of the wings. Though I see them during the day every spring in my groves, one is more apt to see them at night, drawn to an outdoor light or to a window. Usually by the time you find one in daylight, it is nearing the end of its time. Its wings are beginning to tatter, and its ability to fly is much decreased. You can at this time safely "collect" the lovely creature since without a doubt it had already laid its eggs. But should you find one newly emerged from a cocoon, leave it be. The larva of the luna moth is quite beautiful, too—a 3-inch green caterpillar with six pink or green tubercles bearing yellow bristles. Without hickory or walnut, the caterpillars may feed on beech, birch, persimmon, gum, willow, or other hardwood trees.

The cecropia moth is a very large silkworm moth with a wingspan of up to 6 inches. The moth is brown with a white crossband, bordered in red with a red spot near the apex of each forewing, a white spot in the center, and red, blue, and yellow tubercles on the body. The caterpillar is pale green, up to 4 inches long, with the red, blue, and yellow tubercles seen on the adult. Both are beautiful enough to take your breath away. The larvae do little harm; the adults eat nothing. I am appalled that some garden bug books give instructions to "control by destroying cocoons." Even if by some strange twist of the biological food chain the caterpillars become so numerous as to start hurting oak trees (their principal food, although they will eat leaves of other common hardwoods), the thing to do would be to collect the cocoons and sell them! There are people making a nice business out of raising silkworm moths. (See a very interesting book, *How to Talk to Birds and Other Uncommon Ways of Enjoying Nature,* by Richard C. Davids [New York, Alfred A. Knopf, 1972], chap. 4.) If you see a large gray cocoon, whether it be of the cecropia, the Polyphemus moth discussed below, or even the luna moth, clip off the branch and put the whole thing in an *unheated* garage where neither bird nor mouse can get to it. If you can't so protect the cocoon, leave it in the tree, where it will have a better chance against the birds than in your garage against the mice. After the moth emerges the next spring—a fantastic show in itself—you might want to save the cocoons. That's where silk comes from.

The Polyphemus moth is another silkworm only a little less strikingly beautiful than the cecropia. It has brownish yellow wings with a pinkish band across them, and blue "eyes" on either hind wing. The larva is 3 inches long, green, with an oblique yellow line on the sides of each abdominal segment except the first and last. Each segment sports six greenish gold tubercles. The larvae feed on oak and other hardwoods but are not harmful, only delightful.

The promethea moth, better known as the spicebush silk moth, is more common than the above two moths and smaller, but still a treasure in your tree grove. The moths are not as beautiful as the larger ones—the female reddish brown with a distinct white line across the middle, and the male brown to black with more of a zigzag line—but the caterpillars are gorgeous. These measure about 2 inches long, are bluish green in color with black shiny tubercles in the middle, two pairs of bright red tubercles on the second and third segments from the head, and a pair of yellow tubercles at the other end. A black line outlines a "face"—false eyes and nose to my imagination—at the back end of the worm.

The zebra swallowtail butterfly is somewhat rare, which may account for my fascination with it. It is smaller than a monarch and a striking combination of black, white, and red. Its favorite food is papaw leaves, which is probably why you don't see many of them. I have planted papaws as much in hopes of attracting this butterfly as for the fruit.

The saddleback caterpillar (*Sibine stimulea*) is the kind of gaudy creature that we usually associate with the tropics. Yet it is a fairly common Atlantic Coast worm seen from New England to Texas and at least as far inland as Ohio; we found them in our grove last year. The caterpillar is reddish brown with a green saddle that has a smaller purple brown patch inside it, bordered in white. Though lovely to look at, the insect can sting from the tufts of spines at either end, and the resulting pain is very irritating for awhile. The caterpillar feeds mainly on oak and wild cherry, and sometimes on common ornamental bushes of various kinds. But it is not an injurious pest to any plant.

There are, of course, many other harmless butterflies, moths, and insects of great beauty, depending on which region you live in. Learn to treasure them all, and they will be your faithful companions, bringing you pleasant solace in their yearly visitations.

CHAPTER 12

FUNGAL, BACTERIAL, AND VIRAL DISEASES

We customarily look upon fungal diseases as aberrations on the face of nature. But fungi all perform a necessary and beneficial service: They aid in the decomposition of organic matter. Without that decomposition, life could not go on. It may be difficult to look with that much detachment at scab attacking your favorite apple tree, but at the same time it is not difficult to realize that a fungicide has to be, by definition, a most antibiological, and therefore dangerous, chemical. If fungicides really worked effectively, all life would come to some unimaginable state of pickled standstill.

Fortunately, perhaps, sunlight is an effective fungicide. I wonder how often a spray application gets credit for saving a crop when actually it is hot, dry, sunny weather after spraying that really closes down those threatening rot or blight spores. Spraying is only momentarily effective, if at all, and then only if done and continued all through the growing season before the fungal infection becomes established. Meanwhile, new strains of

240

some fungi, especially scab, appear to be growing more resistant to the more or less continuous spraying schedules of commercial orcharding. What's more, in very humid climates, or in years of high humidity and rainfall in regions of moderately humid climates, especially where heavy nitrogenous fertilizers have been applied, no fungicide approved for orchards will control fungal diseases satisfactorily. In the backyard grove you might just as well save your money and pray for sunshine.

In places where fungal disease is an overwhelming problem, the backyard grove-owner has only one really satisfying choice, a choice not open to the commercial grower. Plant the food trees acclimated to your humid climate, where environmental adaptation has worked to protect native fruits from fatal fungal disease. Quit fiddling with the others. So often fungal problems are the result of us indefatigable human beings trying to force our wills on the environment. There may be situations where this willfulness is praiseworthy, but not when growing food trees. There are plenty of fruit and nut varieties that you can grow in the humid eastern states, so why waste time trying to grow others when the odds are 50 to 1 against you? If we had spent the last three centuries developing scab-immune apples instead of just the last 20 years, we would now have so many good immune varieties that we might not have to spray for scab at all. Instead, we stubbornly grow the good apples that are susceptible to scab and so the whole eastern fruit-growing region begins to lose out in competition with the dry West, where these undelicious Delicious apples don't get scab. What if all apple production moves to Washington and similar dry climates and then a vicious new disease runs rampant *there*? Then you will not even be able to buy a hard, bounceable Red Delicious when you go to the grocery.

With much the same streak of stubbornness, we continue to grow English filberts (hazelnuts) where mildew attacks them badly. We can (so far) control the mildew with sprays, so work in developing better-tasting American filberts lags. And selected American varieties really are quite good *now*.

But I don't expect to persuade intrepid Americans with this kind of fatalistic philosophy even in their backyards, at least not until they grow old enough to see the wisdom of metering out their available energy sparingly, so that there's enough for all of the worthwhile jobs. Instead, I'll try to give some sort of rundown on the "safer" fungicides now in general use. If you have a tree you love and blights are killing it, and you are going to waste the time to try to save it, you might as well know the choices. Not much has been written about fungal disease for the home grove-owner, but I have found *How to Control Plant Diseases in Home and Garden,* by Malcolm Shurtleff, to be the easiest to understand and fairly helpful though, unless it has been revised, its chemical products are outdated.

As I have said, sunlight is the only ecologically safe fungicide I know of and also the only effective one. But continued applications of Captan or Cyprex can prevent bad outbreaks from occurring, given halfway decent weather. There are others, of course, but these two are most often mentioned by orchardists as being relatively safe for insects. Captan is better in this regard than Cyprex, as I understand it. (I used to use a lot of Captan but I couldn't see where it made that much difference, so I quit.) Sulfur, which some organic growers use and think is safe because it is a naturally occurring substance, is highly toxic to some beneficial insects, as I already mentioned. However, none of the fungicides so far mentioned, natural or commercial, are directly toxic to humans or animals and so are safer, as far as we know, than say DDT or the organophosphate broad-spectrum insecticides. Phenyl mercury materials, on the other hand, are effective sometimes against scab (they "burn out" the scab, as the saying goes), but they are very toxic to humans.

That leaves the copper fungicides as perhaps the least objectionable. Bordeaux is a very old one, and still fairly effective for mildews and leaf blights. Some "organic" commercial fruit growers are most apt to choose it when they either must spray or lose the crop. Bordeaux is a mixture of copper sulfate and lime with water. You can buy it or mix your own and save money. The hydrated lime can harm foliage. That is why horticulturists who use copper often prefer fixed copper rather than Bordeaux. Use it cautiously, if you must use it at all. The traditional way of making Bordeaux is to mix 4 pounds of copper sulfate, 4 pounds of hydrated lime, and 50 gallons of water. To make small amounts, dissolve 2 ounces of copper sulfate crystals in a gallon of water, and then mix that with another 2 gallons of water into which you have stirred 2 ounces of lime. The idea is never to mix highly concentrated solutions of copper sulfate and hydrated lime together.

The use of sulfur in an organic pest-control program continues to be a controversial practice. Commercial growers who want to grow fruit as organically as possible without incurring heavy losses from fungal disease, defend sulfur, especially in the newer liquid formulations such as Thiolux and THAT Flowable Sulfur. They believe that these fungicides are least likely to have harmful side effects. Liquid sulfur formulations are only slightly harmful to predator mites, they say, and if used with restraint, these formulations will not unduly harm predators of scale pests. Sulfur as sulfate has no beneficial or adverse effect on insect predators and parasites, they argue. And finally, because sulfur is a natural substance, they maintain that it is justifiable in an organic program. The same argument is given for copper, and some organic growers use liquid copper formulations for fungicides. Thus, according to the logic of this point of view, Bordeaux mixture would be a safe, or at least the safest possible, fungicide to use.

Organic purists demur. Copper will build up to toxic levels in soil if used for a long time. It doesn't go away. Sulfur, even as sulfate (or especially as sulfate), in sprays or in fertilizers, is highly toxic to earthworms at it breaks down to sulfuric acid. More importantly, they say, the sulfuric acid engendered in the soil by the presence of sulfate compounds upsets the proper balance of soil organisms, especially soil fungi, and slows the breakdown of organic matter into humus.

What neither side seems to have argued yet is what effect any fungicide, natural or man-made, has on the natural balance of above-soil fungi. Harmful fungal diseases seem to have fungi that "prey" upon them, just as insects prey on other insects, but these discoveries are only now being made. What effect does even a "safe" fungicide such as Bordeaux have on this balance?

A better answer than fungicides is whenever possible to plant tree varieties resistant to the blights, mildews, and rots that are customary to your area. With that in mind, here's a list of the more common fungal diseases you will inevitably have to cope with. There are many, many others, but if you concentrate on adapted tree varieties for your area, you should avoid serious problems. In fact, though what follows is going to sound very discouraging, even the common diseases are seldom going to deprive you of any significant portion of your food supply. If you do decide to use fungicides, read the labels. For example, don't mix Captan with oil sprays. Don't spray Captan on Red Delicious when the leaves are young and tender.

COMMON FUNGAL DISEASES OF TREES

SCAB

If you touch a lighted match to a piece of paper but withdraw it before the paper actually kindles, you leave a brown, welted spot that looks very much like a scab infection when it first appears on apple leaves. If wet weather continues, the spots grow to blackish blotches (though not like the sooty mold that grows on leaves sticky with aphid honeydew). Eventually, if the disease increases in severity, the leaves wither and fall off. If all the leaves fall off two or three years in a row, the tree can die. Fruit on scab-infected trees show the same scabby lesions as on the leaves and, in advanced infections, the apples are wrinkled, warty, misshapen, and nearly useless. Even a mildly infected

Photo 12-1—Apple Scab. Rodale Press photograph.

apple won't sell because people don't know any better, but often the scabby part can be peeled off, and the apple is still perfectly good to eat or process.

Rain or a heavy dew is necessary for scab spores to be discharged and to spread. Therefore, scab is bad in rainy weather, especially, it seems, after a dry early spring. Temperature and humidity combine to affect the seriousness of a scab outbreak, and scientists are working out methods to help growers accurately gauge that effect ahead of time. For instance, when the temperature ranges between about 60° and 76°F, a nine-hour rainy spell might well set off an infection if scab spores are present. But if the temperature is only 40°F, it would take a rainy period of 48 hours to set off an infection.

This knowledge can be important to commercial growers by allowing them to save some scab-spraying costs, and they should be aware (and are) that detailed information regarding scab projections based on weather is available through their land grant college horticultural departments. But since no one can predict the weather, commercial growers usually go ahead and spray, anyway. They do so because once you see a scab infection, it is very difficult to control even with an eradicant (which must be sprayed within 72 hours of an outbreak). By the time an infection is present, spraying it will only help control secondary infections later on.

The time to control scab, therefore, according to the philosophy of commercial orcharding, is before an outbreak by using a protective fungicide rather than an eradicant. The least objectionable fungicides for this purpose are Captan and Cyprex. The latter seems more effective, but new strains of scab seem immune to it. Cyprex (like Captan) does have a lesser toxic effect on beneficial insects and fungi than most fungicides, and it is relatively safe for humans, plants, and animals. Remember, though, that Captan can hurt Red Delicious early in the year and should not be mixed with oil in dormant sprays.

For the grove-owner, a far better answer in humid regions is to grow scab-resistant varieties, not just for apples, but for all fruits and nuts.

There are scabs that infect all fruits and nuts. Some scabs are bacterial in origin, not fungal, but they are of minor importance. Some leaf spots, leaf blights, and rot disease look like scab. Diagnosis can be tricky and should always be done at the tree, not through the mail or over the phone.

FRUIT ROT

Fruit rot makes a convenient catchall phrase for various rots, molds, and blights, such as botrytis blight, brown rot, gray mold, rhizopus rot, and various other colloquial and scientific names for fungi that decompose fruits and nuts before you can harvest them. Stone fruits—peach, plum, nectarine, sweet and sour cherries, and apricot—are most affected. The main route of infection of brown rot on peaches is through the open blossoms. The spore usually remains dormant until just before harvest when the fruit sugar level rises, which creates conditions ideal for growth of the fungus. This often explains severe preharvest brown rot epidemics even though the weather has been fairly dry, and even if fungicide was used. Often the fungi gain access through holes opened by insects, such as plum curculio and oriental fruit moth. Wettable, 80% sulfur is probably the safest control chemical unless it leads to scale outbreaks. Captan is a second choice if you must. I can only say that during years when brown rot was bad on my peaches in the humid Philadelphia area neither sulfur nor Captan controlled it, and when I quit spraying, in drier years we harvested plenty of peaches.

Photo 12-2—Brown Rot on Cherries.
Rodale Press photograph.

When shopping for stone fruit trees, look for varieties with resistance to brown rot (see Stone Fruits, Chap. 14). I'm not too sure any stone fruit has much resistance in a rainy year, but some have the reputation, anyway. Since stone fruits sometimes come fairly true to variety from seed, your best approach would be to scout your area for trees that have remained healthy for many years and plant seed from them.

POWDERY MILDEW

Powdery mildew is a good descriptive name for a very large family of fungi. It appears as whitish or grayish powder on leaves. If you try to control it by spraying, you will do a lot of spraying because there's a mildew or two for nearly every plant species in humid areas. Good air circulation, dry weather, and resistant varieties keep powdery mildew from becoming serious in backyard situations. But in humid areas an attack might cause some branch dieback or russeted fruit. Bordeaux is the "old reliable" spray.

BLACK KNOT

Black knot is mainly a disease of plums, but it also attacks cherries and sometimes apricots. The characteristic symptom is an elongated black swelling on the branch, usually only on one side of the branch. The ugly swelling can be as much as a foot long, but it is usually much shorter. At first the knots are olive green and feel quite like bark. Later they become harder and

Photo 12-3—Black Knot on Plum. Photograph by John Colwell from Grant Heilman.

blacken. The twig or branch often dies, and in severe cases the whole tree dies. You may find insects in the swelling when it is older, but they have nothing to do with the infection.

Spores from last year's knots reinfect the tree, so the more assiduously you amputate infected branches, the better. Pruning away the knots will not necessarily stop the spreading of the disease during the current season, however. Prune new swellings in May if you see them, but by all means get all of them during the winter before they can reinfect the tree next spring. Cut about 4 inches below the knot before bud burst in the spring, and then burn the cuttings.

CHERRY LEAF SPOT

Yellow speckles on cherry leaves turn into holes and the leaves drop prematurely when cherry leaf spot attacks. If the disease continues severely for a few years, the tree may die. But before you panic and grab the Cyprex spray, give nature a chance. In my experience I've had cherry leaves get spotty by late summer many times, and I haven't seen one die as a result yet. Cherry leaf spot does not affect the fruit directly, though of course it would, indirectly, if the tree diminishes in vigor. If you have only one or two trees affected, you can help by raking up the fallen leaves and burning them, say the experts. I don't know of anyone who has actually ever done that. Raking shriveled cherry leaves is sort of like trying to comb up a pile of dandruff.

Photo 12-4—Cherry Leaf Spot. Photograph by Runk/Schoenberger from Grant Heilman.

SOOTY MOLD

A rather common family of fungi, sooty mold grows on honeydew secreted by aphids on tree leaves. Sometimes sooty mold is referred to as black mildew. It is most common on apples but wherever aphids, psylla, and other honeydew-secreting insects feed, sooty mold will sometimes be found. Except in the most severe infestations, permanent harm does not follow (although the aphids themselves may harm the tree), but fruit becomes cosmetically impossible to sell. The black smudge washes off, however, and the apple is usually still quite edible. Dieback can occur on cherry branches weakened by the aphids and then covered with the fungus. Control by suppressing the aphids and the ants that herd them, as discussed earlier.

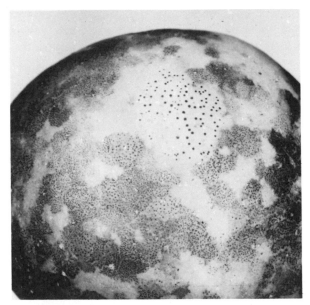

Photo 12-5—Sooty Mold on an Apple. Rodale Press photograph.

RUSTS

As with other fungal diseases, there's a rust strain for many, if not all, of the plant families. The one of most concern to orchardists is cedar-apple rust, an affliction of apples, crabs, hawthorns, and related species where juniper, or red cedar especially (which is a juniper), grow nearby. When the fungus spends part of its life cycle on its alternate host, red cedar, it appears as bright orange, gelatinous fingers. When it affects apple trees, apple leaves become spotted with yellow orange rust. Fruit may have orange spots, too, become disfigured, and drop early.

Many apples are resistant to rust. Cedar-apple rust is not usually as bad a problem as the beginning orchardist is led to expect, even when the worst of conditions prevails. I have visited an orchard bordered by red cedar trees for many years. The owner tells me every year that he intends to cut down the cedar trees because of the danger of the rust, but he never does, and sprays only minimally to control it. He gets lots of apples, including Yellow Delicious.

In the South, rusts on stone fruits rely on several wild plants such as buttercup, anemone, and hepatica, as host plants. Yellow spots on tree leaves become purplish or bronze, with brownish pustules forming underneath. Controlling alternate hosts helps to control the rust.

Photo 12-6—Cedar-Apple Rust on Red Cedar Branch—The globelike gall of cedar-apple rust forms on cedar during rainy spring to infect apple trees later. USDA photograph.

Photo 12-7—Effects of Cedar-Apple Rust on Apple Leaves—The leaf on the left is normal; the right leaf has been damaged by cedar-apple rust. Rodale Press photograph.

Many other fungi can cause problems in the tree grove, including root rots, crown cankers, heartwood rots, wilts, and minor blights. Sometimes the cause is winter injury and the fungus is merely cleaning up dead or injured tissue. Sensible sanitation, such as cleaning up apple mummies that are harboring black rot, or removing affected parts before the canker or whatever spreads, is the best defense. For root rots, more prevalent in the South, soaking bare-rooted stock in 122°F water for ten minutes before planting is an effective help.

BACTERIAL DISEASES
FIREBLIGHT

Fireblight is the most serious and the most common problem where apples and pears are grown. Its telltale sign is a rapid browning and wilting of terminal growth. Branch tips look exactly as if they were scorched by fire. In mild cases, only a few branch tips die; in severe cases nearly all of them do. When the blackened branch tip bends downward to look like the curve of a shepherd's crook, you know you've been looking at fireblight for sure. Winds spread the disease, as do splashing rain and flying insects.

Antibiotics sprayed before an infection, at the very early bloom stage, protect the trees sometimes. But once fireblight has

Photo 12-8—Fireblight on Apple Leaves. Rodale Press photograph.

ɔtruck, it is futile to spray with expensive streptomycin applications. In some cases a weak Bordeaux spray at blossom time has helped to curb blight.

Surgical removal seems the only course after infection, although even this procedure is not necessarily effective, nor is it

Photo 12-9—Fireblight Damage to Tree Branches. Rodale Press photograph.

253

always practical. Cut off all infected branches at least 12 inches below signs of visible infection, then paint the stub with a wound dressing and disinfectant. Disinfect pruning tools between cuts by dipping them in a 70% solution of denatured alcohol or the equivalent. A disinfectant for fireblight trimming tools that is cheaper than alcohol and very effective is one part Clorox and five parts water. Keep the tools oiled at the end of each day to keep them from rusting.

Researchers at the University of West Virginia report that among some experimental sprays they tried in 1977–78, a 4% solution of Clorox sprayed from bud break to bloom reduced incidences of fireblight strikes per tree.

Don't give up on a tree hard hit by fireblight. In the spring of 1979, our county suffered a severe attack. I saw backyard trees which survived quite well although enveloped by scorched terminals. On one small tree that looked nearly dead at first, the owner religiously cut off all infected terminals and, when the fireblight continued to spread, he cut off more. Amazingly, the tree recovered with the advent of hot, dry weather, and grew well from the few unaffected terminals and from spurs below the amputations. By midsummer, the tree appeared normal to anyone who had not seen it before pruning, and it produced a bushel of apples in spite of everything.

We found that the blight harms some varieties more than others. Jonathan was hardest hit. Trees on dwarf rootstock were also hard hit, no matter what the variety. An unusual steady, cold rain for three days seems to have triggered the attack. It seems to have struck worse where dwarf trees had been tip-pruned and fertilized according to the book. My own little orchard, where nothing is done by the book, was unharmed. The only blight I had was on one Lodi branch, grafted to a wild apple tree on the edge of the woods. There were two branches to the graft, and the other branch remained healthy.

The severity of fireblight seems to be connected not only to moisture but also to nitrogen fertility, since lush growth is most frequently affected. Many growers try to avoid fireblight by not using extra nitrogen and by growing grasses around trees to take up extra nitrogen from mulches or naturally rich soils.

BACTERIAL SPOT

Bacterial spot is a widespread and destructive disease of stone fruits, especially peaches. It may show itself by various

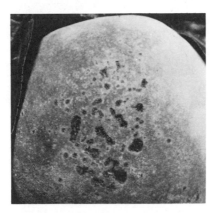

Photo 12-10—*Bacterial Spot on a Peach. USDA photograph.*

symptoms, descriptively called bacterial canker, shot hole, or gummosis. It often appears as irregularly shaped, ovalish cankers on the bark that are rough and raised, and they sometimes look water-soaked. In advanced gummy conditions, the cankers smell sour. Buds and new growth may appear wilty and blighted. Fruit develop sunken, black spots, hence the name. Many nurseries now advise customers of their varieties for sale that have high susceptibility or some resistance to bacterial spot.

Many more bacterial diseases affect tree parts, including roots. Normally they are not serious backyard problems, and there's not much you can do about them anyway.

VIRUSES AND VIROIDS

The least understood classes of plant pests are viruses and the more recently discovered viroids. Viroids are smaller than viruses and can rarely be seen, even with high-powered, electron microscopes. Stone fruits alone have over 50 viral enemies, and there are various strains of each, with new ones being discovered regularly. There's no spray chemical to control viruses directly, although in some instances one might spray for an insect carrier (or vector, as it is called) of the virus. This generally has not been very effective because some insects can transmit the virus just by landing on the plant, even if they die as they land. Other insect-transmitted viruses require that the insect feed on the plant for infection to occur since the virus is carried in the insect's salivary glands. Spraying has not been effective in controlling little cherry virus (a viroid), which nearly wiped out the cherry orchards in the Kootenay Valley of British Columbia in the 1940s and is again becoming prevalent. Says an article in a 1979 issue of an orchard magazine: "Once a vector has been isolated, steps can be taken to eradicate the pest before it destroys the trees. The carrier may be an insect, a bird, or even man himself." One hopes that no man unfortunate enough to be found carrying the virus would be eradicated. Emboldened by that hope, one might further point out that eradicating a guilty bird or insect might not be much more practical, either.

Grafters warn that the easiest way to introduce viruses into your orchard is to accept scionwood indiscriminately from other orchardists who are unaware that viruses are present in their trees or who have no way of testing their stock. An infected graft can infect the whole tree quickly. Buy or trade scionwood only with sources that recognize viruses, or with nurseries and arboretums that can guarantee virus-free stock. Or take your chances. When I find wild trees that are apparently healthy, or trees that have stood 65 years in old abandoned orchards, apparently productively, I don't think that's much of a risk to take.

A usual tip-off to virus is a yellowing, curling, or paling of leaves *early* in the growing season while other trees are growing rapidly. But diagnosis is extremely difficult since many viruses produce look-alike symptoms. "Yellows" refers to a distinct group of viruses, but the term is used very carelessly. "Mosaic" has become another catchall term for any number of viruses. One stone fruit virus family is simply called X-disease. All symptoms can easily be confused with nutritional deficiency, herbicide drift, arsenic toxicity, or fungal problems. You need a plant pathologist to make a proper diagnosis, and if the infection is bad, removal is the only "cure" for the tree. Some viruses probably infect most fruits most of the time, but fortunately are not lethal or even noticeable sometimes, other than through a decline in production or fruit size, a size that may seem "normal" to the grower or to the area.

Phony peach is a recurring, troublesome disease in the southeastern peach-growing regions of the nation that shows the complexity of viral problems. Scientists now believe it is caused by a microorganism of the *Rickettsia* genus that can be carried from tree to tree as a parasite of certain leafhoppers. But the microorganism seems primarily associated with the tree roots, not the top, and whatever the vector, the disease is presumed to be viral in nature. Scientists know that it is present in most wild plums and advise not growing any plums near peaches where phony peach is a problem.

When infected, a tree's growth is stunted, the leaves are a deeper green than normal, the tree blooms earlier than usual, and fruit is abnormally small and poor tasting. Trees must be removed to keep the disease from spreading. This includes pulling up and removing the roots, too.

If wild plums are the source of the problem, it makes me wonder sometimes if the plant families may not be at war with each other occasionally. For centuries the wild plums have proliferated in the South. Plant collectors who are members of the North American Fruit Explorers tell me that some of the wild plums are very delicious, very worthy of propagation and development, but that most of the good ones have been destroyed by the onslaught of civilization. Maybe the wild plums are trying to tell us something. We are ignoring the wild plum that through its long evolution established a secure niche in the natural ecology of the region. We substitute in its place the foreign peach, which is attacked by at least 40 viruses, not to mention innumerable bugs and fungi. The peach is presumed to be a much higher quality fruit to human taste, and so it warrants the expenditure of millions of dollars. The result? No good wild plum varieties have been saved and developed (all the universities I know of who had wild plum breeding programs have bulldozed under their germ plasm), and no good peaches exist in our stores, either. I can vouch for one thing: A good wild plum has better taste by far than any supermarket peach I've tried to bite into in the last ten years. If I were a Chickasaw plum, I'd fight back, too.

PEACH, PEAR, AND PLUM DECLINE

"Decline" has become an easy malapropism for "we don't know what this disease is." Pear decline is now serious in the Northwest. When Old Home pear, a rather low-quality pioneer pear from Illinois, is used as a rootstock, the trees seem to survive decline better. The regular commercial varieties on oriental or French (quince) rootstocks seem particularly susceptible. Peach decline has been bad in the Southeast where it is sometimes called peach short-life because trees are dying well before their time. Peach tree short-life is thought to be caused by a virus spread by certain root-feeding nematodes. For awhile, declining vigor of peach trees was thought to be associated with bacterial canker, which leads to a condition generally referred to as gummosis. But gummosis is another of those important-sounding words that can describe any number of conditions in which gummy substances are oozing from the tree.

Scientists have recently discovered that the principal kind of pear "decline" disease in the West is caused not by a virus at all but by an organism called a mycoplasma. Since antibiotics sometimes cure animal diseases caused by mycoplasmas, they've injected tetracycline directly into the infected tree trunks after fruit harvest. Transfusions repeated over two or three years brought improvement to thousands of trees. But since the disease is being transmitted by pear psylla, the long-range effectiveness of the antibiotic transfusions is still in question. It seems more likely that resistant rootstocks are a cheaper solution in the long run.

Viruses remain a mystery. Canadian pathologists reported a few years ago that they had discovered two Newton apple trees planted in 1935 that were entirely free of all common apple viruses, an extremely unusual situation. The Newton variety has been in existence at least for 200 years and there is no satisfactory explanation as to how these trees could remain virus-free for that long, *if* viruses spread naturally. The scientists suggest, as other scientists have noted before, that perhaps viruses do not spread naturally.

If they do not, then man is spreading them, either directly or inadvertently, through his manipulation of the environment.

PART III

ENJOYING THE HARVEST

CHAPTER 13

THE APPLE FAMILY

In dividing fruits and nuts into categories for the convenience of the reader, I hope, I hesitate even to tiptoe over the finer points of the classification system that has occupied so much of horticulturists' time since the days of Aristotle. My categories are not necessarily perfect according to botanical correctness, but there's method in my seeming madness.

All of the common fruits, in the North if not the South, basically belong to the rose family. But these fruits are divided into at least two distinct branches, no pun intended: "pome" fruit and "stone" or "drupe" fruit. The pome group consists mainly of apples, pears, and quince, while the stone group embraces cherries, peaches, plums, and apricots. The differences between the two groups, without getting too technical, are obvious: pome fruits have edible flesh around clusters of seeds in carpels inside cores, while stone fruits have one pit or seed per fruit (the actual seed is the kernel inside the pit).

Instead of talking about pome fruit, I prefer to use the term "apple family" to include other closely related fruits not generally thought of as pome fruit. I include them for the practical reason that they are generally susceptible to the same diseases and pests as the apple and may respond to some of the same management techniques that the apple responds to. For exam-

260

ple, when you know that apple and loquat are related, you are not surprised to learn that codling moth attacks both plants. When you know that serviceberry and apple are related, you are not surprised when both are attacked by the same fungal diseases. When you know that pear and hawthorn are closely related, you are not surprised that someone has succeeded in grafting pear to hawthorn.

The apple family consists, then, for purposes of the home grove-owner, of the following food trees: apple and crab apple of the *Malus* genus; pear of the *Pyrus* genus; hawthorn of the *Crataegus* genus; saskatoon and serviceberry (also called shadblow, sarvistree, and Juneberry) of the *Amelanchier* genus; quince of the *Cydonia* genus; medlar of the *Mespilus* genus; loquat of the *Eriobotrya* genus; and many shrubby trees such as mountain ash whose fruits play supportive roles in feeding wildlife and birds in the home grove.

APPLES AND CRAB APPLES

Apples are the most reliable of the high-quality fruits for northern groves, and now that warm climate apples such as Granny Smith are being introduced into this country, the fruit can be grown nearly everywhere there is sufficient rainfall or irrigation. Although afflicted with many pests, the apple in its range is by and large less susceptible to its enemies than other domesticated fruit, except for some citrus. But its chief advantage to the home grower, it seems to me, is the amazing variety in which the apple is available: varieties early and late; varieties so distinct in taste one from another as to seem like different fruits; varieties durable enough to last even in common storage so that it is possible through skilled management on the homestead to enjoy fresh apples nine to ten months a year.

In earlier years, these advantages were appreciated more than they are today. Even 30 years ago Americans in the North could not enjoy the amazing variety of fruit that travels from far away which they now enjoy all winter long. Instead, they had their special apples for eating fresh in summer, fall, and winter; their special blends of juices for cider, applejack, and vinegar; their favorites for baking, for stewing, for pies, for jellies, and for butters.

Illus. 13-1—Apple (Baldwin).

What we lost in transition was not only a lot of good homemade pies but also the varieties of apples that made those foods so good then. Apple products today often seem so bland by comparison. Fortunately, the home-grove movement is bringing back many of these older varieties. All we have to do now is reacquaint ourselves with their peculiar and particular advantages and disadvantages.

Which varieties are *really* the choicest? You might as well ask which is better, Ford or Chevrolet. *Tot capita, tot sententia*—as many heads, as many opinions—or perhaps, as many taste buds, as many opinions. I was once persuaded to be a taste panel judge of apple varieties grown by members of the North American Fruit Explorers, a good-natured contest they hold in connection with their annual meetings. There were a great many more varieties involved than I, at the time, knew existed. I tasted all afternoon, eating bits of cheese between apple slices to clear my taste buds. I don't recall which varieties "won" the contest, anymore. Nor do I have a distinct impression of liking any one of them significantly more than the others—they were almost all flavorful. But what I do remember, what in fact came almost as a shocking revelation, was the degree of difference and distinctiveness in flavors in the many old and all-but-forgotten varieties. This difference is what we have been losing in commercial apples, which yearly become more standardized for marketing convenience.

I think, therefore, that it is fruitless (again my apologies for the pun) to try to assemble even a group of the best-tasting apples. Nor do I think it makes too much sense to argue over which varieties are the best for cooking, best for pies, or best for cider. Instead, you must do your own tasting and select accordingly, being mindful that flavor is not the only criterion of taste—texture enters into it, too. Also be aware that a variety may produce better flavor if grown in one region rather than another. With those two caveats, the following *general* rules may be helpful.

1. Apples vary in flavor depending on their tartness—their acid content. The more acid in the apple, the tarter, and the better it will maintain its flavor in cooking. Acid apples generally "cook down" better than sub-acid apples. So Red and Yellow Delicious are rarely used as cooking apples because they are low in acid. However, because Red Delicious apples have very distinctive tastes of their own that some people like, they have become the leading eating apple, for better or for worse. (Actually, some strains of Red Delicious, picked ripe from the tree, are truly delicious despite my nasty remarks to the contrary. It is only because new strains of Red Delicious have been bred to a skin so tough that they take a shine like leather, then held in CO_2 storage until they taste like a wet dishrag, and turn brown inside after three days on the grocery shelf, that I malign them.) For what it's worth, the best apples for cooking in most opinions seem to be the ones of medium acidity, and these are the very ones that are also the favorite eating apples of people I have asked. (See list of favorites below.)

2. Early apples (early anything) do not have the full flavor of full-season apples that ripen more slowly through a longer period of sunlight. I've been told there's an old variety (unavailable from commercial sources) called Irish Peach that is an exception, but I doubt it.

3. Just because an apple is an old favorite of King Louis the Whatever from Wayback does not mean it is necessarily any better tasting than the latest offering from the USDA horticulturists. Nor is the contrary necessarily true. Many new, improved varieties taste blander than what we have now, because these apples are not developed for taste, but for looks.

4. In my opinion and in that of many other orchardists, the better tasting a fruit is, the more it is attacked by bugs and fungal disease. This is true of pears more so than apples, although good apples suffer increased attack, too. So when you decide to set out some of those old-fashioned varieties that taste so good but are no longer grown commercially, be ready for some

263

disappointments. Though the only reason the old variety may have been abandoned was because of its color or lack of color, that variety may also have been very susceptible to some pest. Cox Orange Pippin may be the best apple nature ever gave us, but it is prone to disease. The English raise it, anyway, and some U.S. backyarders have good luck with it, but be forewarned. Tompkins King and Grimes Golden, two high-dessert-quality apples, are subject to killing collar rot and should be grafted onto other rootstock. Wolf River, an old favorite cooking apple, likes to rot on the tree. Baldwin is especially susceptible to bitter rot. Chenango Strawberry rots on the tree rather than ripening, according to the old *Five Acres and Independence* by M. G. Kains (New York, Greenburg, 1935). Jonathan, a good modern variety, gets fireblight easily. Some apples have been abandoned by commercial growers mostly because they won't bear heavily, or they bear only biennially. Esopus Spitzenburg, an old apple much praised by collectors today, is a shy bearer, which may not be a disadvantage to the home grove-owner.

5. The later the apple takes to mature, the better it will keep in storage. There are probably exceptions, but that is generally the case. Yellow Newtown doesn't ripen fully until it has been in storage for a couple of months.

6. An apple that the trade says is good only for cooking is likely not really great for anything. This is my prejudice backed by the biases of a few other people familiar with baking and cooking apples. York and Rome apples are cooking apples, and they are okay, I guess, but because of Yorks and Romes I at one time decided I'd rather eat oranges and bananas. But the point I want to make is that Yorks or Romes can be great apples if the cook who is using them is a great cook. Or to put it more clearly, the apple *variety* is not the main ingredient of a good apple *pie*. The crust is. If the crust is no good, no apple can save the pie. But with a good lard crust, almost any apple is tolerably good. There is no use in growing apples if you are not going to eat homemade apple pies, and there is no using eating homemade apple pies if you do not know how to make a good lard crust. You cannot state the good life in a simpler equation. You cannot buy good lard (or you seldom can, anyway), so raise a pig or make friends with someone who does. Feed the pig cull apples. As John Williams Streeter said at the turn of the century (*The Fat of the Land*): "The orchard is better for the hens and hogs and cows and they are better for the orchard. These industries fit into each other like the folding of hands . . ."

Nevertheless, I am going to list a number of varieties that, year in and year out, apple fanciers mention as the really "great" apples, the apple equivalent of baseball's Hall of Fame, so to speak. For some of the information on these varieties, I'm indebted to the wonderful catalog of Southmeadow Fruit Gardens that Robert Nitschke puts out, and who sells many, if not most, of the old varieties mentioned here. Another source of old apples is the Worcester County Horticultural Society. (See the Appendix for both addresses.) All apples listed below are what knowledgeable people call, individually, "one of the best."

Cox Orange Pippin is considered perhaps *the* finest apple in other parts of the world. But since it is a rusty orange in color rather than shiny red, Americans mistrust it. Nitschke says Cox grows fine for him in Michigan, but the variety is disease-prone. Many seedlings of Cox are favorite varieties in their own right, as is its parent, Ribstone Pippin. This is another indication of my contention elsewhere in this book that it is worthwhile to grow a few seedlings every year. Cox seems to be an excellent variety to work with in this regard.

Roxbury Russet is a late winter apple of medium acid and distinctive flavor. Greenish to yellowish brown, it's often mentioned as a good cider apple, also.

Yellow Newton or Newton Pippin is yellow with a pinkish blush and ripens after storage. It's best from February to May, and is a very renowned apple in all historical treatments.

Tompkins King originated in New Jersey but is considered a good apple for the Midwest. When I ask, this is the apple I most often hear referred to as the best tasting.

Calville Blanc D'Hiver or White Winter Calville is grown in France and served in good restaurants as a dessert. It is pale green with light red spots on the side facing the sun. Nitschke says it contains more vitamin C than oranges.

Esopus Spitzenburg was Tom Jefferson's favorite apple, and it has been a favorite, at least of writers on the subject, ever since. It is bright orange red with gray and yellow spots, and thought to be the parent of Jonathan. This is a late apple and a choice dessert variety.

Ashmead's Kernel, an ugly-looking apple of excellent taste, does well in the Midwest.

Fameuse or Snow is one of my favorites, though I know people who think it's only so-so. It's a sweet apple, but aromatic.

Golden Russet is similar to Roxbury Russet.

Westfield-Seek-No-Further is a creamy yellow apple

striped with dull red. It's very much an old favorite, distinctively flavored (sharp), and with an aroma all its own.

There is another class of apples often referred to as the old "sweet" apples that is distinctive enough from the preceding (except for Fameuse) to merit its own classification. Though sweet, these apples are not necessarily low in acid content and so, unlike Red and Yellow Delicious, they can make good cooking apples. Tolman Sweet is an example of this kind of apple, a late apple that has been a longtime favorite. Sweet Winesap is another. Pound Sweet is one of the best known of the class.

Among the very tart apples, Duchess is best known and a favorite of those who like very tart apples. Duchess is considered too tart for a dessert apple, but as Lewis Hill points out in an article in *Organic Gardening and Farming* (September, 1971), in New England restaurants Duchess apple pie is often priced higher than an ordinary pie. He also says the Duchess is more insect and disease resistant than other varieties he grows.

Of the apples still fairly easy to buy in nurseries, the following always get high ratings:

Northern Spy is a very old variety, still going strong, although the trees on standard rootstock may take ten years to begin bearing. It is worth waiting for. On dwarf roots, it bears much sooner.

Rhode Island Greening is an excellent all-around apple. If it were red, it might be tops in the market.

Macoun is a McIntosh-type apple. All McIntosh are good eating apples but do not store well. Macoun happens to be my favorite. It must be picked a little early. Once completely ripe, it loses taste and snappiness, in my opinion.

Stayman Winesap apples are excellent keepers, and in my house are considered the best apples for all purposes. My wife says if she could have only one apple it would be a Winesap. Old Virginia Winesap is a variety for which I can find no nursery source. It makes far and away the best applesauce I have ever tasted—at least if the applesauce is made by Mrs. Rosalind Noble who, with husband Harrell, knows all about living in a grove of food trees in southern Ohio.

Grimes Golden is again becoming available. An excellent dessert apple that's fine for cooking, too.

Granny Smith is reputed to be the best all-around apple for warm climates, and good in the North where frost does not come early.

Mutsu is a Japanese apple (called Crispin in England, where

it is a great favorite) of rather recent origin that is highly praised by growers and gourmets, too.

HARVESTING HINTS

Taste in apples often depends critically on time of harvest, as pointed out in the case of Macoun. Only experience can teach you when each variety in your climate should be picked, but general ripening dates are helpful (see Chap. 2). Horticulturists have tried to use pressure gauges to determine with mathematical precision the proper time for harvesting apples. Generally speaking, when an apple will not resist 12 pounds of pressure, it is by these calculations "ripe." At a resistance of 15 pounds of pressure, the apple is suitable for picking, depending more or less on variety. Again according to this method, many of the better-keeping apples should be picked at a resistance of 18 to 20 pounds of pressure for storing.

There are problems with this method. Fruits of many varieties do not ripen all at once, so pressure testing of a few apples won't necessarily give readings that apply to all of the apples on the tree that day. Testing, therefore, is impractical. Besides, people's tastes differ. In July, I like to eat Yellow Transparents that are still green.

Other indicators of apple ripeness useful to the small grove-owner are as follows:

1. Seeds turn from milky white to dark brown.
2. Flesh tastes sweet, not a coat-your-tongue starchiness.
3. On yellow varieties, the skin color will begin to "break" from green to pale yellow.
4. A few apples (the ripest) may drop.

In picking apples, especially if they are not fully ripe, care must be taken, or else you will strip off some of next year's fruit buds along with the stem. Or you can pull the stem out altogether, which can shorten storage life if decay sets in where the stem pulled out. You should sort of *lift* an apple off the branch rather than pull it. Lift with a gentle twist and a flick of thumb or finger against the stem. There's a little knack to it that's easy to learn. If the apple won't come off with that maneuver, it most likely is too green yet.

If you are picking from the ground, you can pick into a bucket or even a box. *Lay* the fruit in the container; do not drop it even from a short height. Apples bruise very easily. Up in a tree, you should pick into a bag over your shoulder so that you have both hands free. When emptying your sack into a box or other receptacle, do not pour the apples in. Gently turn the bag upside down in the box and *slowly* pull the bag away from the apples to reduce bumping to an absolute minimum.

The long-handled cage pickers that allow you to pluck individual apples from the ground are okay if you are physically unable to climb a ladder, but cage pickers are otherwise a slow and unsatisfactory way to harvest.

Using a ladder to harvest fruit is more difficult than harvesting from a dwarf tree where no ladder is needed. But a few simple lessons in ladder handling will reduce the job considerably. Place the bottom of the ladder against a solid object or, better, have a partner hold it. Then, beginning at the other end, walk the ladder to a vertical position, hand over hand. Move a ladder from one part of a tree to another, or from tree to tree, in a vertical position. Once up, a ladder is fairly easy to move about so long as you don't let it tip over beyond its center of gravity. In placing the ladder in the tree, always approach the tree with the *edge* of the ladder facing the branches, not the broadside. The edge can easily be slipped between outside branches to a desired position, where it can then be turned and leaned, broadside, against a branch. Withdraw the ladder by again turning it edgewise to the tree.

SUSCEPTIBLE AND RESISTANT APPLES

References to susceptible and resistant varieties have been made throughout this book. The summation that follows should be read with a grain of salt or two. As any plant pathologist will tell you, there is no such thing as an apple completely immune to fireblight, and resistance can be a sometimes observation. Even the new scab-immune apples are not immune to all types of scab. Resistance may be seen in a variety in one area and not in another. That is why reliable apples for one area may not always be listed for another area, as noted in Chapter 2. Nevertheless, the following lists, which have been drawn from many sources, including word of mouth, may be a useful guide where conditions are normal. In all cases, it's better to grow wild seedlings or grafts of good quality fruit that have survived many years in your area.

Resistant to Scab
> Liberty, MacFree, Nova Easy-Gro, Prima, Priscilla, and Sir Prize are the scab-immune varieties that have been released for market. More are on the way. In addition, Adanac, Akane, Astrachan, Baldwin, Earliblaze, Golden Delicious, Jonathan, Macoun, Red Baron, Spartan, State Fair, Transparent, Tydeman's Early Red, and Wagener have some scab resistance. Chehalis, Grimes Golden, Jonafree, and York Imperial have high resistance.

Highly Susceptible to Scab
> McIntosh, Northern Spy, Red Delicious, Rome Beauty, and Winesap are the most susceptible of currently grown varieties. Possibly, many other of the old varieties also are highly susceptible, though we have no reliable new data because these varieties aren't grown widely now.

Resistant to Fireblight
> Liberty is highly resistant, according to the New York State Fruit Testing Association at Geneva, New York. Ben Davis, Black Twig, Grimes Golden, Northwest Greening, and Stayman Winesap are somewhat resistant.

Highly Susceptible to Fireblight
> Beacon or Duchess, Golden Delicious, Jonathan, Sir Prize, Wealthy Rome, and York. Any tree on M 9 or M 26 dwarfing rootstock becomes more susceptible, since these rootstocks themselves are blight susceptible.

Resistant to Cedar Rust
> Liberty, Prima, and Priscilla.

Partially Resistant to Cedar Rust
> Duchess, McIntosh family, Red Delicious family, and Winesap.

Highly Susceptible to Cedar Rust
> Golden Delicious and Rome.

Resistant to Powdery Mildew
> Golden Delicious and Liberty.

Highly Susceptible to Powdery Mildew
> Cortland, Jonathan, McIntosh, and Rome.

MAKING CIDER

Of the many uses of apples other than eating out of hand and table desserts, making cider is still probably the favorite. Indications are that in earlier days cider and stronger alcoholic beverages made from apples were the most important products of the orchard. Certainly earlier generations went to far more trouble than we do today to brew various fermentations. What we call sweet cider they would have recognized (barely) as bland apple juice. What they called cider was closer to brandy or at least applejack, a kind of apple wine people hereabouts make by adding raisins and brown sugar to cider and letting the mixture ferment under controlled wine-making conditions. Here's one of the simpler recipes, from a 1770 book by Alexander Hogg, reprinted in a facsimile edition in 1976 by Longship Press, Crooked Lane, Nantucket, MA 02554, called *The Farmer's Wife or The Complete Country Housewife:*

Procure a number of codlings, as juicy as you can get, but not too sweet, nor quite ripe; let them be laid in hay or straw that is very dry. When they have laid three days, cut them in quarters and take out the hearts, then let them be bruised and put into clean water, with a few blades of mace and a handful of the tops of rosemary; mash all these together, and put to every 12 gallons, 2 quarts of Rhenish wine; when it has boiled two hours, let it be drawn off and set to cool, and it will be fit for use almost as soon as it is cold.

What we make for cider today is unfermented apple juice. Taste will vary dramatically with the kind of apples used. A mixture or blend of apples of varying acidity usually makes the best cider, but what blend you use will be the result of the trial and error of your own experience with the apples you have. The mildly acid apples that taste best to you will make the most satisfactory cider. Or, mix both acid and low-acid apples. Green apples, that is, unripe apples, make bland cider. Low-acid apples alone (such as Delicious) make even blander cider. Overripe apples may have lost the most efficient portion of juice they once had. Bruised apples, if the majority of all apples used, will make the cider tend to turn to hard cider too fast, or worse, turn it sour if the weather is fairly warm. Dirty apples will not help the taste, and sometimes they make it worse. On the other hand, you need not be too fussy—your cider apples don't have to be perfect, nor will an occasional wormy apple hurt. But by the same token, the cleaner and the higher in quality the apples are, the better the cider will taste. As with computers: garbage in, garbage out.

Apples must be mashed, ground, or otherwise pulped before pressing. You can use one of those old hand-cranked corn shellers, or a tractor-powered hammer mill. Most cider lovers buy a regular press with grinder atop it. Many are on the market. In our case, five neighborhood families went together to buy one. This way, the not inconsiderable cost is shared, and cider-making days tend to become relaxed parties nearly as enjoyable as the cider itself.

In most areas, you can haul your apples to a large commercial press and, at minimal cost, get your cider squeezed without the hard work of doing it yourself. Cider mills are excellent places for asking others for cider recipes. One old farmer told me the best way was to mix in about 10% pear juice, something I intend to do if my pear trees ever grow large enough to give us extra fruit for such experiments.

We love cider fresh and sweet and drink most of what we make before it gets past that sharp, tangy "beady" stage of sweet cider. One small barrel we keep for "hard" (dry) cider and vinegar; the rest that doesn't get consumed quickly, we freeze in plastic gallon jugs to stop fermentation. We never use preservatives or pasteurization to arrest fermentation. The warmer the room temperature, the faster the cider will ferment. That's why we make the biggest share of our cider very late in the year (around November 1). The cider barrel in the garage stays fairly cold in November for most years. What cider remains over winter freezes some, and then thaws, and the result is sometimes very good hard cider (if you like hard cider) occasionally approaching almost a champagne taste.

When fermentation is allowed to continue, hard cider becomes vinegar. The liquid will look quite unappetizing as it works, developing a cloudy "must" or a layer of scum, or both. This is the "mother" of vinegar and can be saved to put into the next batch to insure quick fermentation for vinegar. Strain through several layers of cheesecloth to get a clear vinegar.

When working with fermenting juices of any kind, leave room in your containers for the liquid to bubble up and expand. During the time of most active fermentation, allow some means of escape for gases, too, or you may get an explosion. I don't fiddle with fancy air locks, anymore. I just fill my keg about four-fifths of the way up, and leave the stopper not quite tight in the bunghole on the topside. The keg lies on its side with a wooden spigot at the head of the barrel for filling glasses or jugs.

APPLE BUTTER

Apple butter has been a mainstay dessert in farm homes since the time of Johnny Appleseed. Making it is arduous but worth the effort. Apples are peeled and cored (using hand-operated peelers and corers makes the job much easier), then sliced and mixed with cider at a ratio of about one part cider to two parts apples. This mixture is then boiled. After it begins to thicken, you need to stir almost constantly to keep the contents from burning. The boiling and stirring reduce cider and apples to a consistency of a smooth sauce or butter.

The best way to make apple butter is the old-fashioned way, for which you need a copper kettle, a pile of wood to burn, and a long-handled wooden stirrer so you can stand back from the fire and stir the butter without getting blistered. There are two kinds of stirrers: one's a simple paddle affixed at a right angle to the end of the handle; the other is a more sophisticated set of blades that churn around the kettle with the back-and-forth action of pulling and pushing the handle. The first is quite equal to the task and easy to make or find, still, at farm sales. Copper kettles are expensive, new or antique. Copper seems to have been used regularly, although iron is sometimes mentioned. Aluminum leaches into cider, giving it an off-taste, and perhaps maybe even making it dangerous.

At the apple butter festival at Barner Grove Lutheran Church near Liverpool, Pennsylvania, the people make 250 gallons at a crack, boiling all night and finishing at about noon the next day. Here the practice is to boil about half of the water out of the cider before adding the apple slices. They use 40 bushels of sliced apples to about 700 gallons of cider. Some apple-butter makers add the apples as soon as the cider begins boiling. According to the method described in *Stocking Up* (Emmaus, Pa., Rodale Press, 1977), you do not necessarily have to peel, slice, and core the apples, either, if you strain out seeds, etc., later on. Some recipes call for adding honey or a bit of cinnamon, cloves, and allspice to taste. Some even add quince and orange peels for flavoring.

According to Robert Nitschke's catalog (mentioned earlier), orchards of Pumpkin Sweet apple were set out in early Ohio times for the purpose of producing large quantities of apple butter.

DRYING APPLES

Apple slices can be run onto a string with a large darning needle; the strings are then hung to dry in a warm attic or near a stove for a few days, then the slices can be bagged and stored indefinitely. Dried apples were our usual winter snack when I was a child. They make good pies and other desserts, too, when reconstituted with a little water. Years ago the old Fall Russet was considered to be a good apple for drying.

Also, apples can be sliced and dried in the sun under cheesecloth. The cheesecloth keeps bugs off the fruit, although pioneers believed that insects hastened the drying by eating the juicy moisture from the fruit. Really serious fruit-lovers of yesterday built "dry houses" in their orchards—small buildings about 8 feet square with a wood stove in the middle, and with the walls lined completely with shelves. Here they dried all fruits, including cherries, by the heat of the stove, which, in such a small room, efficiently dried considerable amounts in a few days.

Solar dryers and fueled dryers of a wide assortment are available today. Small solar dryers are simplicity itself. My son built one with a wood back, a wood bottom, and a slanting-glass face, much like a small cold frame. With the sun shining brightly, the box easily dries a batch of any fruit (strawberries, we find to our surprise, make the most delectable dried fruit) in two to three days.

CRAB APPLES

There are over 600 species and cultivars of crab apple in the northeastern part of the United States alone. For ornamental purposes, you have many choices in shape—columnar, round, oval, or flat-headed, if that's important to you. Fruits run to every shade of yellow, orange, and red, and blossoms from white through pink to red to dark red. Crabs are especially desirable because, in addition to their lovely blossoms in spring, dense foliage in summer, and fruit that often makes excellent jelly, the brightly colored fruit hangs on into winter. This can mean that your tree will be decorated in December with a flock of cedar waxwings, or even Bohemian waxwings, eating gluttonously away—a sight sure to gladden the most winter-depressed heart.

Crabs are also one of the best pollenators of most other apple varieties.

The problem with crabs is that they are beset by all of the pests that plague apples. Some commonly available varieties or strains are very susceptible to fireblight and scab, the nemesis of the apple business. Fortunately there are ongoing programs at our universities to develop resistant strains. The results of a multi-state survey coordinated by Penn State in the 1970s revealed that many of the highly publicized crabs were not resistant to all five of the leading fungal rascals: scabs, fireblight, powdery mildew, cedar-apple rust and frogeye leaf spot. Those recommended as outstanding varieties with resistance to these five diseases include:

Adams, pink flowered (single) with carmine red fruit about half an inch in diameter, maturing in September–October. The report (1976) gave Adams Nursery, Inc., Box 525, Westfield, MA 01685, as a source of stock.

Beverly, with single pink blossoms and bright red fruit that hangs through winter. The fruit is almost too small to be practical as a human food source. Sources given: Studebaker Nurseries, Inc., New Carlisle, OH 45344; Sherman Nursery Co., Charles City, IA 50616; Eisler Nurseries, 219 E. Pearl St., P.O. Box 70, Butler, PA 16001.

Centennial, with single white flowers. The fruit is attractive bright red over yellow and about 2 inches in diameter. Centennial makes a good cooking apple, and so should be the first choice of the home grove-owner looking for both food and

Illus. 13-2—Crab Apple.

ornamental beauty. Sources given: Mount Arbor Nurseries, P.O. Box 129, Shenandoah, IA 51601; Boyd Nursery Co., Inc., P.O. Box 71, McMinnville, TN 37110.

Robinson, with single crimson blossoms. The fruit is red and about ⅝ inch in diameter. Source given: C. M. Hobbs and Sons, Inc., 9300 W. Washington, Indianapolis, IN 46231.

In old orchards you will often find crab apples of a fairly large size that were used primarily for spiced apples. A spiced apple lover I know insists that only these old varieties make really good spiced apples. If you keep your eyes open as you drive around in the fall, you can usually locate such trees. Most of

Photo 13-1—Crab Apple Tree—Growing almost to jungle density, crab apple trees thrive in many of the abandoned pastures north of Philadelphia. Rodale Press photograph.

them have to be scab and fireblight resistant or they would have died long ago.

In some areas there are many wild crab apples from seeds scattered in abandoned fields by birds eating from ornamental plantings. In the area just north of Philadelphia there are old pastures that have become jungles of crab apples of many strains, some of them excellent for cooking jelly, and even not too bad for eating out of hand.

Some crabs are extremely hardy, like the old Dolgo crab used as hardy rootstock for apples. They will grow in extremely cold northern and plains regions where even the hardiest apples have a tough time.

Crabs incline to heavy sucker growth and dense branching. To keep a tree looking nice, you need to prune hard—although the pruning seems to make the tree sucker even worse.

PEARS

The most popular pears for eating out of hand or for desserts are those that ripen in the fall. A second kind is the small Seckel-type pear that, in some areas, is hard to find in commercial trade, although some are delicious. The third type is the winter pear, so hard at harvesttime you can barely bite into it. In storage, winter pears ripen and can be used for cooking.

Examples of the first type are the Bartlett, Anjou, Bosc, and Comice (slow to reach bearing age—12 to 18 years) of commercial trade. Others are Clapp's Favorite, Parker, Flemish Beauty, Lincoln, Ewart, Aurora, Gorham, Orient, Maxine, Moonglow, and many others. For the home garden, Dr. R. A. Norton at the Northwestern Washington Research and Extension Unit at Mt. Vernon recommends for that area Aurora, Bartlett, Comice, and Elderado. The University of Kentucky recommends Maxine for Kentucky. The New York Agricultural Experiment Station was recommending, in 1971, Aurora and Gorham for the home garden. Dr. Howard Rollins, Jr., at Virginia Polytechnic Institute likes Moonglow, Magness, and Maxine for the backyard in his area.

Almost all horticulturists, at least in the East, recommend Seckel pears for the backyard, in addition to those listed above. Seckels are small, juicy, a little gritty, but delicious. Trees will last forever—my father-in-law has one that has appeared to be dying for 20 years and is believed to be nearly 100 years old. Its

276

Illus. 13-3—Pear.

fruit is incomparable, better than the taste of the Seckel I grew. Different strains of Seckel, or soil and climate, may account for varying taste. Chapin is another Seckel-type pear recommended for home orchards. It is earlier and larger and not quite as good. Some Seckels appear to be resistant to fireblight.

Winter pears are Kieffer and Old Home. Neither are much good for eating, but they make good canned fruit. Both are extremely hardy, and Kieffer will grow in the South, too. Dumont, Winter Nelis, and Dana Hovey are other winter pears of a somewhat better quality recommended for the home orchard. Old Home is resistant to fireblight and pear decline, and is being used for rootstocks and interstems more than as an eating variety due to its small fruit. Since many pears are not completely compatible with the quince that is used as a dwarfing rootstock for pear, Old Home is grafted as an interstem between quince roots and varietal scion, thereby imparting a degree of fireblight resistance to the variety. In the home grove, it is my feeling that Kieffer ought to be grown because it is so trouble-free. Kieffer is gritty and bland eaten raw, but canned it's as good as any pear. In addition, there is no foliage more beautiful than a Kieffer's, flaming orange even into November here, when there are few trees still in leaf.

But though Kieffer is trouble-free, and Seckel is a little mouthful of honey, there is nothing to compete with the taste of a properly ripened Bartlett-type pear. Harvesting pears correctly is the key to proper ripening. Unlike most backyard fruit, the pear will not reach its optimum taste if allowed to hang on the tree until it's ripe. And if picked too green, it will be gritty. (Seckels are not so critical in this regard.) A Bartlett pear is picked when it is *nearly* ripe. The color of the pear is the best indication. When the background skin color changes from a dark green to a light, yellowish green, the pear is about ready. The fruit stem should separate from the spur with a gentle *lifting* twist. The fruit itself should still feel fairly hard. You know when the time is near if you know the number of days from blossoming to "maturity," information that is usually included in catalogs from good nurseries. Here are a few examples: Clapp's Favorite, 112 to 114 days; Bartlett, 122 to 125; Flemish Beauty, 126 to 129; Seckel, 138 to 148; Kieffer, 145 to 148. Climate—a spate of unusually cold or hot weather—can throw these reckonings off and so are only general indications.

But proper harvesting time is only half the secret to a good pear. If you want to eat them as soon as possible, ripen them in a room where the temperature is between 65° and 75°F and humidity is about 80 to 85%. To maintain such high humidity, pear-lovers sometimes drape a wet cloth over the ripening pears. When the pears are to be stored for winter use, the proper temperature is 30°F, too cold for most refrigerators or common storage rooms, with 80% humidity. When the pears are taken out of this storage and kept at room temperature and high humidity, they ripen in 10 to 14 days to a quality as good as a "fresh" pear.

Since most homeowners do not have storage facilities just right for pears, they do the best they can. Keep the pears as cold as you can and, more important, keep the humidity high. Your pears will still last until Christmas. Winter pears, such as Kieffer, will last longer without the optimum temperature and humidity, but they do better in cooler, humid storage. Pears will pick up odors from onions, other vegetables, or mold. Store them in a sealed polyethylene bag to keep out odors. If the storage room is very much above 38°F, though, the pears may mold in the sealed plastic.

A pear is ready to eat if the flesh at the stem end gives slightly when you press on it firmly. The stem end ripens first. Of the better-tasting pears, Bartlett, Bosc, Anjou, Devoe, and Winter Nelis keep well. Nancy Bubel, in her book *Root Cellaring* (Emmaus, Pa., Rodale Press, 1979), says Clapp's Favorite will not keep at all.

Manage pear trees as you do apples. Pruning is usually much less of a job with pears. Most trees, especially on quince, like to grow straight up rather than out, and you may want to use limb spreaders on the branches.

As I said, old-timers mixed a little pear juice with their apple cider. Or you can make pear cider. The ancient beverage, perry, was fermented pear juice along with the juice of a few crab apples. After squeezing and straining the juice, yeast was added and allowed to work for a few days. Then the perry was racked off and bottled. If you try this, don't seal the bottles tight until you perfect your methods, if ever. If the juice continues to ferment, you might be the victim of a minor explosion due to the tightly lidded bottle.

HAWTHORNS

Hundreds of hawthorn cultivars exist, most of the domestic ones being susceptible to fireblight. Fireblight does not seem to infect hawthorns when they are used in isolated ornamental plantings, and so people do not think the trees are susceptible. But the disease ran rampant a few years ago at the Ohio Agricultural Research and Development Center at Wooster. Even the experts couldn't control it. All the Upright Single Seed Hawthorns and Autumn Glory strains on trial there were killed. Downy Hawthorn and Lavalle Hawthorn were damaged.

A new variety, Ohio Pioneer, appears to have high resistance. This is a thornless variety. White Thorn, the wild thorn pest of our pastures, does not get fireblight as often (unfortunately, most farmers would add) as hawthorn rust, which is very similar to cedar-apple rust. Wild White Thorn is a beautiful tree, produces a heavy fruit crop that at least 19 species of bird eat, and can be used to make an impenetrable hedge in the manner of European hawthorn hedgerows. It likes to take over pasture fields, however, and is therefore the bane of farmers everywhere. Once rooted, the trees are almost impossible to kill by mowing. In days when farmers cared for only a few acres, there was time to lay out and maintain beautiful hedge fences and, at the same time, keep them from spreading into pastures. Today, there seems to be no time for such amenities, and our lives are the meaner for it.

There's a substantial body of evidence that the hawthorn fruit is good for the heart, especially the white-berried European

Illus. 13-4—Hawthorn.

hawthorn. Flavor varies from strain to strain, from tree to tree, but in my experience none of the northern varieties can be rated as more than survival food or medicinal food. One species, *Crataegus pinnatifida,* an Asian variety commonly grown in China, does grow tasty fruit.

T. O. Warren in Mississippi, the well-known wild-fruit collector and propagator, has spent a lifetime studying and collecting wild varieties of mayhaw, the popular name for southern hawthorns. He grows about 20 varieties that he thinks have enough promise to be developed into domestic fruits. He believes there are at least 20 more deserving of culinary interest, too. "Mayhaws make a delicious jelly much prized by those of us who were brought up on it," he writes to me. "The juice will keep in the refrigerator for months and still be good for making jelly. . . . Some are good right off the tree, mellow and aromatic . . . not dry and bland like the northern kinds." Warren says that unlike domesticated fruit, our native wild types require no spraying because of resistance inbred over many centuries. Mayhaws, he says, only contract fireblight when brought close to pears and apples, and then not seriously.

Using any of the common grafts, pears can be grafted to hawthorn. The graft union will not always persist, however. As with apricot on plum, stress sometimes can cause the graft union to break.

Southmeadow Fruit Gardens, already mentioned, offers *C. succulenta,* a hawthorn long reputed to be juicy and flavorful. It is dried for winter use by western Indian tribes.

SASKATOONS AND SERVICEBERRIES

At least two members of the *Amelanchier* genus can be important fruit trees in certain regions: *Amelanchier alnifolia,* the saskatoon, a shrubby tree now being developed almost as a bush; and *A. laevis,* a small tree growing wild throughout the eastern half of the country.

The saskatoon has only recently been developed as a commercial fruit, but it was long used by Indians (for pemmican), early Plains settlers, and gardeners in modern times. The "berries" are good eaten fresh, in pies, in other desserts, canned, frozen, or as wine. The saskatoon makes a fine ornamental hedge, too; it is beautiful, very attractive to birds. Fruit size varies from about ⅜ inch up to ⅝ inch on improved cultivars. Some are white fruited but most are bluish when ripe.

The special value of the saskatoon is that it is extremely hardy, will tolerate dry northern Plains climates where few fruits grow, and is adaptable to a wide variety of soils. In its northern and dry western habitat, it so far has suffered only minor injuries from bugs and fungal diseases. *So far,* regular spray programs have been unnecessary in commercial plantings, but if history is any guide, as more orchards are established this clean situation will change. Since the fruit is native and has built-in resistance to native pests due to thousands of years of evolution, it may

Illus. 13-5—Serviceberry.

281

always remain fairly easy to manage, especially in mixed back-yard groves.

Saskatoons spread by suckering and so are easily increased. Make sure the suckers have developed their own roots before trying to transplant them. If individual plants are set about 6 feet apart, their suckering will form a solid hedge in about four years. As single shrubs or small trees, set plants about 8 feet apart in all directions and cut out suckers. Some varieties will grow up to 18 feet, but most can be kept 6 to 8 feet tall with pruning.

Remember that saskatoons are susceptible to most of the diseases that apples suffer from, especially if you try to grow them in warmer, humid regions south and east of their northern Plains and Canadian Plains habitat.

Harvest the "berries" as you would blueberries. Except for wine, the berries are best used when just barely ripe and still a little tart. Fully ripe, they have a higher sugar content for wine, less vitamin C, and are not quite as juicy or flavorful.

Some older varieties of note (new ones are coming along): Smoky grows about 8 feet tall, has large, very sweet fruit in long clusters, and suckers readily. Pembina grows up to 10 feet tall, does not sucker as much as Smoky, and has good-tasting fruit. Smoky and Pembina are two varieties most often recommended. Altaglow has very showy foliage, deep purple, red, and yellow in the fall. Berries are white. The tree grows to 18 feet and is self-sterile. The blue-fruited varieties pollenate it readily. Forestburg has larger fruit on the average than Smoky, but is not quite as flavorful.

A. laevis and *A. arborea* are various forms of a small tree known through the hills of east central United States as the sarvistree, shadbush, or shadblow, the latter two names originating because it bloomed when the shad were migrating upstream in eastern rivers. Sarvistree or serviceberry has a number of folk explanations of doubtful authenticity, one of the commonest being that it was planted at grave sites in early days as part of the funeral service.

The tree blooms beautifully in early spring, and the blue maroon fruits are fairly good eating, fresh or processed. The early fruit lures birds away from cherries and is higher in vitamin C than even citrus. In the fall, the tree's leaves change to various shades of yellow and crimson, and mine at least has proven to be extremely winter-hardy, having passed unscathed through the two worst winters on record. So far, it has not been injured by any bug or disease, either.

A. grandiflora is the type developed by plantsmen for ornamental purposes. They like to call it "apple serviceberry" since it is closely related to the apple. *A. grandiflora* needs to be pruned carefully in early stages to train it to a single stem or small tree. It has a spreading habit and should not be used in a narrow space such as a street planting, say landscapers.

In the wild, serviceberries will struggle along in partial shade, but they grow much better in full sunlight. Every back-yard grove will benefit from this early-fruiting tree.

QUINCE, MEDLAR, AND LOQUAT

Quince is a peculiar fruit, and the only species in its genus, *Cydonia*. It is hardly edible raw. Stewed quince or quince jelly is another matter, a taste distinctive enough and loved enough by some to keep this ancient tree still in vogue. So distinctive is the fruit's aroma that *Taylor's Encyclopedia of Gardening* says it should not be stored with apples or pears, its first cousins. Among devotees, the best varieties (practically the only varieties) are Orange, Smyrna, and Pineapple. The Angiers quince is the French variety used as dwarfing rootstock for pears.

Quince trees may grow up to 25 feet, although they usually are shorter. They bear regularly and sometimes heavily, and since the trees are self-fertile, one is usually enough for home use.

Illus. 13-6—Quince.

Illus. 13-7—Medlar.

Yellow when ripe, quinces will hang on the tree until after frost, but it's best to pick them a little before maturity for better keeping in storage. Though hard, the fruit bruises easily, so handle carefully.

The medlar is an old English fruit, seldom grown in this country. It does not ripen until picked in the fall and stored in a cool place. It will finally soften and turn from a greenish russet color to brown, says Nitschke's Southmeadow Fruit Gardens catalog. As with so many old and rare fruits, Nitschke does not fail to have a medlar. He sells the variety called Nottingham.

Medlars are hardy, good only for jellies and other table desserts. In merry old England, people traditionally ate medlars with wine.

Illus. 13-8—Loquat.

The loquat, *Eriobotrya japonica,* sometimes called oriental plum, Japanese plum, or Japanese medlar, grows where citrus grows. Of all the food trees that make good ornamentals, the loquat ranks at the top of the list, its evergreen and symmetrical growth a pleasant addition to any grove. Improved varieties are fine eating, I'm told. The birds like them, too, as loquats are one of the first fruits (noncitrus) to ripen in sunny California and Florida. Many varieties are available in the South. Gold Nugget is a newer one. Champaign, Tanaka, and Thales are older ones. The loquat is susceptible to codling moth and even fireblight, just as apples are. Temperatures below 20° F can kill it. Seed is available from the Redwood City Seed Company (see the Appendix for address), but only in May and June. The seed must be fresh to germinate well. A loquat can bear in three to four years from seed.

CHAPTER 14

STONE FRUITS

We find it cheaper to buy peaches from nearby commercial orchards, sometimes pick our own, can them, or go without. . . . But . . . no one should be without pie cherry trees. The sour, or pie cherry, is as reliable and foolproof as dandelion greens.
P. Alston Waring and Walter Magnes Teller, Roots in the Earth *(New York, Harper and Brothers, 1943)*

The stone fruit family, all members of the *Prunus* genus, includes all the peaches, cherries, plums, apricots, and almonds. The following list includes the species of interest to food tree growers:

Almond, *P. dulcis*
Apricot, *P. armeniaca*
Cherry plum, myrobalan plum, *P. cerasifera*
Chokecherry, *P. virginiana*
Damson plum, *P. domestica insititia*
Hansen's bush cherry, *P. besseyi*
Japanese plum, *P. salicina*
Nanking cherry, *P. tomentosa*
Peach, nectarine, *P. persica*
Plum, *P. domestica*
Sour cherry, *P. cerasus*
Sweet cherry, *P. avium*

Wild species of interest:

Beach plum, *P. maritima*
Chickasaw plum, *P. angustifolia*
Sand cherry, *P. pumila* (occasionally found in Great Lakes
region)
Various fence row plums (at one time cultured, with some
selections named Gold, Hammer, Hawkeye, Queen, Terry;
unavailable from commercial nurseries), *P. americana,
P. hortulana, P. munsoniana, P. nigra*
Wild black cherry, *P. serotina*

PEACHES AND NECTARINES

For all practical purposes, peaches and nectarines are the
same fruit. Peaches have fuzz; nectarines don't. The latter is
more susceptible to brown rot and any other malady that affects
peaches. Culture for one is the same as for the other. Whatever I
say about peaches applies to nectarines unless otherwise noted.

Peaches are a most interesting fruit for the home grove-
owner because of their seemingly unlimited potential for producing new strains and varieties. Seedling variability is possibly not
as great as in apples—in fact, peaches come true to parent stock
more frequently than apples, which makes their propagation by
seeds less of a gamble—but this variability is still remarkable. In
addition, peaches can abruptly and mysteriously produce new
strains by bud variation, resulting in sports and mutations the
cause of which science can't yet explain. Darwin, years ago,
pointed out these mysteries: nectarines can come from peach
seeds and peaches from nectarine seeds; peach trees can produce
nectarines and nectarine trees produce peaches; and both the
nectarine from a peach tree and a peach from a nectarine tree
may henceforth come true to seed! Furthermore, either a peach
or a nectarine tree is capable of producing individual fruits that
are half fuzzy and half fuzzless.

Peaches are either white or yellow, although some varieties
of either may tend to be quite reddish. Peaches are either
clingstone or freestone. Clingstone flesh literally clings to the
seed and must be cut or bitten away, whereas the freestone seed
falls easily away from the flesh with a gentle pry. Usually,

freestones are the only kind you find for sale nowadays because they are easier to eat and easier to process for other table fare. Most of California's peaches for processing are clingstones, however.

But we clever humans have paid for this convenience a thousand times over. As we have seen, the peach is one of the most disease-prone fruits in the North, as well as being difficult to grow from zones 5 northward because of bud and blossom frost-tenderness. These difficulties apply much more, however, to the big, yellow, modern peaches than to the little, white, juicy clingstones called "naturals" by horticulturists. "It is the big, yellow, hybridized, freestone peaches that are prone to diseases and have to be sprayed so much," says Bill Johnson, whose commercial peach and apple nursery in Georgia offers a good selection of old peach varieties. "The clingstones get worms sometimes, but they do not get diseases. We do not have to spray them much. But you see, everyone wants to eat big yellow freestones."

For eating fresh and for other home uses, the yellow freestone peach is not that much better than the white clings to justify such a universal switch to the former. Today few people even know what a fresh cling peach is, fewer have tasted them, and until recently you could seldom buy nursery stock. Yet the little white "naturals" hold the key to the possibility of a totally unsprayed peach, hardy enough for even Minnesota, with good taste, too. Get any group of peach-lovers together over the age of

Illus. 14-1—Peach.

40 and they will soon reminisce fondly about the juicy, delicious white clings that grew on trees that were never sprayed. Such a tree grew on the farm next to ours when I was young. It was large enough to hide three boys gorging themselves with peaches from the watchful eyes of my Aunt Stella, who happened to own the tree.

It was from Dr. E. M. Meader, the famous plant breeder (now retired) at the University of New Hampshire, that I first learned, or relearned, a high regard for these little white cling-stone "naturals." Dr. Meader urges everyone to be on the lookout for any still growing on old farms or in fence rows because they are, if not practical trees in their own right, possibly valuable genetic material to cross with better-tasting peaches for hardiness and disease-resistance. Dr. Meader developed the Reliance peach, one of the hardiest of the newer varieties, after he was able to locate two white seedling peaches in Minnesota that were extremely hardy. Little white clings like these are what he calls "heirloom" peaches. Early farmers raised the original trees from seeds and kept planting the seeds of the ones that survived the winters. With peach trees, which are mostly self-fruitful, seedlings can finally evolve through successive plantings that are genetically stable. That is, they will come true to the parent stock most of the time.

Some yellow freestone peaches come fairly true from seed. Lemon Free is considered to be one of them, an old variety not available commercially. I know a seedling of Lemon Free growing in my home village, the seed of which comes true to the parent and makes a nice late peach. For all I know, this is the same variety as Hollister, an old Ohio peach that J. Orville Nicholson, a fellow Fruit Explorer writing in the *Pomona,* says is a cross between an heirloom white cling peach now practically extinct and Lemon Free. Hollister, says Nicholson, comes true from seed.

I often plant peach seeds, getting trees that vary from purple-leaved varieties with tiny white clings that are not very hardy or vigorous, to trees that produce fine yellow peaches, though, so far, none of the white cling I'm looking for. Sometimes the seeds germinate, sometimes they do not. I just plant dried seeds in the fall about 2 inches deep in a row. Some say seeds should not be dried out altogether, but they should be kept in a coolish place after removing the flesh. Some stratify the seed by keeping it slightly moist in plastic bags in the refrigerator over the winter for spring planting. Some growers gently crack the outer pit of the seed, but not enough to harm the inner skin of the pit that surrounds the kernel, thus hastening germination without stratifying. I think the best way is to eat the peach and press the seed into the ground with your heel immediately. That is certainly the easiest way.

I'm sure there are various sources for clingstone peaches, but the commercial sources I currently know of are the Johnson Orchard & Nursery and Southmeadow Fruit Gardens, mentioned earlier (see the Appendix for addresses). The Johnsons sell Indian Blood Cling, which Bill thinks could be a native American peach but is generally believed to be the seedling of an ancient French variety; Mayflower, a very early clingstone (two months before Elberta ripens!) known at least since the 1880s in South Carolina; White English, another extremely old variety; Hagan Sweet, originating from a seedling found growing in the wild; Yellow Indian, a yellow clingstone; Heath Cling, a white cling that seems to have originated in New York; and Peento, which is a weird, flat-shaped peach brought from China as seed. Out of nine varieties of peaches, Stark Bro's sells one clingstone, their Sure-Crop.

The Johnsons seldom spray the clingstones much (in fact, they have successfully reduced spraying in their yellow peach orchards by half) and say the Hagan Sweet responds best to only minimal spraying. In 1979, a very wet year for them, the Hagan Sweet with *no* spraying at all was only slightly affected by brown rot.

Southmeadow Fruit Gardens offers a great variety of old white and yellow peaches, though most are freestone or semi-freestone: Champion (white); George IV (white); Early Crawford (yellow); Oldmixon Free (white); and McKay (a very hardy yellow). In nectarines, Nitschke of Southmeadow says his area is too humid and that brown rot often gets the fruit, but for an older variety with some resistance, he suggests Morton. Johnson introduced a new nectarine named Miss Georgia 1980 that he thinks is very promising. Not having ever raised nectarines successfully, I remain biased. If you want to grow nectarines, I say move to California. A peach tastes just as good, for my money.

It is interesting to note that varieties mentioned above are all seedlings from seedlings. Even more telling, Elberta and Belle of Georgia, probably the best yellow and white peach, respectively, that you can grow (that is, if I haven't convinced you to grow old cling seedlings by now), *each came from seeds from the same tree, and that tree came from a seed of Chinese Cling* planted by Samuel H. Rumph of Marshallville, Georgia, in 1870. It's something to think about.

In addition to Elberta and Belle of Georgia (the latter refuses to grow for me in Ohio because of our cold winters, but it seems to be hardy for other people in the North), Redhaven is a reliable and good peach where peaches grow. Late Crawford is again appearing in catalogs; it was once considered an excellent peach. Reliance is known for hardiness, though it winterkilled in Ohio in '77 and '78 when temperatures dropped under $-10°F$. If you live where peaches are normally raised, you should find out which varieties people in your area like to grow. There are many, many of them. For example, the Official Program of the 1978 Nashville Lawn and Garden Fair mentions Early Julie, a peach developed by Dr. Neal McAlpin and Tennessee State University. This peach ripens in May, 45 days after blossoming! Dr. McAlpin has developed several varieties for Tennessee, but any like Early Julie would be risky farther north.

Peaches are an excellent fruit to freeze, in my opinion, maintaining taste and texture better than any other. They are also easy to dry and, for my taste, they're much more enjoyable than dried apples. Fruit leathers, another excellent way to preserve fruits, are best when plenty of peaches are added. Fruit leather is not hard to make. The pulp from juicing peaches, apricots, prunes, apples, or other fruits is sweetened and spread about ¼ inch thick on a lightly oiled cookie sheet. In about two weeks at room temperature the pulp will have dried and congealed to a leathery consistency that can be lifted easily off the sheet. Fruit leather will keep in good condition for a year or more.

The small, white clingstone peaches seem to have come from two different sources historically—and a bit of that history might persuade you to look further into their value. The Spanish brought peaches to Mexico and the Southwest, and northern Europeans may have brought others to the East Coast. At any rate, Indians both in the Southwest and in the East had extensive peach orchards at the time of American settlement, and historians are not quite sure yet whether all the peaches came from Europeans initially or not.

Hopi and Navajo Indians both cultivated the peach at least as early as 1629, according to Stephen C. Jett's "History of Fruit Tree Raising Among The Navajo" (*Agricultural History*, vol. 51, no. 4, October, 1977, pp. 681–701). All through the 19th century the Navajo tribes cultivated very large orchards, and most of the peaches were like those described by a 1907 traveler, quoted by Jett, "small white fruit with rosy cheeks and are delicious to the taste, maturing in early October." During the wars with the Navajo tribes, the great, loving American White Father allowed American soldiers to destroy hundreds of these peach orchards, but the Navajos later replanted many of them.

The peach evidently takes very well to southwestern sand dunes if the ancient skills of Indian farmers are followed. Gary Nabhan, Department of Plant Sciences at the University of Arizona, who also works with the Hopi Indians, has sent me photos of remarkable trees that grow lush and healthy in what looks like pure sand to an Easterner, on only 6 to 10 inches of rainfall per year. The trees are often grown right in the fields with other crops, especially blue maize, a corn that endures dry climates. No irrigation water is used. Trees are not sprayed. The Navajos raised thousands of peach trees for three centuries without spraying. Also, brown rot is no problem because of the arid climate.

Early American settlers on the East Coast planted peaches wherever they went, and records show that the trees grew and produced marvelously. Elwood Fisher, writing in the *Pomona* ("A History of Peach Culture in Eastern United States," Fall,

Photo 14-1—Peaches Grown with Blue Maize in the Southwest— Indians spaced peach trees far apart in the arid soil of the Southwest, and the trees prospered. Photograph by Gary Nabhan.

1977, pp. 185–91), quotes an early clergyman who wrote in 1756 that he was amazed at the vigor and the number of peach orchards: "Peach trees stand within an inclosure by themselves; grow even in the stoniest places *without culture.* The fruit is the most delicious that the mouth can taste, and often allowable in fevers. *One kind, called clingstones, are considered the best . . .*" (emphasis added). In another passage, Fisher quotes Forsyth, a horticulturist writing in 1803: "Peaches ripen . . . in succession, one sort coming after another, from July to November. . . . They are generally divided into clear-stone and cling-stone peaches. . . . *But of all peaches, perhaps of all fruit, there is no equal in flavor to the American Heath Peach, a cling-stone.*" (Emphasis added.)

CHERRIES

Sweet cherries differ from sour cherries not only in taste, being decidedly sweeter, but also in firmness. Sweet cherries are more plumlike in texture, while sour cherries are juicy. Sweet cherries are no hardier than peaches and just as difficult to grow in zone 5 and colder. Humid weather causes brown rot on them even faster than it does on peaches. Birds adore the red and black varieties, which are the best tasting. And then when you are almost home free with a crop, heavy rains can cause the cherries to burst open; it's called cracking. Cracking can be reduced by applying a dishwasher soap spray (1 quart to 100 gallons of water) to the trees a week or so before harvesting. Since a tree may yield several hundred pounds, losing 50% to brown rot and other problems still leaves quite a harvest.

SWEET CHERRIES

Although I don't recommend that everyone grow sweet cherries, there are ways in which this delectable fruit might be made practical for the home grove. The yellow and yellow red varieties are not eaten extensively by birds, and Napolean (perhaps better known as Royal Anne) has an excellent taste, which, sad to say, the pure yellow varieties such as Gold do not have. Small dwarfed varieties now being developed make bird protection with screening more practical (see Chap. 10).

To counter fungal diseases and frost tenderness, there are possibilities one never reads about in popular horticultural publications with the exception of the *Pomona*. The first is to look around the area where you live and see what is growing in the way of sweet cherries. My town certainly is not good sweet cherry country. In fact, a few years ago I would have said flatly that none grew here. But I now know of at least three *large* trees, trees that obviously have been here for many years. In each case, they produce tremendous crops, more than the birds in the nearby yards can eat. One has a yellow pink fruit, probably a Royal Anne. The other two have dark red fruit and I believe they are Duke-type cherries, which are a sort of juicy sweet cherry, somewhere between a sour and a sweet cherry in taste. Needless to say, these are the kinds of trees that should be propagated for backyards in this area.

The other possibility is perhaps even more intriguing. At our former homestead in Pennsylvania, in the overgrown brushland behind our place, I found a cluster of cherry trees that did not answer to the description of any of the wild cherries native to the area. They were obviously miniature sweet cherries—very dark red to almost black, sweet, and somewhat juicy, but the flesh over the seed was hardly half as thick as on a regular sweet cherry. Finally, in reading over the cherry species in *Taylor's Encyclopedia of Gardening,* I found the clue that subsequently led to identification: "*Prunus avium,* the common sweet cherry . . . is often an escape, and is then sometimes known as the Mazzard cherry, used mostly as grafting stock."

When horticulturists say "escape," they mean a domestic plant that goes native—it escapes to the wild, so to speak, where it naturalizes and finds a survival niche in the botany of a locality. Mazzard, as a rootstock, can escape two ways. If the grafted tree dies, the hardier, tougher Mazzard rootstock often sends up its own new sprout which finally becomes a tree and fruits. Birds then scatter the seeds in abandoned fields, fence rows, and woods' edges, and trees then grow there. Or perhaps the seeds of a regular sweet cherry, scattered by birds, come up as seedlings that are throwbacks to Mazzard-type stock. In any event, what I had behind my place was a stand of Mazzard cherries. Since my experience eating sweet cherries was somewhat limited at the time, I thought these were very good despite their small size. We enjoyed them fresh and as jelly. When my own trees in the yard fruited, I realized how much better in quality they were. The difference was more one of inconvenience at working with the smaller Mazzard cherries. Taste was about the same. But the important point is that these smaller, naturalized cherries were available year after year without one bit of spraying or care of any kind, while we never ate one ripe black cherry from the yard because of the birds, and in three out of six years, the yellow variety and yellow red variety succumbed to brown rot, and in one other year, froze out.

Which is better—to have small sweet cherries or not to have any? The idea of sweet cherry quality is wonderful, but quality has become an accomplishment attained only at great cost by a few specialty growers and a few consumers who can afford to buy the fruit. We practical grove-owners aren't that particular. We only want trees that deliver the goods without our having to fog the trees with a costly, dangerous array of chemicals. No one has told us about these lower quality but dependable kinds of sweet cherries. Certainly, for eating out of hand, which is about all sweet cherries are good for, anyway, a mouthful of these little ones is just about as enjoyable as a mouthful of the plumper ones.

If you live where black sweet cherries grow well, Bing is a preferred, fine variety, though subject to cracking in rainy weather. Black Tartarian is a good backyard variety, and Schmidt is a good choice for the home grove as well.

SOUR CHERRIES

Tart cherries, or pie cherries, are much more reliable fruit and are more preferable than sweet cherries for establishing backyard groves. Unlike most sweet cherries (of which Stella is the exception), sour cherries are self-fertile and so you need to grow only one. One big tree is plenty, unless you make lots of cherry juice, preserves, and canned or dried cherries along with your pies. When the tree is small, you can cover it against birds, and when it is large, in most situations it will have more than enough fruit for you and the birds. The best practice is to start a tree every ten years. With a large tree and a smaller one coming on, you will usually get enough cherries for yourself under any circumstances. Pie cherry trees often die when they are between 15 and 20 years old—at least around here they do—so, if you plant every ten years, you'll always have another ready to take the dead one's place.

Not many varieties of sour cherries are sold: Montmorency and Early Richmond are two old-timers; Meteor and North Star, newer ones. North Star is sort of naturally dwarfed, so it's a good tree if you must cover your cherries against birds every year. North Star is not as good a cherry to eat as Montmorency.

The nursery catalogs would have us believe that sour cherries are all about the same in taste and quality, but this is far from true. I have about concluded that everything sold as Montmorency isn't the same strain, because some young trees I've sampled have fruit that's not nearly as high in taste quality as some older trees that we gather our cherries from in our village. New trees have smaller, more sour fruits, and they ripen very slowly, sometimes not ever getting to the full, rich, dark red color of a really great sour cherry. On the other hand, the two ancient trees I eat from in our village grow cherries nearly twice the size, have a darker hue, and when they're fully ripe, they're quite sweet to eat. One of these trees is known to be 80 years old and the owner believes it to be 100, quite remarkable for tart cherries here. The fruit is unusually large, and the owner once sent a sample to a leading nursery to see if the proprietors were interested in propagating it. The nursery replied that the cherry did seem to have fine quality, but that currently the nursery was interested only in cherries that would ship and process well—a revealing reply. Seeds from this tree grow into trees that have good cherries, but not so large. Even so, they have better dessert quality than North Star or some of the cherries I see passing for Montmorency.

Montmorency is a very good cherry, or, at least, was originally. In locations where worms are bad, I would have one Early

Illus. 14-2—Cherry (sour).

Richmond and one Montmorency. Early Richmond matures a good week ahead of Montmorency, and so the time from blossoming to maturity is spread out that much longer. The cherry fruit moths fly out to lay their eggs on a rather precise schedule depending largely on the coming of warm weather. If the moths come early, they will lay eggs on the Early Richmond; if the moths come late, they will lay on the newly forming Montmorency fruit. That's the theory at least. In any event, the infestation usually will not be bad, if my experience is typical. In general, I see little need for spraying sour cherries in the backyard.

Wormy cherries tend to redden up a little quicker, which are the ones most apt to be eaten by the birds. The birds fill up in the early part of the season and leave you the best, fully ripened cherries late in the season.

BUSH CHERRIES

The small trees of Nanking cherry and Hansen's bush cherry must sell very well, because most popular catalogs offer them. These fruits have a place: They will grow in cold, dry northern Plains areas where not much fruit will survive. It is for these areas that they were developed. Nanking cherries (red) taste almost as good as regular sour cherries, but are smaller. Hansen's bush has blue black fruit, little to eat in my opinion, although the plants make an attractive hedge and windbreak valuable for birds. Both plants are used as rootstock and dwarfing rootstock for other, more desirable *Prunus* fruits, although they are not always satisfactory as such. The biggest objection to both is that they are susceptible to brown rot. Hansen's bush is very susceptible in the humid East, and Nanking only a little less so.

Selections of bush cherries have been improved and named for the Plains. Gurney, Henry Field, and other nurseries with customers in the northern Plains states can be depended upon to carry these improved strains.

WILD BLACK CHERRIES AND CHOKECHERRIES

The ideal tree grove is not complete without a black cherry tree or two. Taste of these seedy little cherries varies. Some are surprisingly good and make excellent jelly, though it is tedious to

297

make. Birds in northern groves rely heavily on these fruits in late summer. I have black cherries all around my grapes and raspberries. I'm sure the birds don't bother these fruits much because they have been gorging on wild black cherries. Wild black cherry juice makes a good cough syrup or a flavoring for cider. But the chief reward for growing black cherry trees is the beautiful wood, second only to black walnut in value. If you do any hobby woodworking at all, or want to make extra money from grove lumber, grow a few wild cherries. Grow them on the higher ground, and leave your deep black loam for the walnut.

Chokecherry is a smaller tree of little value other than for bird food. The cherries are never as palatable as are some wild black cherries. I grow a chokecherry bush on the edge of my garden for two reasons. The first is because this particular little tree, which my son found growing in the woods, blooms very early with the most delicious scent ever to waft on the spring air. I want to enjoy it while doing spring gardening work.

The second reason I keep it next to the orchard is because the experts say one must religiously destroy all chokecherry and black cherry trees in the proximity of orchards where plums, cherries, and peaches are grown. The reason is that the scientists have found certain mycoplasmas, some sort of semiliving pathogens in these wild plants, particularly chokecherry, that are at least potentially dangerous to the domestic trees. Or so the theory goes. At the same time the scientists admit they know very little about these viruses. In the absence of fact, someone ought to being doing just the opposite of what the scientists say, and so in this case, that someone is me.

But believe me, I'm not a bit worried. Why? The peach tree closest to the chokecherry is the peach tree that I found growing wild on the woods' edge about 100 feet away from where the chokecherry previously grew. I gather that they both occupied the same grove for a number of years. For the same reason, I have planted a wild plum (another anathema) in the orchard, close by the other peach and plum trees. They're only a little closer than the distance that wild plums have grown from tame ones in this neighborhood for 100 years. As mentioned in Chapter 12, scientists aren't sure just how all viruses do move around, even though in some cases they are carried by certain leafhoppers and aphids. But another theory says viruses do not migrate naturally from tree to tree.

So who knows? I am incensed by experts going about and eradicating plants that have grown healthfully in this climate for thousands of years. Even when you do find a "deadly" virus in a wild plant, I do not know of a single instance where the eradication of all of the wild plant was ever proven to have stopped the spread of the disease. Quite the contrary is true in southeast peach orchards. It reminds me of the age-old caution against planting black raspberries next to red raspberries. I've been doing it now for 13 years without unusual trouble. How many more years do I have to go to prove that theory wrong? And if my raspberries do contract some disease that eventually kills them, will it mean, after so long, that it had anything to do with the proximity of one kind to the other?

PLUMS

In our neighbors' yard there is a plum tree that produces fairly well without any spraying or care of any kind. In fact, the tree has lately been sorely mistreated. New owners, who arrived in the winter, thought the tree, which had grown sprouts all around the base of it because of lack of care, was an overgrown lilac bush. With the fervor of new homeowners they therefore trimmed the heck out of it, the better to make it look like a bush. Results? The mutilated tree fairly dripped with luscious purple fruit the following year. I observed it all with a sense of wonder, and came back to this desk realizing how stupid it is to write books on "right ways" in the face of a fickle nature. But that episode says reams in favor of the old purple plums. Plant them, neglect them, hack them, and keep a couple of bushel baskets handy to catch the abundant crop!

There are so many variations of what we call plum that categorization is difficult. Horticulturists used to talk about European plums (mostly blue and oval) and Japanese plums (mostly red and roundish), but today there is a third group of "hybrid" plums that combine (they hope) red-plum flavor with blue-plum hardiness.

Of the European plums, Stanley is the best known and still one of the best of the blue plums. It can be used for prunes too, and is hardy in zone 5. Italian, Blufre, Valor, Lombard, and Earliblue are others. Damsons and so-called gages are also included in this group, although they are much tarter and useful mostly for jellies and preserves. Giant Damson and Shropshire Damson are two well-known ones. Of the gages, greengage is the old reliable, a greenish yellow plum with high-dessert quality.

299

Southmeadow Fruit Gardens offers a good selection of other old gage and European plums.

Few of the European plums are safe in zone 4. Mount Royal is the only one the University of Wisconsin recommends for northern Wisconsin. Another hardy blue plum is the little Dietz, which often does not live long. But John Bonn, a Fruit Explorer in Wisconsin, tells me the seeds come true to parent stock and so one can easily keep new trees coming on.

All the European plums mentioned above are self-fruitful. Japanese plums often are not (see Chap. 3), and hybrid plums are all self-unfruitful and many are even cross-unfruitful. When buying them, you need to read carefully and make sure one that you get will pollenate the others. Toka will pollenate the other hybrids. But the way to be safe no matter what is to grow a wild native plum with the hybrids to make sure that pollenation occurs. South Dakota is such a native red yellow plum commercially available. You can depend on nurseries like Gurney, Farmer, and Henry Field to carry these hardy hybrid plums. Other varieties are Underwood, Pipestone, Superior, and Ember. For zone 5 and south, Ozark Premier is a well-known hybrid, more like the Japanese plums.

Japanese plums do better in zone 6 and warmer and some of them, like Santa Rosa, which is very susceptible to bacterial spot, will grow with care in the humid East. Many of them will take zone 5 temperatures, though I think them risky that far north. Early Golden, Methley, Abundance, Shiro, and Burbank are typical varieties. Methley is self-fruitful, which is unusual in Japanese plums.

BUSH PLUMS

Buying small trees of ornamental but edible plums can be as trying an experience as buying bush cherries. There are all sorts of these plums from wild regional favorites to hybrid, commercially marketed "cherry plums." Most of the latter look better in catalogs than they are, while some of the former are better than they look in the fence row.

The beach plum is revered by local people on the Atlantic Coast who make jelly out of it. Sometimes a favorite strain that a gardener has propagated finds its way into small local nurseries and is offered for sale. "Actually, if you take the beach plum away from Cape Cod, it makes no better jelly than any other plum," Dr. E. M. Meader, the famous plant breeder mentioned earlier in this chapter, told me one time with a twinkle in his eye.

"But those of us who have lived on the East Coast have a certain sentimental and romantic attachment to the beach plum."

I suppose that's true of the Chickasaw plum in the South, too, although T. O. Warren, whom I've quoted earlier, a man who has spent a lifetime studying the wild fruits of America, insists that the best fence-row selections really are good—for eating out of hand or making jelly. "Most strains have crossed with other introduced species and the chance cross pollenation hasn't improved them for the most part. But fruit hobbyists should always be on the lookout for a good wild Chickasaw. This fruit merits a place in the backyard orchard, even though the trees tend to bloom early and get caught by late frosts sometimes."

Norman Hansen, a Fruit Explorer in Iowa, studies other wild American plums and, like Warren, cultivates them in his orchard. *P. americana* and *P. hortulana* grow commonly across the Midwest and North in wide variety, and the better strains were at one time named, propagated, and sold by nurseries under such names as Terry, Gold, Queen, Nellie Blanch, Hammer, and Hawkeye. Research stations bulldozed out their clones of native plums for the most part, says Hansen, and now he is endeavoring to track down survivors and preserve them on his farm. He says some of them are quite worthy of backyard production.

The influence of Meader, Warren, Hansen, and others led me to start looking in my own area for good wild plums. I was easily persuaded because I remember delicious wild plums in Minnesota where I lived for awhile some years ago. I recall that they were not only good to eat but made an alcoholic beverage with a powerful persuasion of its own. So I began tasting every wild plum I found. Two things will surprise you if you try exploring for fruits. The first is that there are so many that you just never noticed before. The second is the wide variation in taste. I have found this true in all cases, even of wild grapes, but with plums the difference is considerably significant. Of two small trees I found adjacent to each other, the fruit in the first case was barely edible and, in the second, worth eating. The skins of these small plums are generally tough, but some strains are almost as sweet as honey inside. Needless to say, I dug up a sprout of one, and it is now growing in my orchard. As I explained above, if you fear viral infections on your peach trees, bringing wild plums into the orchard is not the right thing to do.

A favorite item of the technicolor catalogs is the "Manchurian" or "Siberian" plum, sometimes labeled *Prunus salicina* hybrid, whatever that means. All that label tells you is that the plant is some form of Japanese plum crossed with something else. These plum-types come (or are supposed to come) from a very hardy seedling brought back from Harbin, Manchuria, about 30 years ago to western Canadian research stations, where work has been going on continuously for many years in an effort to find hardy fruits for the coldest regions. These plums are described with adjectives such as "juicy, super-hardy, exotic, delicious," but because of seedling variability what you may actually end up with could be dry, bland, and not so hardy. Or you make get lucky. A Fruit Explorer in Saskatchewan, Percy Wright, tells me he planted some Manchurian plum seedlings a few years back and got what he called "amazing luck." Of the eight he planted, he said, four were worthwhile for experimental purposes (which means, if you know dedicated Fruit Explorers, the trees died). Two, however, were "oustanding in hardiness and flavor." Two out of eight is a good batting average for an experimenter, but a homeowner paying good money for plants might not think so.

Hybrid "cherry plums" also thrive beautifully in the technicolor ads. They are crosses of wild sand cherries and various oriental plum cultivars. As with the bush cherries, they are very susceptible to brown rot and are therefore satisfactory on the dry, windy plains but doubtful anywhere else. Compass, Oka, Opata, Sapa, and Sapalta are named varieties. Sometimes they are called cherries and sometimes plums. They're not bad eating and good for sauces and preserves.

Plum trees are very sensitive to herbicides, says the Univer-

Illus. 14-3—Plum.

sity of Wisconsin. A word to the wise is sufficient. I have known growers who almost killed their trees simply by using grass that had been sprayed with weed killers for mulch.

There are dwarf forms of plum trees on the market, but plum trees are small, anyway, and, except in unusual situations, dwarfing hardly seems necessary. You can keep a tree small by pruning. The myrobalan plum is the chief rootstock for apricots and plums, especially European plums. Halford peach is used as rootstock for Japanese plums.

Plums soften when they are ripe. Don't pick them hard, even if they look deep blue and ready. Plums do not store fresh very well. The blue ones will keep a few weeks in sealed plastic sacks, the red ones hardly at all.

APRICOTS

The best-tasting apricots grow in California and other areas where dry, not-so-cold climates are favorable for them. Michigan can grow a few commercially, as well as New York, by relying on varieties such as Goldcot and Alfred, which are quite hardy and self-fertile. There's an apricot tree locally that produces a crop nearly every year, and this is the coldest kind of climate you can find and still be in zone 5, believe me. It's a point for debate as to whether these apricots match in taste a sweet Tilton or Blenheim raised in the California sun, but Eastern apricots are picked when ripe rather than when green for shipping, as often is the case in the West.

But there's hope. In Wisconsin there's a little heirloom apricot that farmers kept growing in Door County for years. Fruit Explorers familiar with it say it tastes good and comes true from seed. The Sturgeon Bay Research Station of the University of Wisconsin at Sturgeon Bay has these trees under test. At Beltsville, Maryland, where even the experts have trouble raising apricots, researchers are looking at late-blooming varieties from Italy and elsewhere. The idea is to develop apricot varieties that don't bloom so blooming early. Invariably, apricot trees in the North lose their crops because of cold weather at blossom time.

Robert Kurle, the Fruit Explorer who grows all kinds of apricots in the Chicago area, believes that poor fruiting of apricots is due as much to lack of pollenating bees during cool blossoming times as to the cold weather itself. He thinks that, by being self-fertile, Alfred and Goldcot will alleviate this old problem because pollenating insects won't have to move around so much to do their job. Sungold and Moongold, the new super-hardy varieties from Minnesota, are self-infertile and must be planted together. Kurle suggests grafting them into the same tree to permit easier pollenation.

Another successful backyard apricot grower, Dr. Elwood Fisher in Virginia, trains his trees to Y shapes on a trellis and each arm of a Y overlaps the arm of the tree next on the trellis, which also helps pollenation.

Both Kurle and Fisher think that apricot rootstock is best for apricots, and they both grow their own seedlings. Apricots may come true to parent stock (Moorpark is noted for that), so Fisher plants seeds of any of his many varieties that show signs of desirable late-blossoming or other advantages. After the seedling grows for a year, he cuts the whip back to about 18 inches tall, forcing the tree to develop two forks. On one fork he will graft a variety that he has collected, while he lets go the other fork to see what the seedling produces. Later on he can cut the seedling fork off if it does not produce good fruits. But if it does, he cuts off the other fork if he wants to and transfers the variety on it to another seedling. This seems to me an excellent practice, allowing the backyard grove-owner to test seedlings without losing years of fruiting.

Apricots will grow in light or heavy soil, but it must be at least fairly well drained. Curculio may infest apricot as much as

Illus. 14-4—Apricot.

plum. The trees respond to mulching very well—Fisher says the only fertilizer his get is the mulch as it rots. Bacterial canker may be a problem, and there's no cure. Try to avoid wounds in the bark where crown gall can enter. If you plant apricots in soil recently used for tomatoes, brambles, or other crops that might harbor verticillium fungus, you run a greater risk of the fruit being infected with blackheart.

Hardy varieties other than the ones already mentioned are Scout, Stella, Sundrop, All Red, Roma, and Skaha. Some of these aren't available yet as far as I know.

Tilton, Blenheim, Perfection, Moorpark, and Derby are standard commercial varieties and are good-tasting.

In the East, Fisher has high praise for Skaha, but I don't think it is commercially available. He also lists later-ripening apricots that he thinks are good ones: Hardy Iowa, Nugget, Hungarian Giant, Hungary's Best, Maylar Iran, Perfection, Stella, Wenatchee, Shipley's Blenheim, and Sweetheart. Stella and Maylar Iran are his favorites. The first is available from Bountiful Ridge Nurseries in Maryland, the latter from nowhere I know. Sweetheart is a new variety from Stark Bro's. I have two young ones in a sheltered nook of this cold zone 5 area and so far they have grown well.

What do you do about apricot varieties you would like to try that aren't available? Join the North American Fruit Explorers. Join state fruit-and-nut hobby grower groups. You will become acquainted with other collectors. By and by, you will learn how to graft. New friends will open all sorts of avenues to hard-to-obtain varieties. There is no shortcut. If I mention a certain curious variety and tell of a gardener who may have a few extra ones for sale, then the poor guy is inundated with requests that he has neither the time nor ability to satisfy. Very often some of the eager folk who chase after different varieties do not know how to take care of them yet, or get a scion to graft or a seed to germinate. Join the organizations and learn. That's what I'm doing. In the meantime you can practice the arts of plant collecting in your own area. The fruits and nuts you find growing in your own climate will often prove the most satisfactory for you, anyway.

Currently, the best known of the apricots is Sweetheart, which has sweet, edible kernels in the pits. The North American Fruit Explorers call such apricots *alpricots* because the edible kernels resemble almonds, although the kernels are only about one-third the size of almonds. In the North an alpricot is the most practical way to grow your own almonds (see below). Sweet kernels in apricots are not really uncommon and occur regularly in plantings of seedling apricots. Work on the edible-nut apricots is in progress, especially at Canadian research stations.

ALMONDS

If a sweet-kerneled apricot is not enough to satisfy your itch for a homegrown almond, plant Hall's Hardy almond. But be prepared for a disappointment. This variety is rather hardy even in the warmer parts of zone 5, but the trees do not produce regularly, and the nuts, in my experience, never come close to matching the quality of a California almond. The almond needs a dry, mild climate, and even in California, where it is grown commercially, orchardists have to worry about cool weather in the spring. Even chilly weather without frost can harm almonds.

I don't recommend almonds for home tree groves except in California where almonds do well, and perhaps in Texas and other favorable spots in the Southwest. Culture is the same as for peaches. The two fruits are very similar. Instead of flesh, the almond has a hull. The bloom, the size of tree, and the pests are all about the same. Nonpareil, Mission, and Peerless are the old standby varieties.

Almonds will not do well even in Florida. The climate is too humid in the East. But I suppose there are exceptions to prove that rule.

Illus. 14-5—Almond.

One of the worst pests of almond is the navel orangeworm. The female moth lays her eggs in the crack where the almond hull splits as it approaches maturity. The larvae hatch and feed on the kernel and the hull, safe from sprays. Scientists have recently discovered that a beneficial nematode, *Neoaplectana carpocapsae Weiser,* parasitizes the larvae effectively enough that it may become a good control. The nematode actually releases a bacterium that kills the orangeworm. The same nematode also parasitizes codling moth in Mexico, where the nematode was discovered.

CHAPTER 15

CITRUS FRUITS

Citrus fruits may be grown successfully in the home grounds with little or no control of insects and diseases. Fruits produced without pesticide sprays may be very poor in external quality as the result of damage by several mites, insects, and fungus diseases. Although these unattractive fruits may have little eye appeal, this external damage usually has no detrimental effect on internal fruit quality. And the appearance of the tree may suffer, but seldom will trees be critically damaged by most citrus pests. Natural biological control will assist in maintaining pests at low population levels.

If I asked you to guess who wrote the above quote, you would probably reply with the name of your favorite organic idealist. If you happen to grow oranges commercially in central Florida, more likely you would give the name of the person you deem the biggest environmental crackpot in the United States. Either way, you'd be wrong. This quote comes verbatim from a bulletin of the Cooperative Extension Service of the University of Georgia, a group given more to pragmatism than idealism, and certainly not known for wild-eyed crackpot notions. You know in your heart that if the Extension Service says it's so, it must be so. There has never been such an institution, supposedly ruled by objective scientific standards, that has historically been so rigorously suspicious of anything smacking of "organics." Citrus trees make ideal home-grove trees because of less

308

trouble with bugs and disease, but only where they are acclimated. If you have the space and two strong persons around, you can grow citrus in pots in the North and move them in and out with the weather. But this doesn't pay a busy home grove-owner. He's got enough to do without ruining his back trying to lift a heavy, potted tree.

In the backyard, citrus by and large require less pruning, too, unless you want to shape them to espalier forms, to which the more dwarfish varieties readily take. But otherwise you need to prune a citrus tree much less than an apple tree. It will grow good scaffold branches naturally, and you will only have to decide which to leave as the lowest. Most citrus are self-fertile, another plus for the backyarder, who need not therefore worry overly much about pollination. (The Clementine tangerine and the Orlando tangelo are not self-fertile.) What's more, many times citrus will come true to seed—enough so that it can pay to plant the seeds of tangerines, at least. Seeds need not be stratified but should not be allowed to dry out before planting. Nor are citrus fruits bothered much by birds, a situation that sounds divine to us Northerners. The worst animal pest of orange groves is the *Tourist* genus, particularly the species *Callous thief. T. Callous thief,* upon approaching an orange tree, removes himself from the four-wheeled carapace in which he normally lives, grabs as many oranges as he can stuff in pockets or buckets, scurries back inside his carapace, and speeds away. The most effective control is a lead spray from a shotgun, although you may have difficulty getting a license to use it. Unfortunately.

INSECTS AND DISEASES

In no area of fruit growing is the difference between home-grove methods and commercial-orchard methods more pronounced. That is why the commercial grower will find it so hard to accept the Georgia Extension Service advice to homeowners at the beginning of this chapter. *T. Callous thief* is but one of his many worries. A host of mites, scale insects, aphids, fruit flies, and nematodes threaten him daily. In central Florida, orange trees grow as far as the eye can see in an almost completely artificial environment. The sand that holds up the trees is almost completely devoid of organic matter and nutrients, and the trees are fed entirely with artificial fertilizers. In such

309

circumstances, it does not surprise an organic farmer to find out that a nematode-caused disease known simply as "citrus decline" can run rampant, wiping out whole blocks of trees. There is no cure or chemical control that will kill the nematodes without hurting the trees. The trees are bulldozed together, burned, and the land kept idle for three years. Then trees are replanted with fingers crossed in hope. The home grove-owner normally plants in soil enriched with organic matter rather than in pure sand. A high organic matter content is a known detriment to many kinds of nematodes.

Despite insect and disease problems, citrus seems better suited than, say, peaches for organic commercial production, and there is a small but growing trend in this direction. Organic producers want changes made in the fruit standards for interstate shipment since their oranges may be smaller and cosmetically inferior enough not to pass existing standards. The industry as a whole wants to make sure the organic producers don't try to sell their fruit as "better." In no other fruit do these arguments over cosmetic appearance of the fruit seem more absurd. Orange market standards have historically played up to the ignorance of the Northern housewife and househusband rather than educating them with the facts of life. A perfectly ripe orange can be green as grass in color and still be wonderfully delicious. The orange coloring comes from cool temperatures, and if the temperatures don't cooperate, the trade does not hesitate to add coloring to juice or skin instead of telling buyers that they are paying extra for something they don't need. But that's the way the world turns. Another example is the blood orange, a favorite in Europe that grows well in Florida. But the delicate American housewife (or so the marketers have talked themselves into believing) objects to slicing open an orange that appears to be bleeding because of the juicy red streaks in it.

Now along come a few independent thinkers who believe they can sell an honest orange, perhaps green- and brown-splotched orange on the outside, but just as tasty on the inside as any other orange of its kind, and how pious become conventional orchardists. An orange not up to "standards" might wreck the market, they fear.

One of the most feared pests of citrus is the citrus blackfly, and the history of its control so far makes another interesting commentary on the weakness of chemical approaches. A first infestation reported in Brownsville, Texas, in 1955 was eradicated with chemicals. But a new infestation was discovered there in 1971. In a report published in *Texas Agricultural Progress,* Spring, 1978, C. F. Ketner and J. G. Rosier of the USDA Animal and Plant Health Inspection Service observed: "In spite of intensive control efforts, chemical control did not produce acceptable results even though some trees received more than 30 applications of insecticides. By 1974, the citrus blackfly was reproducing rapidly and expanding its range."

Scientists then closed off locations in Brownsville to the usual chemical-spray programs and began releasing parasites of blackfly brought in from Mexico. The release began in 1974. Blackfly populations continued to increase into 1975, but the researchers kept their cool. Sure enough, by the fall of 1975, blackfly populations began to decrease and continued to do so. "The success of the biological-control program may be judged on the basis that there have been no documented production losses in commercial groves due to citrus blackfly infestations during the 1976 and 1977 crop years," concluded Ketner and Rosier in 1978.

On a small scale, as in a backyard situation, blackflies can be caught in effective numbers with "sticky traps"—yellow cards or disks coated with a sticky substance (as described in Chap. 11 for apple maggot moth control). Blackfly researchers have been using standard, plastic, disk-shaped traps made for that purpose, but, recently, entomologists at the Citrus Insects Research Laboratory (509 West Fourth Street, Weslaco, TX 78596) found that yellow, plastic, coffee-can lids work just as well at half the cost.

CLIMATE FOR CITRUS

Even though they're situated in the ideally best climates, commercial orchards are more prone to frost problems than home groves north of them, because of the marketing schedule. A commercial grower in Florida wants to harvest oranges as many months as possible and has Valencia-type varieties ripening in early spring. This means he has fruit hanging on the trees during the coldest part of the year, where a dip to 28°F might kill them. The home grove-owner can avoid this danger to some extent by growing late-fall and early-winter maturing fruits. Oranges grow well in Ohio loamy clay, but of course we have to pot them and keep them inside all winter. In fact, citrus will grow in a wide variety of soils so long as the soil is well drained.

Because of climate, there is only a relatively small portion of the country where good-tasting citrus is ideally suited, and even in these areas—south-central Florida, about four southern counties in Texas, and southern California, Arizona, and New Mexico—periodic cold spells sweep through and kill whole crops and sometimes whole orchards. I will therefore limit advice on what varieties are best suited for the home grove to the hardier kinds of citrus that can extend the citrus range into Georgia, the Gulf States, and even northern Texas.

The least hardy citrus are limes, lemons, and citron. Even a temperature in the high 20s can injure or kill a tree. Slightly hardier are sweet oranges and grapefruit, which incur major damage to the wood when temperatures fall to the low 20s. Hardier still are the tangerines and mandarins, and especially the satsuma-type tangerines, which can withstand temperatures to 19°F and possibly lower on hardy rootstocks. Hardiest of all the commonly grown citrus is the acidic citrus, kumquat, which will survive to 15°F. But remember, this applies only to the wood. Fruits freeze at 28° to 30°F.

That's the simplest rule of thumb. Homeowners are advised to purchase trees on *Poncirus trifoliata,* a hardy wild orange that sometimes will extend some hardiness to the variety to which it is grafted. Major Collins, the Georgian and North American Fruit Explorer who has worked hardest to develop hardier citrus for Georgia, reports in the *Pomona* that his satsumas on *P. trifoliata* endure 15°F temperatures, and his Meyer lemon, 20°F. Texas A & M horticulturist George Ray McEarchern reports that Changsha tangerine in Texas has survived freezes of 10°F. T. O. Warren, the well-known Fruit Explorer with whom I correspond, reports that a Changsha tree he has tested in Mississippi survived 7°F. It is grafted on *P. trifoliata.* The leaves all blackened and fell off, but to his surprise the tree bounced back with warm weather and produced 24 fruits the next year.

Citrus crosses and hybrids are numerous, and a division such as mine above is oversimplified. For the backyard grower, however, it will serve better perhaps than a long drawn-out discussion of the difference between tangerine and mandarin, or citranges and citrangequats. The following suggestions come mostly from the University of Georgia, but they are corroborated by the general literature and what I have learned from correspondents and Fruit Explorers.

TANGERINES AND ORANGES

Without discussing the technicalities of what a tangerine is and what a mandarin is, the satsuma-type is most generally recommended for homeowners, especially on the colder fringes of the citrus range. Unlike wilder and hardier citrus strains, satsumas are sweet and delicious. Like any tangerine, they have a slip skin and divide into sections. There are few seeds. Owari is a recommended variety. Grow it on *P. trifoliata* rootstock whenever possible for extra hardiness. Where climate is "iffy" (and this is good advice for all citrus threatened by cold), bank dirt up around the trunk at least a foot above the graft. If the tree freezes back, there will be enough varietal trunk left to send up new branches. Satsumas are self-fruitful.

Of the more typical mandarin-tangerine fruits, Dancy, Ponkan, and Clementine are well-known varieties and recommended for something less than the coldest citrus regions. They ripen late and so are more subject to winter cold while still on the tree. Hybrid tangelos ripen earlier, are somewhat cold-hardy, and may be a better risk. Orlando is a recommended variety for the backyard but needs another tangerine to pollinate it. In Texas, Changsha tangerine is recommended. It has only one fault. It is quite seedy.

Where sweet oranges will grow, that is, in the normal orange range and not on the northern fringes of the range, Hamlin is a

Illus. 15-1—Orange.

recommended juice-type for the backyard. It ripens in late fall ahead of cold weather. Of the navel types, Washington, Dream, and Summerfield are recommended for the home grove, though southern Californians have newer ones probably as good or better.

The juice oranges are grown mostly in Florida, and the navels in Calfornia, but both can be grown in either place in the backyard. Varieties proliferate like apple varieties and with names just as picturesque: Parson Brown, Valencia, Magnum Bonum, Lue Gim Gong, Osceola, Majorca, Homosassa, Lamb Summer, Sanford Blood, Maltese Oval, Pineapple Orange, and so forth. An excellent and highly readable introduction into commercial orange production is John A. McPhee's *Oranges* (New York, Farrar-Strauss & Giroux, 1967), written before he became so famous. The book details how orange production in the United States has become the envy of other fruit industries and, whether by intent or not, also shows the not-so-enviable impact that commercialized oranges has had on the ecology of Florida, a place that was very close to a true Garden of Eden before the arrival of colonists.

GRAPEFRUITS

Grapefruits are no hardier than sweet oranges, perhaps even less. If you are fortunate to live where they will thrive, Marsh, a white seedless, and Ruby, a red seedless, are recommended for home plantings. Connoisseurs of quality grapefruit believe, however, that nonseedless whites, such as Royal and Triumph, are better to eat. Texas A & M released Star Ruby a few years ago and touted it as the best of the seedless reds.

LEMONS, LIMES, AND KUMQUATS

There are not many places where the climate is practical for commercial lemons, but the Meyer lemon is much hardier by comparison. If grafted onto hardy rootstock and protected from cold, drying winds, it will grow farther north than the usual lemon range. It makes a very attractive small tree, and the lemons, I am told, are nearly as good as regular lemons. It will grow as far north as southern Georgia.

314

Illus. 15-2—Lemon Tree; Lemon, Kumquat, Grapefruit, and Tangerine.

The lime is practical for an even smaller area than lemons, but horticulturists have found one way to move its range farther north. They crossed a lime with a kumquat, resulting in what is now called a limequat. Limequats are smaller plants, more bush than tree, and are as hardy as tangerines. Eustis is the most popular variety so far. Growers say that limequats make a perfectly adequate substitute for limes for table use. If limequats make frozen daiquiris as good as the ones a south Florida lime grower made out of limes for me one time, then by all means you more northerly Southerners should grow them.

The calamondin is a type of acid citrus that will also grow where tangerines are hardy, and can be substituted for lemons and limes for culinary purposes.

Finally, the kumquat is recommended for home groves because it is the hardiest of all decently edible types of citrus. Eat fresh, skin and all, or make jellies and marmalade. Nagami, Marumi, and Meiwa are the best-known varieties, the latter being the most popular.

CHAPTER 16

MINOR FRUIT TREES

In searching out the unusual and offbeat kinds of fruit trees to grow in his grove, the eager backyard food-producer must weigh not only the advantages but the disadvantages of any particular species. The question foremost in his mind must be: If it is a minor fruit, *why?* Invariably there's a good reason why these fruit trees are not widely grown. The local farmers of long standing may not even know why they don't grow a particular fruit, other than to say, "Well, the old folks said it didn't pay." Their knowledge, or lack of it, is embedded in traditional wisdom, and the newcomer, armed with his books but no experience, violates that wisdom only at some risk. More than likely, for all of his knowledge, he has much to learn from the traditional wisdom. Agriculture is full of true but sad stories bearing out this lesson.

Of course, sometimes a new idea or a new plant is a genuine boon to proven food-production practices. Or a scorned native plant with a little improvement may indeed take an honored place in the backyard grove. Or occasionally a plant fallen into disuse may again become worthy because of a change in current farm economies. For any or all three of these reasons, the minor fruits discussed here, at least the ones that are native and acclimated to a particular region, may fit into your grove.

Be aware that only the best varieties will come close in taste to apples, oranges, peaches, plums, and cherries. Be even more aware that most minor fruits have a flaw that you will have to

316

reckon with sooner or later: They like to spread by suckering from roots, or spread uncontrollably by seed, much more than regular fruits. In conditions favorable to them, these fruits can become pest trees or weed trees. In certain situations, particularly where wild waste ground is not being used to any other advantage or is too poor or erosive for other uses, this spreading habit can be a distinct advantage. But in pastures or sod orchards, understand that you will have to control this spreading with regular mowing and a ready spade to dig out unwanted seedlings.

On the other hand, these fruits, in their native habitat, are quite resistant to insects and diseases. They have pest enemies, of course, but you can plant an orchard of persimmon, papaw, and mulberry, along with some native plums, wild apples, crab apples, perhaps a fig, and in the South, a few citrus, and get enough fruit to eat every year without spraying at all.

PERSIMMONS

AMERICAN PERSIMMON

In the Ohio River Valley, in rich bottomland, a wild persimmon tree can grow very large—over 100 feet tall. But on less fertile ground, competing with other trees, persimmons tend to remain small to medium-size, with slender trunks. The leaves are exceedingly attractive to my eyes, anyway. Closely related to ebony, persimmon's very hard wood is used for golf club heads, for loom shuttles, and is in increasing demand for expensive veneer. It makes a good fence post, too. The fruit is characteristically yellow to orange, although the skin may be tinged bluish or gray on an orange background. Individual fruits should be clipped from the tree or picked very carefully to prevent tearing branchlets. Normally, the fruit ripens, falls, and is picked off the ground too soft for shipping, that is, if a commercial market existed for it. American persimmons (*Diospyros virginiana*) are found on the market only locally where the demand for them is traditional. The pulp can be easily frozen and shipped, however, to make or flavor a variety of foods. Persimmon bread, cake, cookies, and ice cream are excellent and could be sold widely I'm sure, particularly the ice cream. The University of Maryland makes it at the dairy store on campus. I love most any ice cream, but persimmon is one of my favorites. The flavor is distinctive and far removed from any of the lingering astringency in the fresh fruit.

The taste of a good persimmon when ripe is somewhat like a plum. Perhaps the best description I could give is that it's a combination of honey and plum. Texture is that of a soft plum. Only the very best persimmons lack some faint residue of the astringency that characterizes unripe persimmons so strongly. Anyone who has bitten into a green persimmon, or one not quite ripe, seldom will try persimmon again. Folklore says that frost takes away the astringency, but this is not true. A quality persimmon ripens to sweet nonastringency well before frost. A poor persimmon will remain astringent right under the skin and around the seed even after hard freezes. Both taste and ripening time vary markedly from tree to tree.

Almost any additional description of persimmon trees bears exceptions. Generally, the trees are male or female, and both are necessary for good pollination. But some male trees also have female blossoms, and some trees are self-fertile. The named variety Meader is a self-fertile seedling nurtured by Dr. E. M. Meader, a Fruit Explorer whom I've mentioned in Chapter 14. Meader planted a couple hundred seeds of Garretson (one of the better, named varieties) from which three survived the cold winters on his farm in New Hampshire. He transplanted the three, and one survived. Not only is Meader self-fertile, but it is nearly seedless. Seedlessness is another variable among American persimmons. Some have up to 12 seeds, some less, some none. Early Golden, John Rick, and some other good, named varieties are also somewhat self-fertile.

Southern strains of American persimmon have narrow leaves and northern strains have broader leaves, but both can grow in the South. The more southerly strains usually have larger fruit—up to 2 inches in diameter compared to a 1-inch average in the North—and the number of quality-tasting persimmons you are apt to find in the South is greater than in the North.

Persimmons are taprooted and survive tenaciously, even on poor ground. Early settlers considered them weed trees since they can take over a field if not controlled. A similar species, the Texas persimmon (or Mexican persimmon), has become a nuisance in southwestern parts of that state, at least to cattlemen. (There are tree-lovers who think that planting Texas persimmon may be a better use of the land than as range.) The cattle, reportedly, scour (suffer diarrhea) on the persimmons. On the other hand, American persimmons are considered a good fattening feed for hogs, mules and calves, and were used that way for many years. J. Russell Smith's book, *Tree Crops,* is full of testimony on the practicality of persimmon trees in pasture for this purpose.

One of my own experiences with persimmons is worth noting. In north central Ohio where I live, the persimmon is quite rare, and I have long thought that the climate was too cold for them. The persimmon likes zone 6 and warmer, and this is a cold zone 5. Then a farmer only a couple of miles away, learning of my interest, took me to his persimmon grove. His farm has been in his family continuously for 140 years. He told me that the grove comes from *one* seed his great-grandfather brought back with him from Georgia during the Civil War. Even before I visited the grove I was greatly intrigued. If the grove came from one seed and fruited crops regularly, as the farmer said, it must be a self-fertile strain. Secondly, if I know my Ohio farm boys, great-grandfather would not have gone to the trouble of bringing a persimmon seed all the way back from Georgia unless the fruit had really tasted wonderful to him.

The grove stands on a poor clay knoll in a pasture overlooking a river. The trees are smallish, slender trunked, wide enough apart from each other for easy walking, and they admit enough light so that even some grass grows among the trees. Continuously pastured for many, many years, the grove seemed a delightful place to walk. It had not "taken over" the pasture, but had spread, by suckering, perhaps to a quarter acre in size over a period of 120 years. There were no fruits on the ground and only a few still clinging in the tree, a sure sign that the taste was good to both cows and wildlife. I tasted and was delighted. I could discern no lingering astringency, only the not unpleasant, cloying honey-plum flavor. The fruits were small, hardly an inch in diameter, though it is likely from what I've heard from other Fruit Explorers that in its original habitat, on better ground, the persimmons might have grown larger.

Needless to say, I have planted seed and will try to transplant stolons (suckers) from this grove. One of my purposes in searching out minor fruits is to find some *useful* fence-row tree that livestock would not eat. I suspect cattle do not crave persimmon leaves (unless they're starving, no animal I know will eat papaw leaves, but I've been told goats will nibble persimmon leaves) and in every other respect, the tree seems to have few objectionable side effects. The climate is just unfavorable enough so that the persimmons don't sucker *vigorously,* if my neighbor's grove is an example.

Propagating persimmons is difficult. A neophyte goes through three levels of awareness about persimmons (about everything, actually). First he hears about the fruit from reading a book such as this and believes he has discovered The Promised Fruit of Paradise. He orders nursery trees, both the common seedlings offered and a few named, grafted varieties. All of them die. In the meantime, he eats a few persimmons from a wild tree he finds that pucker his mouth so that he cannot whistle for three days. Then he enters the second level of awareness—that persimmons are not, after all, The Promised Fruit of Paradise. But assuming that he is one of the few fruit enthusiasts with real persistence, he tries again. This time he plants seeds as experienced persimmon growers had told him to do in the first place. He plants them in place so he doesn't have to move them later. If they grow the second year, he grafts on scionwood from the best, named varieties or from choice trees that he has located in the wild. (The best, named varieties for scionwood are Early Golden, John Rick, Meader, Garretson, Ruby, Craggs, and Florence— T. O. Warren says Florence is lousy, but J. C. McDaniel, another foremost authority on persimmons at the University of Illinois, recommends it among others, which probably means that persimmons taste differently when raised in different areas.) Now this onetime neophyte is in the persimmon business. Now he is at level three in awareness: Some persimmons are great some of the time, but any persimmon might be a flop at any particular time.

In planting seed, do not let it dry out. Eat the persimmon and plant the seed, no more than an inch under the soil. Winter freezing should stratify it enough for germination, but not always. You can store seed in plastic bags in the freezer or refrigerator over winter, too. Don't put water in with them. If still moist when wrapped, they will be fine.

Persimmons graft easily, say those who have done it. A simple splice graft does the trick, as does a whip and tongue.

Transplanting persimmon trees (or papaw trees) is most difficult because the trees from nurseries or the ones you try to dig up in the woods are often stolons without sufficient root development. But even grafted trees are inclined to die in transplanting. All kinds of reasons have been suggested to explain this, but I know one way to avoid the problem most of the time. Plant hard-to-transplant trees in virgin soil. I reserve the edges of my woods for such trees. With good care the trees survive better than when planted in the old farm fields or in

Illus. 16-1—American Persimmon.

ordinary orchards. Also, tree seeds come up better in virgin soil. I have my own theories about this, as I have explained elsewhere. It is my firm but sad belief that it would take thousands of years of reevolution to return our heavily farmed soils to the state of pristine, ecological fertility capable of supporting the tremendous variety of plant life that nature intended it to. The longer we continue on our present course, the fewer species will be able to survive on these soils. Somewhere along the line man himself will become extinct, or nearly so, and then the slow process of rejuvenation will begin again.

By the time you read this, a book on persimmons should be available called *Persimmons for Everyone,* published by the North American Fruit Explorers. It contains not only everything you ever wanted to know about persimmons, but scads of recipes for making use of them.

Henry Hartman offers scionwood and seedlings at the Jersey Chestnut Farm (see the Appendix for address). The selection, Gehron, in Louisiana, comes from Louisiana Nursery, Sunset Road, Opelousas, LA 70570. It is self-fertile, but you'll be better off with two trees no matter what the variety. The Louis Gerardi Nursery and Talbott Nursery (see the Appendix for addresses) usually have a few grafted trees to sell.

ORIENTAL PERSIMMON

Diospyros Kaki, the oriental persimmon, Chinese persimmon, or Japanese persimmon, is a larger, far showier fruit than the American species, but there is disagreement among enthusiasts over which actually tastes better. *D. Kaki* is firmer when ripe, however, and can be picked off the tree and shipped, so it has entered into commercial trade as fresh fruit. In addition, there are some strains of *D. Kaki* that are nonastringent, or nearly so. Astringent strains are often treated with ethylene to reduce bitterness since, commercially, the fruit often must be picked before it is completely ripe, when the fruit is still astringent. (You can reduce astringency at home by enclosing a number of persimmons in a plastic bag with an apple or two. The ethylene from the apples "absorbs" the bitterness to some extent.) But even so, some people claim they can detect a lingering astringency on commercial oriental persimmons that makes them compare unfavorably with a tree-ripened, quality, American persimmon. In places where persimmon-lovers can get both high-quality varieties ripe from the tree, they often score the oriental as having as good or better a taste as the American persimmons.

Since the American persimmon is the hardier of the two (orientals are risky north of zone 7), the backyard grove-owner probably ought to choose American over oriental. Since the oriental is usually grafted to the American for rootstock, grove-owners in zone 7 and south might train forked trees with one American branch and the other one oriental. Cross pollination might produce what the fruit-breeders have long tried to develop—a hybrid having the best advantages of both.

The best place to grow oriental persimmons is in the mild area of California and similar southwestern climates, although good trees also are reported in Gulf Coast states. For the general grove-owner, the experience of Dr. James B. Shanks of the University of Maryland might be most appropriate. Shanks has been collecting persimmon varieties from all over the country and testing them at the Wye Institute on Maryland's Eastern Shore, a zone 7 climate with considerable winter variation in temperature that can be disastrous to semihardy plants such as oriental persimmon. Of the varieties on test, Shanks says survival rate during the severe '77 and '78 winters was good. (See Bulletin No. 5532 of the Maryland Agricultural Experimentation, Department of Horticulture, College Park, MD 20740.) In general, he finds culture of the oriental not unlike that of the American and notes that oriental is hard to transplant, too.

Based on his experience, Shanks recommends the following varieties for a zone 7 type climate such as the Eastern Shore. Varieties astringent until soft-ripe: Eureka, Great Wall, Kyung-sun Ban-Si, Peiping, Pen Saijo, Sheng, Tamopan, and Tecumseh. Varieties that are nonstringent, "sweet" types: Fuyu, Gosho, Jiro, and Smith's Best. The latter is a selection from J. Russell Smith's plantings in Virginia. Shanks and others have high praise for it. It is what the trade calls a "chocolate" persimmon, meaning it ripens to a dark brown black color. In fact, there is a California variety called Chocolate.

Some of these varieties are sold by nurseries now. Bountiful Ridge Nurseries has Tamopan, Eureka, Fuyuaki (which, I believe, is the same as Fuyu—both are nonastringent), plus Tanenashi, which is astringent until fully ripe. Another possible source I would check if I lived in the South would be O. S. Gray Nursery, Arlington, TX. As an established member of the North American Fruit Growers, you could soon learn of many private sources of scionwood, too.

The feeling I get from talking to people experimenting with persimmons is that the American is a more practical tree to grow. If for no other reason, it is a more dependable bearer. The best news I've heard yet is of a relatively new discovery, a persimmon that appears to be a cross between *D. virginiana* and *D. Kaki* with some of the advantages of both. It is called Eureka (not to be confused with the Eureka variety mentioned above), and it is being propagated for sale now by Paul M. Goodwin of Goodwin Nursery (see the Appendix for address). Goodwin says the tree was hybridized by J. E. Fitzgerald more than 50 years ago. "It will grow anywhere *D. virginiana* will, according to him, *if* it is budded or grafted above ground level," says Goodwin. "I have found this true so far, and have heard from other members of the Northern Nut Growers Association of a Eureka grafted high in a native clump of *D. virginiana* doing splendidly." Goodwin is in the process of experimenting with various buds and grafts at different heights above ground level, and he hopes to have trees for sale in quantity before much longer. He sent me color photos of the persimmon—certainly it is as beautiful as any *D. Kaki*, as the large fruit ripens to almost a deep red from golden orange, with, according to Goodwin, "the most delicious sweet taste of any persimmon."

PAPAWS

Papaw enthusiasts say that if plant breeding were to be concentrated on papaws for several centuries as it has been on apples, a fruit better than apples might result. Their evidence is the papaw itself. Without any breeding improvement at all, it tastes far better than the sour little apples from which today's apples were developed.

The papaw tastes somewhat like a banana and is often called wild banana, Michigan banana, or Nebraska banana. If you really like bananas, you should like papaws; the taste of either is a bit too cloying for me to want more than one at infrequent intervals. As one of my neighbors likes to put it, "Papaw pie is wonderful, but one a year is enough." Though some books counsel eating papaws when they're fully ripe and the skin is dark brown, they actually taste better a little before that, when the skin is yellow. The crushed seeds contain an alkaloid that is poisonous, but, of course, animals (especially raccoons) eat them all the time and the seeds go right through their bodies. Wild cherry seeds are also mildly poisonous but go harmlessly through the birds that eat them.

Corwin Davis, considered a leading authority on papaws, once told me that most papaws are not worth growing because the taste is poor. He tries to convince anyone who will listen to eat good, named varieties and to keep checking every wild tree for better ones. Davis sells seeds and sometimes a few grafted trees in his retirement and has a selection named after him. Typical of his salty honesty, he does not think Davis is the best. He prefers Sunflower, Taytwo, Overleese, and Taylor. Finding a good wild papaw, according to Davis, is about a 1,000 to 1 shot.

Illus. 16-2—Papaw.

324

Papaw is an intriguing fruit, as much because of what we don't know about it as what we do know. It is a tropical fruit that somehow has become acclimated to cold climates as far north as eastern Nebraska and southern Michigan. It has very large, long leaves. Its early spring green flowers turn purple as they mature. The best guess as to how a tropical fruit found its way north is that it came with the Indians. Presumably, Indians in the early migrations from Central or South America brought the tree with them. These Indians, who, according to some theories, developed into the Mound Builders who practiced an advanced form of agriculture, are thought to have planted the papaw as they migrated northward, always taking with them the trees that survived in the current climate.

Paul Thompson, a fruit expert in California who has studied the papaw for a long time, doesn't believe that theory. He says, "Indian cultures may have distributed the papaw more widely, but I'm of the opinion that it originated in North America, and the migrating tribes found it when they came."

The papaw certainly *acts* as if it were a foreigner—that is, few insects and animals seem to have any ecological link with it. One of the few insects that shows much interest in eating the leaves is the zebra swallowtail butterfly, a somewhat rare butterfly that itself looks as if it came north from the tropics. The papaw is difficult to get pollenized because it starts blooming earlier than when most bees are active. Bees are not particularly attracted, anyway. Veteran papaw growers have learned that certain flies, especially those attracted to dead animals, will pollenize the papaw. One grower I know advises placing a small, dead animal under the trees in spring. Another grower hangs dead fish in his trees, which attract greenbottle flies. The flies in turn help with the pollenation.

As with persimmons, papaws are best planted by seed. Plant the seed before it dries out or hold it over winter in the refrigerator in a plastic bag. The seeds are slow to germinate and may not come up until July, or sometimes the following year. Papaws seem to survive the first year or two better in partial shade. They will continue to grow in partial shade in later years, but they do far better in full light. They prefer rich bottomland, although I have found them growing on mountainsides in Kentucky.

Unlike persimmons, papaws bloom early in spring when frost may kill the blossoms. But some blossoms continue to form later, so some fruit usually survives.

325

Some growers say that papaws graft fairly easily, but I think that is because these fellows are experienced grafters. Graft them as you would apples, but don't expect too many takes until you become skilled at the task. Grafting is, at any rate, the best way to get a good variety started. You can buy scionwood much more often than grafted trees. Do not plant seeds more than an inch deep—just under rotted mulch is best. If you plant in a bed for later transplantation, move them soon after they germinate. Once the taproot gets down into the soil, the tree is very difficult to move. Small sprouts around an established wild tree are usually suckers coming up from the roots. If you cut the root that leads back to the mother tree, the stolon on it will develop its own roots faster than it would naturally (or it may die). A year later you can safely move it. Bring as much dirt along as you can. I have noted earlier, with persimmons, that if you plant in virgin soil, your chances will be better. That's also true of papaw and any other fruit, too.

The most complete treatment of the papaw that I know was published in the 1974 yearbook of the California Rare Fruit Growers (vol. 6), available at $6 plus 50¢ postage. (See the Appendix for address.)

MULBERRIES

Taste and dessert quality among mulberries vary tremendously, also. The white mulberry, *Morus alba,* is the most insipid. The American native mulberry, *M. rubra,* a reddish to black fruit about an inch long, is sometimes not bad at all. We have a large tree in our woods, and some of the neighbors enjoy its crops. I think I would, too, if it were not for the quarts and quarts of other berries I eat instead at the time. Raspberries take away any desire I might otherwise have for this fruit. On the other hand, these mulberries are there in the woods every year in great abundance from no labor of mine. These are not as bland as the white types and can make fair desserts, especially if mixed with another, tarter fruit. A homesteading family of my acquaintance dries mulberries and uses them in muffins as a substitute for blueberries. They're good, too.

One of the problems with mulberries is the nomenclature. The white mulberry can have black fruit. The old Russian mulberry, as it is called (*M. alba* 'Tatarica'), is reddish to black. Weeping forms of mulberry that you see as beautiful little trees in front of older homes are forms of white mulberry, though the fruit is black. One on the lawn of the grade school I attended has not changed in size, as far as I can tell, in 40 years. We used to hide inside its weeping branches and stuff ourselves on those mulberries, and I still manage to eat a few off it every year. They are fairly good, to tell the truth, and I think no one bothers to pick them anymore because we are spoiled with ample supplies of apples, oranges, grapefruit, raisins, and bananas, none of which were plentiful on home tables 40 years ago. But I think kids no longer care much about such fruits because the fruity taste we once craved now is supplied in many other ways, not the least of which are soft drinks. Even the poorest kids can guzzle fruit-flavored sugar water today.

Because some white mulberries are black, knowledgeable fruit growers with roots in other countries complain that what is often sold as black mulberry in the United States is really white mulberry. The true *M. nigra* is not found in this country except, say some, for a few so-called "Persian" mulberries, brought in from Italy years ago and grown in California. These mulberries are supposed to be far superior in taste to common mulberries. Among the mulberry testers in the North American Fruit Explorers, certain mulberries grown in Iran and Afghanistan, both black and white kinds, are considered to be of excellent taste. The Explorers hope that these will someday be available in this country.

Illus. 16-3—Mulberry.

In the meantime, two of the better varieties of common mulberry seem to be the Illinois, which has been sold by the Louis Gerardi Nursery, and the Wellington, from the New York State Fruit Testing Cooperative Association (see the Appendix for addresses). Other varieties of long-standing reputation are Hicks, Downing, and Black English. All the named varieties seem to be crosses between white and red mulberries.

Mulberries are among the toughest of trees. They make good windbreak material on the most barren, windswept plains of the Dakotas. They are excellent pioneer plantings on ruined, eroded soil. They transplant easily, and they are easy to start from cuttings. The wood makes good fence posts and firewood. The fruit makes excellent hog and poultry feed. For all of its rapacious growth—I have a young tree that added 4 feet of new growth on the branches in virgin soil last year—the tree does not spread much by suckering, and only mildly so from bird-scattered seed.

Mulberries are susceptible to scale attacks and some insects in the South. In the North, I've never seen one attacked by anything except birds that were after the berries. The weeping forms are very attractive as lawn trees without any of the faults of other weeping tree forms. An excellent backyard tree, it will lure birds away from better fruit. But don't plant mulberry trees over sidewalks or patios, or the kids will track the squashed berries into the house.

FIGS

The commercial fig industry is almost strictly a processed-food business. Fresh figs are very hard to handle and so remain pretty much a backyard food.

Though fig trees survive and fruit even in the Great Lakes area, they are practical for food only in the South—zone 7 and south. Among the two kinds is the Smyrna-type fig, which requires a special insect to pollenate it and is grown almost exclusively in California. Smyrna figs have a somewhat higher dessert quality and are the ones sold in commercial trade.

The other figs, grown from Texas to Georgia and the Carolinas, set fruit without pollenation. Of these varieties, Celeste and Brown Turkey are most often recommended. Texas Everbearing and Kadota are sometimes added to recommended lists. Brown Turkey is somewhat better tasting, according to most, but Celeste has an advantage over the others that makes it the first choice among backyard fig growers. On most varieties, the end of the fruit is open; that is, it has an "open eye" into which fruit bugs can crawl and ruin the fruit, or excessive moisture can enter in rainy periods and split the fruit. Celeste has a closed eye, and thus the problem is avoided. Other names for it are Celestial, Celeste Violette, Sugar, Small Brown, Malta, and Blue Celeste. My correspondent of many years now, Eck Bozeman in Louisiana, who sends me delicious, canned Celeste figs every year, says the Celeste has other favorable properties. It does not break dormancy as easy as some and therefore does not start growing during an unusual warm spell in late winter and then freeze back.

Trees are fairly easy to propagate with cuttings. A new tree can be trained to a central leader shape, but many backyarders prefer to cut back the main stem and encourage several shoots to grow up at ground level. Three or so are saved, and the tree is trained to three or more low, spreading trunks. If freeze-back occurs, this form seems to encourage quick, new shoot replacement, and the shoots soon fruit.

Ants that carry mealybugs into the trees can be controlled the same way as with aphid-herding ants on apples. Keeping trash cleaned up from around trees helps.

Many old-timers believe trees bear better if planted next to the wall of a building. I've heard of both a sunny wall and a north

Illus. 16-4—Fig.

wall as preferred sites. An explanation from a University of Georgia bulletin may account for this belief—and then it may not, too. According to the bulletin, in deep, sandy soil, figs are often bothered by a soil nematode, but not so much on clay soils. If sandy soils are prevalent, says the bulletin, planting a fig near a building helps because the tree's shallow roots grow under the building into soil free of nematodes.

If you are harvesting a lot of figs at once, wear gloves. The juice can irritate your skin after a while. Pick, keeping the stem on the fruit. Celeste does not have to be skinned, but most other varieties do. A big fig tree can produce 60 to 80 gallons of fruit in one crop.

The shortleaf fig, *Ficus laevigata,* is native to Florida, and should be preferred there, for the backyard, since it is more trouble free. It bears small fruit, about ½ inch across, that ripen to a red color. Though more of an ornamental, the fruit is sweet and quite edible.

JUJUBE

From time to time, excitement flares up over this oriental fruit (*Ziziphus jujuba*), commonly called Chinese date, and then subsides, as yet another generation of hopeful advocates realizes the tree's shortcomings. The fruit is rather dry and bland, although good if dried and eaten with a sweetener, in which case it resembles a date.

Illus. 16-5—Jujube.

Flesh of the fruit is green; the outer skin when ripe is brown with perhaps splotches of yellow and orange. The shape varies from round to oval to pear, and the size is about that of a small apple. It grows best in the dry, hot Southwest, from Oklahoma and Texas to California. Trees grow and produce fruit, however, in such diverse locations as Tifton, Georgia, and in the Morton Arboretum in northern Illinois. The U.S. Southern Great Plains Field Station at Woodward, Oklahoma, has worked with jujube extensively. Check the horticulture department at Oklahoma State University for the latest reports.

Jujube trees of reported merit grow in the Gulf states, but most experimenters I have talked to, or those whose reports I've read in the *Pomona,* are negative. Fruits by and large just don't taste that good. The tree is usually quite thorny, and some trees will sucker badly. T. O. Warren, after working with jujube for some years, gave his "final opinion" in 1977: "I have delayed now for six years giving the trees the axe—hoping. But in the end I know I will."

Jujube enthusiasts regret such reports, believing that the fruit needs only breeding development to become a popular addition to the home grove and to commercial production. Time will tell.

AUTUMN OLIVE

John English, a farmer and Fruit Explorer near Bloomington, Illinois, first taught me to sample autumn olive berries whenever I had a chance. Sure enough, some tasted quite good and would obviously make excellent jellies as well as a nice snack while I walked around the farm. And some, as he said, tasted bitter. And also, as he said, the birds knew the difference.

The Soil Conservation Service has been energetically pushing the Cardinal strain of autumn olive for wildlife plantings. My brother and I planted a bunch of them many years ago and are living to regret it, despite the very good effects of this plant. In addition to wildlife feed, it is excellent bee graze, and is one of the few nonleguminous plants that fixes nitrogen in the soil. But birds gorge on the berries and scatter the seed, which starts new plantings everywhere just as vigorous and almost as offensive as multiflora rose. The size of the thorns on autumn olive varies, but some have very nasty thorns indeed. A word to the wise is sufficient.

BLACK HAW VIBURNUM

If I had to do it over again, I would have planted black haw viburnum, not autumn olive, for wildlife food. This viburnum does not spread so rampantly (although it does sucker). It resembles a small apple tree. The fruits are dark bluish when ripe, about the size and shape of an olive. They're good munching on a hike and good for wild animals. The little trees will grow into a sort of natural hedge. They are available from Southmeadow Fruit Gardens, mentioned earlier.

CORNELIAN CHERRY

All dogwood berries are well liked by birds, even the bluish white bitter berries of red osier dogwood. But cornelian cherry (*Cornus mas*), also known as check cherry, has berries that I enjoy eating out of hand. On the campus of Wooster College in Wooster, Ohio, there are some cornelians with an excellent taste. The "cherries" are oval or elongated rather than round, but of about the same size as a sour cherry.

Illus. 16-6—Cornelian Cherry.

OGEECHEE TUPELO

This small tupelo tree (*Nyssa ogeche*) is known colloquially in the Southeast as "lime tree." Traditionally, the fruits are gathered and made into jelly. The tree is very localized, growing mostly in swampy areas of the Southeast, mostly along the Georgia-Florida border. I mention it because it is one of the few fruit trees that grows well in wet soil. The tree is related to dogwood. The leaves are shiny green, the fruit red, up to 1½ inches long. Southern grove-owners with swampy areas should find it inte⁻esting. I know of no nursery sources.

TROPICAL TREE FRUITS

In the national view, only a very small part of the United States mainland has the proper climate for tropical or subtropical fruit trees. But because of the large number of people spending winters in these warm areas, and retiring there, a few words of instruction are in order. If nothing else, the Northerner moving south will be delightfully amazed at the large number of trees that produce food in places such as south Florida and southern California.

If you have not grown up with them, tropical fruit trees seem so exotic that you assume they demand a different kind of care and knowledge. Ordinarily, they don't. The same common-sense pruning and fertilizing practices that are useful with apple and peach trees apply also to tropical fruit trees. It is always somewhat amusing to leaf through a book or encyclopedia on tropical fruits and read under nearly every entry the same obvious type of instruction: "Plant in a fertile, well-drained, sunny location." Most gardening books could be reduced in size by one-third by putting the following statements in the introduction: "Unless otherwise noted, all fruit trees discussed herein grow best in fertile, well-drained soil in a sunny location when protected from cold winds and when mulched regularly. Prune out dead and diseased limbs and bad crotch angles." To repeat this noninstruction owlishly under every variety discussed is an insult to the intelligence of the reading public.

OLIVE

No one who lives in an olive-producing region of the world would list the olive under a heading of "minor fruits." The olive, in fact, should be honored with the first and longest chapter in books of this kind, since it represents a good argument for a stable agriculture built on tree farming and the best example of all of using food trees on land that would otherwise be nearly worthless.

But, though a leading fruit of the world, the olive grows and fruits only in a small portion of the United States—the dry, hot valleys of southern California and Arizona. Worldwide, most olives are processed for oil, but in this country the relatively few grown are used mostly for food and in martinis. Though little work has been done on it yet, olive oil would be a great though expensive fuel after further processing. In our Southeast, the tree makes a nice ornamental, but the climate is too humid for it to set fruit of any significant amount.

Olive trees will last for 500 years, and some still alive are known to be over 1,000 years old. The development of the olive makes an interesting model for those pioneers in this country who seek to upgrade some of our native, pest-resistant fruits to economic value. The olive off the tree is too bitter to eat. The typical person today would simply discard it and go on to something else. But because the olive is so wondrously adaptive to certain parts of the world, an earlier, so-called primitive man "made do" with it. Instead of trying to bring in some exotic tree with tasty fruit to those areas, countless generations of humans kept working with this bitter-fruited tree that would grow in very dry, almost desert conditions, and never die. They learned that acidulous treatment would take away the bitterness and

Illus. 16-7—Olive.

leave a tasty and very nutritious fruit. Lye, lactic acid, or a strong brine is used today. The oil is pressed from seeds and pulp. It must be aged until it becomes mild enough to the taste, in about six months.

Olives will start from cuttings. History says that the Roman Legions inadvertently spread the trees by using branches as stakes for their horses. When they rode away, the stakes rooted.

You can also start olives from seed. Craig Dremann, of Redwood City Seed Company, is the source for seeds I know of. Dremann says the seed should be sown in a mixture of three-quarters sand and one-quarter soil. Clip off the point of the seed at the pointed end to encourage faster germination. The soil should be moist at first, and then it should be maintained fairly dry. Germination may take as much as five months, but usually occurs in a little over one month.

The tried and true varieties in California are Mission, Mansanillo, Sevillano, and Ascolano. In Florida a tree called Madagascar olive (*Noronhia emarginata*) is grown as an ornamental, but it is not a true olive. Fruit is a little over an inch in diameter, dark purple when ripe. The pulp around the seed is edible.

CALIFORNIA BAY OR LAUREL

I have a small bottle carved out of Oregon myrtle, a most beautiful wood, but only lately have I learned that Oregon myrtle is the same tree as the California laurel (*Umbellularia californica*). In some localities it is also called pepperwood or peppernut (not to be confused with the California pepper tree) because the seed has a peppery taste, and when it's ground it can be used as a condiment in that way. Dremann tells me that the seed, when roasted, is delicious. But more interesting than that, he says the flesh tastes like avocado, to which it is related. Varieties could no doubt be developed with thicker flesh and substituted for avocado. The range of the former is considerably more extensive than the latter.

AVOCADO

At least three groups or races of avocado (*Persea americana*) comprise the ancestry of present-day hybrids and crosses:

Mexican, West Indian, and Guatemalan. The leading varieties in California are Hass, which ripens in spring-summer, and Fuerta, which ripens as a fall and winter crop. Florida varieties, mostly or partially West Indian origin, include Dupuis, Pollock, Simmonds, Nadir, and Waldin, which mature from June through September. Fall varieties include Booth, Hicks, Hall, and Lula. Winter varieties are Choquette, Monroe, and Taylor. Thus, it is possible to grow avocados in their range nearly all year long.

Varieties are not usually self-fertile, especially in the crosses, and you should be sure to plant varieties that will pollenate each other. For example, according to *Taylor's Encyclopedia of Gardening,* Booth and Lula are compatible, as are Waldin and Pollock, and Fuerta and Lula. Check with your nurseryman when you buy. Two different varieties are not necessarily compatible.

Seeds germinate easily. A seed suspended in a glass of water so that the seed just touches the water's surface will root and can then be potted.

BANANA

Only in parts of southern Florida do bananas (*Musa sapientum*) fruit well enough to be practical, but where they do grow, they are a good choice for the backyard. George Geiger, a correspondent from south Florida, regularly raises them organically, using lots of composted grass clippings for mulch and fertilizer.

Bananas sucker from the main root clump, and backyard growers prune out all but about four of these for fruiting stalks. After a stalk fruits, it's finished and should be cut out in favor of a young stalk. The trick is to keep a steady succession of stalks coming on. From scratch, it takes a year to a year and a half to get fruit. If a stalk end does freeze, usually it will not fruit. Best to cut it out in favor of a new stalk. Even in south Florida it pays to grow the tree in a spot protected from north winds.

Cavendish is the most widely grown variety. Hart's Choice, or Lady Finger, is an old favorite. Orinoco, or horse banana (also called hog banana), is a hardier kind. About every five years the roots can be dug up, separated, and new rhizome cuttings can be planted.

Geiger says that a banana ripened on the tree tastes much better than store-bought, which probably won't surprise even

Northerners, since the same seems to be true of most fruit. Bananas can be cooked and fried, too, something many Northerners may not know.

DATE PALM

Commercial dates (*Phoenix dactylifera*) are produced in California, Arizona, and Texas, in specific areas where the critical amount of heat occurs. Very hot, dry weather combined with ample irrigation grows the best dates. Raising the fruit commercially is an exacting process. Trees are male and female, and groves—called gardens, colloquially—are laid out as blocks of female trees surrounded by a row of males. Hand-pollenating is often done, too, to insure heavy fruit set. Fruit bunches are thinned then, if necessary, and tied. Later the bunches may be covered to protect them from possible damaging rain at ripening time. Harvesting begins in September and lasts until about Christmas.

In an interesting article in *Organic Gardening and Farming* magazine (November, 1969), Lee Goldman describes how Lee Anderson controlled the date beetle in his Coachella Valley groves: ". . . the date beetle spends the winter among the fallen dates. These supply food and lodging for free and the beetle emerges in the spring to become a pest. 'We tried to combat this problem by having all fallen fruit picked up by hand, then fed to our hogs,' says Anderson. 'This proved costly, so we tried turning the hogs into each 10-acre tract after every picking. They cooperated beautifully—getting their exercise and part of their food at the same time—and cleaning the date garden of possible winter housing for the beetles.' Now a herd of 150 pigs is run through regularly after harvest to clean up drops and prevent insects from overwintering.

"Next step [in controlling the date beetle] . . . is to hang buckets on each date palm tree . . . filling them with melon rinds, tomatoes, or any fruit which ferments—the date beetle's preferred diet. Soon the beetles leave other areas of the garden and flock to the bait in the buckets, where they are simply scalded with hot water once a week."

The most commonly grown date varieties are Khadraw, Deglet-Noor, Medjool, Barhi, Zahidi, and Halawy. Dates are especially low in sodium and hence are a good food for the hypertensive.

MANGO

The climate for mangoes (*Mangifera indica*) is suitable in the southernmost parts of Florida, although some are grown in southern California. The trees will grow fairly well in sandy soil. Fruit of the improved varieties is sweet, somewhat like a peach, but more cloying. Blossoms are a beautiful ivory to red, and the fruit ranges from green to yellow through orange and sometimes purplish red.

The trees make fine shade trees, but around homes they are usually kept pruned back to 40 feet or less. A 5-inch-diameter fruit, falling from the 80-foot height to which the tree can grow, could be dangerous to your health. The varieties most often planted are Keitt, Tommy Atkins, Irwin, and Kent. Keitt and Kent average 24 ounces in weight of ripe fruit and are considered the best in quality. Julie is a variety that comes true from seed.

GUAVA

Seedlings of guava grow wild in southern Florida. Some taste very good, some not so good. Improved varieties from the University of Miami and elsewhere are usually much better. Guavas grow easily from seed. Propagate good varieties by air-layering.

The odor of the common guava (*Psidium guajava*) puts some people off, but other than that, the fruit makes good jelly and preserves, and is used in relishes, too. The fruit is pear shaped and whitish yellow. Being high in pectin, the fruit makes lots of jelly per pound of guava, and the plants are very prolific.

The strawberry guava (*P. cattleianum*) is red, as the name indicates, spicier, but smaller than the common guava.

Improved varieties include Red Indian, Ruby, Miami Red, and Miami White. The Caribbean fruit fly is becoming a real problem for guava.

LITCHI

The litchi or lychee (*Litchi chinensis*) has been cultivated in Florida for only about 40 years, but has proven itself as an excellent backyard food tree. It grows only about 35 feet tall, with evergreen leaves, panicles of greenish white flowers, and red fruit when ripe. The fruit is delicious, sub-acid, sort of like a grape in texture and flavor. When dried, it resembles a raisin and is called litchi nut. Brewster is the old reliable Florida variety. Unfortunately, the tree does well only in frost-free areas.

PAPAYA

Virus problems torment growers of papaya (*Carica papaya*) in Florida. The fruit is a true tropical and will not tolerate below-freezing temperatures, either. The fruit is melonlike, yellow orange, musky, and sweet, and well worth growing if you are situated properly. Seedlings naturalize away from commercial and backyard plantings, and these trees usually have inferior fruit. But check them out. Trees are usually male or female, but some are both. Solo is the main variety, and as often as not comes from Hawaii for the commercial market. Unripe fruit can be cooked as a vegetable. Papaya juice is used as a meat tenderizer, too.

CHERIMOYA, SWEETSOP, AND CUSTARD APPLE

Cherimoya (*Annona Cherimola*) is a tropical tree that can be grown in California from Santa Barbara southward. It will grow in south Florida but doesn't produce well there. Fruits may weigh up to a pound but are usually half that size or less. The fruit has a custardlike texture and is eaten fresh. The bumpy-skinned fruits are superior to the smooth-skinned varieties. Since the cherimoya can't be shipped, it has not been commercialized to any great extent and is available only locally.

In Florida, sweetsop (*A. squamosa*) grows better than cherimoya, tastes almost as good, but is even more perishable when ripe. Nevertheless, for zone 9 in Florida, it is a better backyard tree. Another relative, *A. reticulata,* called custard apple or bullock's-heart because of its shape, is also edible, but inferior to the other two.

MINOR TROPICAL FRUITS

Here's an additional list of minor tropical fruits that you will want to investigate if you have a permanent residence in zone 9.

Acerola, *Malpighia glabra*
Baobab, *Adansonia digitata* (edible, but not much good)
Beach screw pine, *Pandanus tectorius*
Black sapote, *Diospyros digyna* (a type of persimmon)
Brush cherry, *Eugenia paniculata*
Canistel or eggfruit, *Pouteria campechiana*

Carambola, *Averrhoa Carambola* (Highly recommended by Marian Van Atta in her *Living Off the Land,* a subtropic handbook which I highly recommend to all grove-owners in the tropical parts of the United States. She mentions the varieties Golden Star, Newcomb, Peisy Tao, and Thayer. Her handbook at this writing is available from Marian Van Atta, P.O. Box 2131, Melbourne, FL 32901.)

Ceylon gooseberry, *Dovyalis hebecarpa*
Coconut, *Cocos nucifera*
Coco plum or icaco, *Chrysobalanus Icaco*
Coffee tree, *Coffea arabica* (very iffy; needs special protection from cold weather)
Common screw pine, *Pandanus utilis*
Geiger tree, *Cordia Sebestena*
Governor's plum, *Flacourtia indica*
Hog plum, *Spondias Mombin*
Indian jujube, *Ziziphus mauritiana*
Jackfruit, *Artocarpus heterophyllus* (edible, but not much good; the cooked seeds are prized in the tropics)
Jambolan, *Syzygium cumini*
Jelly palm, *Butia capitata* (Julia F. Morton [*500 Plants of South Florida,* Miami, E. A. Seeman Publishing, Inc., 1974] says the jelly palm is actually hardy to Virginia.)
Limeberry, *Triphasia trifolia*
Passion fruit, *Passiflora edulis*
Pigeon plum, *Coccoloba diversifolia*
Pomegranate, *Punica granatum*
Provision tree, *Pachira aquatica*
Red ironwood, *Reynosia septentrionalis*
Rose apple, *Syzygium Jambos*
Saw palmetto, *Serenoa repens*
Spanish plum or red mombin, *Spondias purpurea*
Star gooseberry, *Phyllanthus acidus*
Surinam cherry, *Eugenia uniflora*
Tamarind, *Tamarindus indica*
Tropical almond, *Terminalia Catappa*
Wine palm, *Caryota urens*

The yearbooks of the California Rare Fruit Growers (see the Appendix for address) are another good source of information on tropical fruits.

CHAPTER 17

WALNUTS AND HICKORIES

The walnut family includes hickories, pecans, walnuts, butternuts, and heartnuts, and all of them are managed in somewhat the same manner. All exhibit wide variation in nut quality in the wild. All produce wood of value. The edible nuts of these trees are almost all delicious, save for some pignuts and bitternut hickories, and provide a source of balanced protein. All of the native species produce nuts dependably in their range without spraying, although the alternate-bearing habit (producing nuts only every other year) is characteristic of all species. About half of the hickory nuts on any given tree in any given woodlot are liable to be wormy. Even then, a couple of trees will produce more good nuts than a family needs. High-quality pecans in intensive cultivation are susceptible to almost as many profit-cutting ailments as apples. But individual trees in backyard situations usually get by without spraying. Very large mature trees are beyond the backyarder's ability to spray, anyway.

Why our native nuts have never become popular with the suburban homeowner outside of the pecan-growing areas of the South is one of those mysteries for which I have heard only one adequate explanation. Black walnuts, hickory nuts, butternuts, native pecans with northern-hardiness, and other wild nuts have had little immediate potential for commercial sale, so their improvement has not been a matter of pressing concern at land

341

grant colleges and agricultural research stations. It is sort of like the young person looking for a job. He can't get hired until he has experience, and he can't get experience until he gets hired. So, too, hickories and black walnuts won't sell profitably until improvements in breeding take place, but funding for improvements won't come until the nuts start selling profitably. As a result, today more and more people who have turned to gardening and then to growing food trees can't find good supplies of trees that have been grafted to improve nut varieties.

What is available almost always comes from a few small nurseries or devoted amateur backyard growers who belong to the Northern Nut Growers Association (NNGA), or to the many state and regional associations of amateur nut growers. These hobbyists seek out and collect exceptional varieties, grow, graft, and hybridize them in their backyards, and in general go about enthusiastically trying to convince anyone who will listen that the *best* varieties of native nuts are well worth growing and are far superior to the run-of-the-mill woodlot tree. Doug Campbell, a past president of NNGA, a man I quote often because I've rarely met anyone so enthusiastic about "groves of trees to live in," has a theory about why more people don't grow native nuts in their yards. It's not so much that the people don't know anything about nuts, he says, *but that they know so many things that aren't so!*

Among the false nutlore, Campbell gives a few examples: (1) "You can't get a good nut tree from a seedling."—Not always true, by far, and especially not true with chestnuts. (See the next chapter for discussion of chestnuts.) (2) "You can't graft chestnut trees successfully."—Not so. Grafts take hold much of the time. (3) "You can't grow pecans in the North."—He showed me delicious pecans grown near Lake Erie in northern Ohio. (4) "You can't grow a producing hickory in less than 20 years."— Campbell has two Fayette shellbarks in his Ontario grove that were planted as 14-inch-tall transplants and that started bearing nuts five years later. (5) "You can't get good crops of nuts from a hican."—Campbell says the varieties Des Moines, Burton, and Henke produce fairly well and regularly. (6) "You can't produce shellbark hickories which crack and release the kernels easily."—A myth, says Campbell, and I certainly agree. Keystone and Fayette both crack out easily, he says, and I know several wild trees that also crack out as well or better than most shagbark hickories. (7) "You can't make a commercial return on nut crops in the Northeast."—You can on chestnuts, says Campbell.

I can add a few more beliefs that ain't necessarily so. (8) "It takes too much time to crack and pick out wild nuts."—Not if you have a variety that cracks well. Proceed by first cracking out a whole pan full of hickory nuts, *then* sit down (before the fire) and pick out the "whole halves" and other large pieces from the shells. Don't try to pick out every tiny piece of nutmeat. That's what takes the time. Black walnuts pick out even faster because the nut pieces are bigger. (9) "Black walnut hulls are too icky. Hulling the nuts stains my hands for weeks."—If you begin harvest right after the nuts fall, one bop of a hammer on the soft, green hull will release the nut enough so that you can pick it out cleanly, wearing a rubber glove on your other hand. But an easier way is to gather the walnuts in green hull and scatter them on your driveway where the car will run over them to and from the garage. The tires hull the walnuts, rain washes most of the brown stain away, and the sun dries them. Wear rubber gloves when you pick them up to avoid lingering stain. (10) "We don't like nuts well enough to bother."—Are you sure? Take any cookie recipe you can make and put hickory nuts in the next batch and watch what happens when you serve them. Try a native pecan-butter-and-jelly sandwich on your kids. Or a black walnut cake. Or a hickory nut pie. Or butternut ice cream.

HICKORY-PECAN

Of all the tree fruits and nuts, none hybridize naturally so freely, and so your chances of growing a nut like the mother tree from seed are slim. But that is no reason to be so hard on hickory and pecan seedlings the way horticultural specialists often are. *Taylor's Encyclopedia of Gardening* goes out of its way on several different pages to call *Carya* seedlings "useless." In natural hybridization, there is as much chance that the cross may be better than the parent as there is that it will be "useless." Truth is, the seedling *usually* produces a tree different, but of similar quality, from the parent. Only where the parent is one of the exceptional choice varieties does the seedling fail to measure up, but even then it may equal the normal wild tree in quality. It certainly is not "useless" to the homeowner.

In fact, nuts from old, stable groves of hickories or mature pecans usually produce nuts similar to the mother. (Not exactly,

343

Illus. 17-1—Hickory (Shagbark).

though; I don't think I have ever found two trees in the same hickory woods with identical nuts.) It is only where high-quality papershell pecans are being developed in the South that seedling variability becomes a real pain. It took nature who knows how many years to develop a Stuart pecan (but it was a seedling, don't forget). Man then assumes that in a few short years he can breed even better pecans using Stuarts and other selected varieties as parents. Most offspring are inferior (but not useless). At the W. R. Poage Pecan Field Station in Brownwood, Texas, only nine new varieties were put on the recommended list in the 38 years before 1970—nine out of several thousand seedling crosses. But some seedlings get the axe (literally) simply because they are alternate bearing. As I have mentioned earlier, homeowners can harvest enough nuts for two years and still freeze one year's supply. In my own case, in the woodland I frequent, there are some trees producing one year and some another. Alternate bearing is undesirable for commercial growers but not useless to the backyarder.

The reason I harp on this point is that nut trees of hickory and pecan species are difficult to transplant. They have very long taproots. Seeds are easy to plant. I'm aware that Southerners transplant pecan trees even 5 to 6 feet tall. That demands a huge hole or special nursery preparation, but I doubt this would be successful even half the time with hickories. On three and four footers I have tried to transplant, the taproot was longer than the tree! Plant nuts. Nourish seedlings. Then if you become really hell-bent on growing the very best varieties, graft on scions to your seedling. It is far easier to get scions of native nut selections than trees, anyway. But leave a branch of the seedling to see what kind of nut it makes. It is not a bad idea with pecans to have two or three varieties on a tree, anyway, because pecans will then pollenate better. There is an added advantage to this method, at least with hickory. Since some hickories do take years to produce nuts (12 or more), grafting on scions from a mature tree can mean nuts from the graft in two years.

In the long run, it may be wise to plant nuts, whatever one's chances with the seedlings. For example, right beside my typewriter this morning are 18 "northern" pecans, just arrived from some NNGA friends. These come from trees discovered in 1978 by Doug Campbell and NNGA associates along the Mississippi River between Burlington, Iowa, and Dubuque, Iowa, *200 miles north* of any previously known existing groves of native pecans. Thousands of people cooperating in the NNGA program are planting nuts from these trees in their northern groves and backyards. We all hope that we are working with the genetic pecan material that will produce, among the thousands of nuts planted, one or more varieties that are truly hardy in the true North. I could't resist eating one of the nuts. It is as sweet as Campbell said and, though smaller than a good papershell pecan, more flavorful and as easy to crack. The trees they come from are easily a hundred years old; some may be twice that. They represent centuries, perhaps eons, of slow, natural development and intelligent selection by Indians of the Mississippian culture. I planted the seeds with awe, even humility. I'm helping to preserve a genetic code of priceless value, all but destroyed by the thoughtless, rapacious bulldozing of thousands of acres of wild pecan groves on the Mississippi floodplain—for corn. The corn is traded to Russia for worthless dollar bills. And for every bushel of corn traded, three bushels of soil go down the Mississippi River, lost forever.

Horticulturists distinguish at least five main species of hickory: *Carya ovata,* the shagbark; *C. laciniosa,* the shellbark, often called king nut, big nut shagbark, or bullnut because of its larger size (about the size of a walnut); *C. glabra,* pignut; *C. tomentosa,* mockernut; and *C. cordiformis,* bitternut. The first two have the best nuts. In a typical oak-hickory woodlot, you will find all sorts of gradations between the species—so much so that I find positive identification sometimes to be difficult. Shag-

barks and shellbarks have thicker, easily hulled husks. The
others have thin hulls that often stick rather tightly to the nut.
Not all bitternuts are necessarily so, and pignuts may be bitter,
too. Taste them all. Flavor ranges from a nutty banana taste to
almost a sharp, walnut taste. Before gathering quantities of nuts
from under any tree, crack half a dozen or so. If most are wormy
or dried up, move on to another tree. Nutmeats with dark skin
are strong tasting and will not keep. The desirable nutmeats
have a white or pale ivory skin and are firm and plump. These
will keep well. With the nut stood up on its side edge, a tap or
two with a hammer on top should crack it. On desirable nuts, the
shell is thin and will often crack in two, allowing you to lift or
pick out the nutmeats in two "whole halves." Small-size nuts
that will readily crack out into two whole halves are more
desirable than large nuts that will not.

The shape of hickory nuts varies from tree to tree. Some are
long and skinny, and suggestive of pecan. Some are flattish and
ovoid; some nearly square. Out of a woodlot containing perhaps
50 hickories, you will generally find only five with really first-
rate nuts in all respects. Baby these trees. Cut out competing
trees around them to allow in plenty of sunlight so that they
branch out well and produce abundantly. (Invariably, the best-
producing trees are already growing in a sunlit glade or at the
edge of the woods.)

Of all the more common northern hardwoods, hickory is by
far the best firewood. If you cut a green hickory, it will usually
send up new shoots. When about 3 inches in diameter, these
sprouts make good handle material. Prune the hickory to one
sprout and allow it to grow into another tree. When cutting down
a dying hickory, you will usually find at least one young shoot
growing up from a root nearby, or from the old crown. Fell the
old tree carefully so as to preserve this little sproutling and, as
nature intended, it will become the replacement tree.

Pecans are divided into two groups, "native" pecans and the
improved "papershells" that are selected from nature, or newly
hybridized varieties for commercial orchards. The designations
are confusing. All pecans are more or less native. All are more or
less "papershell," too, in that the shell is far thinner and easier to
crack than other *Carya* nuts. "Native" pecans are sometimes
called northern pecans, although that designation more precisely
refers to those varieties of pecan with enough hardiness to grow
in zone 6 and possibly zone 5. These hardier varieties are
generally of less quality than the improved southern varieties

grown in abundance in Georgia, Texas, Arizona, and other southernmost states. When a nut grower uses the phrase "native pecan" in Oklahoma and Kansas, he is referring to natural stands of pecan that have been converted into commercial groves. This practice is common, or was common before bulldozers tempted farmers to knock down the magnificent old pecans along the river bottoms of the southern Mississippi and its tributaries in favor of corn and soybeans.

If you live where the best southern pecan varieties flourish, by all means you should choose them over "native" pecans. These varieties, however, generally speaking are more susceptible to diseases (scab) and to various insects than are native pecans, as is so often true of the highest-quality varieties of fruit. Georgia and Texas are the leading regions for these varieties, and Arizona is good if you have plenty of irrigation water. Pecans like lots of water. The University of Georgia suggests that backyarders grow Stuart, Desirable, Elliott, Farley, and Gloria Grande, as these varieties do not require the intensive management of most papershell pecans. There are many others, and the place to inquire about new ones is the W. R. Poage Pecan Field Station, P.O. Box 579, Woodson Road, Brownwood, TX 76801.

For other growers, particularly those of us trying to establish groves to live *in* as well as *from,* the native pecan is a far more practical choice and promises some degree of success even into zone 6. "Northern" pecans selected from native stands, such as Colby, Peruque, Chief, Duvall, Giles, Hodge, Starking Hardy Giant, Steuck, Sweeney, Fritz, and Witte, possess a surprising degree of hardiness. As with apricots, their chief drawback is that they flower early when frosts in the North are still apt to kill the blossoms. But I have seen Peruque trees produce reasonably well along Lake Erie (zone 6 next to the lake), in northern Ohio.

Anyone willing to go to the bother of running orchard heaters under his pecan tree on cold April nights can grow Peruque pecans anywhere that peaches grow. The newly discovered "northern" pecans along the upper Mississippi may perform even better. Part of the secret of why these trees produce so abundantly as far north as Dubuque is their great height—the flowering limbs are high above the settling frosts of spring. The higher air is moved by breezes more often, and also its temperature is moderated by the expanse of river water nearby.

The first thing to keep in mind when planting a pecan is its eventual size. On good river-bottom land, pecans grow very large, so that old-timers figured on a final tree population of only six per acre. Today most growers aim for 30 per acre and then finally thin down to 15. A mature tree needs a space 70 × 70 feet, but the best rule to follow is simply not to let limbs of adjacent trees grow into each other.

At its field station at Chetopa, the University of Kansas has done much experimenting with improving native stands of pecans. Researchers advise the following steps if profitable commercial production is the ultimate goal. First, clear out all other oak, elm, ash, etc., in the wild stand. Next, thin the pecans out, too, so that none touch each other and enough room is secured for adequate sunlight and easy movement of machinery through the grove. However, take your time with this thinning job—as much as three years. Young tree trunks that have been in their own shade for a long time may sunscald if exposed suddenly to bright sunlight. But the biggest reason for thinning slowly is to make sure that you keep the trees that produce the best nuts. This takes checking and comparing the trees over a period of at least a couple years. If the only tree in a particular space is a poor one, you can start a new tree or, as is the customary practice, you can cut it back and graft on good varieties. Bark grafts and side cleft grafts are most often employed.

The trees are pruned as they grow in order to maintain 15 to 20 feet of lower trunk free of branches at maturity. Such branches should be pruned off before they reach 2 inches in diameter to preserve the value of the eventual sawlog that can be sold if and when the tree is cut down. Pecan has become valuable wood.

The homestead grove-owner might think twice before following exactly the course outlined above. If you do not want to try to operate a highly profitable, native pecan grove, but only wish for a few trees from which to eat and sell a little, you can learn which trees in your woods produce the best nuts and then clear out only those trees adjacent to the choice ones. Keeping a variety of trees in the grove rather than just a pure stand of pecan will guarantee a wider variety of all biological life and will help to deter or slow down the spread of pests to which a pure stand is more vulnerable. Even if you do want to establish a commercial grove, but only one of limited size, this course can sometimes be followed. For example, if you want an acre of pecan trees to harvest, and have a 5-acre native stand crowded with other kinds of trees, try this: Instead of thinning out one acre to a pure stand of trees, preserve the best acre's-worth of pecans on the entire 5 acres, then thin and clear out brush, etc., only around them. Maintain on the other parts of the 5 acres the best edible oaks, walnuts, maples (for sugar), or other food trees native to your area. Eventually your woodlot becomes what I call a "food-wood" that requires little or no spraying or cultivation.

Many farmers use their pecan groves for livestock pasture, too, to increase their return. On creek-bottom land, which is subject to erosion, the grass saves soil, too. Fertilizer helps both trees and grass. Usually some commercial fertilizer is used, but manure would be as good or better. Where the trees are smaller, or spaced widely apart so that plenty of sun strikes the grove floor, legumes can be grown with the grass as a natural supply of nitrogen for the soil. In the South, crimson clover is recommended, or vetch, and sometimes even sweet lupine, where sandy soils predominate. Blue lupine makes an excellent cover for the pecan grove on such soils, but it is not a good grazing crop. Rye or perennial ryegrass often is sown as a grass, but any grass that does well on your soil is preferable. Ideally, the area right under the tree ought to be mulched or cultivated shallowly, but this is seldom practical for the owner of a native stand.

Thinning native stands has been found to triple nut production. Something considerably more than that can be gained by adding fertilizer, but it is doubtful whether the extra cost in material and labor could be justified for the backyarder or homesteader. Besides, heavy applications of nitrogen invariably produce negative results in the form of increased fungal and insect attack, and in colder, humid climates, nitrogen induces late growth that's subject to winterkill.

HICAN

As the name implies, the hican is a natural hybrid cross of hickory and pecan, and it has some of the hardiness of the former and some of the nutmeat size of the latter. It often produces less than either, though not always. The newly discovered James hican and others give promise of a great future for hicans, though good, grafted trees are difficult to get at present. Other varieties include Palmer, Pleas, Underwood, Westbrook, and Burton.

WALNUT

The native American black walnut, *Juglans nigra,* grows throughout the eastern half of the United States, its presence usually denoting the richest soils. It will grow and bear nuts well on poorer sites, however, so long as drainage is no problem. But on poor sites the tree grows more slowly and only to half the regal height and girth that it achieves on deep river-bottom soil. Therefore, when contemplating a walnut plantation primarily for an ultimate profitable sale of lumber for veneer, only the deepest, richest soils should be chosen. On such sites, a walnut at 60 years of age, at today's veneer prices, can be worth $2,500 or more if the trunk is clear of knots, branches, and other defects.

The Persian walnut, *J. regia,* often called English walnut (although there is nothing English about it), can be divided into three somewhat different groups according to degree of hardiness. One group that is quite frost tender is grown commercially almost exclusively in southern California. Eureka, Ehrhardt, and Placentia are "old reliable" varieties in this frost-tender group. Farther north in California and continuing up the coast into Oregon, the bulk of the English walnuts is grown, using varieties somewhat more hardy and requiring somewhat colder weather during winter dormancy. Carmelo is a very large variety recommended for the backyard (it is not a heavy producer, usually) in coastal western climates. It is available from Sierra Gold Nursery, Yuba City, CA 95991. Other varieties are Spurgeon (one of the hardiest), Hanoka, Franquette, Concord, Payne, and Blackmer.

Illus. 17-2—Walnut.

The third group is usually referred to as the Carpathian walnuts, of which good varieties produce nuts in zone 6 and even protected spots in zone 5. Varieties of somewhat less quality (that is, with shells that are thicker and harder to crack than those of commercial English walnuts) grow and fruit in zone 5 and possibly protected spots in zone 4, though late freezes that far north might kill blossoms in most years.

The Hansen variety seems best for northern areas where Persian walnuts are practical (zone 6). The walnut is small, but the shell is easier to crack than that of most commercial English walnuts, and the nutmeat so fills the inner cavity that you get nearly as much as you would from a larger nut. The taste is excellent, the equal of any California walnut. Off the tree or naturally dried it is even better, since artificial drying tends to add a bit of bitterness to the taste of walnuts. Art Weaver, near Toledo, Ohio, along Lake Erie, has two acres of Persian walnuts in his backyard. In addition to Hansen, he has good luck with Fately No. 5 and Broadview, a much larger nut than Hansen. Most of his trees are grafted onto black walnut, which Weaver feels makes them grow more vigorously.

Persian walnuts fall from the tree free of the hull and so are far nicer to harvest than black walnuts. Weaver picks his up from the ground with a homemade scoop—a tin can nailed to a stick—which saves bending over. With a little practice handling it, the scoop helps to speed up harvesting considerably. He dumps the nuts into an inexpensive plastic laundry basket, lowers them into a barrel of water, and sloshes them up and down vigorously several times to clean them. Floaters are usually bad, and these are skimmed off and discarded. Then he puts the nuts into shallow racks for drying.

Other named varieties of Carpathians are: Silvis, Metcalf, Orth, Merkel, Dr. Moss, Wallick, Breslau, Ward, Robinette, Springlake, McKinster, Prize, McGuire, Street, Fickes, Buckeye, Burtner, Kentucky Giant, Nelson, Wilmoth, Sauber, and Lake. The English or Persian walnuts typically offered by nurseries are unnamed varieties—seedlings rather than grafted trees. You might get a good nut that way, but more likely you'll only get a fair one. These trees are generally very hardy, however, and any nut at all is better than none. Seedling trees I have observed bear nuts that have rather thick shells, but the meats are good nonetheless. In cold zone 5 climate, such as in my neighborhood, the trees bear well about one out of three years, depending on the severity of spring frosts.

My experience with Carpathian walnuts is that the named varieties, at least Hansen and Broadview, are quite a lot better than common seedlings. But in black walnuts I have not yet seen a named variety that *significantly* surpasses the selected wild trees from which I harvest nuts in the woods. I have a hunch that the varieties may perform differently in different soils or climates. I have heard nut authorities question the reputed superior quality of such old-time favorites as Thomas and Stabler. There is also the possibility that a seedling of one of these varieties that is similar to the parent but not *exactly* like it became confused with it. At any rate, if you live where black walnuts are common, you may be as well off selecting your own favorite tree from the woods as buying a Thomas, Stabler, Ohio, Emma Kay, Elmer Myers, Ten Eyck, Sparrow, Cook, Schrieber, Lambs Curly, Burton, Clermont, Clark, or Vandersoot.

Assuming you live near a typical eastern hardwood forest, you can be choosy in selecting the trees from which to harvest your year's supply of nuts because you will have quite a number of trees to choose from. Even the most rapacious lumberman shuns walnuts growing in fence rows where wire of old fences is so often embedded within the trunks of the trees. Test half a dozen nuts or so from every tree before gathering the nuts under it. Does the nut come freely from the green hull after it falls to the ground? If not, the nut is probably not well filled. (If you harvest later in the season when the hulls have rotted around the nuts, this rule does not apply, since the hulls may not come off easily then, even if the nut is well filled.) While they're still in the hulls, are the nuts all of about the same diameter? If hull size varies, most likely the smaller nuts are not well filled. Does the nut, freed from the hull, crack easily? Do the nutmeats come out easily? (Some will, even when undried, but you cannot really judge the ease with which a shell releases its nutmeats until the nut has been thoroughly dried.) Is the skin of the nutmeats dark or light colored? If dark, the nuts will not keep well—the nutmeats will shrivel and turn bitterish in storage. Collect only from trees with nutmeats that are white and plump, as with hickory nuts.

Hull black walnuts as described earlier. You can wash the nuts to make cracking them later an easier, cleaner job. I know one family who washes them in a cement mixer. I just leave mine on a barn or shed roof, or on the driveway, where fall rains wash them off fairly well and sunshine dries them. Then I store them in a cool, dry basement for cracking through the winter.

There's a difference of opinion on the best way to crack a black walnut. Since the intricate inner-wall structure of black walnut shells varies from tree to tree, experiment, and then choose the best method for the nuts you are cracking. Generally speaking, I have found that standing the nut on one end and hitting it squarely on the other end disintegrates the shell best. But sometimes, standing the nut on the side edge, as you would do with a hickory nut, works better. Commercial black walnut crackers use internal force to explode the nut shell.

Black walnuts, unlike hickory nuts, are seldom wormy. Shuckworms work only in the outer hull, and though resulting hull damage may indirectly affect the quality of the nutmeats, the effect is normally minimal. The meats may contain a pinkish orange fluid between the layers of nutmeat, however, a condition referred to as "amber." If nutmeats contain a lot of amber, they generally will not keep and often have an off-taste. If you have a choice, move on to another tree.

The black walnut makes an ideal tree for the homestead grove because it can combine well with other food-producing homestead enterprises. The black walnut has a curious beneficial effect on certain grasses grown around it, especially fescue and bluegrass, and so makes a good tree to grow in combination with livestock pasture. No one is yet sure exactly what causes bluegrass, for example, to grow well under walnut trees, but the theory is that the toxic substance, called juglone, released by walnut roots subdues competing weeds and weedy grasses but does not affect the bluegrass. Thus, the grass grows better without competition from the weeds. The fine leaves of the walnut do not block sunlight from the grass to any growth-inhibiting degree, either. Juglone seems to be toxic to some legumes, though, but not others, so one must choose his pasture mixture with care. Alfalfa and lespedeza seem particularly affected, but not red clover and little Dutch. Farmers' experiences, even with alfalfa, differ; some farmers claim that alfalfa, too, grows well near walnut trees. At any rate, some livestock producers are dotting pastures with walnut trees without significantly reducing the amount of pasture available. When they are small, the trees, of course, must be protected from cattle, although in my experience if the cattle have access to other trees and brush they will not bother walnuts. A cow must be very hungry to eat walnut leaves.

The trees in such a pasture, or in any stand with eventual harvest for veneer lumber as the goal, should be pruned so that a nice clean trunk is maintained up to at least 9 feet. Pruning higher than that increases the value of the tree as lumber, but if you also intend to harvest the nuts commercially, pruning beyond 9 feet significantly increases the time before you can perform the first commercial harvest. Pruning above that height also increases labor considerably.

The Hammons Products Company in Missouri, which produces black walnuts commercially, is experimenting with the ultimate multi-cropping system involving walnuts. Between newly started seedlings, the company grows soybeans and wheat for about 10 years until the trees are large enough to hinder grain production with shade and extending branches. Then the grove floor is seeded to forage, mainly fescue, and livestock is grazed there until appreciable nut production occurs at about 20 years. Grazing may continue longer during the years of heavy nut production. The University of Missouri projects profits on such an operation, after the eventual sale of the trees as veneer lumber occurs 60 to 70 years from the start of the grove, at from 13% to 18% return on investment, a rosy picture indeed. The flaw in this plan, according to some walnut growers, is that the trees don't produce enough nuts to justify commercial harvest at current prices. But the Hammons people say, with confirmation by the University of Missouri, that selected trees that are fertilized and protected from disease produce three times the crops of typical woodland trees, and, therefore, do make money. Marketing is integral to the scheme, too. Hammons sells not only nutmeats, but also sells the shells to Detroit, where they are used as an abrasive to smooth and polish piston walls. The company is also working with ground walnuts as a protein feed supplement for cattle.

When pruning a seedling tree to grow into a straight, unflawed trunk, the rule is to keep between one-third and one-half of the height of the tree in crown (branches). If you try to cut off all of the side branches on, say, a 5-foot tree so that it grows straight up faster, you may weaken the stem too much, and the tree will bend over. In small tree trunks, there will be crooks. The tree will straighten these slight twists and turns as it grows. Make sure that it is growing up straight overall, and keep one dominant leader rather than allowing the tree to fork into two main branches. If the tree persists in growing crooked, whack it off at ground level, and a new shoot or shoots will quickly spring up. Prune off all but the straightest.

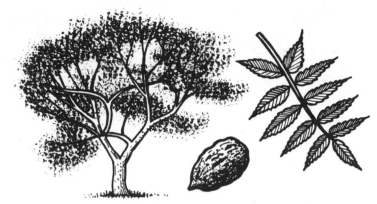

Illus. 17-3—Butternut.

BUTTERNUT

The butternut (*Juglans cinerea*) is the hardiest of our native nuts. It makes a nice lawn tree by sporting leaves that are somewhat wider individually than black walnut leaves and, hence, cast nicer shade. The nuts themselves are not as messy in the hull as black walnuts, and usually are not as numerous, either. The nut is a bit harder to extract from the hull, but the hull, though sticky to the touch, does not stain your skin as black walnuts do. The nut is oblong rather than round. The taste is delicious, somewhat milder than black walnut. The wood is a lighter color of brown (butternut is sometimes referred to as white walnut), is not as strong as black walnut, but makes desirable furniture nonetheless.

Both butternuts and black walnuts can be tapped for syrup just as maples can, though the quantity is not as large as in the latter. But in pioneer times, the butternut especially was tapped frequently for sugar. Named varieties include: Craxezy, Vancycle, Kenworthy, and Ayers.

HEARTNUT

The heartnut (*Juglans sieboldiana*) is not particularly hardy, especially in the northern reaches of the Carpathian walnut range. This walnut has the decided advantage, however, of easily coming out of the shell in one piece when cracked. This Japanese walnut is not grown much and is used perhaps more as rootstock for Persian walnuts than as a tree in its own right. Like the oriental persimmon, it has its enthusiasts, but it seems to offer no advantages over other walnuts grown with less effort in its range. Schubert is a well-known variety, from a tree grown in Illinois.

CHAPTER 18

OAKS, CHESTNUTS, AND BEECHES—THE FAGACEAE FAMILY

OAK

Acorns have provided staple food for more people in human history than steak and strawberry shortcake have. Entire Indian cultures in California, not to mention generations of Europeans, flourished on a diet principally made up of acorns. Nonetheless, because some acorns contain excessive tannin, it behooves writers on such matters to point out that an acorn can be slightly toxic. Up goes the caution flag. Experts who have never eaten an acorn feel obliged to warn somberly that acorns "have been reported to cause poisoning in humans." So you are warned, although I personally believe that it is as needless a warning as ever got warned. Malic acid in green apples is sort of toxic, too. It will give you a stomachache, which I suppose comes under the definition of "poisoning." Anyone who can eat enough bitter acorns to get tannic poisoning would have to hate himself exceedingly. I sample acorns from nearly every oak tree I pass under, and believe me, even the most contrary child won't eat many of the bitter ones. And if they did? Deer, turkeys, hogs, blue jays, and other birds thrive on them. I would just love to check out the details of any case where acorns "caused poisoning in humans."

Nevertheless, acorns will never be a popular nut, such as pecans or hickory nuts, because of the bitterness. Of course, if our civilization were as advanced as the western Indian civilizations, we would know how to avoid the tannin and make use of one of the most abundant of natural foods—instead of cutting down the forests that hold the key to our biological survival. Some varieties of oak produce acorns that contain little tannin or none and can be eaten fresh or roasted without the leaching process that's used on a bitter acorns. Most of the white oak group, as it is called to distinguish it from the black oaks, produce nuts quite edible to fairly tasty, with little or no leaching. White oaks produce acorns on the annual new growth, and their leaves have rounded lobes. Black oaks (including red oaks) produce acorns next year from buds that grow this year, and have pointed leaf lobes. The common white oak, *Quercus alba,* and the mossy-cup or bur oak (*Q. macrocarpa*) are two of the best for edible acorns in the East. Fred Ashworth, the famous plant breeder—who talked me into sampling acorns in the woods—told me the story of the Ashworth bur oak he propagated and sold for years. As a very young man, he was once on his way to town with horse and wagon to deliver the morning's supply of milk from the family farm when he stopped

Illus. 18-1—Black and White Oak Leaves and Acorns.

under a bur oak tree along the road for lunch. He didn't have much to eat with him and decided to try some of the acorns off the tree to blunt his hunger. To his surprise, the acorns were quite good and sweet and he continued on his way, satisfied. Later he began propagating the tree. We need a few more Fred Ashworths in this country.

My own experience in sampling acorns from the white oak group is that those with red or pink splotches on the shell are the sweetest. I never like to try to identify the oaks in my groves too closely because they do not resemble the descriptions in the books exactly. I have an idea that these old oaks are products of hundreds of years of hybridization. Sometimes the difference between white oak and swamp white oak is not distinct, nor is that of red and scarlet oak. But these reddish-splotched acorns are fair tasting raw. Roasted, salted, and buttered, they are tolerably good.

In the West, the California live oak acorn, *Q. agrifolia,* was highly prized by the seed-gathering Indians of California, according to Edward K. Balls in his *Early Uses of California Plants* (University of California Press, 1962). According to Balls, Indian families hoped to collect 500 pounds of acorns per year, although they were not always successful. The valley oak, *Q. lobata* (a white oak), is also a good variety for edible acorns. Craig Dremann, mentioned earlier, has found a tree with acorns that approach cashews in taste, he says. Other species with noteworthy acorns are: shin or mountain oak, *Q. Gambelii;* the blue or Douglas oak, *Q. Douglasii;* and the holly or holm oak, *Q. Ilex.*

As survival insurance, Indians also gathered the bitter acorns of various black oaks because these acorns keep well in storage. Leaching was not the bothersome task it is today, but an integral part of daily life. The raw acorns were ground into flour, then put into baskets or other strainerlike containers and placed into springs of running water. The tannin, being soluble in water, washed out. The process might take a few hours or a couple of days, depending on the amount of tannin in the meal.

Edith Van Ellen Murphey, in her *Indian Uses of Native Plants* (Mendicino Historical Society, 1959), describes a more elaborate leaching process.

After the acorn meal was ground, it was leached to take the bitterness out in the following manner: a frame was prepared with incense cedar twigs laid overlapping, like shingles on a roof; the acorn meal was spread out on the frame, and water poured through the meal repeatedly, until the meal turned pink, when it was dried and kept until used. The cedar twigs gave a spicy taste to the meal.

Perhaps the most practical way today to leach acorns is to steep them in hot water. A bulletin from the University of California gives these directions: Place shelled raw acorns (before grinding into meal) in boiling water until the water turns to the color of strong tea. Repeat the process until the water remains clear instead of turning brown. Allow the nuts to dry and then bake slowly in shallow pans in a low oven, 275°F, mixing in butter and salt and stirring occasionally to prevent burning, until the acorns no longer taste raw. When cooled, the acorns make a tasty, salted nut to munch on.

The ground meal, raw or roasted, makes a heavy but nutty-flavored bread. (We always mix in about one-third part or more of conventional flour when we experiment with concoctions such as this, to keep the bread lighter.) The Indians made a gruel or soup out of the raw meal. The meal is better, to my taste, if made from roasted nuts.

Cracking the meat out of acorns is sometimes easy, sometimes not so easy. I haven't tried it, but I believe acorns could be roasted and popped or peeled out of the shells much in the manner of chestnuts (see below). Otherwise you usually can crack them out with a nutcracker, like a pecan.

Acorns come in all sizes and shapes. Don't expect them always to fit the description of a particular species given in the books. Oak trees do not read many books, and hybridize to suit themselves. Size of nuts within the same species can vary by as much as 1 inch.

CHESTNUT

Of the several strains and species of chestnut, the American (*Castanea dentata*) and the Chinese (*C. mollissima*) are the most interesting to the grove-owner. From these two species, and sometimes also from the Japanese chestnut (*C. crenata*), hybrids and crosses are being developed in hope of achieving a chestnut with the taste and timber value of the American and the blight resistance and nut size of the Chinese and Japanese. These attempts have been something less than totally successful, but hybrids that resemble mostly the Chinese parent, or selected

Chinese varieties, produce nuts of good quality and even commercial profitability. In the East the little chinquapin or chinkapin tree (*C. pumila*) is a wild tree with distinct grove possibilities. It is susceptible to the chestnut blight, but instead of dying completely, a few shoots will die and those remaining in the clump grow more vigorously and produce nuts. Nuts are small and only one to a hull, so total production is less than that with other chestnuts. But the chinquapin makes a good wildlife food and a handy snack on a fall walk. Louis Gerardi Nursery (see the Appendix for address) is the only nursery I know of that sells an improved chinquapin, "American Hybrid A."

Native to California are two other close relatives to the chestnut, also called chinquapins, but which belong to a different genus, *Castanopsis*. These produce nuts much like the chestnut and are delicious when roasted. One is the giant chinquapin, and the other is the golden chinquapin.

Some old American chestnut stumps still send up sprouts. I have seen some along the Appalachian Trail reach a height of 25 feet and bear nuts before they die. In fact, the number of struggling sprout-trees in the Pennsylvania forests (and I assume elsewhere in chestnut country) is surprising, even encouraging. One continually hopes that nature will find a way to even the score against the terrible blight (*Endothia*) that restless man, ever about his mischief, accidentally brought to this country from the Orient at around 1900. It subsequently laid waste to one of the most magnificent stands of timber the world

Illus. 18-2—American Chestnut.

was ever fortunate enough to be blessed with. Chestnut is one of the strongest and most durable woods for its weight, nearly indestructible in the weather, and vast herds of hogs once shared the nuts along with innumerable wildlife animals. What is especially tragic about the decline of the American chestnut is that it was especially adapted to shaley, acid soils in Appalachian highlands—soils not able to support a tillage type of agriculture. Here, if any place, a tree agriculture based on chestnut made perfect sense, economically as well as ecologically, but man managed to wreck it all in a few short years.

Some hope does now exist—coming from nature, not from man. European chestnut, a species very susceptible to *Endothia,* too, has been ravaged by the blight since man managed to carry the disease there in about 1920. But over 30 years ago, a scientist already reported that some infected chestnut trees in Italy seemed to be recovering from the blight. No one paid any attention to him—science was too busy nurturing the notion it could halt the disease by its own methods. Then a few years ago, plant pathologists began following up those reports and made an amazing discovery. A hypovirulent strain of *Endothia* was attacking the normal strain! Blight cankers were healing, and the trees were becoming healthy.

Since then both France and Italy have been busy inoculating infested trees with this naturally occurring blight control. As with all cases of biological control, this one cannot work *completely,* because if the blight were wiped out, the hypovirulent strain would have nothing to live on and would die out, too.

Illus. 18-3—Chinquapin Chestnut.

The ideal situation is achieved when the hypovirulent strain can keep the regular blight strain so weak that the tree keeps on growing in fairly good health. One can hypothesize that had an effective fungicide been invented to control the blight, the hypovirulent strain might never have appeared, and no natural control would have been achieved.

In the United States, the new strain has not been easy to naturalize. When a blight-infested tree is inoculated, the canker heals and the tree recovers in many instances, but the hypovirulent strain won't yet persist and spread to other infected trees. Optimism is still high, however. What's more, a native American hypovirulent strain seems to be at work in certain chestnut stands in Michigan, where groves have not been affected as much by the disease as farther south. Foresters have always thought that the relative isolation of these trees was their protection, but others now believe hypovirulency is at work. Time will tell.

In the meantime, the hybrid American-Chinese trees are the practical choice. One problem with improved varieties is that grafted trees often die after transplanting. Most backyarders may be as well off to use selected seedlings from good trees, or simply to plant seeds from such trees, since chestnuts often do come true from seed. They also germinate easily *if* planted before the nut dries out completely. The best way is to take a nut out of the hull as it falls from the tree and plant it. If you have to store nuts, store in a cool, moist place. A dried-out chestnut won't germinate very well.

Chestnuts are fussy about where they will grow well. They like a slightly acid soil that is sandy or gravelly. Unless they are extremely well drained, heavy clay soils will often be inadequate, and probably ought not to be chosen if commercial production is a goal. I've noticed that chestnuts do well where the more acid-loving trees, such as laurel and pine, proliferate. On good, clay-loam soil of neutral or near neutral pH, you don't find many chestnuts.

Nor will chestnuts withstand severe winters. Zone 6 is as cold an area as you can grow dependable crops. Here in a cold part of zone 5 my chestnut trees froze in 1977, '78 and '79 but persisted in growing back every year. Still, I don't foresee nuts from these nondescript seedlings. Despite the risks, I've instead put my hope in a hybrid, grafted Ford's Sweet that was discovered in Kentucky. Ford's Sweet is a chestnut with some American quality to it, and I purchased it from Leslie H. Wilmoth

Nursery (see the Appendix for address). But I don't have much hope for it in my clay soil. There is a producing chestnut tree in my hometown, so I figure I have a chance. A wiser course for me to follow would be to plant seeds from the hometown tree.

Orrin, Crane, Nanking, Armstrong, Mossberger, Abundance, Kerr, and Ford's Sweet are varieties, that are available. There are many more named varieties, and new ones are available nearly every year.

When harvesting chestnuts, wear gloves to protect your hands from the bristly hulls. But be thankful for those hulls. In places where squirrels are a problem, the prickly hulls deter the rodents from gathering the nuts before they are ripe, at which time the hulls split open. But the grove-owner can swat the nuts, hulls and all, off the tree with a stick a little before they mature. Store the burr-covered nuts in a cool place where they will slowly dry until the burr cracks open, enabling you to extract the nuts. Otherwise, you can wait for the nuts to ripen on the tree and fall, some out of the hulls, some still partially in the hulls.

To roast a chestnut, cut or prick a small hole through the shell first. Otherwise, as the nut heats, the pressure of the steam inside will make it pop or explode like a buckeye in a bonfire. Leave one or two nuts unpricked in the batch you are roasting. When you hear them pop, say old chestnut-lovers, you should allow the batch to roast one minute more, and they are then ready to eat. Of course, let them cool a little first.

Some people like raw chestnuts and dry them to a kind of rubbery consistency. If dried completely, the nut becomes quite hard and can be ground into flour. The roasted nut can also be ground into flour and added to various pastries.

Peeling unroasted chestnuts is difficult unless you heat them. Slit the nuts' scab sides (the light-colored part opposite the nuts' points), spread the nuts, scab sides down, in a single layer in a pan, and place in an oven preheated to 230°F for four minutes. The hulls shrink and force raw nuts into the slits you have made. By squeezing at the pointed ends, the nuts usually pop out. Such nuts can be stir-fried a little, as a crunchy addition to salads. Boiled and then mashed, they resemble mashed potatoes with a nutty flavor.

BEECH

The beech tree, another genus of the Fagaceae family, contains several species of merit for the home grove. The Euro-

Illus. 18-4—Beech.

pean beech, in its many beautiful and showy strains, gets more attention as an ornamental, but the American beech, *Fagus grandiflora,* is a better nut-producer. Beechnuts are delicious, but small and tedious to crack open. The best way is between your teeth, like a sunflower seed. The trees do not fruit every year, and when they do, blackbirds, blue jays, and many other fall-migrating birds may eat most of the nuts before you get to them. The greedy birds, however, drop about as many nuts as they eat and save you the impossible task of climbing into those huge, majestic old trees to gather nuts yourself. About every third year you can gather enough nuts to snack on through the winter. We used to roast them, which makes them taste better yet.

The only improved selection of American beech I've heard about is the Jenner beech. Again, it was Fred Ashworth who found it in the wild, and because of its somewhat larger-than-usual nuts, he propagated it for sale. As far as I can find out, trees of Jenner are not available at present.

If you find seedling trees growing in the shadow of beeches that produce extra-nice nuts, you can transplant them. They transplant fairly easily and, if you find them standing in the deep shade of a healthy beech, they probably will not survive there, anyhow.

CHAPTER 19

MINOR NUT TREES

HAZEL

It is doubtful that the hazel should be called a "minor" nut tree. Its range, at least, is very widespread. Besides the ubiquitous American hazel, *Corylus americana,* there are regional native hazels such as the California species, *C. rostrata* var. *californica.* European and Asiatic species, of which the "European" filbert of commerce, *C. maxima,* is the best-tasting, have been introduced into this country. Hybrids of the various hazels and selected, improved varieties are grown commercially along the coasts of Washington and Oregon, where the climate is favorable, and to a minor degree in the East, where the climate is not so favorable. Barcelona is still probably the leading variety, with new crosses between Barcelona and Ennis, Hall's Giant, Daviana, and others showing much promise. Weather is a limiting factor for all of them. In Oregon, the cold snap of 1972 all but killed off a promising variety called Gem, and even harmed Barcelona. Butler and Hall's Giant survived the cold the best.

One of the problems with European filberts, particularly in the East, is a hazel blight carried by American hazels that is not harmful to them but devastating to the European species. For this reason, the American grove-owner is wiser to grow selected American hazels. Some authoritative gardening books describe the American wild hazel as being "of little value," which makes me wonder how many hazelnuts those authors have eaten. Though smaller than commercial filberts and occasionally slightly more acrid in taste, wild hazelnuts are generally good, can be harvested in quantity without undue effort, and require little care in the yard, except for pruning back the suckers to keep the plants from spreading too much. I have gathered wild hazelnuts in northern Indiana and northern Ohio, zone 5, and in zone 4 of Minnesota, where temperatures plummet to −20°F with chilling regularity. The Minnesota nuts were very delicious raw, the Indiana ones only a little less so, and the Ohio ones fair to good. When hazelnuts of less than the best quality in taste are roasted, they are delicious. I noticed that the bulletin on wild foods put out by the University of California says the same about wild *C. rostrata* in that state.

You will find wild hazels in fence rows, along country roads, and at the edges of woodlots. They need the sun and will not compete with heftier hardwoods. Often little more than a bush, they will grow in rich soil to 20 feet or so, usually in fairly dense stands of sprouts that spread out from a central root clump. In the wild the little trees are quite nondescript and easy to miss until you train your eyes to look for catkins next to the elmlike leaves. The catkins are especially visible in spring and fall when leaves are just coming or just going. The nut clusters, encased in green hulls that turn brown at maturity, resemble curled-up leaves and are even more difficult to spot. The mature clusters fall to the ground where they mix and blend so well with the debris of leaf and twig that they almost disappear.

Size of nut varies as much as quality of taste. If you find a bush with nuts larger than the customary marble size, you can

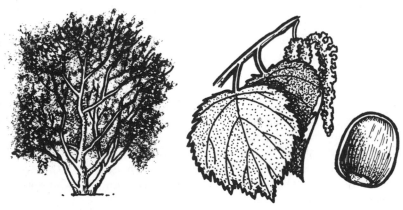

Illus. 19-1—Hazel.

dig up some of the smaller sprouts that have established their own root systems quite easily from around the edge of the stand. These sprouts are easy to transplant. I dig them up with a shovelful of dirt and plop them in a new hole rather hastily and unceremoniously, and I've not lost one yet.

They grow just about as fast from seed. I put the seed in the refrigerator over winter, or in the deep freezer for a few weeks, and plant. Germination success I've experienced is about 50%. I would put them directly in the ground in the fall, but I fear squirrels would eat them over winter.

Once growing, you can let a plant run via its suckers into a hedge. Or you can prune all suckers and develop a single tree trunk. Expect nuts in three or four years, if not sooner. They crack out with a hammer or nutcracker just as a commercial filbert does.

Winkler is the best-known named variety from wild selections. Rush is another. Potomac, Bixby, and Trizel are varieties of filbert crossed with American (and other) species.

Ornamental corkscrew, purple-leaved, and bronze-leaved species produce fewer nuts, but are desirable dual-purpose landscape plants (see Chap. 5).

MACADAMIA

Macadamia nuts will produce in zones 8 and 9. A tree of them might well turn out to be the most financially lucrative square footage in your grove, since the nuts are very expensive to buy. With good reason. Production methods in Hawaii, where most of the commercial macadamia nuts are grown, read like an ecologist's nightmare. The tree (*Macadamia ternifolia*, but in Hawaii more often *M. integrifolia*) is native to Australia where it is called Queensland nut, and adapts to Hawaii only under great protest. So great were the problems in growing it that for many years its culture languished on the islands. But as more people learned how delicious the nut tasted when cooked in coconut oil, a few venturesome agribusiness-types decided that the consumer would pay for them, hang the cost. Tracts of 1,000 acres and more were hacked out of the virgin forest with bulldozers and planted to macadamias. Then growers learned that the trees could not stand the force of wind and had to plant windbreaks of pine around the groves.

These large groves are almost completely mechanized.

(Small growers still harvest by hand.) Chemicals to counteract a host of nutritional, fungal, and insect problems are unleashed upon them, often by plane. One grower for a large company, writing in the *Fruits Varieties Journal,* 30 (4):110–15, reports: "An aerial contractor applies our fertilizer as needed. We have applied over 124,000 pounds of fertilizer in a single day, requiring over 100 touchdowns by the pilot."

To facilitate mechanical harvest, the large growers at first maintained a bare orchard floor, which quickly led to erosion on the steeper slopes. They put sod strips between the trees to help counter that problem. The sod is mowed and the bare ground under the trees is sprayed with herbicides. The trees sucker badly. Dieback is a serious and somewhat mysterious problem. A mite called broad mite is controlled effectively with sulfur, but if the pesticide history of other regions repeats itself here, eventually there will be an outbreak of some bug whose predators are also being controlled by the sulfur. Blossom blights are another problem, held at bay with regular soakings of Benlate and Difolatan, often from airplanes. But biological controls are being brought into practice, too; a troublesome stinkbug is now controlled fairly effectively with an introduced parasitical fly.

In the good old days the airlines used to serve free macadamia nuts. I know why they no longer can do that. I bought a few last winter that were priced, if I remember correctly, at over six dollars a pound. I tried to buy one-eighth of a pound, but one-fourth was the minimum order. With the horrendous expenses involved in trying to grow macadamias in spite of Mother Nature, not much profit is made yet by growers, as I understand it. As much as I love the nuts, I wonder exceedingly if the whole deal is worth the whole cost.

Sometimes the nuts, which are extremely rich, anyway, seem to be more oily than at other times, in which case you cannot eat many of them at one time. I suspect that there is some overcooking being practiced. If you have your own, experiment. Coconut oil is cloying enough the way it is. Perhaps less cooking or using another oil would produce better results. I've an idea that roasted macadamias would be a true fruit for the gods, but out here in the humdrum corn belt we don't see raw macadamias very often, so we don't get a chance to roast any.

The tree is beautiful to look at, too. The evergreen leaves resemble an odd-shaped holly or a shingle oak. Clusters of white, creamy blossoms dangle in the spring breezes. Trees remain rather small. You'll have better luck in California than Florida, where the trees usually do not set much fruit. The disadvantage of the nuts is that their hard shells cannot be cracked with an ordinary nutcracker. The wild hogs in Hawaii quickly learn which trees have the thinner-shelled nuts, and in the hogs' forays on the plantations, they go directly to those trees and crunch happily away.

PISTACHIO AND SUMAC

The Anacardiaceae family is most interesting for the seemingly diverse but closely related plants in it. Pistachio, sumac, and mango (see Chap. 16) are members, and so is poison ivy. This fact may explain why birds love poison ivy berries though you and I can't go near them.

Very few regions are adequate in the United States for pistachio, unfortunately. This most desirable, inch-long nut thrives on sandy ground in dry climates where winter is a bit chillier than in true tropical regions but still very mild in general. Trees are male and female, and you need both unless you graft a male branch into a female tree. One male tree to 12 females works out well in commercial plantations. Bronte and Aleppo are good nut-bearers; Kaz is a good pollenator. *Pistacia vera* grows to 20 to 30 feet tall. *P. chinensis*, Chinese pistachio, is a larger tree, used for ornament or as rootstock for *P. vera*.

The staghorn sumac (*Rhus typhina*) is the only American species that can qualify as a tree, and then it is usually only a small shrubby tree. The reddish cluster of seeds at the top of

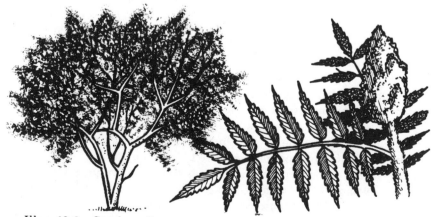

Illus. 19-2—Staghorn Sumac.

each shoot in a clump can be steeped in water, chilled, and sipped as a summer drink that tastes much like lemonade. Staghorn sumac is easy to tell from poison sumac. The latter has white seeds in a sprawling bouquet rather than the tight, upright cluster of red seeds on staghorn.

PINE

All pine seeds (*Pinus* genus) I know of are edible, but only a few are large enough for practical gathering as nuts. The following is as complete a list of the latter as I have been able to compile from various books on native foods.

Bull pine, western yellow pine, *P. ponderosa,* is found in the American West.

Chinese white pine, *P. Armandii,* is a delicacy in China.

Coulter pine, *P. Coulteri,* is also found in the American West.

Digger pine, *P. Sabiniana,* is from the American West.

Italian stone pine, *P. Pinea,* is called pignolia in southern Europe; it's very good.

Korean pine, *P. koraiensis,* is an important food in Korea.

Lace-bark pine, *P. Bungeana,* is adaptable to most of the United States.

Limber pine, *P. flexilis,* grows in the American West.

Piñon nut pine in several species:

    P. edulis

    P. cembroides var. *monophylla*

    P. cembroides var. *Parryana*

Even today, these nuts, especially the first two, are important enough to be harvested from the wild for commercial markets. There are other minor *P. cembroides* eaten locally, especially in Mexico.

Sugar pine, *P. Lambertiana,* grows in the American West; the sap, which is sweet and also good to eat in limited amounts, acts as a mild laxative.

Swiss stone pine, *P. Cembra.* A valued food in Siberia, says Tyozaburo Tanaka in *Tanaka's Cyclopedia of Edible Plants of the World.* Swiss stone and Italian stone pines will grow in the eastern part of the United States.

Torrey pine, *P. Torreyana,* has very large nuts, collected by California Indians for centuries.

371

The piñon pines, in their range, are excellent choices for the home grove. *P. edulis,* the state tree of New Mexico, is the principle pine nut of commerce and an attractive ornamental. Its range is mostly the southwestern states of New Mexico, Arizona, Colorado, and Utah. *P. cembroides* is found mostly in southern California and Nevada. Neither are hardy in the true North. Both were basic foods of Indian civilizations. Both are good raw or roasted and make a fine meal. The seed or nut of the *P. cembroides* species varies from ½ inch to ¾ inch; that of *P. edulis* is about ½ inch. The total value, especially of *P. edulis,* is best appreciated if discussed along with juniper, the other food tree with which it is naturally associated in its range.

One characteristic of the piñon seldom mentioned is that it does not produce nuts every year, and in some areas only about once every five years. When they do fruit, writes Ric Lassiter from Colorado: ". . . they make nuts in earnest. Last year (1980) all the piñons, as if they could talk with each other and plan these things, produced pollen. Great yellow green clouds of pollen billowed up from the trees. Everything—cars, people, pavement, chickens, dogs, cats, and, we hoped, other piñons— was pollenated. In a good nut year, the ranchers tightened their fences and put up new Keep Out signs in a futile attempt to fend off the piñon pickers. Piñon nuts sell for over $2 a pound and they're very easy to pick—just shake the tree and the nuts fall out of the cones. The folks here roast them in the sun or in the oven to keep them."

Illus. 19-3—Pine (Red Spruce).

JUNIPER

Some 40,000 square miles, mostly in New Mexico and Arizona, were once (and still are for the most part) a solid and stable forest of piñon pine and juniper in which Indian cultures flourished for 20,000 years. I emphasize this forest association because it makes a good model in the idealistic search for a grove of trees to live in. Quincy Randles, describing this huge forest association (the largest of all in the United States) in the 1949 Yearbook of Agriculture, entitled *Trees,* writes: "The piñon-juniper forest is usually open, and the openings among the trees are occupied by the grasses and shrubs. The short stems and broad crowns of the individual trees usually of one species of piñon and one or more species of juniper give the forest a pleasing appearance." Pleasing, yes, and really parklike without one lawn mower or landscape architect involved. Over 40,000 square miles of such natural parkland existed, to which man adapted his ways for 20,000 years until a "smarter" white civilization came along. The pine nuts were the "grain" of that stable Indian culture, the juniper berries its fruit. For meat, it relied on the wild turkeys, which lived mostly on the juniper berries, and the deer and antelope that grazed the grass and shrubs and ate the pine nuts, too. For houses and utensils, they used the light but soft juniper wood, which their primitive tools could shape. For fuel wood, both the juniper and piñon served well. In addition, they raised a little corn, squash, and other vegetables, but never at the expense of the grove. It was a permanent agriculture particularly adapted to the fragile soil and climate system upon which it was built. In such dry climates, other agricultural methods are precarious, built on irrigation and fertilizers. When the piñon forests are bulldozed out in favor of cattle range, the grass grows for a few years, withers from drought and overgrazing, and erosion sets in. Or the grass is maintained only at tremendous financial and ecological expense. Once gone, the piñon-juniper forest is difficult to bring back. Randles says in the article cited above that it takes ten years to add an inch to the diameter of these trees in this dry climate.

The junipers most often found with *P. edulis* are the one-seeded juniper, *Juniperus monosperma;* Utah juniper, *J. uta-hensis;* alligator juniper, *J. pachyphlaea;* and the Rocky Mountain juniper, *J. scopulorum.* Alligator juniper is the only tall tree in the group. All four are referred to colloquially as cedar, just as *J. virginiana* is called red cedar in the East. Berries or nuts vary

373

from ¼ to ½ inch in size and are sweet enough to eat. They contain more vitamin C than citrus. However, for food, *J. californica*, a species native to California, is better, having berries as large as ¾ inch in diameter, and oblong. The fruit is dry but sweet. Distillers use these berries as well as other juniper berries, particularly the Sierra juniper (*J. occidentalis,* another California native), in the production of gin.

This matter of gin has led me to a theory not altogether facetious. I no longer worry that cattlemen, developers, and the press of population will ever destroy the juniper forests altogether. The juniper will be the last tree to go, in fact. How so? If you were to select the most influential group of people in this country, I don't know what computer breakout you would use, but I would isolate those businessmen and decision makers who believe they cannot survive without a martini or two a day. Faced with a loss of good gin, I am positive men would finally figure out a way to bring the bulldozers to a grinding halt in our forests and woodlots.

The eastern red cedar is common and widespread in the eastern half of the country. Farmers in its vigorous range consider it more a weed tree than a useful tree because it can spread rapidly in pastures if it's not controlled. But dotted over pastures, red cedar is quite beautiful, and because it usually grows narrow and tall, it makes an excellent fence row and windbreak tree. Its ecological value is that it is a pioneer plant, spreading over impoverished and eroded hillsides and preparing the way eventually for the hardwood forest to come back. Its berries are edible—survival food in winter if one ever runs short of conventional vitamin C sources—and much liked by a dozen

Illus. 19-4—Juniper.

or so bird species. A grove designed to draw birds should include red cedar. The trees also make excellent nesting sites and winter protection for birds. Red cedar oil from the wood and leaves is used in medicine and perfumes. The heartwood makes good fence posts. We have often used them for Christmas trees, a tradition that comes from my wife's Kentucky family farm. I think at one time over a dozen families all rooted in that farm, cut their red cedar Christmas trees there, and gathered mistletoe growing on the walnut trees. These are the kinds of fringe benefits that reward the keepers of home groves.

LEGUME TREES

Whether you think of the fruits of legume trees as nuts or beans, there may be specific situations in which you might want to consider them for the homestead food grove. There are many minor legume trees with edible fruit, particularly in the tropics, but only three apply to a wide enough range to mention here: carob, honey locust, and mesquite. (Black locust is an excellent soil-builder and fuel wood, but not really a food tree except indirectly, as a honey tree for bees.) These legume trees all have heavy, durable wood, produce beans that are edible and potentially, if not actually, valuable, and are all pioneer plants. That last characteristic means that they will establish themselves on poor land, since they are able to manufacture nitrogen from the air to help them grow and to help other plants around them grow. But because of their pioneer toughness, they can be and often are pest trees in the eyes of farmers and ranchers. Mesquite and honey locust especially are a bane to conventional agriculture, and it is only lately that the benefits of these trees have begun to be appreciated.

CAROB

The carob tree may be the oldest cultivated crop tree. References to carob farming occur as early as 1500 B.C. in Egyptian records. Within its range—roughly the climate in which oranges grow—it is an excellent source of natural sugars, protein, and other commercial products. On the island of Cyprus, for example, commercial growers harvest carob beans for processing into glues.

In the United States you are most likely to find carob trees in California, where they have been grown for nearly a century.

The carob survives well as a street tree, and the kids can snack on the ripe pods. Dark brown at maturity, the pods are very sweet and are used, among other ways, as a substitute for cane sugar, particularly in chocolate. California carob-lovers, however, make a point of telling "foreigners" such as myself that carob can stand on its own as a food and does not have to be mixed in that "advertised chocolate stuff." "If handled right," says Bee Williams, who has worked with carob in marketable items since 1961, "carob can stand on its own merits. I did my teething on a carob pod. If you grow up that way you learn to love carob right off the tree. And there are many dishes you can make with it."

She does not, however, advise neophytes to try to process carob into powder themselves, at least not at first. "Best to buy the powder, I think. Making it is lots of work and disappointment until you learn how."

Williams has operated a carob-tree nursery for years, but says that "by the time your book comes out, I may be out of the business." She has one of the best and largest private libraries on carob culture around, however, and is willing to share her information. As of now, her business address is Carob Products, P.O. Box 5084, Walnut Creek, CA 94596.

Dremann's Redwood City Seed Company, mentioned earlier, is one source of seed (see the Appendix). Dremann believes that carob grown from seed will tolerate temperatures a little colder than its normal range. But if winter temperature gets much below 25° to 28°F, the trees won't fruit.

HONEY LOCUST

Closely related to carob, and looking remarkably like it, the honey locust (*Gleditsia triacanthos*) offers possibilities for specific situations in the home grove. I feel a bit hypocritical saying that, having just spend a number of winter days cutting down every honey locust I could lay my axe to. My reluctance about honey locust results from the very thorny character of most wild trees. The thorns are a menace to tractor tire, livestock hoof, and human foot, no matter how well booted. Veneer buyers tell me that honey locust wood is beautiful and would be desirable as veneer, but lumbermen won't go near the trees for fear of puncturing expensive tires on their trucks. When you fell a honey locust, the long thorns fall off everywhere, and even bucking the limbs into firewood is unpleasant, although the wood is excellent fuel. The thorns seem to have a poison in them, too. Whenever I get stabbed by one, which has been frequently, the puncture burns more than the tiny wound seems to justify.

The answer seems simple enough. Grow thornless cultivars, many of which are available as lawn trees now. The drawback to that solution is that the lawn cultivars of thornless honey locust have been bred not to bear fruit either, and so do not help you toward your goal of growing more food, at least not directly. Sometimes you can find a naturally thornless honey locust—I have one in my woods—which can be increased and propagated elsewhere.

Not altogether to my astonishment, the high-bred, fruitless and thornless, ornamental honey locusts seem to be very susceptible to a host of insect enemies, something not at all true of wild honey locusts, at least not here in Ohio. I've seen mimosa webworm do a number on a wild honey locust, but for the most part these wild trees grow with awesome speed, vigor, and total disdain of bugs and blight. The ornamental cultivars, on the other hand, are, in the words of a Purdue Extension bulletin, "popular with the insects": leafhoppers, aphids, and plant bugs. These pests eat the first growth of leaves so that the tree doesn't come into full leaf until midsummer. Eventually, continual attacks weaken the tree, and it becomes easy prey for borers and diseases.

For the food grove, you will do better to look for trees that have been improved or selected to produce pods with high sugar content, as feed for livestock. Back in the '30s, some land grant colleges and, especially, Tennessee Valley Authority (TVA)

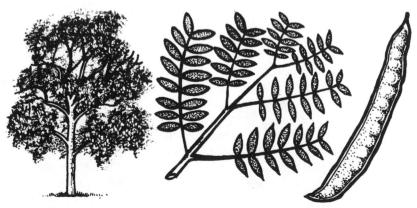

Illus. 19-5—Honey Locust.

started honey locust breeding work as a way to reclaim worn-out farmland profitably. The best current source of information on these trees is the Appalachian Regional Office of the International Tree Crops Institute, U.S.A., Inc., Route 1, Gravel Switch, KY 40328. Greg Williams has been in charge there, and he tells me that he and his workers have been busy collecting promising honey locust varieties from the wild, and from the stocks preserved at the National Arboretum and by TVA. Milwood is the best known of these varieties, purported to contain an unusually high sugar content.

The reason for recurring interest in honey locust is the tree's tremendous capability for producing protein and carbohydrates. Though not as rich in sugar as carob, honey locust pods make very respectable statistics in the livestock nutrition tables: about 27% sugar on the average and 12% protein, with per-acre yields far greater than any grain. Moreover, enough sunlight filters through the lacy leaves to make good pasture beneath them, which draws on the extra nitrogen fixed by the tree. The only hitch is a lack of a way to harvest the pods mechanically.

J. Russell Smith, in *Tree Crops,* recounts many glowing reports of cattle fattening on honey locust beans while grazing the grass under the trees. I agree in general from my own experiences, although they have not been as glowing. Where I do not agree, or rather where my cows do not, is in palatability. My horse, cows, and sheep will eat the long green pods that hang down within reach. That is, they will eat *a few.* When there is none to pull off, they will eat *a few* out of my hand, or scattered on the ground. If I feed the beans in their bunks, they will nibble *a few. Unless very hungry,* they will not eat many. They prefer good grass and clover every time. Those accounts that paint a rosy picture of hogs and livestock beating eager paths to the honey locust trees were probably describing animals deprived of good grazing. I would worry about the condition of livestock allowed to get that hungry.

I react to the beans the same way my livestock does. I gather them in the green-pod stage occasionally, shell out the beans, and eat them. Raw, they are quite good, much like a raw pea. But I tire of them quickly. Cooked, the beans are fair. Although they're hardly as good as peas, if I lacked other green vegetables I could get by on them. Again, they are filling. There is a certain taste to them that hinders (rather than satisfies) the appetite. When the pods mature to a dark brown, the sugar in the pod concentrates into an orange pulp that smells and tastes somewhat like banana, only sweeter. As children, we used to eat that pulp in the fall—for awhile. I still do—for awhile. Again, there is what has been described as an "astringent tang" to the sweet pulp that leaves a bitter aftertaste in the mouth. I assume this is the reason my sheep, in early winter when pasture is nearly gone, will eat the dry fallen pods greedily . . . but only for a short time.

Yet one does not have to be as visionary as Smith to see the possibilities that a century or two of breeding might bring about. Certainly, the green honey locust bean is far closer to a good garden vegetable than, in their wild state, most other fruits and vegetables that we've developed. Certainly, too, the long pods are already easier to harvest by hand than most fruit. They would no doubt succumb easily to mechanical harvest if man put his tinkering mind to the job. Imagine a garden vegetable that goes on producing year after year without tillage or planting.

I think that honey locust plantations should be small, not large-scale operations. The trees spread like weeds, and if you decide to grow them, you commit yourself to going over your pasture yearly to hoe out seedlings if your sheep haven't eaten them. This is not a large job; it is, in fact, a pleasant job *if* the pasture is of a size practical for spot-hoeing of this kind. In any event, plant thornless varieties. There is no future in growing the thorny ones. They do not even make a good hedge fence, say the old books. You can't keep a honey locust hedge thick at the bottom. Nor is working on such a hedge like working with hawthorn. Hawthorn thorns are nasty, but honey locust thorns are wicked.

MESQUITE

Mesquite is a pest tree only in relation to the scale of the farming enterprise in which it exists. Some 56 million acres of semiarid Texas plains are being overtaken by mesquite, and the more ranchers try to make these plains hospitable to improved grasses, the better the conditions are for mesquite. I can grow honey locust in a controlled situation on 20 acres of pasture; on 200 acres the tree would spread like a weed and brush over the grass in short order because I could not control its spread. In the same way, a Texas rancher with 10,000 acres is simply helpless before the onward march of mesquite. The most advanced technology fails him, including chemicals. What would easily kill the trees would also kill the grass.

All but admitting defeat, Texas has taken a new and, surprisingly, ecological approach. If you can't beat 'em, join 'em. For centuries the mesquite was survival food for Indians and

Photo 19-1—Mesquite. Photograph by U.S. Forest Service.

their livestock. Even into the 20th century, when labor was still cheap, trainloads of mesquite beans were shipped to cattle feeders. In a land that grew very little of anything, these beans were a sort of manna from heaven. Perhaps by way of new technology they could become so again, even in a land where labor is not cheap. Texas Tech University is finding ways to increase the digestibility of mesquite pulp for livestock feed— the *whole* tree, shredded up. If you can't beat 'em, eat 'em.

Mesquite is an extremely hard wood that's excellent for fuel and fence posts. Allen Wiley, a wood technologist writing in *Texas Forestry Service News* (Spring, 1975), points out that the wood machines well, takes a beautiful finish, and makes quality parquet flooring, pistol grips, carvings, and other items where small pieces can be utilized. The problem with mesquite wood is that the tree rarely grows a log of adequate size for sawing into useful boards. Whole tree chipping, said Wiley, could be the answer for a high Btu fuel, for paper making, and for composition board.

As with honey locust, mesquite beans grind into a palatable meal for livestock. Indians baked bread with it, and we could again, if necessary. The home grove-owner in the semiarid Southwest probably has mesquite whether he wants it or not. If your grove is small enough so you can keep the tree from taking over your property, don't be in a hurry to eradicate it.

CHAPTER 20

SYRUP- AND OIL-PRODUCING TREES

Maples, birches, hickories, walnuts, butternuts, even ashes and basswoods produce a sap sweet enough to make into syrup or sugar for table use. Probably a good many other trees do, too. But only the maples, and possibly birches, produce a sap with enough sugar content to make processing into food really practical. Many syrup-makers would go one step further and say that only sugar maple, *Acer saccharum,* is worth the trouble of boiling down into syrup. But other maples should be considered; box elder, for example, yields a poorer grade of sap but a good flow and is a maple that will grow almost anywhere, including windy, windbreak situations not conducive to sugar maples. We boil syrup from red maples nearly as efficiently as from our sugar maples. The advantage of red maple is that it will grow well on some poorly drained sites—sites otherwise wasted for food use.

MAPLE

Sugar maple is certainly the king of the sugar trees, and both a splendid hardwood and fine lawn tree besides. Not only is the foliage beautiful, but the wood is most useful and valuable as cabinet wood of the highest quality and as excellent fuel wood. Occasionally a tree will produce extremely valuable cross-grain patterns known as curly maple grain, used for gun stocks, violins, and other artful woodwork. Or the grain may form a bird's-eye pattern, also very valuable for furniture. Before you cut up a maple for fuel, or sell it as sawlogs, be sure to have an honest expert check out its true potential value. The best curly and bird's-eye patterns seem to develop on trees grown on stress sites—drier, poorer soil where the tree grows slowly and not necessarily into a straight, large log.

Sugar content of sugar-maple sap varies usually between 2% and 3%—more on trees growing a full crown in the open, as in a yard, less when growing in a tall-trunked forest tree. Howard Kriebel and his associates at the Ohio Agriculture Research and Development Center in Wooster have been developing for 25 years what he calls super sugar maples. These improved strains are capable of producing sap with sugar content of around 4%, double the average for sugar maples in Ohio today. The savings in fuel are very considerable. It takes about 40 gallons of maple sap at 2% sugar to make 1 gallon of syrup. To get the same amount of syrup from one of the super trees would take only 20 gallons of sap, thus saving over half the fuel costs. Selected seedlings of these high-sugar trees are being sold as they become available from the state nurseries. The next batch to be sold,

Illus. 20-1—Sugar Maple, Leaf and Seed, and Red Maple Leaf and Seed.

Kriebel says, is in 1981–82. To order, write: Department of Natural Resources, State of Ohio, Division of Forestry, Fountain Square, Columbus, OH 43224.

If you have a large sugar maple in your yard right now, you should be able to make as much as a gallon of syrup from it. For family use, that's more syrup than you think—it will take a lot of pancakes to soak it up. The point is, one or two trees are sufficient to give you a good taste of syrup, a taste that freshly cooled from the boiling tray is superb and unique. Real maple syrup has an ever so slight husky, barky edge to its sweet flavor that most of us maplers absolutely crave in the spring. In fact, I like to sip it as a drink when about half-boiled down. I have a hunch there's something in maple sap besides the sugar that is very good for the body. I even like to drink the sap right out of the tree when it is hardly sweet at all.

Usually you tap maple trees in late winter or early spring, right on the heels of the first serious thaw. That's about March 5 to 10 here, most years. But any thaw may bring a good sap flow. The one commercial maple farm in our area tapped trees in *January* of 1980! As I was cutting box elders out of an old fence row, they bled from pruned branches as if I'd turned a spigot on. But cold weather soon followed and the sap ceased flowing until March. Since the first run makes the best syrup, it pays to be ready. (Old-timers say January syrup is the best of all.) Once the main sap flow is running, warmish days and frosty nights

Illus. 20-2—Silver Maple.

increase the flow. Or so everyone says. Warm, moist nights will often overflow your buckets with sap, too, I've found.

I should not tell you how we make our syrup because it is mostly the wrong way. There are dozens of books that explain the right way and you should consult these. (The best article I've read for the backyarder is "Maple Sugaring on a Small Scale," by Jack Cook in *Country Journal,* vol. 2, no. 2, 1975, p. 46 ff.) But perhaps by telling you some wrong ways, you will get the idea that you don't have to be an expert to get the job done and enjoy the fruits of your labor.

If you use regular sap buckets, spigots, and covers, you will be gallons ahead, I suppose, but I use plastic milk jugs and homemade spigots. I cut a hole in the side of the jug at the top of the opposite side of the handle. The spigot goes through the hole into the jug, and is thereby covered, so rain can't get in. I drill a ⅝-inch hole 2 inches into the tree on the east side, usually. The hole can be slightly smaller or larger. The book says to tap the south side of the tree for a better sap flow, but I like the east side because the jug is then protected better from our prevailing hard, western March winds and rain. I tap a nail (just barely) into the tree above the spigot and hang the jug by a piece of twine on the nail. The spout sticking into the jug holds it fairly stable when the sap runs.

Photo 20-1—*Sugar Maple Tapped for Syrup—One backyard tree tapped for syrup can give a homeowner enough sap for a gallon of syrup. Rodale Press photograph.*

For spouts I used to ream out sumac branches into hollow tubes. They never seem to work well enough to suit me, so I started splitting the sumac tubes in half, lengthwise, to make two miniature troughs, which worked just fine as spouts. Now I've carved such miniature troughs out of white oak. They are much more durable, and I can drive them tightly into the tap hole without breaking them.

My sisters run plastic tubes from their metal spouts to jugs sitting on the ground around the tree. I'd worry about animals, especially dogs, knocking them over, but my sisters seem to have good luck this way. There's certainly less chance of dirt getting into the sap with this method, but you should strain it, anyway. There is a brown, night-flying moth that always gets into my sap jugs and drowns. The moths don't hurt anything but have to be strained out, of course.

Since we make only a small amount of syrup and the trees are close at hand, collection and boiling aren't a problem for us. The jugs fill up fairly fast on good days, but I can run out there and empty them in a few minutes. We could use the kitchen stove for a gallon or so of syrup, but more than that will make your kitchen begin to sweat like a hard-working horse. We have an emergency stove we keep on the porch ever since the big blizzard when we were four days without electricity and, at that time, without a wood stove, either. This stove is an old-fashioned gas stove that does not require any electricity for start up or thermostat control, as do so many newer ones. We use it mainly for cooking down lard and for boiling off maple syrup. Sometimes you can get old gas stoves for almost nothing. My sister found one that must be 50 years old that she keeps in her garage. I think she paid $15 for it. Bottled gas is not cheap, of course, but neither is any fuel.

Ideally, if you burn wood for heat, you should build an outside, wood-fired boiler large enough to burn up the knotty pieces of wood that are so hard to split into stove kindling. If you use a wood stove in your house, you can boil somewhat more sap inside than you can boil by using an electric or gas stove. Since wood heat typically dries out a house so much during regular operation, the house can benefit from humidity from the sap's steam. I have boiled off sap on a crane over our fireplace, too. It works fine, but the syrup has a slightly smoky taste to it.

Commercially, there are four grades of maple syrup: Fancy, A, B, and C, ranging from a light amber color and delicate taste, to a darker, heavier syrup that comes from the last flow when the weather has warmed up. The best course to follow, in my opinion, is not to worry about grade, but pull the spouts after the first two weeks of good flow. You should have about all of the sap you can handle by that time, and you automatically avoid the late, dark syrup. If some sap still runs out of the hole, don't worry about it. Tapping maples does not seem to hurt them.

Knowing when to quit boiling the sap is the hard part of the task, or at least the part that provokes the most technical advice. If you stop too soon, the syrup will be runny and may not keep as well. Too late and it may crystallize in storage. Of course, if you want to make sugar, you have to boil longer. I don't advise beginners to try to make sugar. First make syrup. Then in a few years, if you want to dabble in sugar, you will have gained the necessary experience.

The syrup is ready when the candy thermometer hits 220° to 222°F. (Another 7° will make sugar, the books say.) Another way to tell is when the syrup sheets off a spoon dipped into it, rather than drips off. I can never tell when dripping changes to sheeting, but people who make candy know all that. I don't really care, because we pull the syrup off the fire when it is still a little runny. I like it that way. You get more that way. You use less fuel that way. It is all gone by the time of the big honey flow in June, so storage is not much of a problem.

The books say not to store maple syrup in glass, but we always have. If the syrup has been boiled a mite too long, it may crystallize, and if it does it may break the jar. We've never had that problem.

The books also say that you must strain the syrup through felt to take out the niter (lime deposit). We've never done that, either. Niter may give the syrup a slightly bitter taste, say the books. I've never noticed. However, the last dregs in a jar sometimes get a slightly grayish scum on them that I assume is the niter. I just keep right on spreading it on my toast.

Incidentally, I don't know how you enjoy eating your maple syrup, but I like the taste so well I don't want anything else interfering with it. Fancy foods made with maple syrup are a waste of maple syrup, as Noel Perrin, the well-known country writer, has so delightfully pointed out in his articles. I tried Perrin's idea: spread the maple syrup on dry, white bread toast—homemade white bread in our case. Delicious. I like whole wheat bread better, but the taste of whole wheat bread competes with maple syrup too much. Pancakes suffocate maple syrup (and my appetite). Next to smearing it on white, home-made bread, my favorite way to use syrup is on hot, homemade sourdough biscuits fresh from the oven.

A caution: When boiling down sap, the first 200 degrees take a long time. But when the syrup is almost finished, don't turn your back on it. You can burn it up very fast after it is almost ready, especially if you are doing only a very small amount. This is a voice of experience speaking.

If you contemplate commercial production on a small scale, you should by all means visit (or work for) a commercial opera-tion. There are many technical innovations in the business you'll need to know about. One, for example, is a new drill for tapping trees that fits on your chain saw.

The innovation that is going to revolutionize the maple-sugar business is just now approaching practical application. For years, scientists have been working with a process they call reverse osmosis, by which they pass the sap through a membrane that takes out some of the water before the sap is evaporated. Reverse osmosis units have been set up in some commercial sugar operations, just in the last two or three years. These large units are very expensive—as high as $20,000 or more—but they can take out enough water to leave a sap with a sugar content of 6%. That may not seem much to you, but it saves over half the cost of the fuel needed for evaporation. With the rising cost of fuel and its scarcity, reverse osmosis units even at that price will pay for themselves quickly and save fuel. And the process has other applications of interest to backyard food-producers, too.

A couple of companies are making small hobby units. Elecprohom, Inc., of Kitchener, Ontario, Canada, is one I've heard about. How well these units work I have no way of knowing, yet, but obviously they will continue to be improved and become more readily available. The best sources of informa-tion I have found on reverse osmosis are the biology and forestry departments at the University of Vermont in Burlington.

BIRCH

In eastern Europe, making syrup from birch trees is a significant commercial enterprise. The European white birch, *Betula pendula,* is commonly tapped, and it yields an average sugar content of 1.5% to 1.8%. Intrigued, Canadians have been experimenting with North American birches, principally the gray birch, *B. populifolia.* They found that gray-birch sap averaged only .76% sugar, probably not high enough for profitable commercial production. Other birches will be studied, no doubt, mainly *B. lenta,* the sweet birch, which has higher sugar content.

The scientists chose gray birch for the first experiments for some sound reasons, however. Gray birch is very plentiful, especially around Macdonald College of McGill University, where the experimentation has been going on. More important, gray birch is one of the first pioneer trees to come back after forest destruction, often in dense stands, note the scientists. Quite possibly the dense birch stands might be considered principally as fuel sources and secondarily as sugar-producing trees. This could be true of other birches, too.

Another advantage of birch from the commercial (as well as backyard) point of view is that harvesting sap from them would lengthen the sap season. Birches begin to flow just as maples begin to quit. Therefore, greater utilization of equipment and a longer sap season could spread costs and increase marketing enough to make birch sap profitable even if production were less efficient than for maple syrup.

In any event, the backyarder in the birch range will want to consider *B. lenta* as one of his grove trees, if not other birches. Where the sweet birch grows, country restaurants traditionally serve birch beer. This root beer-type of drink used to be made from real birch sap. Now artificial flavoring is usually used and

Illus. 20-3—Birch (Paper).

the popularity of birch beer, not too surprisingly, wanes. There are still a few small commercial enterprises that process oil of wintergreen, which is used in medicine and perfumes, from the sweet birch. In Scandinavian countries, where man is thankful for any sweet "fruit" he can wrest from a harsh nature, wine is made by fermenting birch sap.

SASSAFRAS

The Food and Drug Administration (FDA) has banned the use of sassafras oil for root beer because of a possible link to cancer. So, if you've noticed that root beer has a bland, flat taste of nothing but fizz water and sugar, you know why. I believe that 100% of the people who use sassafras eventually die. Since cancer is a leading cause of death in this country, no doubt a statistically significant number of sassafras users die of cancer. I have a hunch the root-beer makers were overjoyed at the FDA's ruling since now they can make root beer cheaper without worrying about hard-to-get sassafras.

The FDA is afraid of milk, butter, and eggs, too. I could, with no trouble at all, call upon any number of healthy septua-genarians and octogenarians who have "taken" sassafras tea as a spring tonic all their lives, but then I suppose one must die of *something* when he or she gets old. Sassafras tea is fun to make. Just peel some bark off the roots, boil in water, steep, add honey or maple syrup to taste, and enjoy. I am willing to wager all the

Illus. 20-4—Sassafras.

gold at Fort Knox that if you do not die of it sooner or later, you will die of something else.

I think that if the FDA was not prodded into this action by root-beer makers, then it probably banned sassafras to show how broad-minded it is. If it banned only man-made test-tube chemicals with toxic ingredients, then why not a few natural foods? People with the same sort of mentality love to point out that there is arsenic in lima beans, solanine in potatoes, etc.—all poisons. They forget conveniently that the lima bean, the potato, and sassafras roots have been evolving along with man for millions of years and that each has learned to take the measure of the other and each has survived handsomely. New, artificial chemicals, on the other hand, are thrown together in a test tube by lab technicians who have no idea what the effect of these substances will be ten years down the road.

A traditional farm practice in sassafras country is to use poles cut from sassafras sprouts for chicken roosts. The aromatic oils (chew a twig for a breath freshener) supposedly repel lice. (Maybe the lice get cancer.) The leaves of sassafras are used as a thickener in traditional southern dishes such as gumbo.

EUCALYPTUS

I wonder if the FDA has tried feeding eucalyptus oil to rats. The oil, eucalyptol, is distilled from the foliage and is used in pharmaceuticals, flavoring, and perfumery.

Eucalyptus is a family of exceedingly numerous trees, most of them having originated in Australia, and many of them now are established in zones 8, 9, and sometimes in protected parts of zone 7. Eucalypti are wonderful trees. They grow surprisingly fast, some to gigantic size (300 feet), and are a favorite shade tree in southern California. Most bloom beautiful fragrant blossoms and are first-rate bee trees. What's more, the trees of many species adapt well to alkaline soils, windy situations, and considerable drought, although they grow better with a good supply of moisture. The wood splits easily and is excellent fuel wood, partly because of the oil content. The tree is being looked at as a possible efficient source of wood alcohol to substitute for gasoline. When cut down, trees send up second growth and, once established, a grove is self-renewing.

Commercial groves are kept in some parts of the world for oil production. For the owner of a fruit grove, the tree is also well

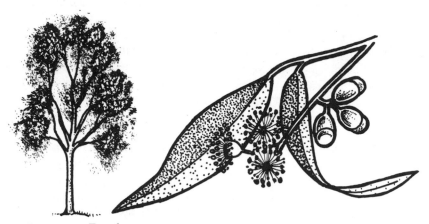

Illus. 20-5—Eucalyptus.

suited for forming a windbreak around fruit trees, at least where wind is a problem. Studies reported in the 1949 Yearbook of Agriculture, *Trees,* demonstrated that on 20 Arizona groves of citrus protected by eucalyptus windbreaks (eucalyptus trees are traditionally used for windbreaks in Arizona because they are well adapted to the region), the financial returns were approximately double that of unprotected groves. With less wind, there was less droppage and other damage to fruit. Bees did a better job of pollenation in the protected groves. (No doubt the fragrance of the eucalypti blossoms helped draw bees to the groves, too.) A 10-acre grove with 1 acre planted to eucalyptus as windbreaks produced more net profit than a 10-acre grove planted entirely in citrus without a windbreak.

Locally, eucalypti are almost always called gum trees. The blue gum, *Eucalyptus Globulus,* is one of the most common and popular trees, although if planted near a sewer the roots will grow into the pipeline. Desert gum, *E. rudis;* mahogany gum, *E. robusta;* peppermint gum, *E. amygdalina;* and lemon-scented gum, *E. maculata,* are other favorites. There are many more. Unfortunately, none are northern winter-hardy.

TURPENTINE ORCHARDS

Though the oils derived from southern longleaf pines and from tung trees are not food, in the South, where these trees

391

flourish, both types of orcharding could someday be an integral part of a homestead grove of trees to live in.

Historically, turpentining has been a method for a small farmer to make part of his living, and many still do. The process is not unlike maple-sugaring in the North, but the trees are cut or slashed rather than tapped, and the sap, or gum as it is called, drains from the cut "face" into special paper bags. The work is done during the hottest part of the summer, which is why farmers who still work the pines are usually older, and inured to work of this nature. "Young people get jobs where there's air-conditioning," one farmer told me disdainfully. "There's still a good demand for turpentine gum. It has higher quality than tar oil. You can make a good living at it if you don't mind sweating and stepping over the rattlesnakes. I expect to see some of the younger ones come back to turpentining when times get too hard to support all those fluff jobs in air-conditioned offices."

A "crop" for a turpentine farmer is 10,000 faces, which generally means 10,000 trees (one face per tree, though large trees can take two), which is considered about all one man can handle. Most farmers don't cut a whole crop anymore. The work is a little easier than it used to be, however. Turpentiners use a special paste over the cuts that keeps the sap running for as much as three weeks per treatment. Previously, acid treatments kept the sap running for only a few days, and it then had to be repeated.

In the '40s and '50s, cattle and turpentining were often combined. The pine stand was maintained thinner than for the best turpentine production, and cattle grazed between the trees. The grazing kept low brush from growing up. Brush covered with fallen pine needles was a bad fire hazard and the cattle-pine combination was thought to be a good practice. Since then, with the sharpening of the demands for "efficiency" in all types of farm production, the practice is not often followed since it calls for fewer than the profitable number of trees and fewer than the profitable number of cattle. In a homestead situation, however, the maintenance of half a "crop" of 5,000 pines spread pleasantly over 300 to 400 acres of pasture on sandy, otherwise low-producing Georgia soil might become very practical again.

Today there's a good business "harvesting" the stumps of huge, old yellow pines cut long ago for lumber. So much resin remains in the wood that the stumps don't rot. The wood is in demand as easy-starting kindling for a new generation of wood-stove users. It's called Georgia Fatwood when advertised in fancy magazines. A person who bought 100 acres of "worthless" pine stumps a few years ago might suddenly find himself well-off in a very unexpected way.

Nor is it lost on anyone in the slash-pine region that turpentine can be used as a gasoline substitute, either as is or with further refinement. A fuel drawn from living trees rather than from row crops might be the only safe ecological way to "grow our own fuel," as the gas-alcohol proponents want to do. Turpentine is presently too expensive to burn in an automobile, but that could change.

TUNG TREES

Tung oil is known as the drying oil of the highest quality for use in varnishes, paints, etc. The Chinese have grown the tree for centuries for the oil, hence its common name as "Chinese wood oil tree." During the Second World War, our sources of tung oil in the Orient were cut off, and the USDA quickly embarked on a program to produce the oil in this country. Tung trees would grow well, researchers found, in a rather narrow, long belt across the lower Gulf States. South of this belt was too warm; north, too cold.

Tung orchards sprang up all across this belt, but just as the trees came into full production, our problems with Japan came to an end. Tung oil again was available via importation at prices

Illus. 20-6—Tung Tree.

cheaper than American tung growers could compete with. To make matters worse for our growers, the tung-tree industry that was initiated in South America at the same time as ours could also produce tung oil cheaper than we could. As a result, the tung business has dwindled. I believe the only market left is Mobile, Alabama. Periodically, someone tries to rejuvenate a tung orchard to go into production again, but almost always meets disappointment.

A tung orchard looks quite like a fruit orchard from the road, blossoming and producing a fruit above the size of an apple. The oil is pressed from the seeds in the fruit. The tung-oil business is another example of a stable agricultural pattern adaptable to the small farm or homestead way of life but rendered impractical because of ulterior financial reasons. If the cost of shipping tung oil from thousands of miles away rises to meet the true cost of burning up fossil fuels in this manner, we may again be in the tung-oil business. Since it is a superior drying oil, at that future time we might reflect as to whether it makes sense to produce so much linseed oil from flax, which requires a system of continuous cultivation, rather than establishing more groves of tung trees. It may be cheaper to produce oils from cultivated crops here and now. But a grove agriculture perpetuates a livable world, while an agriculture of continuous cultivation perpetuates an ever increasing rate of fossil resource consumption and soil deterioration.

APPENDIX

SOURCES OF TREES

The list below is far from exhaustive. I have tried mainly to give a fairly representative list that covers most of the trees discussed in this book. However, when faced with a choice of two that seem equal, I find myself picking the nursery from which I have purchased trees with satisfaction, or a nursery that other tree growers I know speak of favorably. This does not mean that other nurseries are not as good, or better.

Any list of nurseries I've ever seen in any book, including this one, gives but a tip of the iceberg of tree sources. There are hundreds of small local nurseries that grow a limited amount of their own stock, which in nearly every situation will prove to be satisfactory for the backyard grower living in that region. In a recent issue of *The Green Thumb,* a regular bulletin published by the Horticulture Department of the University of Kentucky (Lexington), no less than 38 nurseries were listed as sources of flowering crab apples, of which most of the nurseries I had never heard of before, even though I'm an inveterate catalog reader.

Every state has an association of nurserymen. Its headquarters can be located by checking with the horticulture department of your state university. Many of these local nurseries may not even issue catalogs. Others may. If you can find one within driving distance with trees you want, you can usually save money shopping there in person. In some situations you can save more by digging or helping to dig up your own trees. In any event, this should be your first choice of sources. Use mail order only as a source of second resort.

A good listing of sources of fruit trees can be found in *American Fruit Grower* magazine's annual Buyer's Guide.

(37841 Euclid Avenue, Willoughby, OH 44094). *Organic Gardening* magazine's Reader Service Department (Rodale Press, 33 East Minor Street, Emmaus, PA 18049) has also compiled an extensive list of nursery suppliers.

Some of the nurseries listed below are operated by elderly people, and some are new ventures. It is possible that some of them may not be in business by the time you read this.

Armstrong Nurseries
Box 4060
Ontario, CA 91761

Fruit and nut trees, especially pecan and almond along the latter.

Bountiful Ridge Nurseries, Inc.
Box 250
Princess Anne, MD 21853

Large source of almost all fruit trees, including oriental persimmon, low-chilling apples, old apple varieties; nuts, including pecans, walnuts, hican, hazel, chestnuts, hickory, and butternut; figs.

C & O Nursery
P.O. Box 116
1700 North Wenatchee Avenue
Wenatchee, WA 98801

Fruit trees, natural dwarf sweet cherries; ornamental and shade trees.

Columbia Basin Nursery
Box 458
Quincy, WA 98848

Fruit trees; rootstocks for fruit trees.

Corwin Davis
20865 Junction Road
Bellevue, MI 49021

Grafted papaws and seed; tree supply is limited.

Farmer Seed & Nursery Co.
818 Northwest Fourth Street
Faribault, MN 55021

Fruit trees; saskatoons.

Fiddyment Pistachios
5010 Fiddyment Road
Roseville, CA 95678

Container-grown pistachios.

Henry Field Seed &
Nursery Co.
407 Sycamore Street
Shenandoah, IA 51602

Northern fruits and nuts.

Fowler Nurseries, Inc.
525 Fowler Road
Newcastle, CA 95658

Fruits and nuts; pecans and
almonds for the West.

Louis Gerardi Nursery
Route 1, Box 146
O'Fallon, IL 62269

Northern nuts, including
chinquapin; grafted persimmons; grafted papaw, sometimes; also grafted mulberries and hazels.

Goodwin Nursery
Route 1, Box 97
Kingfisher, OK 73750

Fruits, including grafted
persimmons.

Ernest Grimo
Route 3
Niagara-on-the-Lake, ON,
Canada L0S 1J0

Grafted nut trees; seeds;
seedlings.

Gurney Seed & Nursery Co.
1917 Page Street
Yankton, SD 57078

Wide selection of fruits;
good source for hardy
cherry plums and hybrid
plums.

Herbst Brothers Seedsmen,
Inc.
1000 North Main Street
Brewster, NY 10509

Fruit-tree and nut-tree
seeds.

Hilltop Orchards &
Nurseries, Inc.
Route 2
Hartford, MI 49057

A large nursery that maintains top quality; trees are
in such demand (all fruits)
from commercial growers
that sometimes small backyard orders can't be filled
for a year or so.

Jersey Chestnut Farm
58 Van Duyne Avenue
Wayne, NJ 07470

Good source of chestnuts;
limited production; may
have to wait a year or so after ordering.

Johnson Orchard &
Nursery
Route 5, Box 325
Ellijay, GA 30540

Fruit trees, especially
peaches; old white cling-
stone peaches.

Lawson's Nursery
Route 1, Box 294
Yellow Creek Road
Ball Ground, GA 30107

Old and rare fruit trees;
over 100 varieties of old apples.

Norman & Bonnie
Letsinger
Windy Hills Farm
1565 East Wilson Road
Scottville, MI 49454

Most native North Ameri-
can lawn, food, and wind-
break trees, including nut
trees, honey locust, etc.; a
new venture especially for
homesteaders.

Henry Leuthardt Nurseries,
Inc.
Montauk Highway
East Moriches, NY 11940

Dwarf fruit trees, especially
espaliers.

Lundy's Nursery
Route 3, Box 35
Live Oak, FL 32060

Fruits and nuts, especially
those for tropical zone 9.

Mellinger's, Inc.
230 West South Range
Road
North Lima, OH 44452

Most fruits; ornamental
trees; seeds of many trees;
Juneberry (sarvistree)
trees.

J. E. Miller Nurseries
5060 West Lake Road
Canandaigua, NY 14424

All fruits and nuts; good selection of old apple varieties.

Musser Forests, Inc.
Route 119, Box 340
Indiana, PA 15701

Swiss stone pine; wide assortment of lawn trees.

New York State Fruit Testing Cooperative Association
Geneva, NY 14456

Good source of all fruit
trees, including mulberry,
but sometimes sold out.

Pataky Nursery
610 Hickory Lane
Mansfield, OH 44905

All northern nuts.

Redwood City Seed Co.
P.O. Box 361
Redwood City, CA 94064

Pine nut seeds; other fruit-
and nut-tree seeds.

Southmeadow Fruit
Gardens
2363 Tilbury Place
Birmingham, MI 48009

Fruit trees, especially old
varieties; cornelian cherry,
black haw viburnum; excellent source of old, rare
fruits.

Stark Bro's Nurseries &
Orchards Co.
Box A3441A
Louisiana, MO 63353

All fruit trees; varietal and
seedling nut trees.

Willis Stribling Nursery Co.
1620 West 16th Street
P.O. Box 793
Merced, CA 95340

Fruit trees; nuts, including
walnuts, almonds; pecans in
short supply because of big
demand—this is true (1980)
of most western commercial
nut suppliers.

Talbott Nursery
Route 3, Box 212
Linton, IN 47441

Northern nuts; grafted persimmons; grafted papaws;
some other fruits, including
mulberry.

Leslie H. Wilmoth Nursery
Route 2, Box 469
Elizabethtown, KY 42701

Nuts, custom grafting; limited numbers of pecans,
walnuts, hickories, butternuts, and chestnuts.

Dave Wilson Nursery
4306 Santa Fe Avenue
Hughson, CA 95326

All fruits; walnuts; al-
monds; genetic dwarf fruit
trees.

Worcester County
Horticultural Society
30 Elm Street
Worcester, MA 01608

Scionwood of older-fruit varieties.

FRUIT- AND NUT-TREE ORGANIZATIONS

For the purposes of the backyard grove-owner seeking to develop new ideas in tree-food production as suggested in this book, sources of trees other than regular commercial nurseries can be helpful. Such a source may be your nearest woodland or perhaps an old homestead in your area where a family has lovingly kept old and unnamed fruit trees that produce well with minimal care. Lacking these sources, you may wish to join one or more of the organizations listed below. You will find other members in these organizations full of information on local varieties of interest. Through scion- and seed-exchange programs available to members only, you gain access to rare and/or intriguing varieties of promise.

American Pomological Society
103 Tyson Building
University Park, PA 16802

California Rare Fruit Growers
The Fullerton Arboretum
% Mrs. Patricia Sawyer
California State University, Fullerton
Fullerton, CA 92634

The Home Orchard Society
2511 Southwest Miles Street
Portland, OR 97219

The North American Fruit Explorers
Treasurer Ray Walker (for membership application)
Box 711
St. Louis, MO 63188

The Northern Nut Growers Association
% Richard A. Jaynes
Broken Arrow Road
Hamden, CT 06518

(Many states have their own state nut-growing organizations. You can learn of them through NNGA.)

FRUIT- AND NUT-TREE RESEARCH GROUPS

As interest grows in a stable tree-foods agriculture, research projects are sprouting up in various areas. A few you might find of considerable interest for information pertinent to establishing your own tree grove are listed below:

The Earlham Foodforest Project
Box 1174
Earlham College
Richmond, IN 47374

International Tree Crops Institute U.S.A.
Box 1272
Winters, CA 95694

Tree Crops Research Project
230 East Roberts
Cornell University
Ithaca, NY 14853

BOOKS TO READ

I have not listed all of the good books on individual fruit and nut trees—such a list would be endless. Moreover, most horticultural books on fruit trees pursue the subject from a conventional "orchard" point of view: one plants trees in orderly blocks and endeavors to kill everything threatening to destroy those trees, or an orchardist plants trees artificially dwarfed by rootstock or interstem and then prunes them into grotesque and unnatural forms. I mean no criticism of these practices (many are included in this book), but reading books that assume that these methods are the only way food can be produced from trees will not help you to take the different view suggested in *Organic Orcharding: A Grove of Trees to Live In.* To my knowledge, very few books so far address themselves specifically to the establishment of such a natural grove for the homeowner. I am familiar with only the following:

401

Forest Farming: Towards a Solution to Problems of World Hunger and Conservation, by J. Sholto Douglas and Robert A. de J. Hart (Emmaus, Pa.: Rodale Press, 1978).

Fruits and Berries for the Home Garden, by Lewis Hill (New York: Alfred A. Knopf, 1977).

Nut Tree Culture in North America. Available through the Northern Nut Growers Association, Broken Arrow Road, Hamden, CT 06518.

The One-Straw Revolution, by Masanobu Fukuoka (Emmaus, Pa.: Rodale Press, 1978 [see Chap. 2 on natural orcharding]).

Permaculture Two: Practical Design for Town and Country in Permanent Agriculture, by Bill Mollison. Distributed in this country by International Tree Crops Institute U.S.A., Box 1272, Winters, CA 95694.

The Pesticide Conspiracy, by Robert Van Den Bosch (New York: Doubleday, 1978).

Back issues of the *Pomona,* the quarterly publication of the North American Fruit Explorers, and the *Annual Reports* of the Northern Nut Growers Association, and their quarterly publication, the *Nutshell,* are, in my opinion, extremely helpful.

Pruning Simplified, by Lewis Hill (Emmaus, Pa.: Rodale Press, 1979).

Tree Crops, by J. Russell Smith (New York: Harper & Row, 1978).

Trees for the Yard, Orchard, and Woodlot, edited by Roger Yepsen (Emmaus, Pa.: Rodale Press, 1976).

In choosing books about conventional orcharding, a few old books interspersed in your reading schedule can be of considerable help for the clues they give to raising fruit *before* the chemical era. For example, *The Illustrated Annual Register of Rural Affairs* was published throughout the last half of the 19th century, I believe, in annual softbound editions that were eventually bound together in hardcover volumes. These annuals offer advice on all aspects of agriculture and are especially helpful for the grove-owner because orchards are treated as a part of the *whole* food production system on the farm, which is the way the backyard grove-owner must view his trees. Here's an example from 1877:

The report of the Maine Pomological Society states that Washington Gilbert of Bath had found it profitable to feed corn and small grains to sheep and swine in the orchard, kept there for both destroying the codling moth and keeping up the fertility (by eating fallen apples). He thinks the market product of the animals would pay all the expenses of the orchard. He had seen apples more than double in size by pasturing swine, in a single year.

These old books are difficult to find outside of large horticultural libraries. I have found some by shopping used book stores habitually. One source of older fruit books is Pomona Book Exchange, Highway 52, Rockton P.O., Ontario, Canada L0R 1X0.

My experience is that books from about 1880 to 1945 that deal with a particular farm's experiences in *all* aspects of food production, including fruit and nut trees, give better information for the backyarder than books that are exclusively about fruit production.

INDEX